I0120697

URBAN IMAGINARIES

URBAN IMAGINARIES

Locating the Modern City

Alev Çınar and Thomas Bender, Editors

University of Minnesota Press

Minneapolis • London

Portions of chapter 1 were originally published in Deniz Yükseker, "Trust and Gender in a Transnational Marketplace: The Public Culture of Laleli, Istanbul," *Public Culture* 16, no. 1 (2004): 47–65; copyright 2004 Duke University Press; all rights reserved; reprinted by permission of the publisher. A slightly different version of chapter 3 originally appeared in Nigel Harkness, Paul Rowe, Tim Unwin, and Jennifer Yee, eds., *Visions/Revisions: Essays on Nineteenth-Century French Culture* (Oxford, UK: Peter Lang, 2003). Portions of chapter 5 were previously published in "Favelas and the Aesthetics of Realism: Representations in Film and Fiction," *Latin American Cultural Studies* 13, no. 3 (December 2004): 327–42; reprinted by permission of Taylor and Francis Group, http://www.tandf.co.uk. Chapter 10 was originally published as Maha Yahya, "Let the Dead Be Dead: Memory, Urban Narratives, and the Post–Civil War Reconstitution of Beirut," in *Traumes urbans. La ciutat i els desastres, Urbanitats Digital* 9, Centre of Contemporary Culture of Barcelona, 2006, http://www.cccb.org/transcrip/urbanitats/traumes/tra_cat.htm; reprinted with permission.

Copyright 2007 by the Regents of the University of Minnesota

All rights reserved. No part of this publication may be reproduced, stored in a retrieval system, or transmitted, in any form or by any means, electronic, mechanical, photocopying, recording, or otherwise, without the prior written permission of the publisher.

Published by the University of Minnesota Press
111 Third Avenue South, Suite 290
Minneapolis, MN 55401-2520
http://www.upress.umn.edu

Library of Congress Cataloging-in-Publication Data
Urban imaginaries: locating the modern city/Alev Çınar and Thomas Bender, editors.
    p.cm.
  Includes bibliographical references and index.
  ISBN 978-0-8166-4801-6 (hc: alk. paper)—ISBN 978-0-8166-4802-3 (pb: alk. paper)
1. Cities and towns. 2. Cities and towns—Cross-cultural studies. 3. Sociology, Urban. 4. Social history—1970   I. Çınar, Alev. II. Bender, Thomas.
  HT119.U692 2007
  307.76—dc22   2006035354

The University of Minnesota is an equal-opportunity educator and employer.

This book is dedicated to Richard and Jodi.

CONTENTS

ACKNOWLEDGMENTS

The seeds of this collective work were planted at the International Center for Advanced Studies at New York University (ICAS/NYU), where between 1997 and 2001 most of the contributors participated as fellows of the Project on Cities and Urban Knowledges. Alev Çınar extends her most sincere feelings of gratitude to Tom Bender for having created such supportive, congenial, and intellectually inspiring conditions at ICAS/NYU; the participants had an invaluable experience developing new perspectives, expanding the scope of their research, and starting a scholarly enriching dialogue across disciplines on the topic of the city that culminated in the present book.

She also thanks the Center for Research in Transitional Societies (CRTS) of Bilkent University, particularly its director, Guliz Ger, without whose generous support the conference at Kemer, Turkey (where the authors of this book first gathered) would not have taken place. Thanks to CRTS and the facilities and funds offered by Bilkent University, we had an excellent gathering at Kemer, where a more systematic debate on the questions that guide this book began. Alev Çınar expresses her appreciation and gratitude to the Department of Political Science at Bilkent University and to its chair and dean, Dr. Metin Heper, for enthusiastic encouragement and support toward her ventures into interdisciplinary research and international collaborative projects.

Tom Bender thanks the remarkable staff at ICAS, who provide essential institutional support that sustains the work of the Center; the intellectual commitment and professionalism of Barbara Abrash, the associate director whose counsel was so important to the establishment of the Center; and Jeryl Martin-Hannibal, who assumed the position of administrator at the time of the conference from which this book emerged. He also thanks New York University, particularly the deans of the faculty of arts and science—former dean Phil Furmanski and current dean Richard Foley—for their consistent support and wise advice.

The chapters in this book represent only a portion of the rich discussions and the work presented at the conference at Kemer, and we wish to mark here the important contribution of the whole body of participants in the conference. We thank Carrie Mullen and Jason Weidemann of the University of Minnesota Press for the support and assistance they extended toward the completion of this work.

INTRODUCTION

The City:
Experience, Imagination, and Place

Alev Çınar and Thomas Bender

The ambition of urban theory is the generation of a formal definition of the city and a characterization of the urban experience. Once the city stood out against the landscape, walled and compact, surrounded by a hinterland. As late as the middle of the twentieth century, such a concept of the city—a center and a surround—seemed adequate. But in fact the boundaries of cities, the relations of different groups within the city to a variety of extended meanings and connections beyond the imaginary wall, are both pervasive and distinct. This has become obvious in our own time as cities sprawl endlessly outward, without a clear endpoint, indeed sometimes blending into the next city or a whole region as in the U.S. northeast. Indeed, the matter of definition and of locating the city is so daunting that there is not, as Robert Fishman has pointed out, even a commonly accepted word for the giant social aggregations of our era, while the architect Richard Ingersoll believes that "cities have become impossible to describe."[1]

The chapters in this book respond to this condition by turning away from the conventional markers of the city that no longer seem to mark and take a different approach to the city. They focus on how, amid such ambiguity and indistinctness, the city is nevertheless imagined as at once indefinite and a singular space and on how this space is shared by a population with various cultural commitments and translocal attachments and yet understood as a distinct entity. In other words, rather than focusing on the city's materiality for definition, the emphasis of these chapters is on the city as a field of experience as well as the way social and physical space is imagined and thus made into urban culture. We assume, as

Kevin Lynch did long ago, that urban dwellers and users orient themselves by constructing an imagined city—what he called a cognitive map, which deviates in meaningful ways from the cartographer's map, with its solidity and boundedness. The imaginaries explored in these chapters are richer and more pluralized than those investigated by Lynch, but they serve urban dwellers by locating the city and themselves in it. Our claim is that the city is located and continually reproduced through such orienting acts of imagination, acts grounded in material space and social practice. As such, this book leaves aside, at least for the moment, the general question of definition, accepting the sufficiency of the urban imaginary of those in the city and those using it. We seek to understand those meanings, which may lead by an alternate route to new levels and types of generalization about cities, their internal organization and division, as well as their extension. It focuses on the idea of the imagination in explaining the ways in which a city is conceived so unquestionably and obviously as a single space.

When Benedict Anderson introduced the idea of the imagination as constitutive of national communities, he may not have realized the significance of the depth and scope of his innovation. He restricted his idea of imagination to the formation of national communities. Yet after the "linguistic turn" in the humanities and social sciences, realized after his book was initially published, we can see that this concept may be expanded to explain the constitution not only of nations but also of all sorts of social and political institutions, ranging from the family to the state and, in fact, to all of social reality itself, including space. Indeed, just as nations are imagined communities, it is possible to conceive of cities as imagined places or as an "imagined environment," as James Donald puts it.[2] In fact, the role of print capitalism—the engine of Anderson's interpretation of the emergence of nationalism—may be even clearer in respect to modern cities.[3]

As elaborated by Anthony King in the introductory essay, it is impossible for the city to be experienced in its totality. Any one person's experience of a city is bound to remain limited and partial to a fragment of the city and to their unique perspective of that fragment. Hence, as King puts it, the city "exists only in our heads." This issue of totality and the modern city's resistance to a totalizing account was at the heart of Walter Benjamin's famous "Arcades project." Walt Whitman's poetry makes the same point. If Whitman could not or would not form the complexity of New York into a closed narrative, relying instead on great lists, so Benjamin created not a singular narrative or principle of order for Paris, leaving us instead a remarkable indexing and filing system, especially rich in images, that emphasized the multiplicity of the modern city.[4] Benjamin's ambition to bring the multiple images of Paris into a Marxist social analysis of the city did not reach the closure such an analysis

Alev Çınar and Thomas Bender

implied. By contrast, David Harvey's recent and brilliantly executed *Paris, Capital of Modernity*, a title that evokes Benjamin's famous agenda-setting essay, "Paris, the Capital of the Nineteenth Century," probably comes as near as any Marxist—or anyone else—will to a singular, comprehensive, and theoretically consistent synthetic analysis of a modern metropolis.[5]

Benjamin more than Harvey points to the direction taken in this volume. Once we suspend the assumption that a city is a totality, which implies conceptual and definitional closure, then it becomes meaningful to inquire how cities are imagined in more open ways, more accommodating to translocal connections, internal tensions, and generally loose ends, yet still recognized as distinct from the larger environs, social and physical. To locate, identify, and understand such a city draws the scholar, we argue in this book, toward the imagination and toward the making and remaking of public culture. Such a city culture is a shared, if not unitary, mental image of the city, however limited the particular image of the city that is held by any one urban "shareholder."

These chapters seek to contribute in two ways to our understanding of the imagination as constitutive of social reality in general and of urban space in particular. First, this book looks at how imagination works on a collective basis. Whether it involves the constitution of national communities, or of social reality, or the city itself, the constitutive power of the imagination lies in its collective nature. Although it is obvious that imagining a nation into being involves a collective rather than an individual act of imagining, Anderson's account does not really clarify the relation of the individual imagination to the collective one. Yet, illuminating this difference and connection is vital. It is the *social* production and reproduction of the nation or city that enables the reification and naturalizing of the city or nation that enables its persistence *as a thing* in space and over time. Anderson discusses the origins of a sense of the collective nation, but he does not deal with the social reproduction of that collectivity over time, which involves the interplay of social practices and imagination.

The making of a collective imagination is a public process; indeed, one might well speak of the making of urban public culture. Such a notion is inspired by Jürgen Habermas. His classic work, *The Structural Transformation of the Public Sphere,* is not easily adapted to the analysis of the modern metropolis.[6] First, except for the discussion of eighteenth-century coffeehouses, Habermas does not concern himself with the space of the public, or the space in which public culture is made. Second, as has often been remarked, the public sphere for Habermas is a highly rationalized exchange that is as cognitive as it is communicative. To understand the making of the urban collective culture, a much wider notion of communication and the public is needed, a point made particularly by social historians who have been both inspired by and critical of Habermas's work. Geoff Ely and Mary Ryan in particular suggest a much wider range of participants in the making of urban public culture and many more forms of communication, including simple bodily presence in a public place.[7]

The key focus common to the individual chapters in this book is to examine the ways in which the collective imagination takes place through a wide range of daily practices of urban dwellers. As different chapters reveal, the very practice of daily urban life emerges as the means through which the collective imagination that conjures up a city takes place. The collective imagination operates not only through the written text such as the newspaper or the novel as Anderson suggests, but also through a variety of different media in daily life, which is a vast field of collective experience. These urban experiences involve travels, interactions, and communicative practices of people within a city, which function to weave a sense of connectedness in space and in turn serve to imagine the city as a single place. The sorts of daily practices that are dealt with in this book include popular media, film, art, and trade and market relations or personal networks that function similarly as tools for the building of a collective imagination.

What is common in all these experiences is that they function as the media through which certain collective narratives are produced and disseminated. These narratives tell the story of the city, produce its history, set its many boundaries, define its culture, or hierarchically situate its dwellers around the categories of class, race, religion, sexual orientation, or ethnicity, and map these onto certain city spaces and remove them from others. Indeed, it is through the production and dissemination of such narratives that certain parts of a city or sometimes its presumed totality is marked as old and historical or new, traditional or modern, rich or poor, or as a "black neighborhood," an "upper-class" part of town, or a "gay haven." In sum, we argue that a city is produced and sustained, that is, located, in such narratives that proliferate through the daily travels, transactions, and interactions of its dwellers, thereby shaping the collective imaginary. Each of the chapters here looks at a particular instance through which narratives of a city are produced. While Yükseker examines business transactions among shopkeepers and their customers where a particular narrative of Istanbul and its borders is produced, Fojas looks at film in constituting a certain narrative of Los Angeles; Cohen uses the medium of art to read a specific narrative of Paris; Simone observes popular narratives produced through eating habits of certain drivers in Douala, Cameroon; Jaguaribe looks at novels and film toward the construction of a narrative of the favela in Brazil; and Shami examines narratives of Amman as they emerge in the daily talk of the urban elite.

There are also competing narratives that seek to produce very different imaginations of the same city, as LeVine illustrates in the case of Jaffa–Tel Aviv, where contestation involves not only the boundaries of the

Alev Çınar and Thomas Bender

city, but also whether there is in fact a single city or not. We also see in Çınar's and Roy's work how official discourse itself produces narratives of a city, as they attempt to direct the collective imagination into the conjuring up of a city in certain ways so as to fulfill particular goals of the modernizing state.

The second contribution of this book is to demonstrate the ways in which such collective imaginations are constitutive of not just communities and solidarities but also of space. Just as the "nation" is an abstract concept that is reified through a variety of different representations circulating in daily life, so is the "city." However, it is easier to recognize the symbolic nature of the representations through which the "nation" is reified, due to the highly ambiguous nature of the referent, such that a person (the "national hero"), a piece of cloth (the flag), a statue, a coin, or a piece of land can all be equally effective in conjuring up the image of the nation.

Typical representations of the city are weaker than those of the nation. The reason is partly historical. The consolidation of modern nation-states significantly reduced the power of cities. This subordination of cities to nations in the modern era weakened the potency of urban symbols as well as the political and other forms of power cities had held. As a result, the "city" and the symbolic nature of representational aspects of the city's being are more difficult to acknowledge. Despite the common knowledge that the city is socially heterogeneous and an uneven space that is difficult to represent, it is often naturalized and reduced to a map. This default representation, as one might call it, is often taken for granted, and city maps, with the unambiguous boundaries, are taken as "real," not as representations, something that makes it more difficult to think about the city as a multifaceted imaginary space.[8] Yet, as LeVine and Shami both demonstrate here, maps of a city can be quite inconclusive, ambiguous, and highly contested, thereby revealing that far from being objective, natural, and factual, they are equally metaphorical in functioning as symbolic tools with which a city is reified as a single tangible place in the collective imagination. In addition, other chapters demonstrate that cities are evoked and reified in the collective imagination not just through maps but also through monuments, statues, paintings, novels, films, residential projects, new schemes of urban planning, or even seemingly trivial eating habits.

As these studies illustrate, if cities are constructed through the act of collective imagination, then we need to look for the city in such media of the collective imagination as literary texts, popular media, films, the daily discursive reality of inhabitants, and numerous other forms of the public culture of daily life.

Regardless of the medium of representation, such narratives of the city produced through various acts of collective imagination serve to construct, negotiate, and contest boundaries. Cities are products of many solidarities and boundaries. Not only territorial borders mark a city. A complex web of social, economic, and cultural boundaries operating along class, gender, ethnicity, race, and other lines concertedly shape the ways in which cities are imagined, perceived, and experienced. Such boundaries are present not only on maps, streets, and the physical structures that sustain the imagined city, but also in daily social interactions, habitual practices, images and icons, daily public discourse, and media representations. These boundaries are both internal and external— boundaries that set apart the urban from the rural, that mark and reify national territory and land, that separate ethnically, racially, or religiously defined communities, that organize class differences, that differentiate the local from the global, the inside from the outside, and map all these differences on to urban spaces, neighborhoods, and similar spatial divides.

Individual chapters explore various boundaries that constitute cities, as such boundaries become the sites of contestations and politics. They interrogate the ways in which class, race, gender, ethnicity, religion, alternative nationalisms and modernities, and postcolonial and diasporic experiences are implicated in the making and negotiation of the boundaries that constitute cities. They demonstrate that the search for the city is the search for the ways in which boundaries that constitute cities are produced, disseminated, institutionalized, contested, and negotiated in various instances of daily urban life constituting and continually reproducing the collective imagination.

In sum, rather than asking what a city is, this book asks how one gains access to understanding of the urban imaginary. Where exactly does one look? With what disciplinary combinations? What is the relation of the imagined city—whether in the mind of the urban actor or the scholarly analyst—to the everyday life in cities? Who and what represents that life? Who counts as an urban inhabitant? What are the bounds of the city? What practices of everyday life are relevant? Are there some experiences that more effectively open the city for inspection by the urban scholar and enable representation of the city? Is a city ever experienced in its totality and impartially? Is the scholar, like the urbanite, captured by parts and partiality?

These questions urge us to consider how meaningful it is to talk about the city as a single place where there is a characteristic urban experience. Doubtless, position and condition produce discrepancies in the ways in which a city is perceived and experienced. Indeed, the public culture of a city is an ongoing contest over terrain. Much of the city's social and political dynamic derives from attempts to possess and appropriate this terrain. Of course, the contest is over not only physical territory but also all manner of public spaces (newspapers, schools, places of leisure, etc.). But the prize is always relative influence, legitimacy, and security for the meanings particular individuals and groups, whether formally institutionalized or informal, give to their own lives and to civic life. The result is the constant making and remaking of urban culture as local, private, or public concerns are brought to the broader terrain of public culture. It is a reciprocal process; private concerns brought to the public culture change that culture, even as that culture affects the local and particular solidarities that constitute it. In other words, the ways in which a city is conceived, experienced, and represented are always conditioned by politics.

Motivated by these questions that challenge the notion of a city as a unified and contained thing, the body of work gathered here builds on the assumption that there is no single definition of the "city." The city, we are suggesting, at least metaphorically, speaks back to the disciplines, and what it says depends on where the city is and what aspects of city life are being examined. The starting premise of the book is that it is not possible to represent a city in any impartial and objective way, independent of a context of networks and boundaries and from the many and diverse ways in which the city is subjectively experienced. Of course, assuming that there are as many "cities" as there are urbanites and analysts is reductionist in its own way. There are instances whereby the ideas of the city and urban practices partially converge. The challenge of contemporary urban analysis is thus to locate them even as the restless analyst recognizes the particularity of each perception and representation. But one must begin by opening up the analytical field, and this book seeks to explore and locate different ways in which the city is conjured up in political, spatial, and ideational practices as it becomes the locus of the modern, the national, or the global. If all cities are part of the modern, the national, and the global, their relations to these large categories and solidarities are distinctive to their time and place. Hence a wide range of cities are examined here.

The chapters look at diverse urban experiences in different parts of the world and seek to demonstrate the ways in which collective imaginations become possible through diverse mediums including cinema, market relations, narratives produced via informal networks, literary and textual imaginations, or the official discourse of the state as it is inscribed on the city through various urban development schemes, monuments, and structures. As these studies illustrate, in all these diverse cases, such interventions constitute the city by shaping or contesting its boundaries, its unity, its cohesion, and its singleness.

THE CITY AND ITS BOUNDARIES

The introductory chapter by Anthony King addresses the question of imagination by tracing the different ways in which the "city" has been conceptualized in the history of urban theory. King demonstrates that the imagination of the city depends very much on the specific ways in which the larger world is imagined. In other words, the city is always conceptualized in relation to its externality, even if that externality is internalized and represented locally. As such, cities are imagined in relation to either the colonized society where they emerge as sites of resistance and transformation, or to the metropolitan power where they are conceptualized as sites of domination and assimilation, or to the larger region defined in terms of expanding trade relations and economic activity, or to the larger empire that has shaped and transformed many cities under its reign.

King sets the terms of analysis for the study of the city, which is adopted by the rest of the chapters, in that the attempt to locate the city involves the study of its many boundaries that constitute the city in relation to its externality. Indeed, each subsequent chapter does exactly this by examining the city in question through its boundaries, whether they are founded, redrawn, contested, negotiated, or transformed through the daily interactions of dwellers.

The rest of the chapters address three main themes in relation to cities and are grouped accordingly. The first set of chapters explore different ways in which the boundaries of a city are constructed in relation mainly to its exterior but including as well the ways divisions that may originate outside of the city affect its internal relations. Since cities are identified with place and are largely about spatial relations, place is often assumed to define their boundaries. More and more, however, the city is understood as extending beyond the local, beyond a particular place. At least, it is understood to be embedded in structures, networks, and processes that are larger than it. Since the end of the walled city, the question of what constitutes an urban boundary has been in various ways indefinite, more so now than ever, and these chapters illuminate that issue. They examine the relation of the city to its larger context, to its changing boundaries or extensions. How is the city constituted in relation to its boundaries that separate its exterior from its interior? How does the city contribute to the constitution of its larger context, whether that other context is geographical, ethnic, economic, cultural, or political? What is the extended city's relation to the national state and state system? Questions of the definitions and relations of the "local," "global," and "cosmopolitan" are inevitably raised. In what way is the city present in the global and the global in the urban?

It is not only the sense of place that sets the boundaries of a city but also the movement of its inhabitants. How is the sense of place unsettled by such movement and exchange of the inhabitants of a city with its exterior? What boundaries are at stake when the movement and transactions of city dwellers increasingly involve places and people beyond the local? What are the ways in which spatial and other boundaries that are conditioned by dominant hierarchies of race, gender, ethnicity, or class called into question and unsettled as a result of such expanding translo-cal, regional, and global relations?

Looking at the Laleli district of Istanbul where an informal market is formed between merchants from the former Soviet Union and local vendors, Yükseker draws attention to the city as borderland. According to Yükseker, this area of Istanbul emerges as an urban borderland because it does not belong to a particular nation or a city, but rather the space itself becomes a transnational space. It is transnational not only because the par-ticipants of this public culture formed around trade activity are from differ-ent countries in the region but also because their activity is not regulated and overseen by the state. What constitutes Laleli as a borderland is the unregulated nature of this activity, the ambiguous national affiliations of the constituents of its community, and the constancy of the movement and transnational flow of its constituents. These flows make it impossible to draw any stable boundaries that delineate the nation, its ethnicity, norms of citizenship and belonging, or even the city itself in an unproblematic way.

As Yükseker notes, Laleli is a socially constructed urban space "through the everyday encounters of people in streets, shops, and public places." As she illustrates, a city space is formed through the daily activity and interac-tion of people, whereby a public culture is created that allows for the collective imagination of the city in a particular way, an imagination that comes to be institutionalized through daily activities and interactions. This notion of the borderland as a space that is created within a city shows how borders that constitute a city, or likewise a nation, are fluid, con-stantly changing, and porous, subverting attempts to arrive at unambigu-ous and clearly demarcated definitions of a city. Indeed, a borderland created right at the center of Istanbul as a space that is not really part of Istanbul, as a market that is not really national, and as a public culture whose participants do not necessarily reside in that city nor are citizens throws into question the definability of the city.

Fojas examines the construction and contestations of multiple bound-aries that constitute a city, Los Angeles, through the medium of film. Basing her discussion on an analysis of several Latino films, Fojas exam-ines subtle but powerful ways in which several borders, particularly of ethnicity and class, are produced and contested within the city as she traces them through the travels and experiences of Latinos. She demon-strates that there are at least four borders that are drawn through the daily interactions and movement of immigrants through the city.

First is the border between the national community and the Latin American immigrant where the Chicanos themselves serve as this boundary that separates the national self from its Latin American other. The presence of the Chicano, by competing with and overpowering the immigrant for jobs and belonging, serves to privilege the North American national subject. The second border is that which is drawn between different neighborhoods within the city that recall national boundaries. As most saliently illustrated in the film *The Border,* the border between Mexico and the United States is reproduced within the city between Mexican and Anglo-American neighborhoods. The third is the border that delineates North American national identity, particularly in contrast to the immigrant populations in Los Angeles, as these borders are drawn by immigration policies of the 1990s. Finally, Fojas explores the making of the border along class lines, dividing the city around wealth and poverty. While the wealthy neighborhoods of Hollywood remain inaccessible to them, a whole class of immigrants find themselves in a city that offers nothing but the unlivable conditions of poverty. Fojas draws our attention to another way in which a border city is produced and reproduced through a double representation: both through the experiences of immigrants and also through the medium of film.

Looking at the maps and other visual representations of Paris in the nineteenth century, Cohen examines how the ideology of the modern city shapes the boundaries, imaginations, and representations of the city. Cohen draws attention to the ways in which waterways in Paris, which played a central role in the city's industrialization and thereby were very much part of the daily flow of urban life, have been systematically excluded from various later representations of the city. Cohen argues that this exclusion of the waterways is a product of the specific ideology of the city prevalent at the time, which celebrates stability, unity, and fixity across time and space in contrast to fluidity, disorder, and transience symbolized by waterways. In other words, the dominant ideology of modernity at the time that shapes the construction of the modern city as a place of permanence and solidity leaves no place for waterways in the imagination of Paris. Cohen also illustrates how, during the shifts and changes in the ideology of the city in the twentieth century, when the city came to be conceptualized as a place of flows and fluidity, transience and process, waterways were included back in the representations of Paris. Cohen's account is a brilliant demonstration of the ways in which a particular imagination of a city comes to be institutionalized through maps and other visual representations and how such boundaries are drawn by the dominant ideology of the city at the time. If the prevailing ideology emphasizes constancy and solidity, the boundaries of the city exclude things that are fluid and transient, such as waterways.

COMPETING NARRATIVES OF THE CITY: CONTESTED INCLUSIONS AND EXCLUSIONS

The second set of chapters examines the making and remaking of cities in relation to contested boundaries and techniques of exclusions and inclusions. The boundaries of a city are negotiated not only in relation to its externality but also to its internal others. This occurs in view of a real or imagined global or more specific gaze. A city is made and occurs remade on a daily basis through a complex network of interactions, negotiations, and contestations yielding several competing narratives and images of the city that seek to give it a particular presence and identity. These competing narratives are conditioned by underlying relations of class, ethnicity, gender, race, or religion and seek to attain a hegemonic status, or to sustain an existing hegemony by suppressing alternatives, or to emerge as a counter-hegemonic narrative. These chapters examine the making and remaking of a city around competing images and narratives that seek to either dictate the terms of inclusion and exclusion or otherwise contest existing norms and narratives that frame a city in ways that privilege a particular discourse.

AbdouMaliq Simone's chapter takes us to Douala in Cameroon, which is one of sub-Saharan Africa's largest cities, the significance of which lies in it being a commercial center rather than a place of administrative and political power. In Simone's account, what makes Douala an interesting case is how the construction of this city as a coherent and single place providing its inhabitants a solid sense of community is achieved through locally and spontaneously formed informal social collaboration and networks, rather than through formal governmental interventions and the activities of international agencies, as in the case with other African cities. Simone examines an incident that took place in July 2003 when motorbike drivers, called the *bendskins*, who meet the city's main transportation needs, rallied in protest of police brutality against the *bendskins* and literally shut down the city for eight hours. Simone demonstrates how a sense of community and solidarity is created among Doualans through the spontaneous formation of networks and collaboration that connect distant parts of the city. The specific activity of the *bendskins* as they "steer the roads" of the city functions as the very act by which a sense of the city as a single and connected place is created. Simone also examines the eating habits developed by the *bendskins*, who make conscious efforts to have their meals in different and new parts of the city, and produces narratives of this activity.

These experiences of the city of Douala through the activity of the *bendskins* show how a city is produced through collaboration by its inhabitants by producing and disseminating narratives of urbanity and a sense of urban cohesion. The travels of the *bendskins* in the city serve to weave a sense of social and spatial cohesion, produce and disseminate a common narrative of community, and mark the boundaries of the city. These travels that seek to continuously expand and cover new parts of the city function to map a sense of community onto the streets and diverse corners of the city, which are significant particularly because they serve a boundary-creating function in a place that is not coded, structured, and bound governmentally through engineered urban plans and maps.

Looking at one/two cities of Israel, Mark LeVine brings forth a situation where the lack of such a social cohesion and communal solidarity results in ambiguous boundaries that throw into question the very city status of a city. Closely examining the making of Israel's "World City" Tel Aviv and its controversial city-turned-neighborhood Jaffa, Levine explores how the coexistence of competing narratives of the city throws into question the boundaries that constitute the city and separate it from its surroundings. LeVine demonstrates how Tel Aviv was made by overthrowing and erasing the existing Arab landscape during the British Mandate period. However, while the resulting new space was recognized as a city by its Jewish inhabitants and the British administration, the Arab population living there did not see it as such and instead treated the area as their agricultural land. This failure to create a single narrative of the city among its inhabitants resulted in a lack of correspondence between the image of the city conjured up by its name and the officially delineated place. As LeVine demonstrates, it is still not clear whether Jaffa and Tel Aviv are two cities or one. This ambiguity is particularly apparent in the space between the two cities where parts and patches of land used by Arabs as agricultural land have been turned into suburban residential areas by other city dwellers. These urban and rural patches are so interwoven as to defy all attempts to clearly delineate a boundary that separates the rural from the urban, the city from its surroundings, and Jaffa from Tel Aviv.

Jaguaribe's essay examines overlapping images and narratives of the favelas of Rio de Janeiro and São Paulo in Brazil that are mobilized toward the construction of the collective imaginations of the city and of the nation. Exploring realist literary and cinematic representations of the favelas since the 1960s, Jaguaribe argues that such representations function to produce new images of the modern city as a site of fragmentation, multiplicity, and ambiguity. These realist representations portray the favelas simultaneously as romanticized sites of carnival and entertainment and as dangerous sites of urban life exposing its community to the threat of drugs, shootings, crime, and violence. Jaguaribe suggests that such images are mobilized in order to create the effect of realism and become the media for the negotiation of the coherence, solidarity, and mapability of the city. In other words, we see again how competing images and narratives of the city and its neighborhoods serve to subvert and contest the boundaries of the modern city and are mobilized to challenge assumptions about the coherence and solidarity of city life and its boundaries.

THE CITY AND THE VISION OF THE NATION

The third set of chapters studies the ways in which the city and urban space are related to nationalist projects that fuse the distinct but intertwined aspirations for nation building and modernity. The urban experience often takes shape in relation to questions of belonging and identification. These chapters explore the ways in which the city becomes a site of national identification and the articulation of alternative visions of the nation. It explores the image and identity of a city as it becomes the articulation of a particular modernity or vision of a national future wherein different groups seek a sense of belonging. As the locus of modernity and nationalism, the city becomes the site for the negotiation of what is to be included into the making of the national community and what is to be excluded. This negotiation is often articulated as a question of integration and/or resistance of the particular and historical to the new and modern, the local to the national, the marginal to the center, and the rural and suburban to the urban. How does the city become the locus of identification that provides either a sense of belonging and participation in the national community or an estrangement from it? What are the ways in which cities and city spaces become the main sites from which national identities are forged, nations are built, and issues of modernity and modernization are negotiated? These chapters explore the ways in which the city becomes implicated in the consolidation of the nation-state and the articulation of contending notions of nationhood and modernity. They address questions related to nation building, including citizenship, territorial consolidation, centralization of power, integration and assimilation, or contestations of these as they are articulated spatially, architecturally, and geographically.

Seteney Shami's and Alev Çınar's chapters both examine the city in relation to the nation-building project. While Shami explores the case of Amman, which emerges as an incomplete and disjointed city as a result of the inconclusiveness of the nation-building project in Jordan, Çınar looks at the building of Ankara as a capital city that is the product of a carefully forged and engineered nation-building process.

Shami demonstrates how the urban elite in Amman continually draw their urban identities from other cities in the region rather than Amman. She also shows how the lack of a consistent and hegemonic national project results in the changing of urban planning schemes from one administration to another, which in turn results in the lack of a consistent and overarching urban discourse and hence negates Amman's identity as a city. One of the most revealing signs of this inconsistency and the lack of a hegemonic urban discourse is the continual displacement of the city center that marks Amman as a city with no center.

The significance of Shami's discussion is further emphasized by Çınar's study of the making of Ankara, where the nation-building project initiated and engineered by Mustafa Kemal Atatürk resulted in the construction of a new city in the image of the nation where every statue, monument, square, and avenue was built and named so as to create a new nation and constitute its citizens. Çınar demonstrates how the city of Ankara was built with the central concern of constituting and institutionalizing the founding ideology of the new Turkish state and establishing the state as the agent of modernity that inscribed the nation into space. Examining the building of the city center, erection and placement of monuments, and the making of Atatürk's Mausoleum Anıtkabir and other significant urban sites, Çınar illustrates the ways in which Turkish nationalism, secularism, and official modernism were instituted against their alternatives through the construction of the city, the arrangement of its spaces, the engineering of its appearance, and the regulation of the flow of daily life. Çınar argues that this carefully engineered creation of a new national city and a modern urban life in Ankara was in effect the material consolidation of the new nation.

Looking at the construction of the steel towns of India (namely, towns conjured up by the national state around steel plants so as to provide residential areas for the workers), Srirupa Roy diverts our gaze to new urban spaces that are created by postcolonial nationalism between the center and the boundaries of the nation. These steel towns created "elsewhere," outside the center, also have boundary drawing functions in the sense that they carry and expand the limits of the nation beyond what is constructed at the center. Roy draws parallels between the construction of such steel towns and the Nehruvian nation-building process at the time, such that the steel towns were erected as symbols of "progress and growth of the nation through the planned guidance of the state" toward the fulfillment of the national dream that the new Indian state promised its citizens.

Tracing the trajectory of these towns from promised dreamworlds into sites of disintegrated communal solidarity, Roy explores how these steel towns turned from being sites of the national promise to a "national problem." During the 1960s when most of India was struck by interreligious violence, similar riots and demonstrations also resulted in the rapid disintegration of the communities of the steel towns. Roy argues that the failure of the state to effectively address the issue of interreligious violence in India was replicated in the reform plans of the steel towns, resulting in failed attempts to resolve the communal fragmentation. Roy's account once again demonstrates the ways in which the construction and transformation of cities and urban communities are an integral and constitutive part of the nation-building process.

The last chapter in this section also draws attention to the close-knit relation between the making of a city and nation building. Writing on the reconstruction of Beirut and particularly the city center after the civil war, Maha Yahya explores the place of the city in shaping the contours of modernity and defining national identity. Yahya demonstrates how the rebuilding of the city is inextricably linked to the rebuilding of the nation in Lebanon after the country was torn by a bloody civil war that lasted fifteen years. Yahya illustrates the ways in which the making of a new city center in the absence of a clearly defined national identity involved the careful erasure of all memories of the civil war and of all the deaths— both the deaths of citizens and the death of the city. The post–civil war Lebanese state sought to build a new national identity and history that omits the civil war experience altogether. Yahya argues that this "clean-slate" view of a new national project is reified in the making of the new city center in Beirut.

NOTES

1. Robert Fishman, "Megalopolis Unbound," *Wilson Quarterly* 14 (Winter 1990): 30, 398; Richard Ingersoll, "The Disappearing Suburb," *Design Book Review* 26 (1992): 5.

2. James Donald, "Metropolis: The City as Text," in *Social and Cultural Forms of Modernity*, ed. Robert Bocock and Kenneth Thompson, 417–61 (Cambridge, UK: Polity Press, 1992), 427.

3. See Neil Harris, "Covering New York: Journalism and Civic Identity in the Twentieth Century," in *Budapest and New York: Studies in Metropolitan Transformation, 1870–1930,* ed. Thomas Bender and Carl E. Schorske, 248–68 (New York: Russell Sage, 1994).

4. Walter Benjamin, *The Arcades Project,* ed. Rolf Tiedemann, trans. Howard Eeland and Kevin McLaughlin (Cambridge, Mass.: Harvard University Press, 1999).

5. David Harvey, *Paris, Capital of Modernity* (New York: Routledge, 2003). It is worth noting that while Harvey has Benjamin very much in mind, his proclaimed model is the classic history of Vienna by Carl Schorske, which reveals the dissolution of a common, civic sense in Vienna (Carl E. Schorske, *Fin de Siècle Vienna: Politics and Culture* [New York: Alfred A. Knopf, 1979]).

6. Jürgen Habermas, *The Structural Transformation of the Public Sphere: An Inquiry into a Category of Bourgeois Society,* trans. Thomas Burger and Frederick Lawrence (Cambridge, Mass.: MIT Press, 1989, orig. 1962)

7. Mary P. Ryan, "Gender and Public Access: Women's Politics in Nineteenth Century America," in *Habermas and the Public Sphere,* ed. Craig Calhoun, 259–88 (Cambridge, Mass.: MIT Press, 1992); Geoff Eley, "Nations, Publics, and Political Cultures: Placing Habermas in the Nineteenth Century," in ibid., 289–349. See also Thomas Bender, "Metropolitan Life and the Making of Public Culture," in *Power, Culture, and Place: Essays on New York City,* ed. John Mollenkopf, 261–71 (New York: Russell Sage, 1988); Thomas Bender, *The Unfinished*

City: New York and the Metropolitan Idea (New York: The New Press, 2002), chs. 4, 13.

8. The development of modern maps as the bird's eye view of space, thereby giving the impression of objectivity, is discussed by Benedict Anderson, *Imagined Communities* (New York: Verso, 1983), 163–86.

BOUNDARIES, NETWORKS, AND CITIES

Playing and Replaying Diasporas and Histories

Anthony D. King

The city now stretches across nations, just as migration and diasporic cultures extend nations beyond their geographic territories.

—C. Greig Crysler, *Writing Spaces*

CITIES AND REPRESENTATIONS

As researchers and scholars engaged in representing various aspects of the world to others, we tend to think of "the city" as somehow singular, as some kind of self-contained, bounded entity, a social, spatial, or experientially tangible unit. We reify the city. We give it a name. We may see different cities as separate and isolated dots on a map that locate the city in relation to a larger space, perhaps a state, linguistic, or religious community or a particular geographical, religious, or ideological understanding of "the world."

Yet this kind of (essentially imaginative) representation is quite static and fixed. It is contrary to our own everyday lived experience in at least three respects.

Unless we are city planners, public relations consultants promoting the city as a tourist site, or perhaps acting in our roles as teachers when we imagine it as a singular totality, our daily lived experience of the city where we spend most of our time is, socially and spatially, exceedingly limited. We live, for much of our lives, only in a *fragment* of the city. If

1

we are lucky, this is a dwelling of some kind, an apartment or a house shared with others. In some cases, it is simply a room. If we work away from home, our experience includes the workspace, an office or workshop and the institution to which it belongs; the journey between the two, by car, bus, bicycle, on foot, subway, train; and places where we shop and take our leisure, the different locations we visit each day. These fragments, perhaps neighborhoods, nevertheless, are often the stuff of the narratives and tales of the city, the site of soap operas, the bases of communities and grounds for protests, social movements and group nostalgias, and sites of memory. They form the basis of one kind of urban identity.

For the rest, what is referred to as "the city" exists only in our heads or in the discourses of those who work in the various arts and media: television, the press, theater, radio, films, novels, DVDs. In the succinct phrases of cultural theorist, James Donald:

> To put it polemically, there is no such *thing* as a city. Rather *the city* designates the space produced by the interaction of historically and geographically specific institutions, social relations of production and reproduction, practices of government, forms and media of communication, and so forth. By calling this diversity "the city," we ascribe to it a coherence or integrity. *The city,* then, is above all a representation. But what sort of representation? By analogy with the now familiar idea that the nation provides us with an "imagined community," I would argue that the city constitutes an *imagined environment.*[1]

In the second place, through the development of modern transportation technology, the social and geographical "lived experience" of an increasing proportion of the world's population is not simply of one city but a number of cities (or at least fragments of these). Through the even more explosive growth in innovative communications and information technology, cities both collect as well as connect subjects together, both in terms of intracity and intercity. Their "lived experience" of the urban has further been enhanced and also confounded by the vast proliferation worldwide of information as well as visual imagery of the city, electronic, photographic, and textual. Collective imaginaries of the city, therefore, are necessarily highly complex. One city (or part of one) is imagined through the subconscious lenses of many remembered or forgotten others.

Finally, historically, over the last two centuries, the proportion of the world's population actually living in urban places—many of them large cities—has mushroomed, rising from about 3 percent in 1800 to over 50 percent in the mid-1990s, with a projected 60 percent from 2025.[2] The fixed dots on the map I referred to previously elide the fact that cities are always *in process,* always on the move, always changing, always growing, never static. How do these realities about the nature of cities and our experience of them affect the way they have been conceptualized, collectively imagined, and individually represented by those who think and write about them?

THEORIZING THE SPACES OF CITIES

In introducing their edited collection, *Imagining Cities: Scripts, Signs, Memory,* Westwood and Williams suggest that the notion of imaginaries might relate to "literary productions, notions of urban myth, memory and nostalgia in the city and its environment, or to the sociological imagination re-cast within the changing realm of new technologies and forms of communication."[3] In the West, where the rapid growth of modern cities took place mainly from the nineteenth century, imagining the city was largely about representing it as an object of social pathology. In the early twentieth century, with the development of the social sciences, it was more about making theoretical models, the diagrams of concentric circles relating social forms to spatial forms, produced by members of the Chicago School. After urban studies had been institutionalized as an academic specialization in the 1960s and the (especially, economic) future of Western cities had come under threat, a more sophisticated, self-reflexive urban critique developed. In *Cities of the Mind,* Rodwin and Hollister brought together a series of essays examining the ways in which "images and themes" of the city—rather than imaginaries, though there is an obvious relationship—had been developed in a wide range of the social sciences: geography, economics, political science, anthropology, sociology, history, city planning. The aim of the various essays was to show how the power of the "city of the mind" determines the nature of research and, in turn, influences urban policy.[4] Concern with the *boundaries* of the city, not only in physical, geographical, and social terms, but also more especially in conceptual ones, is central to the task of imagining the city.

Boundaries can be thought of in many different ways. In the most realist sense, they may refer perhaps to the administrative boundaries of the city. Unlike limits, which suggest a connotation of finality, boundaries are there to be negotiated. There are boundaries to what is acceptable or unacceptable behavior. Boundaries mark the space where one thing turns into something else. They exclude as well as include. They mark transformation between sanity and insanity, health and illness, life and death, between acquaintance and friendship, friendship and love. In this essay, however, I shall treat them largely in their reference to social, spatial, and urban worlds.

SPHERES AND BOUNDARIES

In the three decades between the 1960s and the 1990s, we might say that the study and representation of the city went through three overlapping phases that have shadowed not only what has been happening to the physical development of cities on the ground but also the theoretical imaginings of the larger social and spatial worlds in which the city is thought to exist. In an oversimplified way, these might be characterized as the study of the city qua city, imagined in relation to itself or to others similar to or different from it; from the 1970s, the city in relation to the society where it exists; and since the 1990s, the city in relation to the world, or better "worlds." However, it is not just the apparent social and spatial boundaries of the city—often delineated in positivistic fashion by batteries of statistical data—that have changed. Especially from the 1990s, as is evident in the preceding citation from Donald, the very notion of the city, what it is, what it means, how and in what manner it exists, has been deconstructed and displaced into the realm of memory, the imaginary, the subconscious, whether through the rhymes and rhythms of poetry or the virtual space of cybernetics.[5] A burgeoning literature on representations of the city in literature, film, art, theater, the media, and popular culture confirms the overwhelming significance of the city, and urban life in contemporary Western cultures. We see this especially in comparison to the world outside the West, where, despite the persistently rapid growth in the number and size of cities, nonurban, rural populations are still in the majority. However, this literature has also destabilized the positivistic models and theories of the city which had their origin in the influential, but ethnocentric, theoretical work of many Western scholars, of which the sociologists of the Chicago School were the most prominent. What Park, Burgess, and others like them attempted to do by looking at Chicago through a series of concentric circles was to somehow "domesticate" the city, to bring order to it by emphasizing patterns and coherence, to eliminate the chaos, as well as the fear, of what could not be controlled.[6] Closely related to this conceptualization, was the imagination of planners. During a period in which these models of scholarship were dominant in the wider world outside the West, it seemed that the forms and processes of every city had somehow to defer to those of Chicago.

Yet between the 1950s and 1970s, critiques of these universalizing theoretical imaginings of the city began to surface. Scholars in areas both in and outside the West came up with different theories, different forms, and different trajectories for the past and future of cities in their regions. Of equal, if not more, importance, these critiques depended on alternative imaginings of the economic, political, cultural, and social worlds in which the city was thought to exist. For an increasing number of Western and subsequently "non-Western" commentators from the mid-1950s, the world was not one but three: the First, Second, and Third. This was a paradigm that, while increasingly contested, has lasted from 1954 till today.[7] Whether referenced as "developed, developing, or underdeveloped," the "three worlds" were explicitly *not* part of what today we would call a "global imaginary" but part of another form of ideologically inspired world informed by "development studies." Imagined through the lens of specific sets of economic and social indicators, "cities in the developing world" were assessed according to an assumed trajectory of economic growth, as it had taken place in the West. From the early 1970s, "Third World cities," assigned with similar characteristics, were assumed to not only be different from those in the "First World," but also to be quite independent and disconnected from them.[8] Alternatively, cities might be located and consequently influenced by being in "the core," "periphery," or "semiperiphery" of the "capitalist world-system."[9] As the discourse of the latter was supplemented (rather than displaced) from the mid-1980s by the paradigm of "globalization," which, according to one of its principal theorists, represented the "world as a single place,"[10] the concept of "world" and "global cities" developed in parallel.

In the early years of this new theoretical paradigm, globalization as a process was seen as something new, developing only from the 1970s; "global" cities, with their concentrations of capital, multinational headquarters, international banks, financial services, were equally represented as a new phenomenon, the "cotter pins" of the world economy, exercising the capability of global control. Subsequently, however, globalization has been accepted as a more long-term historical process, for some commentators, characterized by archaic, premodern, modern, imperial, and postcolonial phases.[11] This injection of temporality into what is primarily a spatial metaphor has also included the recognition that before the middle of the twentieth century some 85 to 90 percent of the earth was controlled by Europe as colonies, protectorates, dependencies, or commonwealths. In this context, many if not all of what today are being called "world" or "global cities" were the "imperial" and "colonial—often capital—cities" of yesterday. Looked at through these different historical lenses and for different interpretative objectives, such cities are now being reimagined, as "postimperial" or "postcolonial." In short, the nature of the world space(s) in which cities are perceived to exist and how that world has actually come to be "worlded" as such affect the way we think of any city's boundaries and how far they extend and also influence what happens in the city.

BOUNDARIES, GLOBALIZATION, AND THE CITY

At the center of the debate about the impact of globalization on the city has been the emergence of the "world" or "global" city concept.[12] The seemingly positive aspects of this approach have been to extend, almost infinitely, the significant boundaries of the city, taking note of the "global" extent of exchanges and flows that link cities worldwide.[13] Yet just as their Chicago School predecessors, theorists of the world or global city have not escaped criticism; like all systems of classification, categories depend on the use of comparable data drawn from a single universe. In this case, the conceptualization of the world or the "world city" is one principally of the world economy. Prior to the events of September 2001, it has been a universe largely devoid of cultural, religious, and historical difference; national and urban politics; the recognition of weak as well as strong power; and the specter of postcolonial histories that haunt the present of many cities worldwide. Like earlier theoretical models, concepts of "world" and "global" cities have been largely developed on the basis of Euro-American imaginings and Euro-American data, but with less attention to their divergent histories.

It is worth remarking in this context that virtually all of the cities discussed in this collection were at one time, for varying periods from the very brief to the more extended, either the capitals or in the colonial satellites of powerful empires, whether Ottoman, Spanish, French, German, British, or Portuguese. The world in which they exist, therefore, is not simply a singular "global world," devoid of boundaries, limits, or values but, in their various localities, one where different national and local histories, different conceptions of time and memory, and different collective aspirations account for the formation of distinctive alliances and identities.

As an increasing number of scholars have recognized, appropriating the term "global" for the analysis of cities (to say nothing of its liberal proliferation elsewhere) has turned out to be a sloppy and inadequate metaphor. Its sense of totalization and its application to all and sundry has become an excuse for analytical imprecision. As a metaphor, the smooth, circular, and evenly balanced spherical image conveyed by the term represents a form of epistemic violence that disguises the grossly uneven economic conditions and exploitative social relations that characterize the so-called global city.

LOCATING THE CITY

How we imagine the city, its boundaries, and the space in which it exists depends largely on what our interest in the city is and what we want to know about it. As David Harvey wrote three decades ago, "Urbanism is not just the history of a particular city but the history of a system of cities."[14] Seen from an inherently structuralist perspective, the interrelated elements of different systems and structures, at various levels, are more significant than the elements when considered in isolation. We should therefore add to Harvey's reference to the system of cities the economic, political, and cultural spaces in which those systems are embedded. All of these spaces extend the meaningful and significant boundaries of cities. As an example, we might imagine alternative ways of thinking about erstwhile colonial (or also postcolonial) cities in terms of the geopolitical and geocultural space they occupy. In each case, specifying both the spatial as well as the conceptual boundaries raises different kinds of questions.

We can begin by thinking of the city in relation to the colonized society or territory: Bombay in relation to India, Boston in relation to New England, Rio de Janeiro in relation to Brazil.[15] In this case, the city can be seen as a spearhead of economic, political, and cultural penetration and the structural organization or reorganization of the colonized society or territory. Simultaneously, we might examine the resistances from the local indigenous society, the growth of new colonial or indigenous elites, and the development of a distinctive social, ethnic, racial, or religious composition of the city. Our focus, in this case, is primarily at the level of the local.

Alternatively, we may focus our attention on the city in relation to the metropolitan power. Here, thinking about the colonial city can provides insights into the metropolitan society, its institutions and culture, in ways that an examination of the metropolitan society alone does not permit. Metropolitan political and cultural practices and institutions, lifted out of their original social and historical context and transplanted elsewhere, can be seen in a new light. What is specifically Spanish in the planning and architecture transplanted to Havana? How is it different from that in Mexico City? How does the French colonial presence in North Africa impact the development of Paris?

A third avenue is to imagine the city in relation to the boundaries, political or territorial, imposed by the region, which might be a continent or a seaborne trading area such as the Indian Ocean, the Mediterranean, or the Caribbean. Attention might focus on the collaborations or rivalries of different colonial powers, the development of specifically regional economies, and the patterns of migration that help to determine collective identities.

Alternatively, we might imagine the city in relation to the larger space of a transcontinental empire, whether Dutch, Ottoman, Spanish, French, British, or Portuguese. Within the cities of these colonial empires, legal, economic, political, and cultural institutions—such as particular forms of religious practice, urban planning models, language, or educational systems—are shared by all cities within the imperial hierarchy. Yet in each city, such institutions and practices become transformed and hybridized by local conditions and indigenous populations. Each creates its own space, traditions, and practices.

In brief, spatially *locating* the city within different sets of boundaries generates very different questions and very different answers. Where this issue is illustrated with regard to spatial boundaries, it is clear that boundaries can be equally well understood in relation to an infinite variety of conceptual realms—religion, law, politics, expressive activities, ideas about science, medicine, and the natural world, to mention only a few.

MIGRATIONS, NETWORKS, DIASPORAS, AND IDENTITIES

Urban imaginaries are also about the construction of imaginary identities. "Urban" and its antithesis, "rural," are descriptive categories. They describe the nature and attributes of particular types of environment and settlement. To be described as urban supposedly gives some insight into a subject's lifestyle, their habitus. Living in a city, bearing the identity of an Angelino, Berliner, New Yorker, or Delhi-wallah, confers the added value of the attributes of a particular city.

The relatively late recognition of the historical dimensions of globalization has drawn attention to the fact that transnational migration and the existence of global diasporas is not just a recent phenomenon. For example, Pieterse speaks of globalization as "a long term historical process involving ancient population movements, long distance cross-cultural trade, the spread of world religions and the diffusion and development of technologies due to inter-cultural contact."[16] Many of these enforced as well as voluntary migrations were the result of long-term processes of colonization and imperially driven wars, conquests, and displacements, often accompanied by slavery and the use of indentured labor.

Voluntary and forced migration around the world transplanted peoples and cultures from their original places of birth to regions and cities far from their places of origin. In the process, there was planted, in "racial," ethnic, linguistic, gender, religious, and cultural terms, the potential for what in the future would become the flows and spaces of globally created and "imagined" identities that were not necessarily those of "the nation."[17] Two, three, or even four centuries after the initial migrations, through possibilities created by modern communications and transport technologies, these potentialities were to burst into the real and imaginary networked spaces of identity that have extended the boundaries of cities worldwide. Jamaican-born cultural theorist, Stuart Hall, has described in powerful and emotive terms how the social category of "Black" emerged in the 1970s to become a force in cultural politics on both sides of the Atlantic;[18] one of Hall's students, Paul Gilroy, has added to our conceptual vocabulary the notion of "The Black Atlantic" to describe the transnational space in which (especially) Black music culture flourishes.[19] In the early twenty-first century, the popular Indian magazine, *India Today,* circulating widely among the more than 20 million Indian diaspora around the world, coined the phrase "Global Indian," hoping thereby to both create identities and enlist loyalties of people of Indian origin for the economic and cultural interests of their national mother country. The more than 55 million "Overseas Chinese," apparently separated only by water from their ancestral home, form a significant business community, particularly in Southeast Asia. Through the activism of global feminism in recent decades, we can now refer to the political category of "women" world-wide. All are transnational identities and networks that massively extend the boundaries of city politics and the limits of the urban economy. Many similar examples could be cited. The extent of some of these historical migrations we can note from the following.

In the three hundred years after 1550, 14 or 15 million West African slaves were taken to North, South, and Central America, including the Caribbean. From 1620 to 1914, 13.5 million British and Irish moved to North America (part of the 30 to 35 million Europeans who migrated there). From the sixteenth to the nineteenth century, 2.3 million Spaniards went to South America. In Asia, from 1820 and 1914, 22 million Chinese migrated to Southeast Asia, and in the two decades after 1900, 8 million Japanese went to East and Southeast Asia and the United States.

In the second half of the nineteenth century, 3 million migrant workers left India; 5 million Germans and 5 million Italians moved to North America.

In more recent times, after 1947, 15 million Indian and Pakistani refugees moved into what became their respective states. These historic figures underline the citation from Pieterse about the long history of migration in the world.[20]

Ethnicity and "race," their social construction and visual "recognition," does not provide an automatic, essentialized cultural identity. Yet historically, they have been powerful identity features, especially when associated with language, particularly language as a mother tongue.

Yet, language as a mother tongue has also been the outcome of politics and power, of the strength of empires and nation-states and their policies of cultural control. It is these factors which help to explain why, among some 5,000 languages still existing in the world (with about one hundred accounting for 95 percent of the world's population), the most widely spoken as mother tongues not only reflect the numerical size of their ethnic populations, but also the historical facts of European imperialism. As Mignolo points out, 75 percent of the world's population speaks twelve languages, of which six, English, Spanish, German, Portuguese, French, and Italian, are those of the principal European and American imperial powers.[21]

In addition to "race," ethnicity, and language, a further and, in recent times, an increasingly significant layer of real and potential identity formation is obviously that of religion, again, associated with the proselytizing activities of imperialism.[22]

The obvious identity criteria are those of nation, class, and gender. However, in comparison with other criteria already mentioned, we should note how relatively recent, in terms of modern world history, belonging to and deriving one's identity primarily from a nation-state (as opposed to a tribe, clan, region, language, or empire), nationality actually is. Prior to the French Revolution, there were some twenty of what we would today recognize as nation-states. Only in the "nation-forming" phase of world history, from 1815 to the establishment of the United Nations in 1945, did the number of nation-states increase from twenty-three to sixty-seven. During most of the nineteenth and the first half of the twentieth century much of the population of the urbanized (as well as nonurbanized) world belonged to various European and Asian empires. Only in the era of global modernity from the second half of the twentieth century when the nation-state has become the sole form of civil governance recognized worldwide have we seen numerically significant growth in the number of states so that, in the fifty years from 1945 to the mid-1990s, the figure has risen from sixty-seven to over 190.[23]

What this suggests is that the degree of commitment of individual subjects worldwide to the "imagined communities" of nation-states and how important this is in terms of political, economic, or cultural mobilization can vary immensely between "older" and "newer," larger or smaller, and richer or poorer states. Indeed, as the proportion of the urban population of the world increases, with ever fewer in rural areas and ever more in large five or even ten million plus cities, the number of which is predicated to grow exponentially in the twenty-first century, the likelihood of people's identity being primarily determined by their commitment to their *city*, as provider of work and welfare, shelter and sustenance, culture and leisure, is very real. In particular situations, subjects will act according to their identity as Cariocans, Lahoris, or Londoners rather than Brazilians, Pakistanis, or British. In this context, the establishment of a United Cities Organization before the end of the twenty-first century to supplement, if not displace, the functions of the United Nations is more than a pipe dream. After all, few of Europe's politicians and intellectuals were imagining the realistic possibility of European governance and European citizenship in the early twentieth century.

Indeed, cities themselves have been instrumental not only in imagining their own collective identities, but also in imagining the community of the nation. Anderson's concept of print capitalism is essentially an urban phenomenon. Industrial urbanization and the city as a socio-spatial mechanism have been equally instrumental in the construction of other foundational identities, particular those of class, "race," and gender. The formations of nation and class, both in terms of the bourgeoisie and the proletariat, have been inseparable processes from the French Revolution to the present.[24]

What is the significance of these "extramural" (as well, indeed, as "intramural") identities when thinking about the boundaries and the imaginaries of the city? It is these that, through the very particular, historically influenced, global and postcolonial flows and spaces, help determine its politics and its policies, its investments and its cultures. It is these which help explain the similarities and the differences between cities and cultures.

HISTORIES AND CATEGORIES

The tendency in many urban studies to assume that there is a single theoretical frame within which to interpret the form, character, and culture of cities and that this frame can be established on the basis of Euro-American historical experience and theorizing has, despite constant critiques, remained a remarkably persistent assumption. In 1965, the American urban geographer, Norton Ginsburg, well versed in the knowledge of cities outside the West, particularly those in Asia, set out what he described as "the most important question in cross-cultural urban research."

> To what extent are basic differences in culture, even given the spread of "modern Western" technology and values, likely to give rise to different urbanization processes and the creation of cities as artifacts that differ from culture to culture?[25]

Yet almost forty years later, the editors of *Postcolonial Urbanism: Southeast Asian Cities and Global Processes* still find it necessary to counter the view that "cities in Africa, Asia and South America could be understood on the models of cities in Europe, Australia or the United States" and that global urbanism "can be regarded as a uniform or homogenous outgrowth from Europe and America."[26] These comments were prompted by a recent "reader" on "the city," but they could equally apply the criticism to recent publications on "the city" which offer the development of Los Angeles as a suitable paradigm to suggest what may happen to all large metropolises in the future. The task of contemporary city writers seems to be to construct an ever-expanding conceptual terminology to describe and explain the ever-spatially expanding "postmetropolis,"[27] the terminology locked within the ideological-cultural language of the analysis. For contributors to *The City*, this is the "postmodern urban condition" with its references to privatopias, edge cities, splintered labyrinth, exopolis, flexicities, or hyperspace.[28] While these may be appropriate for the spaces of Los Angeles, the history and culture of each city is sufficiently different to require, in addition to the more basic analytical concepts, its own descriptions and categories drawn from its own cultural histories and languages. As Westwood and Williams point out, cities, as well as the distinctive communities within them, construct and inhabit their own senses of time, their own histories.[29]

In this context, the unique historical circumstances of the origins and development of Los Angeles, located in a territory doubly colonized by Europe (first, by Spain; subsequently, by America), the colonizers effectively erasing, or marginalizing, the indigenous population in the process, and creating in the twentieth century the modern, sprawling city of Los Angeles, can hardly be found in any other city in the world. The possible exception is Australia where not only has a brake been put on the elimination of the indigenous inhabitants, but they are also increasingly gaining in political clout. The fact that two cities are territorially extensive gives them nothing in common except that fact itself. Despite the historical evidence that the United States began (and has continued) as a colonial society, though is now an increasingly imperialist nation-state, there is a persistent aporia among many American urban historians to recognize these assumptions in explaining the circumstances of Los Angeles' spatial, ethnic, and linguistic-cultural development, even when 40 percent of the Los Angeles metropolitan region is Spanish-speaking and the remainder mainly Anglophone. Where are the voices, and tongues, of the original, indigenous inhabitants? The appropriate comparative conceptual framework for the imaginative analysis of Los Angeles' development would be one that took into account the colonial urbanization of Latin as well as North America, Australasia, and South Africa. Instead, as far as this particular past is concerned, the city is dehistoricized, decultured, and respatialized in order to leapfrog into a representation of "global space," rather than the "postcolonial" or even "colonial" space in which it might be more accurately represented.

To conclude, the adoption of the term "global" into the academic discourse about cities has created as much confusion as enlightenment. What is evident from many recent studies of so-called global cities, London, Hong Kong, Istanbul,[30] or others, is that different cities have their own understandings and different imaginations of what has been labeled as "global." The nature of that "global" has been constructed in relation to their own histories and has everything to do, both positively and negatively, with their relations to their own regions, their own economies, and their own imaginaries.

NOTES

1. James Donald, "Metropolis: The City as Text," in *Social and Cultural Forms of Modernity,* ed. Robert Bocock and Kenneth Thompson, 417–61 (Cambridge: Polity Press, 1992), 427. See also James Donald, *Imagining the Modern City* (London: Athlone Press, 1999).

2. David Clarke, *Urban World/Global City* (London: Routledge, 1996).

3. Sallie Westwood and John Williams, eds., *Imagining Cities: Scripts, Signs, Memory* (London: Routledge, 1987), 1.

4. Lloyd Rodwin and Robert M. Hollister, eds., *Cities of the Mind: Images and Themes of the City in the Social Sciences* (New York: Plenum Press, 1984), x.

5. See especially the two essays on "Virtual Cities" in part 4 of Westwood and Williams, *Imagining Cities*.

6. Ibid., 3.

7. Leslie Wolff-Phillips, "Why 'Third World'? Origin, Definition, and Usage," *Third World Quarterly*, 9, no. 4 (1987): 1311–27.

8. Early uses of the category are Hugh Tinker, *Race and the Third World City* (New York: Ford Foundation, 1971) and David Dwyer, *Third World Cities* (London: Macmillan, 1974); more recent, David A. Smith, *Third World Cities in Global Perspective* (Boulder, Colo.: Westview Press, 1996).

9. Immanuel Wallerstein, *The Modern World-System: Capitalist Agriculture and the Origins of the European World-Economy in the Sixteenth Century* (New York: Academic Press, 1974).

10. Roland Robertson, *Globalisation: Social Theory and Global Culture* (London: Sage, 1992).

11. Anthony G. Hopkins, ed., *Globalisation in World History* (London: Pimlico, 2002).

12. Anthony D. King, *Global Cities: Post-Imperialism and the Internationalisation of London* (London: Routledge, 1990); Saskia Sassen, *Global Cities: New York, London, Tokyo* (Princeton, N.J.: Princeton University Press, 1991; 2nd ed. 2001); Paul Knox and Peter J. Taylor, eds., *World Cities in a World-System* (Cambridge: Cambridge University Press, 1995).

13. Manuel Castells, *The Rise of Network Society,* vol. 1 (Cambridge, Mass.: Blackwell, 1996).

14. David Harvey, *Social Justice and the City* (London: Edward Arnold, 1973), 250.

15. See Anthony D. King, *Urbanism, Colonialism, and the World-Economy: Cultural and Spatial Foundations of the World Urban System* (London: Routledge, 1990), 22–27.

16. Jan Niederveen Pieterse, *Globalization and Culture* (Lanham, Md.: Rowman and Littlefield, 2004).

17. Benedict Anderson, *Imagined Communities: Reflections on the Origins and Spread of Nationalism* (London: Verso, 1983).

18. Stuart Hall, "Old and New Identities, Old and New Ethnicities," in *Culture, Globalization, and the World-System: Contemporary Conditions for the Representation of Identity,* ed. Anthony D. King, 41–68 (Minneapolis: University of Minnesota Press, 1997).

19. Paul Gilroy, *The Black Atlantic: Modernity and Double Consciousness* (Cambridge, Mass.: Harvard University Press, 1993).

20. *Oxford Atlas of the World,* 4th ed. (New York: Oxford University Press, 1996).

21. Walter Mignolo, *Local Histories/Global Designs: Coloniality, Subaltern Knowledges and Border Thinking* (Princeton, N.J.: Princeton University Press, 2000), 9.

22. The major world religions accounting for 1,667 million Christians of different persuasions, 881 million Muslims, 663 million Hindus, 312 million Buddhists, 172 million Chinese Folk Religion, 18 million Jews, and 17 million Sikhs, according to the *Oxford Atlas of the World* (1996).

23. Anthony H. Birch, *Nationalism and National Integration* (London: Unwin Hyman, 1989), 25.

24. Eric Hobsbawm, *Nationalism* (Harmondsworth, UK: Penguin, 1997).

25. Norton Ginsburg, "Urban Geography in Non-Western Areas," in *The Study of Urbanisation,* ed. Phillip M. Hauser and L. M. Schnore, 311–46 (New York: John Wiley, 1965), 319.

26. Ryan Bishop, John Phillips, and Wei Wei Yeo, *Postcolonial Urbanism: Southeast Asian Cities and Global Processes* (New York: Routledge, 2003), 2. Their reference is to Richard T. LeGates and Frederic Stout, eds., *The City Reader* (New York: Routledge, 2000).

27. Edward M. Soja, *Postmetropolis: Critical Studies of Cities and Regions* (Malden, Mass.: Blackwell, 2000).

28. Allen J. Scott and Edward W. Soja, *The City: Los Angeles and Urban Theory at the End of the Twentieth Century* (Berkeley and Los Angeles: University of California Press, 1998).

29. Westwood and Williams, *Imagining Cities,* 6.

30. King, *Global Cities*; Ackbar Abbas, *Hong Kong: Culture and the Politics of Disappearance* (Minneapolis: University of Minnesota Press, 1997); Caglar Keyder, *Istanbul: Between the Local and the Global* (Lanham, Md.: Roman and Littlefield, 1999).

PART I

The City and Its Boundaries

1

ECONOMY AND GENDER IN THE URBAN BORDERLAND

The Public Culture of Laleli, Istanbul

Deniz Yükseker

In the past quarter of a century, cities have become arenas for the circulation of *transnational* flows of capital, goods, people, and ideas. This is enabled by the receding regulatory powers of nation-states and the widespread access to telecommunications technologies. Urban struggles over resources, places, and meaning that emanate from this process often result in the creation of new social, ethnic, and class boundaries *within* cities.[1] Yet, sometimes, cultural and economic *borderlands* may also be produced through the mobility of goods, money, people, and ideas.

This chapter addresses the creation of such a cultural and economic borderland in Istanbul during the 1990s, at the nexus of transnational movements of goods and people. Migrant merchants and petty traders from the former Soviet Union (FSU) buy and sell from each other in the district of Laleli, creating a marketplace that lies economically and culturally outside the "local" and the "national." This urban space is a borderland in which migrants and itinerants have fashioned a unique public culture[2] that consists of economic, cultural, and gender practices produced through the interactions between transnational groups of people. The ways of doing business in Laleli, marked by the absence of state regulation of economic transactions, are at once an amalgam of the previous economic experiences of the involved people and a product of the unsettling of gender codes. Since there are hardly any preexisting social bonds between the buyers and the sellers in Laleli, informal market exchange is facilitated through makeshift interpersonal relations. On the one hand, exchange is immersed in an eclectic idiom that brings together the actors' know-how with operating beyond the gaze of states and a notion of "trust" that is couched in small business practices in both Turkey and the FSU. On the other hand, in the public culture of Laleli, consensual sexual relationships nurtured by gender stereotypes are often beneficial for business.

The cultural and economic practices in this marketplace lie beyond the "national" and the "local," both because the trade is not formally regulated by the state and because its participants are from different countries and ethnicities. Therefore, the public culture that has emerged in Laleli through social intercourse does not so much belong to any one cultural group as it is the product of a collective imagination in the course of constant transnational movement by persons of diverse citizenship, ethnicity, and gender identity. In this respect, the urban borderland in Laleli also challenges received notions of transnational social spaces woven across borders such as diasporic or ethnic communities. When conceived as a borderland, the contours of Laleli as an urban space cannot be easily defined, since it is the movements of people and their exchanges with each other that bring about this public culture, rather than any local, ethnic, or national attribute. As such, the boundaries of the borderland are porous and shifting, as is the public culture that is the result of collective imagination: The idioms of trust and friendliness and business relations colored by sex are fluid and contingent on the flows of people, goods, and money.

Shuttle Trade

During the 1990s, Istanbul and within it Laleli became a thriving node of a trade network that emanated from former Soviet republics. Every year, tens of thousands of people "shuttle" between Russia and other ex-Soviet republics and cities in the Middle East, North Africa, Europe, and South and Southeast Asia to purchase moderate quantities of goods for resale back at home. The shuttle trade (chelnochny biznes) that takes place between Turkey and the FSU is unregistered for the most part, evading taxes and customs duties, since the involved states are either unwilling or unable to regulate it. Home to the majority of shuttle traders (chelnoki), Russia has allowed billions of dollars of unrecorded imports[3] when the production of consumer goods plummeted after the collapse of the socialist economy at the turn of the decade. The actors of informal transnational trade are mostly jobless or underemployed workers who took up trading when they found that surviving on state incomes or pensions was impossible. Among the shuttle traders who visit Istanbul regularly, those from Russia, the Ukraine, and Belarus are overwhelmingly women, whereas men are more numerous among chelnoki from predominantly Muslim republics.

Turkey does not regulate "suitcase trade" (bavul ticareti)—as unregistered small-scale trade by foreigners is called in Turkish—since the government perceives it as an effortless way to attract much needed foreign currency for the ailing national economy. At a high point in the mid-1990s, suitcase trade "exports" were estimated to be close to $9 billion annually, a significant sum compared to Turkey's official total exports which ranged between $13 and $27 billion per annum over the decade.[4] The Laleli area, which lies in the background of Istanbul's historic districts of Sultanahmet and Beyazit, emerged as a transnational marketplace for traders from Eastern Europe and the Middle East during the 1980s. Formerly a residential neighborhood, dozens of hotels were built in Laleli in the 1980s, attracting tourists from Poland, Czechoslovakia, Hungary, and Yugoslavia as well as from countries in North Africa and the Persian Gulf. The removal of travel restrictions and the collapse of the state-led economy resulted in a stream of shuttle traders from the Soviet Union starting in 1990. Their onslaught brought about a mushrooming of stores that catered to their demands for clothing, shoes, and leatherwear. In Laleli,[5] shopkeepers mediate between small-scale informal manufacturers of apparel and footwear in Istanbul and the Russian-speaking customers who shuttle back and forth from the FSU. In much the same way as the shuttle traders, most of the shopkeepers and their workers in Laleli are not "locals." The majority are Kurds from eastern and southeastern provinces and immigrant groups from the Balkans. As opposed to the shuttle traders, the shopkeepers and workers in Laleli are overwhelmingly male.

The interactions between these two groups of people created the Laleli marketplace. The people in Laleli are often culturally and ethnically strangers to each other. Their unregulated economic interactions resemble clandestine crossings over a border, hence the notion of "urban borderland." This term draws attention to the unique nature of the transnational social space created by the activities of the shuttle traders. Laleli does not host trading minorities or transnational migrants that share a lived or imagined heritage, but rather, it is a meeting point of strangers who collectively improvise an eclectic yet common set of practices in the course of buying and selling from each other.

A growing body of scholarship has emerged around the notion of transnationalism in the last decade. In its version popularized by scholars of migration, the concept of transnationalism refers to the social space created by the border crossing, that is, the economic, cultural, and political activities of migrants between their original and host societies.[6] The thrust of this framework is that *local* communities stretch across national borders through migration thanks to easy access to air travel and communications technologies in our age. There has emerged a parallel body of scholarship on the formation of transnational cultural and political practices, including those of diasporas. According to many scholars writing within this framework, growing transnational connections unsettle our notions of territoriality and national identity, and thus they might also challenge the nation-state.[7]

However, not much has been written on how people on the move, yet who are not migrants or diasporic groups, articulate with or disrupt local, national, and global structures. Specifically, the concern here is with people who crisscross borders regularly in search of a livelihood as petty traders or illegal workers. Such people create translocal social spaces through their interactions with others, resulting not in reproductions of lived or imagined local or original cultures, but rather, eclectic idioms that help them operate in the new setting. This chapter concentrates on the urban social space that emerges when separate groups' paths intersect in the course of transnational movement in a place that lies on the margins of state regulation. Thus, the usual focus on *within*-the-same-group processes as they are enacted transnationally is replaced with a focus on an urban space that is the product of *between*-different-groups interactions.

Laleli does not represent an informal "ethnic economy," where the social ties within an immigrant community might effectively substitute for legal regulation of economic activities.[8] Nor are the shuttle traders reminiscent of historical trade diasporas for whom trade routes were settled by co-ethnic communities.[9] In fact, we might have expected to find patterns of ethnic trading between former Soviet republics and Turkey, given the history of the region. In the nineteenth century, trade around the Black Sea had flourished thanks to ethnic networks built by diasporic groups such as Greeks, Armenians, and Persians.[10] More significantly from the perspective of this chapter, the region was the stage for several waves of refugee flows into Anatolia from the Caucasus, Crimea, and the Balkans in the course of the Ottomans' territorial losses in the second half of the nineteenth century. These groups included Circassians, Chechens, Muslim Georgians, Abkhazians, and Crimean Tatars as well as Turks and Muslims from Balkan countries.[11] Cultural and economic interaction across the region came to a halt in the 1920s, with the formation of the Turkish Republic on the one side and the USSR on the other. When the border gate between the Soviet Republic of Georgia and Turkey was reopened in 1988, for the first time in nearly seventy years relatives and co-ethnics came together. In the ensuing years, Caucasian diasporic groups in Turkey such as Circassians and Abkhazians have rebuilt their relations with their homelands.[12] While some diaspora members made economic investments, others became involved in political movements for independence (e.g., Abkhazia in Georgia).

During the same period, informal shuttle trade from the FSU started to flourish both in Istanbul and along the eastern Black Sea coast. However, the majority of the people who visit Turkey for suitcase trade do not belong to diasporic ethnic groups. Most of them are from Russia,[13] and ethnically they are predominantly Russians. Based on observations in Istanbul and the Black Sea port city of Trabzon, it appears that no "trade diasporas" are involved in suitcase trade between Turkey and the FSU. Lack of co-ethnic trading and the weakness of formal regulation of economic activities have contributed to the creation of an urban borderland in Laleli.

LALELI AS AN URBAN BORDERLAND

This borderland has nurtured the creation of a market culture in the absence of legal and social regulation. The borderland may be defined drawing on both cultural and political economic understandings of this notion. Anzaldúa calls the vague cultural and economic area born of the encounter between bordering societies a borderland. She argues that legal and illegal migration from Mexico into the United States has created "a border culture, a third country." Within this borderland are located the transgressors of sexual, ethnic, legal, and economic "norms."[14] Writing about Mexican immigrants living in a U.S. city, Rouse has suggested that a borderland does not have to be a zone located on the two sides of an actual international border, but that it may also exist in cities where migrants settle and continue to weave relations with their hometowns. He emphasizes that although home and host cities that make up a borderland are "implicated with each other" in various ways, "the line between them never disappears."[15] According to this understanding, a borderland presupposes the existence of a geopolitical line that is simultaneously regulated *and* open to subversion.[16]

In Laleli, a borderland has emerged at the intersection of transnational flows of people in a space where there is hardly any official regulation. Here, the borderland is not so much a "borderline" that cuts through or separates, but rather, it is a "terrain of discontinuity" in which something new is created, culturally and economically. This is a term that Sassen uses in describing the intersection between the corporate economy and the informal economy in a global city as an "analytical borderland":

> Why borderlands? They are spaces that are constituted in terms of discontinuities; in them, discontinuities are given a terrain rather than reduced to a dividing line. . . .This produces a terrain within which these discontinuities can be reconstituted in terms of economic operations whose properties are not merely a function of the spaces on each side . . ., but also, and most centrally, of the discontinuity itself . . .[17]

So, the understanding of the Laleli marketplace as a borderland draws on both Sassen's and Anzaldúa's notions. Thus, Laleli is an *urban* borderland in which a market culture is constructed through the interactions among people from different nationalities, ethnicities, and usually of the opposite sexes. The urban borderland exists not only because of the absence of state regulation of market exchange, but also because it is a "terrain of discontinuity" which engenders activities whose purpose is to fill the absence of regulation. Two different sets of activities take place within the urban borderland. At the economic level, shuttle trade exhibits a degree of *informal* organization beyond state regulation. At the "cultural" level, gender codes and business practices that different groups of people carry with them to the marketplace create a unique public culture.

INFORMALITY IN LALELI

In shuttle trade, legal regulation characteristic of formal international trade is largely absent. This situation is most visible in marketplaces that cater to the foreign shopping tourists. In Laleli, transactions and employment are usually off-the-books. Likewise, the goods are not registered as exports when they pass through Turkish customs. Instead, they are treated as "accompanying baggage" of the tourists. The prevalence of informality does not mean that shuttle trade is disorganized. In fact, it leads to *informal* arrangements to facilitate buying and selling and the transportation of the traded goods beyond the control of states.

For instance, garment manufacturers deliver merchandise to Laleli in the evening in order to avoid Finance Ministry officials responsible for fining tax evaders. Likewise, street vendors and hawkers appear after business hours on Laleli streets in order to escape the scrutiny of the municipal police. In general, the Finance Ministry is prepared to neglect the nonpayment of the value-added tax (VAT) by Laleli suppliers, but since there are no clear-cut policies on this, it is up to individual tax officials and storeowners to negotiate the terms of looking the other way. Thus, Laleli suppliers complain that they have to pay bribes to Finance Ministry officials who visit their stores once per month to check accounting books. Since most suppliers in Laleli are newcomers to this trade, efforts among them to solve the problem of informality are not concerted enough. A Laleli Businessmen's Association (LASIAD) was formed in 1997, with the goals of bringing orderliness to the neighborhood and pressuring the Turkish government to devise a policy to exempt Laleli wholesalers from the VAT. But LASIAD's membership is small compared to the thousands of shops that operate in the neighborhood, and its public voice is weak. It was only in response to lobbying by the well-established Leather Industrialists' Association (an organization that represents the export-oriented and integrated industries of leather tanning and leatherwear) that the government sought to remedy this problem. The Finance Ministry and the Foreign Trade Undersecretariat issued decrees in 1997 that granted enterprises exemption from the VAT if they reported their sales as export earnings. Yet, this arrangement has not benefited small- or medium-scale suppliers in Laleli because of its impracticality and the unawareness of many shopkeepers about it. But it has prompted large-scale entrepreneurs to collaborate with each other to reap the benefits.

Ironically, efforts to create official regulation have precipitated more organization, albeit informal, in activities where such organization is profitable. Perhaps the best example of such informal organization is the cross-border transportation of the goods.[18] In the early 1990s, individual *chelnoki* used to carry heavy sacks full of leather coats, shoes, or garments from stores to their Laleli hotel rooms and from buses to the check-in at Istanbul Atatürk Airport's charter terminal. Alternatively, some shuttle traders from more proximate republics such as Moldova and the Ukraine used to carry all that merchandise back home by bus or train. In either case, traders were obliged to negotiate bribes with corrupt customs officials in their countries. Travel agencies and charter companies quickly noticed the potential for profits in the transportation of goods. By mid-decade, cargo companies emerged that handled the merchandise from hotels in Laleli to all the way through customs in the respective countries. Large cargo companies are partnerships between Russian charter liners and Turkish tourism agencies. They subcontract the hauling of merchandise between Laleli and the airport to smaller firms. Transportation activities are usually off-the-books. For example, small subcontractors are usually unregistered enterprises operating from the basements of hotels. But more significantly, the large companies take advantage of loopholes in existing regulations to facilitate large-scale smuggling. In return for weight-based fees, cargo companies gather merchandise from the shuttle traders and then report it to the Turkish customs as exports, thus enabling them to collect VAT refunds from the government originally intended for Laleli suppliers. Cargo company operatives pay bribes to customs officials at Russian border gates and then deliver the merchandise to the shuttle traders. While this setup has made transportation much easier for the *chelnoki*, it appears that the greatest beneficiaries have been large-scale apparel manufacturers, cargo companies, and large-scale wholesalers in Russia, which collaborate with each other to move millions of dollars of goods under the guise of shuttle trade without paying the corresponding customs duties.[19]

The picture of the transnational shuttle trade network that emerges here is one in which large-scale enterprises are able to collaborate with each other to get around regulations and to replace the lack of an international trade regime in the region with their less than legal operations. In contrast, small- and medium-scale entrepreneurs rely on personal relations to facilitate exchange.

THE PUBLIC CULTURE OF LALELI

Entrepreneurship and employment in Laleli are characterized by the predominance of migrants. Although not large in numbers, the pioneering entrepreneurs in Laleli during the 1980s were second-generation immigrants from Bosnia and Kurds from border towns. These people have brought two kinds of know-how to Laleli, namely language skills and savvy with operating beyond the gaze of the state. Bulgarian Turks and other immigrants from the Balkans can speak Russian and other Slavic languages. Kurds from border towns have another skill: They had previously been operating in a gray zone with respect to the law, having engaged in goods smuggling between Turkey and Iran, Iraq, and Syria.[20] Especially storeowners from Dogubayazit, a town on the border with Iran, emphasized this in conversations with me. When border trade with Iran started to decline in the second half of the 1980s, moving to Istanbul and working in Laleli, where most transactions are unrecorded, had become a reasonable alternative for livelihood. As one shopkeeper from Dogubayazit explained, "[They] were already experienced in dealing with the customs." The same familiarity with informal cross-border trade might be present among a small group of Syriacs with goldsmith and jeweler backgrounds in the Grand Bazaar as well as some Arabs and Kurds, all of whom are from the multiethnic province of Mardin on the Syrian border. Interestingly, Bosnian immigrants share with the Kurds the familiarity with informal trade. A Bosnian hotel owner commented that the earliest Bosnian shopkeepers in Laleli were "used to police beatings." This was because Bosnian salespeople in the Grand Bazaar and Beyazit had been trading with East Europeans in the late 1970s when all the foreign currency transactions were considered black market dealings and hence illegal. Thus, like the smugglers from Dogubayazit, Bosnians used to operate in a gray zone with respect to the law.

However, recent migrants are more numerous in Laleli. The majority of the shopkeepers and workers in the marketplace are Kurdish. Many of them are among internally displaced persons (IDPs) who have sought refuge in cities including metropolitan Istanbul in the past ten years because of the civil war in the southeast.[21] Another large group is ethnic Turks from Bulgaria who were among the 200,000 people that emigrated in 1990 when the former communist government wanted to change their names.[22] Bulgarian Turks have mostly become salespeople and interpreters in stores. Among the Kurds, the younger and the poorer have become porters and street vendors. The more resourceful, those who had some start-up capital, have opened apparel and leatherwear stores.

The *chelnoki* who shuttle to Istanbul regularly, especially the women, have something in common with the Laleli shopkeepers. They are also experienced with operating in economic gray zones. The majority of *chelnoki* in Turkey are from Russia. Women comprise a significant segment of the unemployed and the underemployed in Russia.[23] Scholars agree that during the "transition to market economy" women have become disprivileged in the labor market, suffering from cutbacks both in sectors that require higher education and in the low-wage feminized industries. Governments have not been forthcoming with retraining and reemployment programs or small business development incentives geared toward women.[24] Under these conditions, they have been pushed to the informal and small-scale trading sector in the absence of meaningful opportunities for wage employment or business development.[25] There is a pattern of continuity between women's overpresence in the informal economy today and their role within the "second economy" (unofficial economy) under socialism. As the social services provided by the state and the official distribution system deteriorated in the 1970s and the 1980s, many people sought to obtain services in the second economy, which operated parallel to the state-owned socialist economy. Women's role in this process was crucial as they gradually developed networks and skills to deal with the changes.

Hence, Laleli brought together people most of who were marginalized from formal wage employment and formal entrepreneurship in *both* Turkey and the FSU. Kurdish and immigrant shopkeepers and salespeople in Laleli operated on the margins of the formal economy in Istanbul. Female shuttle traders were pushed out of the state sector, but were not allowed into the privatized structures of the post-Soviet economy. The interactions between members of economically marginalized groups, often of the opposite sexes, led to the emergence of specific economic and cultural practices in Laleli.

The cultural and economic interactions among disparate groups in this urban borderland have produced a unique public culture. Following Zukin's analysis of the cultures of American cities, here public culture refers to the social construction of an urban space through the everyday encounters of people in streets, shops, and public places.[26] According to her, not only shopping malls and business districts, but also marketplaces are spaces where distinct public cultures are built or represented. The public culture in Laleli is the product of the intertwining of disparate gender codes and cultural practices in the urban borderland. Thus, this public culture is brought about by not only economic transactions, but also social and gender relationships that underlie market exchange. There are two interrelated elements of the public culture in Laleli. One pertains to the creation of an idiom for facilitating business whereby "strangers" come to "trust" each other. The other important element of the market culture in Laleli is the gendered nature of business relations between male and female entrepreneurs.

The lack of safeguards on trading and the pervasiveness of informality lead merchants to seek ways of minimizing uncertainty. A time-honored way of circumventing this problem is creating repeat trading patterns through cash and credit flows between pairs of buyers and sellers.[27] The fact that buyers and sellers in Laleli are strangers renders this mechanism a very unique process since there is no possibility of enforcing contracts, payments, and deliveries. The *chelnoki* and the shopkeepers usually engage in trade with the same people regularly and boast of friendly and trusting relationships with each other. Yet, their expressions of trust are often intertwined with complaints about the breach of it.

Storeowners and traders in Laleli often stress the same point: The most important trait of an entrepreneur is being trustworthy in the eyes of both suppliers and customers. Some shopkeepers were unequivocal in expressing their confidence in their trade partners. The owner of a large shoe store in Laleli thought that "Russians" (meaning people from the Slavic republics of Russia, Belarus, and the Ukraine) were "perfect" people. "They are well educated, honest, and sincere," he asserted. He had such faith in their honesty that he said, "I am Turkish, yet I am sorry to say I will not sell another Turk shoes on credit. But I will sell on credit to Russians." Sometimes when a customer was short of cash, he said he let her make the payment after she sold the shoes back home. One Kurdish apparel store owner in Laleli (previously a dairy merchant in the southeast) put the issue of trustworthiness in starker terms: "There are hardly any bad people among Russians. They are much more honest than we are. Christians do not cheat. But Muslims do." He explained that sometimes his customers would pay for half of the goods they bought and pay back the rest during their next trip to Istanbul. Yet, at the other extreme, there are merchants whose businesses were jeopardized by too much faith in their customers. Shopkeepers who delivered merchandise based on promises to pay in the future sometimes found that their trusted trade partners disappeared.

On the side of the buyers, some *chelnoki* said they completely trusted their Turkish[28] trade partners. Shuttle traders who expressed faith in the storeowners commented that Turkish people are usually "fair," "good," and "honest." But others expressed less than full trust, citing the sale of defective or low quality merchandise as the reason.

Thus, the stress on the indispensability of trust for both the *chelnoki* and the local merchants is intertwined with grievances about the lack of it. Does trust really exist in Laleli? If so, does it denote a single thing? Trust in this marketplace is not what economic sociologists refer to as "enforceable" trust, which helps business run smoothly thanks to the enforcing power of social ties within an ethnic, immigrant, or diasporic community.[29] If a shopkeeper runs away with down payments without delivering the goods or if a *chelnoki* disappears without paying for delivered merchandise, there is no social network (such as an ethnic community or a trade diaspora) to right the wrongdoings in the networks of shuttle trade. Neither does trust refer to a societal characteristic, whereby it is assumed to be a generalized moral principle.[30]

In this transnational marketplace, trust has developed as an idiom that "greases the wheels" of commerce in the absence of legal, societal, or community-level institutions. This idiom is a hybrid between the Turkish understanding of trust (*güven*) in small entrepreneurship and Russian understandings of trust and reciprocal exchange (*blat*) nurtured within the social networks of the second economy (and subsequently the informal economy). Furthermore, it is enmeshed in the experience of the participants of the marketplace in operating in legal gray zones.

In Turkey, small business operates on *güven*. This principle suggests that buyers and sellers mutually assume risks when they do business with each other based on lagged payments. An apparel manufacturer remarked that Laleli operated on the same principle. "There may be ebbs and flows. [The garment industry] is risky business. Trust and risk-taking go together." He explained that in the chain from manufacturing apparel to wholesaling and retailing it each person counts on (trusts) the next one in line for successful sales. If there is failure at the final loop of the chain, it reverberates down the line. Thus, payments in all steps depend on the overall performance of the market. Then, trust in small-scale trade and production in Turkey does not denote an enforceable norm or a moral principle, but rather, interdependency between the actors in taking risks together.

Trust is also an important tenet in small-scale activities within the nascent market economy of Russia, although it is completely missing among the new capitalists. The "transition to the market economy" in the former Soviet Union and specifically in Russia has been a bifurcated process. On the one side are the "New Russians," a predominantly male group of entrepreneurs who have been the main beneficiaries of the privatization of state companies and had access to capital by virtue of their previous positions within the Soviet bureaucracy. To a great extent, big private business in Russia is entangled with the mafia and protection rackets.[31] Thus, far from a reliance on trust, Russia's new capitalism substitutes the lack of effective formal regulation with the use of force, that is, organized crime. On the other side are people who seek to complement wages or earn a living by resorting to petty entrepreneurial activities, ranging from selling small items at subway stations to shuttle trading abroad. Small entrepreneurs usually evade taxation and therefore official regulation,[32] while simultaneously struggling to stay away from protection rackets.

Market practices in Russia today are influenced by the ways of doing things that people were accustomed to within the second economy of the Soviet period. Especially one practice stands out in this respect, the *blat* system of informal transactions. *Blat* is a form of exchange characterized by reciprocal dependence, and it engenders mutual trust over the long term. It entails the exchange of "favors of access" to public resources among people who have social relationships with each other (such as kinship, friendship, mutual acquaintance).[33] Given constant shortages in the Soviet economy, *blat* was used widely by people to exchange anything from repairs to information about new deliveries in a supermarket. Reciprocity based on *blat* exchange has survived the socialist economy. Especially women rely on such resources for operating in the uncertain setting of the post-socialist economy. Since contract laws are de facto useless because of the administrative chaos in Russia, people resort to other methods in order to do business. If large entrepreneurs use protection rackets to enforce contracts, for the small business owner, one's word is more important than a contract on paper. In this environment, women petty entrepreneurs boast of their trustworthiness in business relations, a trait that they have nurtured through barter and exchange relations in the Soviet period. On the other hand, they also admit that sometimes they may have to "use their femininity" and present themselves as attractive women when dealing with officials or with racketeers in order to keep their market stalls or get trading licenses.[34]

In Laleli, the participants of the market enmesh the disparate understandings of trust in Turkish and Russian small informal business practices and their experience within the informal economies of their respective countries. Hence, the market culture in Laleli is an amalgam of small business practices in the two countries. None of the transactions involve written contracts, nor are they recorded. Apparel manufacturers sell merchandise on credit to Laleli storeowners, expecting that they would be paid when the goods are sold off. Similarly, shopkeepers sometimes give goods to Russian-speaking customers partly on credit, again on the assumption that they would be paid when the *chelnoki* sell out the merchandise. Nevertheless, storeowners said they usually would not sell on credit above half of the total value of a batch of merchandise. The risk in giving too much credit became obvious during downturns in shuttle trade. In the wake of the economic crisis in Russia in summer 1998, about one third of the shops in Laleli went bankrupt, according to observations in the following summer. Storeowners who relied on sales on credit were the first to go under. Yet, the shopkeepers and shuttle traders interviewed still emphasized the importance of having long-lasting business partners. *Chelnoki* indicated that they sought to shop from the same stores on each visit, and they trusted those people with whom they had been doing business for several years. Likewise, shopkeepers said that they sometimes gave merchandise on credit to a customer whom they trusted, that is, if she was a regular customer. What is noteworthy here is that many entrepreneurs actually conceded that, when the market almost collapsed after the Russian economic crisis, some of their regular business partners (both shopkeepers and *chelnoki*) disappeared—with undelivered merchandise or without paying for purchases. But once trade started to pick up the next year, buyers and sellers found themselves *new* "regular partners."

So, the notion of trust in Laleli is more of an eclectic idiom that helps business run smoothly. It is not enforceable since an overarching "social structure" such as an ethnic, immigrant, or diasporic community does not back it up. "Regular" clients and partners are susceptible to change during economic crises. Thus, the trust that is created through repeat trading is not so much a social norm as it is a lubricant for undertaking business. Precisely because trust operates as an idiom rather than an enforceable social norm, trustworthiness and untrustworthiness, honesty and dishonesty are always intertwined in the public culture of Laleli. Indeed, malfeasance occurs between buyers and sellers who consider each other friends or at least regular business partners. This is to be expected since people who do business with each other casually (without prior socialization with each other) would not trust the other for lagged payments or delayed deliveries and therefore would conclude the deal right at the spot.

The entanglement between trust and malfeasance can be observed most clearly when trade relations are coupled with sexual relationships between male shopkeepers and female shuttle traders. In the uncertain and unregulated environment of Laleli, sexually charged encounters and intimate relationships between some buyers and sellers constitute one way in which market exchange is immersed in social relations. However, gender relations between Turkish nationals and shuttle traders are as much the product of the borderland in which these people operate as the notion of trust itself is. Thus, in the course of interaction between men and women in the marketplace, gender codes and stereotypes are entangled, contributing a unique aspect to the public culture. In order to understand the role of gender in exchange, we must have a closer look at gender relations in Laleli.

SEXUAL RELATIONS INTO BUSINESS RELATIONS

A parallel process to the flourishing of shuttle trade in Eastern Europe and the former Soviet Union during the 1990s was the burgeoning of prostitution in the region. Criminal rings reportedly organize much of prostitution from Eastern Europe,[35] but it also takes place through the flows of petty traders and undocumented migrants. In Turkey, towns along the eastern Black Sea coast and certain districts of Istanbul gained a reputation during the 1990s for the presence of "Natashas"—as women considered to be engaging in prostitution are derogatively called in Turkish. In coastal cities such as Trabzon, Ordu, and Rize, the exchange of sexual favors probably exists in a continuum of survival activities by poor petty traders from the neighboring Caucasian republics and southern Russia.[36]

However, this phenomenon has been blown out of proportion by the Turkish national media, fueling prejudices against women from the region as a group. Enmeshed with conservative sentiments against sexual relations out of marriage, even consensual sexual relationships between the local men and foreign women are often viewed as prostitution.

Likewise in Istanbul, the media contributed early in the decade to the creation of an image of Laleli and the adjacent district of Aksaray as centers of prostitution. The *chelnoki* were presented in sensationalist newspapers and television shows as traders-plus-prostitutes. In fact, suitcase trading and prostitution in the neighborhood are separate activities with separate participants. Nevertheless, the media image of Laleli and the constant presence of blonde, light-complexioned women with outfits that Turkish men consider to be revealing certainly symbolically distinguish this district from other places in Istanbul. Therefore, in addition to its economic aspects, the public culture in Laleli also has a unique gender dimension. Gender codes and stereotypes are entangled in a way that propels cross-cultural sexual relationships as well as friendships, both of which, in turn, help facilitate business.

For many men, this neighborhood symbolically and sometimes physically offers more "liberal" relationships with women such as the possibility of having consensual sex without the obligation of long-term commitment or marriage. Doing business, becoming friends, or getting sexually involved with a "Russian" woman is one of the attractions of working in Laleli for some men. Shopkeepers frequently praise Slavic shuttle traders' physical beauty and liberal behavior, and some acknowledge that they have "Russian" lovers. This may have several consequences from the perspective of doing business. On the one hand, an exchange relationship between two people can sometimes be immersed in sexual/romantic intimacy. The story of a young Kurdish shopkeeper is illustrative of this point. This man had a Ukrainian girlfriend who worked as a salesperson in Laleli. Eventually, the woman decided to go back permanently to the Ukraine, while the man started sending batches of leatherwear to her for sale at a marketplace. Thus, a long distance romance had turned into a business partnership. In another example, a married shopkeeper had a lover from Russia. Apparently, the woman was also married. She frequently flew to Istanbul to buy goods and exclusively shopped from his store. In this case, a business partnership corresponded to a clandestine long-distance relationship.

On the other hand, sometimes sexual attraction between a shopkeeper and a female *chelnoki* gives a business advantage to a woman. A young shopkeeper originally from Bulgaria conceded that he sometimes gave merchandise on credit to his Russian girlfriend. "But it wouldn't exceed several hundred dollars," he stressed. Yet, because he was "soft-hearted," he also lent money to other female customers when they complained of having run out of money. A leatherwear storeowner was rather candid about his sexual liaisons with "Russian" women. He said he had slept with potential customers on several occasions, but when sexual intimacy was coupled with business, he was the one in a disadvantageous position. "Then I was obliged to compromise my trade," he remarked, saying that he would be more likely to sell goods on loan or give a discount to a woman to whom he was sexually attracted. In this vein, I heard stories in Laleli about shopkeepers who were "fooled" by female suitcase traders' beauty, gave them too much credit, and jeopardized their business.

Although the majority of shuttle traders are women, there are many among them who are accompanied by husbands or boyfriends, who complain about unwanted sexual approaches by men in Laleli or who describe their interaction with the shopkeepers as "based on mutual respect." Likewise, many merchants speak critically of the harassment of women on streets, and some even attribute the decline in the numbers of *chelnoki* in the last few years to the behavior of unruly men.

In fact, the importance of gender relations in Laleli goes beyond the issue of sex and romance. Gendered images of the shuttle traders not only pertain to their sex appeal, but also to their traits as entrepreneurs. Turkish men in Laleli are impressed with the entrepreneurship and personal characteristics of the *chelnoki*. I heard storeowners on numerous occasions say that "Russian" women were hardworking, "active," energetic, and "cultured," qualities which they contrasted with Turkish women. Observing well-educated shuttle traders carry heavy sacks, travel long distances, and sell goods in open-air marketplaces in cold weather to earn a living, the store-owners thought that in Russia women were "active" and men were "passive." Entrepreneurship, a field that is dominated by men in Turkey, earned for these women respect in the eyes of their business partners in Laleli. In contrast, men considered their Turkish wives to be "passive," and this made women's labor in the household and in waged employment invisible.[37] Respecting their business partners in this way, Laleli storeowners were usually ready to form friendly relations with customers. For instance, they would help the women shuttle traders find suppliers, show them around the city, take them out to dinner, and help when the women have trouble with the police or customs. Thus, another aspect of the market culture in Laleli that underlays exchange relations was the nurturing of friendships between buyers and sellers, in general, and men and women, in particular.

Conclusion

The Laleli marketplace in Istanbul is an urban place that is bounded not so much by its physical location in Istanbul and Turkey, but by the social practices of the people who frequent it and who are in constant transnational movement. The nature of this social space is not shaped by the interactions of a single ethnic or migrant community, either. Rather, Laleli is an urban borderland, a zone where people from different countries and ethnicities and often with uncertain belonging to a nation-state meet each other for engaging in trade. This urban space should be seen as a borderland in a second sense as well: The economic and social interactions among the involved people are marginal to the "mainstream," that is, to the "formal" economy and the norms of gender relations in Turkey. Therefore, as people engage in gendered business and interpersonal relations, they also collectively construct a transnational social space that is located at the border between formal and informal, local and foreign, and sexually permissible and promiscuous. However, this borderland is not a line that separates. Precisely because of the lack of state-level formal or community-level informal institutions within which trade can take place, the participants of the borderland have fashioned a public culture that is an eclectic amalgam of gender codes and market practices that they bring with them to Istanbul. On the one hand, this public culture consists of a makeshift idiom of trust that helps the initiation of repeated acts of buying and selling and hence nurtures friendly relationships. On the other hand, such interpersonal relations are often colored by the entanglement of gender codes and stereotypes. Nevertheless, the elements of this public culture (notions of trust, friendliness, romance, etc.) are fluid to the extent that they are collectively imagined by the inhabitants of an urban borderland, which is itself bound to shift in the course of the flows of people, goods, and money, rather than being defined in terms of a physical place.

NOTES

The chapter is based on the fieldwork I conducted in Istanbul, Moscow, and Trabzon in 1996–1997, and back in Istanbul in 2001 and 2002. The research consisted of nearly 150 open-ended interviews with shopkeepers, suitcase traders, and other entrepreneurs in the three cities and a nonrepresentative survey with 168 suitcase traders in Istanbul. The fieldwork in 1996–1997 was funded by a research award from the MEAwards. I would like to thank Caitrin Lynch and Kelly T. Brewer for their helpful comments on a previous version of this essay.

1. Saskia Sassen, *Globalization and Its Discontents: Chapters on the New Mobility of People and Money* (New York: The New Press, 1998) and *The Global City: New York, London, Tokyo* (Princeton, N.J.: Princeton University Press, 1991); Çağlar Keyder, ed., *Istanbul between the Global and the Local* (Lanham, Md.: Rowman and Littlefield, 2000).

2. I borrow the term "public culture" from Zukin's work on cities (Sharon Zukin, *The Cultures of Cities* [Cambridge, Mass.: Blackwell, 1995]).

The sense in which I employ this term also partially draws on the way the editors of *Public Culture* have originally described it. Although my emphasis is on everyday urban practices rather than on art forms and cultural products and services, I underline the *translocal* character of public culture, as Arjun Appadurai and Carol Breckenridge also have ("Why Public Culture?" *Public Culture* 1 [1988]: 5–9).

3. For instance, the OECD estimated that unregistered shuttle trade imports accounted for about one fourth of Russia's total imports of $84 billion in 1996 (*OECD Economic Surveys: Russian Federation 1997–1998* [Paris: Organization of Economic Co-Operation and Development, 1997]).

4. Since 1996, the Central Bank of Turkey makes estimations of shuttle trade exports. At a high point in 1996, the Central Bank figure was $8.8 billion. Suitcase trade exports declined significantly after the Russian currency crisis of 1998 to a low of $2.2 billion in 1999. They recovered slightly to over $3 billion in 2001 (State Planning Organization, 2002, http://www.dpt.gov.tr).

5. In the past several years, shuttle trade activities have spread to peripheral neighborhoods of Istanbul where garment and leatherwear production takes place. But Laleli is still the symbolic center and the hub of all suitcase trade-related activities in the city.

6. Linda Basch, Nina Glick Schiller, and Carol Blanc Szanton, *Nations Unbound: Transnational Projects, Postcolonial Predicaments, and Deterritorialized Nation-States* (Langhorne, Pa.: Gordon and Breach, 1994); Alejandro Portes, Luis E. Guarnizo, and Patricia Landolt, "Introduction: Pitfalls and Promise of an Emergent Research Field," *Ethnic and Racial Studies* 22 (1999): 217–37; Thomas Faist, *The Volume and Dynamics of International Migration and Transnational Social Spaces* (Oxford, UK: Oxford University Press, 2000).

7. Stephen Cohen, "Diasporas and the Nation-State: From Victims to Challengers," *International Affairs* 72 (1996): 507–20; Arjun Appadurai, *Modernity at Large: Cultural Dimensions of Globalization* (Minneapolis: University of Minnesota Press, 1996); James Clifford, "Diasporas," *Cultural Anthropology* 9 (1994): 302–38; Ulf Hannerz, *Transnational Connections: Culture, People, Place* (London: Routledge, 1996).

8. Alejandro Portes, "The Informal Economy and Its Paradoxes," in *The Handbook of Economic Sociology*, ed. Neil J. Smelser and Richard Swedberg, 426–52 (Princeton, N.J.: Princeton University Press, 1994).

9. Philip Curtin, *Cross-Cultural Trade in World History* (Cambridge: Cambridge University Press, 1984); Fernand Braudel, *The Wheels of*

Commerce: Civilization and Capitalism 15th–18th Century, vol. 2 (New York: Harper & Row, 1982); for modern day parallels, see Mamadou Diouf, "The Senegalese Murid Trade Diaspora and the Making of a Vernacular Cosmopolitanism," *Public Culture* 12 (2000): 679–702; David Kyle, *Transnational Peasants: Migrations, Networks, and Ethnicity in Andean Ecuador* (Baltimore: The Johns Hopkins University Press, 2000).

10. Donald Quataert, "The Age of Reforms, 1812–1914," in *A Social and Economic History of the Ottoman Empire, 1300–1914,* ed. Halil Inalcik and Donald Quataert (Cambridge: Cambridge University Press, 1994); Eyüp Özveren, "A Framework for the Study of the Black Sea World, 1789–1915," *Review* 20 (1997): 77–113.

11. Kemal Karpat, *Ottoman Population 1830–1914: Demographic and Social Characteristics* (Madison: University of Wisconsin Press, 1985).

12. Seteney K. Shami, "Prehistories of Globalization: Circassian Identity in Motion," *Public Culture* 12 (2000): 177–204 and "Ciscassian Encounters: The Self as Other and the Production of the Homeland in the North Caucasus," *Development and Change* 29 (1998): 617–46.

13. For instance, in 1996, around 1.5 million people visited Turkey by air from the Russian Federation, whereas the number of visitors from all other former Soviet republics was around 500,000 people (*Devlet Hava Meydanları İşletmesi Yıllığı* [State Airports Administration Yearbook] (Ankara: DHMİ, 1997)).

14. Gloria Anzaldúa, *Borderlands: La Frontera. The New Mestiza* (San Francisco: Aunt Lute Books, 1987), 11.

15. Richard Rouse, "Mexican Migration and the Social Space of Postmodernism," *Diaspora* 1 (1991): 8–23.

16. Clifford, "Diasporas," 303–4.

17. Sassen, *Globalization and Its Discontents,* 102, footnote 19.

18. The following discussion of transportation is based on information I gathered from Laleli suppliers and manufacturers and small cargo firms. The large transport companies whose operations were legally questionable refused my requests for interviews.

19. Shuttle traders can pass unlimited amounts of goods as "accompanying baggage" through the Turkish customs under a 1992 decree. At the Russian customs, *chelnoki* can pass some of that merchandise without paying taxes (up to $2,000 until August 1996 and up to $1,000 after that date). For merchandise above that value, they have to either pay the full amount of the customs duties or negotiate a lower amount through bribes.

20. The smuggling of goods between Turkey and Iran, Iraq, and Syria has been a widespread phenomenon throughout the republican period. In 1979, separate agreements between Iran and Turkey and between Syria and Turkey allowed formal trade among border provinces. When border trade came under official regulation, smuggling to and from Iran and Syria declined. However, the informal border economy among Turkey, Iran, Iraq, and Syria still exists.

21. Hundreds of thousands of Kurds were evicted from their villages and towns in the southeastern region during the military campaign against the Kurdish insurgency in the first half of the 1990s. For the discrepancies in the estimated number of IDPs, ranging from 400,000 to 3 million, see Bilgin Ayata and Deniz Yükseker, "A Belated Awakening: National and International Responses to the Internal Displacement of Kurds in Turkey," *New Perspectives on Turkey* 32 (2005): 5–42.

22. D. Vasileva, "Bulgarian Turkish Emigration and Return," *International Migration Review* 26 (1992): 342–52.

23. Sue Bridger, Rebecca Kay, and Kate Pinnick, *No More Heroines? Russia, Women and the Market* (London: Routledge, 1996); L. Rzhanitsyna, "Women's Attitudes toward Economic Reforms and the Market Economy," in *Women in Contemporary Russia,* ed. Vitalina Koval (Providence, R.I.: Berghahn Books, 1995).

24. Linda Attwood, "The Post-Soviet Women in the Move to the Market: A Return to Domesticity and Dependence?" in *Women in Russia and Ukraine,* ed. R. Marsh (Cambridge: Cambridge University Press, 1996).

25. Martha Bruno, "Women and the Culture of Entrepreneurship," in *Post-Soviet Women: From the Baltic to Central Asia,* ed. Mary Buckley (Cambridge: Cambridge University Press, 1997).

26. Zukin, *Culture of Cities,* 11.

27. Clifford Geertz, *Peddlers and Princes* (Chicago: University of Chicago Press, 1963).

28. I use the word Turkish to denote citizens of Turkey rather than people of Turkish ethnicity.

29. Portes, "Informal Economy."

30. For instance, Francis Fukuyama, *Trust: The Social Virtues and the Creation of Prosperity* (New York: The Free Press, 1995); Robert D. Putnam, "The Prosperous Community. Social Capital and Public Life," *The American Prospect* 13 (1993): 35–42.

31. Claire Sterling, *Thieves' World: The Threat of the New Global Network of Organized Crime* (New York: Simon & Shuster, 1994).

32. G. Schroeder, "Economic Transformation in the Post-Soviet Republics: An Overview," in *Economic Transition in Russia and the New States of Euroasia*, ed. B. Kaminski (Armonk, N.Y.: M. E. Sharpe, 1996).

33. Alena Ledeneva, "*Blat* Exchange: Between Gift and Commodity," *Cambridge Anthropology* 3 (1996/97): 43–66.

34. Bruno, "Women and the Culture of Entrepreneurship," 69–71.

35. Bridger et al., *No More Heroines.*

36. Chris Hann and Ildiko Beller-Hann, "Samovars and Sex on Turkey's Russian Markets," *Anthropology Today* 4 (1992): 3–6.

37. Part of the discrepancy in Turkish men's perceptions of Slavic and Turkish women's work stems from the devaluation of women's labor within the private sphere—the household—whereas entrepreneurship belongs to the public and male realm. This discrepancy in perception looks all the more paradoxical when we consider the fact that a significant proportion of informal laborers in the small-scale garment industry in Istanbul are women. For an ethnographic account of how women's labor in family-owned garment workshops is trivialized by male kin, see Jenny White, *Money Makes Us Relatives: Women's Labor in Urban Turkey* (Austin: University of Texas Press, 1994).

2

Borderlined in the Global City (of Angels)

Camilla Fojas

Many critical Latino films based in Los Angeles during the 1980s mark a distinct turn in the vision of the global city; they challenge its reputation as a center of cosmopolitanism and multiculturalism, a place where difference is celebrated and experienced, and as a sovereign location of hospitality and refuge for the stranger and the immigrant. Instead, many Latino films link the national borderline with barriers faced by Latinos in the city. Films such as *El Norte* (Gregory Nava, 1983), *Born in East L.A.* (Cheech Marin, 1987), *Stand and Deliver* (Ramón Menéndez, 1988), and *American Me* (Edward James Olmos, 1992) associate segregated urban space with border politics and immigration policies built on typologies of inclusion and exclusion and other schizoid dyads of colonialism: citizen and alien, "legal" and "illegal," white and "of color," developed and underdeveloped, first world and third world, and civilization and barbarism. The perceived boundaries among neighborhoods are depicted as national boundaries. For instance, those living in these neighborhood republics are represented as objects of police and INS surveillance and control—while middle-class Anglos are objects of police protection. Los Angeles border films align the national border with urban issues of citizenship and belonging to show how the border casts long shadows into the city.

After a number of cultural and political changes, most notably the North American Free Trade Agreement (NAFTA), the Immigration Reform and Control Act of 1986, and the rise of new technologies of communication, the border imaginary in the city was presented differently by filmmakers. By the late 1990s, the anti-immigrant phobia and hysteria of the 1980s is eclipsed by an uninterrupted history of migration from Mexico and other parts of Latin America,[1] which returned Los Angeles to its Hispanic heritage.[2] As neighborhoods change, immigrant settlements disperse, and communities go cybernetic, the social and economic boundaries of the 1980s might manifest differently. Partly as an effect of the rise of the "Hispanic Hollywood" and the success of films such as *El Norte,* Latinos had consolidated what Renato Rosaldo calls "cultural citizenship," or the social and cultural practices that establish place and belonging for marginalized populations. Latino cinema is a vital foundation for new forms of membership both as cultural texts of historical value and as individual film texts that demand transformative modes of engagement. By the 1990s, Los Angeles was viewed as a beacon of social and cultural changes that would lead to new conceptions of national identity.

To explore the impact of cinema on urban space, I consider *El Norte* to examine a popular configuration of a divided city and *Bread and Roses* (Ken Loach, 2000) to explore the new vision of Los Angeles in the contemporary context. These two films have plot similarities and telling divergences. Both share a similar story of border crossing with a Los Angeles destination, but each offers a distinct view of the city and its communities. Each film gives a different map of the city where borders and boundaries shift along with forms of belonging and cultural citizenship.

El Norte is a major force in film history and a cornerstone of Latino cinema that continues to have wide appeal and influence; it was nominated for an Academy Award for "Best Original Screenplay," named an "American Classic" in 1996, and targeted for special preservation by the Library of Congress. The story, based on the Mayan creation myth Popul Vuh, documents the travels of two young Guatemalan siblings posing as Mexicans in their journey through Mexico to the United States. Rosa and Enrique aspire to the free upward mobility promised by the media-induced mythos of *el norte,* yet they face permanent exile in the city, where their mobility is limited and they are neither free nor accepted—"no somos libres . . . no somos aceptados." Their participation in the economic life of the city is not sufficient to grant greater social membership or a sense of belonging. Their predicament represents the tension between the labor needs of the global city and its reputation as a place of refuge against a larger national mood of immigration restrictions and nativist sentiment. The story illustrates how the policies and politics of the city are complicit with those expressed at the national level during a time of heightened nationalism and immigrant phobia.

El Norte is one of the first films to explore the political forces behind immigration patterns in an effort to stem the rising immigrant phobia of the 1980s. During this era, U.S.-backed Central American civil wars and massive debt in Mexico and the rest of Latin America drove many from their homes seeking refuge and economic liberation in the north; many of these emigrants followed a well-worn path and pattern of short-term labor migration cultivated by the Bracero program of the 1940s. Roughly concurrent with the changes to immigration policy in 1965, the Bracero program was ended, and the migration of labor became criminalized by new border policies.[3] As a result of a historical force of habit, a large labor population continued to migrate; the only difference was a lack of legal permission to do so.

The 1980s witnessed a rise in the numbers of undocumented immigrants who subsequently became scapegoats during a nationwide recession, unprecedented inflation, and high unemployment rates. There was intense public pressure for Congress to "get tough" on undocumented immigration, which led to the Immigration Reform and Control Act of 1986 and later to the California-based SOS "Save Our State" ballot measure Proposition 187 in 1994—deemed unconstitutional by a California federal judge for blocking access to education for the children of undocumented immigrants. Proposition 187 paved the way for the 1996 Illegal Immigration Reform and Immigration Responsibility Act (IIRIRA), which denied due process to undocumented immigrants, and the 1996 Personal Responsibility and Work Opportunity Reconciliation Act, which restricted undocumented immigrants from many social services and barred legal immigrants from Social Security and food stamps.[4] Immigration reform has become increasingly punitive by rolling back benefits for all immigrants regardless of legal status and subsequently rendering citizenship ever more exclusive and difficult to obtain.

Immigration reform reflects and justifies a cultural image of the immigrant as a pernicious socioeconomic liability. According to Leo Chavez, from 1965, the year that national origin quotas were dismantled, to 1999, the cover images from various popular news magazines told compelling stories about immigrant incursions as economic and political burdens.[5] In a study that complements the work of Chavez, Otto Santa Ana reviews the imagistic language of metaphor in popular news stories and finds it typical of warmongering rhetoric where incoming populations are described as violent forces of invasion and intrusion.[6] These critics agree that mass media expresses popular opinion, which in turn helps shape and subsequently enact policies. Popular images and discourses about immigration aided in the creation of new policies and the intensification of those already in place. In the 1980s, Hollywood joined in with neo-Western border films commandeered by vigilante border patrolmen heroes who promised to stop the traffic of "illegals": *Borderline* (Jerrold Freedman, 1980) with Charles Bronson, *The Border* (Tony Richardson, 1982) with Jack Nicholson, and *Flashpoint* (William Tannen, 1984) with Kris Kristofferson. *The Border* begins in Los Angeles, but only briefly; the main character, Charlie, migrates to Texas and makes the easy transition from border agent in Los Angeles to border patrolman along the Texas border, a powerfully symbolic move that links enforcement in the global city to the reinforcement of the national border.

Latino cinema responded to the bad publicity by showing how the complex symbology of the border is projected onto all Latinos regardless of immigration status. This is most apparent in the popular comedy *Born in East L.A.*, where the humor derives from various circumstances of mistaken identity when Rudy, a citizen of East Los Angeles, is deported to Mexico after he is caught in a factory raid trying to pick up his cousin. Based on many actual occurrences, Rudy is a victim of the immigrant phobia of the 1980s when citizenship is defined by exclusive notions of race and ethnicity. Though Rudy has a firmly established membership and place in East Los Angeles as a native Chicano Angelino, he is not deemed so by federal authorities; the handling of Rudy and many others like him gives powerful testimony to the 1980s imperative to subordinate urban to national culture.

MIGRATION IN AND TO THE CITY

El Norte begins in Guatemala with workers on a coffee plantation, one of whom we follow as he is driven from home to Los Angeles where his fate will be to serve the coffee he once picked. The workers labor monotonously against the lush and verdant mountains that loom in the background; the end of the work day is signaled violently by a discharged rifle to remind us that these are not representatives of a joyful Juan Valdez picking every bean with gusto. The men include one of the main characters, Enrique, and his father, who will later be shot by the military over land disputes. They are in the middle of a U.S.-backed war against "insurgents" and the peasants that look like them, that is, the *campesinos* who simply want to retain their land and the government that wants to dispossess them of it. Enrique's only option is to flee for the north before he is murdered like his father. He and his sister, Rosa, follow the dream of their aunt for the opportunities and new life offered by "el norte." The coffee is the invisible protagonist and the only character that meets a happy ending as it travels freely from Guatemala to Los Angeles.

Enrique and Rosa cross from Mexico to the United States via unused sewage tunnels, where, in a horrific scene, they are attacked by a horde of rats as the Border Patrol hovers ominously above in helicopters; border officials will continue to haunt them long after this incident. After they emerge from their underworld travel, like their mythic counterparts, they are faced with what they believe is the promise of redemption, suggested in the luminous aerial view of the city accompanied by triumphant orchestral music. This scene is a preface for the final installment in this tripartite structure, where each segment corresponds to a different place. The final destination is announced in the intertitles: "The North" and "Los Angeles." The next image is a disappointment of the expectations of the previous scene. Instead of a clean and promising cityscape full of possibility, we find a city where the palm trees of paradise are bisected by telephone lines against a grey and smoggy sky. A shift of focus from the sky to the ground reveals a windy street strewn with trash and the sign of the Lazy Acres Motel, reminiscent of the Mirador motel of border film *Touch of Evil* (Orson Welles, 1958), precursor to the Bates motel in *Psycho* (Alfred Hitchcock, 1960). Like the Mirador and its Bates kin, the motel seems ominous and isolated on the outskirts of town, and it inspires no confidence that something hopeful or good will occur on its premises. The placement of the motel at or beyond the city limits and the limits of modernity emphasizes the characters' marginality; the location bears no resemblance to the "postmodern" city that harbors it.

The siblings' experiences constitute a map of the city that dramatizes what Soja has called the "geography of capitalism," the spatial dynamics and tensions that marginalize and ghettoize populations.[7] In *Postmodern Geographies*, Soja describes the importance of reasserting space into the social sciences by using Los Angeles as an exemplary model, claiming, in an eponymous chapter, that "It All Comes Together in Los Angeles." He describes how Los Angeles duplicates and embodies many other cities, how it "seems to be conjugating the recent history of capitalist urbanization in virtually all its inflectional forms."[8] The spatial restructuring of Los Angeles is a result of economic developments that made it the "world's largest job machine" in the 1980s, specifically for the growth of several industries, the garment industry and its proliferation of sweatshops— where Rosa is employed, the high technology industries, and the defense industry. The region is also marked by simultaneous deindustrialization and de-unionization that resulted in deeper economic divisions as unemployment rates rose along with crime rates and poverty and a deepening housing crisis. These changes lead to an increasing economic and social atomization and segregation of urban populations "both at the place of work and the place of residence."[9] This analysis is born out in *El Norte* at every turn, dramatized in Rosa and Enrique's experience of an economically segregated city, though, at the same time, the analysis objectifies marginalization as merely an effect of postmodern urbanization.

Elizabeth Mahoney, citing Doreen Massey's similar analysis, criticizes Soja's broad-based and overly generalizing theoretical perspective as one that perpetuates the marginalization it identifies, not only by putting Los Angeles at the center as the model of models, but also for totalizing minority populations from a theoretical position of mastery. Mahoney exposes the contradiction between the theory and the practice of the city as the site of difference; "If we look at Soja's *Postmodern Geographies*, we can see . . . his concern with difference, otherness and critical 'ghettoization', and, on the other hand, the continuation of such 'ghettoization' within the text."[10] Though Soja provides a detailed account of the spatial restructuring of Los Angeles in the 1980s, he never fully characterizes the lived experience of the "sites of difference" generated by the "geography of capitalism"; he never provides a map for the metaphor. Soja claims to include many different points of view, asserting that "the perspectives explored are purposeful, eclectic, fragmentary, incomplete, and frequently contradictory,"[11] yet Mahoney insists that the overarching view is that of the omniscient theorist engaging a "rhetoric and practice of mastery over the urban spectacle."[12] Mahoney is concerned with how conventional urban discourses and their attendant spatial paradigms reproduce relations of power. She uses individual cinematic narrative texts to illustrate specific challenges to dominant spatial paradigms; each example is one discrete critical moment that is part of a larger history but that does not essentialize the difference it marks. Perhaps urban cinematic texts better dramatize Soja's spatialized historical narratives of difference. They explore unique itineraries, perspectives, and subjective experiences within and across social spaces; they give voice and image to those living and working in the noniconic and peripheral areas of the city. For instance, El Norte is focalized through the marginal perspectives of immigrant male and female subjects whose movement in the city is determined by the uneven dynamics of globalization. Enrique and Rosa's respective itineraries delineate the various social, political, economic, racial, and gendered spaces bisected by a national border imaginary, conveying a different city map for Latinos who face various daily impasses.

At every turn the siblings find a split between their media-induced expectations and their actual experiences of the city. Rosa and Enrique's ideas about the North are drawn entirely from popular media, from their aunt's Buen Hogar magazines that associate the United States with all the modern conveniences and opportunities for upward mobility, where everyone has a flushable toilet and electric lights and may buy a car with no money down. What they discover is less impressive. In their room at the Lazy Acres Motel, they do find the toilet and lights, but the conditions are atrocious and almost unlivable. This is just the beginning of an uneasy introduction to the big city. Rosa and Enrique encounter a city split between those who are full citizens—who enjoy the right to flourish, free speech, and mobility and who benefit from the rule of law and social services—and those who are dispossessed of both rights and place. Rosa and Enrique are denationalized; their forced migration and subsequent experience in the city deprives them of "un lugar," a space that is both a home and a place to flourish. They belong nowhere, neither in Mexico nor in the most diverse and Latino city of the United States; everywhere they go, they encounter impasses to the fulfillment of their happiness.

Rosa's alienation inspires a longing for home that becomes the stuff of hallucinations and dreams. Yet her dreams are tainted by the contradictions and disappointments she faces in the city. She dreams she sees her mother in the kitchen making tortillas and telling her of the economic reality of life in "el norte," and on another occasion, she sees her father in a garden offering her a basket of flowers that is soiled by a dead catfish—a symbol of the man-fishes into which the twins transform in the Popul Vuh—a fateful sign of Rosa's imminent death, but also a hopeful sign that she will soon transcend this earthly life. Rosa herself remarks on her deathbed that only in death might she find a place, *un lugar,* a home.

The national border emerges in the city in many ways, but most dramatically through the insistent presence of immigration officials and the constant threat of deportation. Rosa and Enrique live in constant fear of "*la migra,*" and both are driven from their first jobs by INS raids. Mike Davis calls this linking of border surveillance technology to urban space the "third border," indicating both the border in the city and the movement of the southern national border toward Los Angeles, apparent in the northerly migration of border technologies in the "INS" checkpoints found on the way to Los Angeles. But the border greets Latinos in the city as well, where they are tacitly restricted from the use of Anglo spaces. Davis gives several examples, one of which is the example of the barricade between El Sereno and South Pasadena to keep the largely Latino population of the former out of the latter. Likewise, Gustavo Leclerc and Michael J. Dear locate the river as a borderline separating the Latino east from the Anglo west of the city.[13]

Rosa and Enrique face an illegible city, a space of contradiction that cannot be mastered or made intelligible. The city is alienating in its contradictions, in the segregation of neighborhoods, in the sense of history and its erasure, and in the split between economy and polity. Rosa is mystified by the city's racial polarization evident in the absence of Anglos in her neighborhood, until her friend informs her that they can be found sequestered in their own neighborhoods. She then discovers that she can take free English classes at a local school, classes offered to immigrants to aid in their linguistic assimilation—which she finds completely paradoxical. Likewise, Enrique wonders why a coworker is called a "Chicano" and learns that the term refers to someone of Mexican heritage who was born in the United States. But he also learns that this relatively more privileged status as Chicano, as a citizen, nonetheless relegates him to the same secondary labor market.

El Norte is a story of boundedness, of dreams of mobility against a reality of intransitivity and urban segregation for Latinos in the global city. The two characters are forced from their native countries and lured to the United States by mediated promises of opportunity, only to become further alienated. At every turn, they find themselves on the denigrated side of the divided city and experience alienation as an effect of nationalist typologies of inclusion and exclusion. Their estrangement is not simply an effect of urban-based postmodern fragmentation, but the persistence of a modernist split between nations, between the colonial centers of power and the colonized and denationalized objects of control.

In the end, Rosa dies inconsolable about the lack of place for them in the city, for the experience of always being outside even while participating in the life of the city, whereas Enrique is forced back into the temporary labor market building homes for the middle class, while he himself lives and works in limbo.

Bread and Roses Too

Bread and Roses conveys an alternate vision of the city, less as a place of segregation and limitation and more as a location where collective formations might provide new political identities, rights, and forms of belonging. The city is the place where citizenship is both formed and maintained through political means, where workers organize and demand rights drawn from their participation in local economies—as both laborers and consumers of goods and media. Moreover, the city is an exemplary crucible for political change; it is a beacon that leads the way for the rest of the nation.

Like *Norma Rae* (Martin Ritt, 1979), *Bread and Roses* is the story of a woman's evolution of political consciousness through the labor movement, but unlike the eponymous Norma Rae, Maya's story has deeply transnational features. Maya emigrates to Los Angeles from Mexico to work with her sister at Angel Cleaning Services, a nonunion operation paying its workers less than living wages with no benefits. Maya falls in with a union activist and quickly becomes a leader in the Justice for Janitors campaign, an actual movement organized by the Service Employees International Union (SEIU). *Bread and Roses* goes beyond others of the same type by depicting all the steps and possible pitfalls of labor activism in what Leonard Quart and William Kornblum call the film's unusual mix of "entertainment, political polemic, and . . . Introduction to Organizing 101."[14]

Bread and Roses begins with Maya's dangerous traversal of the border on foot and van ride to Los Angeles. Maya's sister, Rosa, greets her upon her arrival, but without the money to liberate her from the coyotes. Angered, the coyotes refuse to release Maya and drive off, flipping a coin to determine who will get their way with her. However, they fail to anticipate the craftiness of their charge. Using her wit and savvy, Maya escapes the motel where she was taken hostage by pretending to help her captor lather up in the shower, taking his keys and his boots. When he realizes he has been conned, he swears her up and down, looking out the window as she waves his boots in defiance and runs away. This is a new and uplifting image; unlike the tragic siblings of *El Norte* or the desperate deportation of Jennifer Lopez's character in *Mi Familia,* Maya gets away with it, makes us laugh, and reminds the audience that you can pull one over on the forces in power. This scene is a telling preface for the victories to come and a powerful template for the transformative identifications crucial to the urban remapping of the film. For instance, El Norte's melodramatic narrative ending might encourage reconsideration of prejudice through an affective engagement with the protagonists, whereas Bread and Roses adds an insurrectionary force to identification. Each character allegorizes a different stage in political consciousness with the final stage represented by Maya, whose attitude of fearlessness and insubordination performs the activist work of change. She crosses the line separating proper from improper in various ways: She refuses to be shut out of exclusionary spaces, she says and does things not expected of undocumented workers who typically fear exposure, and she refuses to be treated with disrespect. Maya forges both her social and actual mobility; we see her move throughout the city on foot, moped, and public transportation; she, with others, takes to the streets to march for better rights; and she and her fellow workers invade the coveted space of a Hollywood party to make public their exploitation.

Loach does not present an immigrant-phobic city carrying out the imperatives of the nation-state but imagines the global city as the place where national political blind spots might be exposed. For instance, the "borderlessness" of the post-NAFTA era refers not to the limitless opportunities for mobility, but the borderlessness at the bottom of the labor market and the subsequent creation of a new multicultural urban underclass. Angel Cleaning Services is comprised of African-Americans, women, older workers, undocumented immigrants, Central Americans, and Russians who all face the same job insecurity and economic exploitation. These new workspaces are sites of racial and ethnic mixing in a competitive environment of contingency and rollbacks ripe for conflict and divisiveness, a volatile dynamic that the bosses keep active. The workers of Angel Cleaning Services face various strategies of divisiveness and competition from the bosses; they are tricked with offers of promotions for giving names of workers who attend union meetings; they are punished for diminution of physical ability with age; and they are outright threatened with dismissal if they organize or even question company policy or lack thereof. While there might be a number of ways to remedy this situation, one viable solution would be larger political representation and integration of the secondary labor market in the cities where they gather.

The political invisibility of the secondary sector of the labor population is a consequence of a polarized labor market that privileges the professional and management class within the new corporate hegemony in the global cities.[15] For Saskia Sassen, corporations are the "main spaces of authority in today's city," so that claims to social membership and attempts at political visibility are addressed to these locally-based global entities rather than the nation-state. Corporate structures mesh nicely with urban space since the "vertical grid of the corporate tower is imbued with the same neutrality and rationality attributed to the horizontal grid in American cities."[16] Yet corporations undergird a split city; they create an "amalgamated other" excluded from the elite day operations in the corporate towers, except perhaps as support staff.[17] *Bread and Roses* present this "amalgamated other" as the Angel Cleaning Services, the invisible nighttime workforce that cleans the offices of the daytime professional class. These workers are crucial to the operations of the new global economic system, yet their labor is unrecognized. In *Bread and Roses,* the onus is upon the workers to realize their value to the larger system and disseminate this knowledge to other workers and to those in positions of power.

Sassen proposes a new perspective on the global city as a crucial "cog" of globalization, as "command points, global marketplaces for capital, and production sites for the information economy," while it is also the site of the invisible workforce who are "never represented as part of the global economy but are in fact as much a part of globalization as international finance."[18] The global city is the locus of belonging that may have little to do with formal citizenship as defined by membership to the nation-state; instead belonging is forged on the micropolitical level through various often disconnected modes of political visibility. In this case, the workplace is the space where the Angel Cleaning Services workers will secure their rights to a safe and secure livelihood. Urban films spectacularly present these invisible populations and political movements and make a vital contribution to new formulations of local citizenship. Like the eponymous landmark protest in 1912 in Lawrence, Massachusetts—where immigrant workers, mostly women, fought against poverty wages, carrying banners that demanded bread and roses, too— these successful struggles are beacons for other social movements in other parts of the city and nation.

Unlike the divisions and separations represented in *El Norte* and other films of the same era *(Born in East L.A., Mi Vida Loca,* or *American Me),* the cinematic post-NAFTA city is a place where borderlessness is the rule of the day, where the underclass occupies the same spheres and people from the developing worlds are lured to the same low-wage jobs. This is not to suggest that the portrait of a fortified city segregated and charged by class antagonism is waning, rather that a new model is emerging. The new image of the city is the consequence of a number of changes that, in recent years, have transformed both the mobility and opportunities for transit of immigrants in and to the city. The city is viewed as detached from national policies with renewed sovereignty in globalization, where it is the basin of both global movements and global capital. As a result, there are new opportunities for local actors for mobility and political integration. Also, the city map has changed; new migrants to the city are not as bound by earlier patterns of movement. Jerome Straughan and Pierrette Hondagneu-Sotelo find that changes in communication and transportation technologies means that immigrant communities are no longer restricted to particular locations in the city nor are they "defined by territory."[19] No doubt the city is still split in ways represented in *El Norte*, but new ways of traversing the city as well as new patterns of settlement have changed the urban landscape. In their study, Straughan and Hondagneu-Sotelo found that those working class Latinos who did follow the older patterns of settlement did so in a transitional manner, as "launchpads" to places beyond the city.[20]

The changes to global cities do not suggest an absolute sovereignty of the global city from the nation, but a different relationship of city to nation, where the city provides cultural templates for the nation. For James Holston and Arjun Appadurai, globalization has not completely ruptured the global city from the nation but intensified and deepened the gap between them. They give the example of Los Angeles as an urban center that "sustains many aspects of a multicultural society at odds with mainstream ideologies of American identity."[21] This relationship of opposition has become one of leadership, where the city forecasts cultural changes that will transform the exclusive meaning of "American" to include its larger hemispheric vantage.

By the 1990s, a cultural revolution had taken place; Latinos in Hollywood and other forms of media in Los Angeles had begun to reap the benefits of the long cultural history of the city to reassert their rightful place at the center of popular culture—an era often referred to as "Hispanic Hollywood." Gustavo Leclerc and Michael J. Dear claim that it was not just Latino cultural production but the sheer force of the surge in the Latino population that revolutionized and reclaimed Los Angeles. Everything about the city and the state of California from place-names to representatives in city and state governance has the mark of its Latino and Hispanic heritage; the culmination of this heritage is apparent in its current leadership under native Angelino and Chicano Mayor Antonio Villaraigosa. In *La Vida Latina en L.A.*, Leclerc, Villa, and Dear gather various artists and writers who reconstruct the Latino heritage of Los Angeles lost to the "official history" of the city; many turn to the city itself as a vital archive and archeological record.[22] They document changes in the cultural landscape of Los Angeles apparent in "cultural events on the street; in magazines, art, and television; and in universities, homes, and the workplace."[23]

For the Latino Cultural Studies Working Group, these cultural practices, from those of everyday life to linguistic and artistic expression, in the words of William V. Flores and Rina Benmayor, "cross the political realm and contribute to the process of affirming and building an emerging Latino identity and political and social consciousness."[24] They eschew the rigid legal definition of citizenship for a flexible sociopolitical notion of citizenship that is more inclusive and descriptive of Latino realities; "In this way, immigrants who might not be citizens in the legal sense or who might not even be in this country legally, but who labor and contribute to the economic and cultural wealth of the country, would be recognized as legitimate political subjects claiming rights for themselves and their children, and in that sense, as citizens."[25]

Latino cultural productions constitute claims to membership that express and enact citizenship for all Latinos, from naturalized citizens to undocumented immigrants. Films like *El Norte* and *Bread and Roses* are part of the legacy of this cultural citizenship; they are part of larger social processes of contestation of hegemonic political identities as cultural practices that perform and interpret political belonging. Many films of Latino Cinema locate their stories in Los Angeles because of its unique position as home to the second largest Mexican population outside of Mexico, as well as a sizable population of South Americans and Central Americans. Indeed, almost every film mentioned by Flores and Benmayor as "standard stock in video stores"—"*Zoot Suit, La Bamba, El Norte, Stand and Deliver, American Me,* and *Mi Familia*"—is set in Los Angeles.[26] These films are part of a growing and vital tradition of reexamining global city spaces as the political centers of the nation, as places that dramatize new configurations of North American identities.

Bread and Roses is part of a slate of films that reimagines the city, in part by not making reference to any of the landmark Hollywood Los Angeles films and by making an invisible labor force the central protagonists. Ken Loach is explicit about his desire to show a different Los Angeles, not that of monumental cinematic icons, but one in which we see the everyday life and locatedness of living and working in the city. In an interview with Neil Smith, he gives the following explanation: "The idea of doing a film in Los Angeles was quite interesting, but we wanted to make a film that showed the other side of the city—to tell a story about the Mexicans and ignore Beverly Hills, the swimming pools, the fast cars, and the police chases."[27] He avoids all the icons of Los Angeles cinema, even the East Los Angeles of *Born in East L.A.* or Echo Park in *Mi Vida Loca*; instead, urban blight and Beverly Hills are traded for unspectacular lower middle class neighborhoods and the unglamorous corporate towers of downtown Los Angeles. Like British critic Reyner Banham's seminal work on Los Angeles, it is the outsider, the nonresident, the undocumented immigrants in *El Norte* or British filmmaker Loach, who offer a fresh vision of the city.

As an English filmmaker with a socialist realist agenda, Ken Loach is not organically connected to the politics of working in Hollywood, which affords him a uniquely irreverent perspective of the industry. Critic Peter Matthews comments on his refreshingly naïve representation of the Hollywood elite: "A supposedly comical episode in which the exploited casuals invade a swank Hollywood party with their vacuum cleaners is so poorly staged it suggests that Loach has never been within miles of such an event."[28] The Hollywood party takes place in isolation. It is full of stars, their agents and lawyers, yet there is not even a hint of paparazzi. The scene of the arrival of the major industry players is eerily deserted and unspectacular. Loach's alienation from the force field of Hollywood disrupts the framing of Los Angeles in its typical fashion, giving the impression that it is relatively easy to infiltrate the insular spaces of Hollywood and that anyone could, and perhaps should, do so. The activists storm the Hollywood party to inform the showbiz elite exactly how little their agents, lawyers, and financiers are paying their janitors. This shaming encounter is so unexpected that it promptly makes the news. Cornered by bad publicity, the building managers have no choice but to capitulate to the demands of the workers.

Prior to *Bread and Roses,* Loach had not ventured onto the U.S. cultural terrain, but it is clear that he has many reasons to choose Los Angeles as the target of social reform for an increasingly rapacious global capitalism. Los Angeles signifies the globalization of corporations and media, but it also represents a vital history of insurrection and political insurgency. For Michael Dear and Steven Flusty—drawing on Edward Soja's precedent, Los Angeles is the best model for understanding and "explaining the form and function of urbanism in a time of globalization."[29] Roger Keil claims globalization "led Los Angeles astray from the trajectory of American urbanism," causing a "redefinition of the very concept of the 'American city,'" not just as a global city, but as the seat of global justice movements.[30] Keil points to the rebellion of 1992 as the origin of decades of diversification of protest movements and struggles located in various global cities around the world; though the event was spurred by a black-white racial politics, a multiethnic and multiracial coalition of peoples rose up in protest.[31] The rebellion became a beacon for urban-based political movements and presented an image of Angelenos as organic social activists. *Bread and Roses* draws on this and other activist legacies; for instance, it draws specifically on the publicity garnered by labor activists in Los Angeles for the successful Justice for Janitors campaign of 1990, followed by a number of other movements, such as the dramatic Hotel Employees and Restaurant Employees (HERE) battles against The New Otani Hotel and when Local 11 president Durazo, joined by Latino celebrities and legislators, brought the largest private employer in Los Angeles, University of Southern California, to its knees for more secure contracts for its veteran catering and cleaning workers.[32]

The key difference of these urban-based global movements and the history of labor organizing on a national scale is the attitude toward immigrant and undocumented labor, one clearly expressed in the film. The new movements are a function and consequence of globalization and its new international workforce. The current president of the Service

Employees International Union (SEIU), Andrew Stern, has argued that unions need to build institutions that are strong enough to match the power of global corporations, which means unions need to reach across borders and become global.[33] The new labor movement connects workers' rights to international human rights, reaching beyond the nation-state to secure workers' rights, since the state guarantees no protections or no rights, for undocumented workers who might be mistreated, subject to dangerous conditions, or fired out of hand.[34] A human rights agenda allows workers to identify injustice and violation of rights and appeal to a larger international tribunal for remedies and change.[35] Moreover, the linkage of workers rights to human rights enables local movements to work both locally and globally at once, but this local work is necessarily city not nation-based. This is a major shift from labor efforts of the past. Helene Hayes, in a remarkable history of the relationship of immigration policy and undocumented immigration, shows that support for nativist and exclusionary immigration policies has consistently emanated from nationalist U.S. labor unions and organizations. Organized labor was behind every piece of exclusionary legislation from the Chinese Exclusion Acts to the "labor certification requirement" of the McCarren-Walter Act of 1952, but the greatest victory for labor was in the transformation of the language of immigration policy from that of labor, from the imperative to fill national work needs, to the ideology of family in the language of "family reunification," thus refocusing the national gaze back onto internal labor markets.[36]

Though *Bread and Roses* is a labor activist film, Loach does not endorse the labor movement wholesale; he remains critical of organized labor's connection to larger state-bound institutions. For instance, Sam is chastised by his boss for getting three injunctions in two days and threatening the economic viability of the organization; "What are you doing here? The lawyers are going insane. I'm trying to keep the executive board off your ass." Sam's boss suggests that it is time to change targets, to which Sam replies, "an easier target," insinuating that Angel Cleaning Services is not a good investment of time or money. Sam taunts, "Not going to have your forty million to give to the Democrats next election?" His criticism underpins a reality besetting labor unions. Labor's influence and dependence on the Democratic Party has increasingly become untenable because, as Sam the renegade labor activist suggests, local city politics is sacrificed to national politics. The union's tie to the Democratic Party limits its political effectiveness and is perceived by many as little more than the hemorrhaging of funds to campaigning—cause of the recent split of the SEIU from AFL-CIO.

Loach does not belabor the critique of union corporatization; he instead foregrounds the collective struggle of the workers in their local conditions. Sam breaks from his paid position as a union organizer to continue what seems like a losing battle against the Angel Cleaning Services company. Like heroes of the old Westerns, the cowboy vigilante who breaks the law is vindicated in the end; Sam achieves victory. In one scene, Sam interrupts the building manager's business lunch and informs him of what his janitors are being paid (without lunch breaks), while taking and eating a lamb chop off his plate. This move is invasive and shaming and, above all, effective. Like the motto of the Lower East Side Collective (LESC) in New York, Sam works "to make life miserable for bosses and bureaucrats" until they capitulate to worker demands.[37] In the end, with Sam and Maya at the forefront, the workers march through the city and end up in the semipublic corporate plaza of the building that employs the Angel Cleaning Services. The workers assert their sociopolitical membership in the city by demanding the recognition of their rights to fair working conditions and insisting that workers fired for union involvement be reinstated. The arc of this success is dramatized in the narrative progression of events and their relation to urban space. In the beginning Maya is forced out of the plaza by security guards, but by the end, she and her coworkers have occupied this same plaza.

Loach draws up an ending in which everyone wins but Maya. Maya is the exemplary political figure in the beginning, but she is a cautionary emblem at the end for taking her political fervor too far. The bosses reinstate the workers, and all workers receive health insurance and holidays. But Maya, who earlier robs a gas station to fund her friend's college tuition, is found culpable of robbery and deported. The story ends as it began, with Maya in transit, but this time heading south. Loach suggests the answer is not in the creation of informal and subversive economies, but in political and civic engagement. *Bread and Roses* does not promote a tactic of transgression or violence, but rather strategizes a means of attaining more far-reaching symbolic effects by staging worker visibility in the city and a savvy manipulation of locally-based global media. The major cities of the United States, where most of the major corporations, institutions, and financiers are housed, are also global media stages. If there are show-stopping protests, it is likely that the rest of the world will hear about it. Like the antics of the Yes Men who infiltrated the World Trade Organization by posing as its members to the media, in *Bread and Roses,* the Justice for Janitors activists infiltrate corporate power from within to expose its institutional injustice and shame its major agents for the television cameras.

El Norte examines the economic and social structure of Los Angeles in the early 1980s before key features of globalization drastically altered the landscape of the city. Rosa and Enrique are victims of unprecedented immigrant phobia in the 1980s; they are drawn to the city by the imperatives of global capital to attract labor but are shut out by the state imperative to control the borders and its labor market, a scenario that creates a gap between local legal systems and the transnational processes of globalization. Though they contribute to the economic life of the city, they never find a space, a home, or a sense of belonging. Their story ends with no resolution to their alienation in the city.

El Norte remains an important foundational text for Latino cinema and a major intervention into Hollywood that paved the way for the cultural revolution of the 1990s, when Latinos gained increasing local and national visibility. *Bread and Roses* continues this revolution; it forges a reflexive relation to the dominant media by charging into the centers of production to dramatize the activist process of place-making through a direct engagement with urban power structures. Rather than a city doomed to Hollywood film and television representations of social divisions, we might reimagine Los Angeles as a powerful template for the creation of cultural membership, for civic and political agencies that impact national political sentiments about the definition of citizenship. Los Angeles is a major locus of Latino cultural citizenship, a place that benefits from the special resources of cultural and racial difference and that profoundly affects national debates about citizenship and belonging for marginalized populations.

NOTES

1. According to the 2000 census of Los Angeles, Latinos constitute 46.5 percent of the population of the city.

2. Jerome Straughan and Pierrette Hondagneu-Sotelo, "From Immigrants in the City, to Immigrant City," in *From Chicago to L.A.: Making Sense of Urban Theory*, ed. Michael J. Dear, 183–211 (Thousand Oaks, Calif.: Sage Publications, 2002), 190.

3. Helen Hayes, *U.S. Immigration Policy and the Undocumented: Ambivalent Laws, Furtive Lives* (Westport, Conn.: Praeger, 2001), 18.

4. Ibid., 7–8.

5. Leo R. Chávez, *Covering Immigration: Popular Images and the Politics of the Nation* (Berkeley: University of California Press, 2001).

6. Otto Santa Ana, *Brown Tide Rising: Metaphors of Latinos in Contemporary American Public Discourse* (Austin: University of Texas Press, 2002).

7. Edward Soja, *Postmodern Geographies: The Reassertion of Space in Critical Social Theory* (London: Verso, 1989), 74.

8. Ibid., 193.

9. Ibid., 215.

10. Ibid., 170.

11. Ibid., 247.

12. Elisabeth Mulroney, "'The People in Parentheses': Space under Pressure in the Postmodern City," in *The Cinematic City*, ed. David B. Clarke, 168–85 (London: Routledge, 1997), 169–70.

13. Gustavo Leclerc, Raúl Villa, and Michael J. Dear, eds., *La Vida Latina en L.A.: Urban Latino Cultures* (Thousand Oaks, Calif.: Sage Publications, 1999).

14. Leonard Quart and William Kornblum, "Documenting Workers," *Dissent* 48, no. 4 (2001): 117.

15. Saskia Sassen, "Analytic Borderlands: Race, Gender, and Representation in the New City," in *Race, Identity, and Citizenship*, ed. Rodolfo D. Torres, Louis F. Mirón, and Jonathan Xavier Inda, 355–72 (Malden, Mass.: Blackwell, 1999), 362.

16. Ibid., 362.

17. Ibid., 363.

18. Ibid., 366.

19. Straughan and Hondagneu-Sotelo, "From Immigrants in the City, to Immigrant City," 187.

20. Ibid., 188.

21. James Holston and Arjun Appadurai, "Introduction: Cities and Citizenship," in *Cities and Citizenship*, ed. James Holston, 1–18 (Durham, N.C.: Duke University Press, 1999), 3.

22. Leclerc, Villa, and Dear, *La Vida Latina en L.A.*, 3.

23. Ibid., 1.

24. William V. Flores and Rina Benmayor, "Introduction: Constructing Cultural Citizenship," in *Latino Cultural Citizenship*, ed. William V. Flores and Rina Benmayor, 1–23 (Boston: Beacon Press, 1997), 6.

25. Ibid., 10–11.

26. Ibid., 5–6.

27. http://www.bbc.co.uk/films/2001/04/18/ken_loach_bread_roses_interview.shtml.

28. Peter Mathews, "Bread and Roses," *Sight and Sound* 11, no. 5 (2001): 36.

29. Michael J. Dear and Steven Flusty, "The Resistible Rise of the L.A. School," in *From Chicago to L.A.: Making Sense of Urban Theory,* ed. Michael J. Dear, 3–16 (Thousand Oaks, Calif.: Sage Publications, 2002), 12.

30. Roger Keil, "From Los Angeles to Seattle: World City Politics and the New Global Resistance," in *From Act-Up to the WTO: Urban Protest and Community Building in the Era of Globalization,* ed. Ronald Hayduk and Benjamin Shepard, 326–33 (London: Verso, 2002), 328.

31. Ibid.

32. Mike Davis, *Magical Urbanism* (London: Verso, 2000), 146–47.

33. See David Moberg, "Labor Debates Its Future," *Nation* 280, no. 10 (2005): 11–14, 16.

34. Lance Compa, "Responses," *Dissent* 52, no. 1 (2005): 66–68.

35. Ibid., 66.

36. Hayes, 25–26.

37. Ronald Hayduk and Benjamin Shepard, "Urban Protest and Community Building in the Era of Globalization," in *From Act-Up to the WTO: Urban Protest and Community Building in the Era of Globalization,* ed. Ronald Hayduk and Benjamin Shepard, 1–9 (London: Verso, 2002), 7.

3

MODERNITY ON THE WATERFRONT

The Case of Haussmann's Paris

Margaret Cohen

The ship that is the seal of Paris calls attention to the importance of boat transport in its history. This importance dates back to the Middle Ages when Paris took shape as an archipelago city, composed of islands and banks united by the Seine. This point is worth pondering by scholars of the nineteenth-century Paris, given the landlocked *topoi* they associate with the development of Parisian modernity. In Walter Benjamin's powerful paradigm articulated on the topography of nineteenth-century Paris, the bourgeoisie emerge from their cosseted interiors and the working classes from their overcrowded *faubourgs* to gather in squares and boulevards that are the backdrop both for revolutionary struggle and for a culture of consumption, media, and the spectacle, spilling from the grand boulevards into arcades, panoramas, department stores, and even the morgue. When Benjamin dedicated a Konvolut to the Seine in his *Arcades Project,* he paid little attention to the river as part of Parisian life. Rather, in a tellingly landlocked vein, he represented the Seine as earth, the riverbed, a chthonic realm entombing the city's secrets and its past.

The minimal attention paid to the waterways by cultural theorists who use Paris to define the traits of nineteenth-century urban modernity contrasts with the historical importance of the city's waterways for its infrastructure during the nineteenth century. Isabelle Bakouche and Jean Millard, among other urban historians, have convincingly shown that not only does the river remain a conduit into Paris and avenue through it in the post-Revolutionary years, but its importance, if anything, also grows.[1] This growth is spurred by the state-organized construction of a network of canals across France in what has been called the *first* great transportation revolution predating the railroads. The extensive modernization and construction of canals strengthened the commercial links of the Seine to the rest of the Hexagon during the first decades of the nineteenth century.

When the railroads became widespread in the 1840s, the Seine lost its importance for passenger travel but maintained its commercial prominence. Railways were without peer for carrying passengers and light goods, but the heavy raw materials essential to the infrastructure of industrialization, such as buildings, machinery, and the coal that drove engines, could much more cheaply and easily be transported by water (even today, it is often forgotten that most of the world's goods circulate long distance by sea). The engineering innovations of the industrial age also facilitated water transport by perfecting canal engineering. When Eugène Belgrand modernized the portion of the Seine that ran through Paris, he eliminated tricky currents and standardized water depth with locks. In doing so, he increased the size of the boats that could navigate safely, along with the volume of traffic. The Ecluse de la Monnaie built on the Seine in central Paris during the Second Empire belonged to a series of movable locks that turned the Seine into essentially an artificial waterway. The Seine also became more easily navigable due to steam power, which increased the maneuverability of the vessels.

As a result, the ports that historically had flourished on the quays in the heart of Paris, such as the Port Saint Nicolas on the side of the Louvre and the Port d'Orsay across the river, remained vital to the infrastructure of the nineteenth-century city. Expanded new facilities sprung up in the suburbs and outskirts of the city. Across the age of the railroads and steam, port freight increased in the Parisian basin from two million tons of goods entering in 1840 to four million tons at the end of the Second Empire and more than five million tons in 1880.[2] This increase in tonnage reflects in part an increase in traffic. In part, it reflects the increased heaviness of industrial materials transported.

Given the vitality of the Seine to the infrastructure of "Paris, capital of the nineteenth century," how do we explain its minimal presence in accounts of the genesis of Parisian cultural modernity? This minimal presence has been influential as well for visions of the modern metropolis that Paris has helped to shape. When scholars pay little attention to the river as part of the modern city, they respond to the river's disappearance from practices of urban sociability in the second half of the nineteenth century, though they do so unthinkingly rather than taking this disappearance as worthy of comment. The disappearance of the city's waterways from urban sociability crystallizes in the 1850s, which is the first decade of the Second Empire, and the era of Haussmannization. In part, it is impelled by Haussmannization, yet at the same time, Haussmannization is itself continuing earlier trends in urban planning, visible both in Paris and in other cities. The erasure of

water-based sociability is further impelled by developments in technological modernization which enable Haussmannization, but which are
distinct from them.[3]

Across the Middle Ages and the early modern era, the Seine was the
commercial heart of the city, and it was a vibrant theater of cultural life.
The cultural role of the Seine ranged from its importance in workaday life
to its use in riverside displays of royal power, from waterside pageants
to the waterside Place de Grève (riverbanks square) used for executions
in the ancient régime. The river remained central to the cultural spectacle of the city in the post-Revolutionary decades. Indeed riverside sociability received new impetus with enthusiasm for the steamboat in the
1810s and 1820s. Parisians' interaction with the waterfront during these
years was spurred by the cultivation of hygiene through water sports
such as swimming and boating. Leisure boating in France maintained the
waterfront's picturesque association with popular life, as is evident in
boater's pirate and sailor fashions and the longshoremen outfits figuring
in costume balls made famous in the caricatures of Paul Gavarni from the
1830s and 1840s.[4]

Figure 3.1. "Après le débardeur la fin du monde!" [After the long-
shoreman costume, the world ends!] from *Le Diable à Paris—Paris et
les parisiens. Le Tiroir du diable* (Paris: J. Hetzel, 1845).

Gavarni's illustrations appeared in the minor descriptive writing on contemporary society that Benjamin termed panoramic literature and that he mined for insight into emerging Parisian cultural modernity. During the 1830s and 1840s, the Seine figured in this literature as a zone of bustling urban sociability. When the prominent fiction writer and essayist, Charles Nodier, authored a lavishly illustrated *La Seine et ses bords* in 1836, he devoted a long section to "the river that is king of the queen of cities." For Nodier, the Seine was at once cosmopolitan and urban, connecting the capital with "our wealthiest provinces" and receiving the "tributes of the globe" through Le Havre and Honfleur.[5] The Seine has a similar character in Eugéne Briffault's "A Day at Swim School," in *Le Tiroir du Diable,* an 1845 sequel to *Le Diable à Paris.* Discussing the boats set up for swimming on the banks of the Seine, Briffault celebrated the glory of a Gallic Venice. "The Parisian loves the Seine like the Venetian loves the Adriatic. . . . It has its ports and canals, its fleet and its maritime population, navigation and vast traffic, its floating trains and its steamboats . . . On this thoroughfare that unfolds in crossing Paris . . . the city sees the goods of its richest provinces crowding at the entrance to the river; all the products of the world flow out its exit."[6]

When panoramic writers like Nodier and Briffault admired the working waterfront as an emblem of global power, they continued the early modern vision of the waterfront made famous by the Dutch genre paintings of port life, as celebrating a city's connection to the trade and consumption networks of the world. They also continued the picturesque aesthetic blending leisure and work that was a feature of this celebration. This picturesque harmony of dock work and boating, swimming and fishing pervades the visual vignettes surrounding the texts. The sketches that accompany "A Day at Swim School" in *Le Diable à Paris* show families and idlers fishing, longshoremen, and leisure and professional boaters.

That this picturesque mixture of leisure and business did not always coexist harmoniously is underscored when Honoré Daumier satirizes riverfront life in one of his caricatures in *"Les Philanthropes du jour."*

The picturesque aesthetic of the waterfront blending commerce and leisure shaped the depiction of the Seine in works with artistic ambition as well. Watercolors of the Seine around Paris were published by the tourist Joseph Turner in the 1835 volume of his two-volume *Annual Tour: The Seine* (1834–35).[7] In the watercolor of *The Pont Neuf and the Ile de la Cité,* monumental Paris is only a backdrop to the lively quay with its families, soldiers, spectators, boatsmen, a coach, and a washerwoman with her bundle. In this image, Turner's visual composition enlarges the quay, extending it "awkwardly out into the river," to create further space for detailing the activities occurring there.[8] Ian Warell observes that Turner used this extension to emphasize that he

Paris, s'il le pouvait, ferait de son fleuve une mer. Que de fois il a sérieusement rêvé ce prodige ! Aussi, comme il traite gravement toutes ses relations avec la Seine ! Il a ses ports, ses canaux, sa flotte et sa population maritime, sa navigation, un commerce immense, ses trains flottants et ses pyroscaphes : voilà pour ses intérêts, pour son travail et pour son bien-être. Sur ce chemin, qui marche en traversant Paris, comme eût dit Pascal, la ville voit se presser, à l'entrée du fleuve, les denrées des plus riches provinces ; à sa sortie, affluent toutes les productions du monde. On a parlé des eaux qui roulaient de l'or ; l'industrie a chargé d'or le sable de nos rivières.

Pour ses plaisirs, Paris a sa flottille, svelte, élégante, légère et pavoisée ; les rivoyeurs et les canotiers de la Seine sont assurément de nature plaisante ; il est sans doute difficile de ne pas rire de l'importance nautique

dont ils affublent leur personne, leurs mœurs et leur langage ; c'est le carnaval sur l'eau. Cependant, sans trop d'efforts, on peut retrouver, dans cette fantaisie poussée jusqu'au burlesque, les traces de l'instinct primitif et des premières amours des rives et du fleuve.

Figure 3.2. Page from "Une Journée à l'école de natation" [Day at swim school] in *Le Diable à Paris—Paris et les parisiens. Le Tiroir du diable.*

Figure 3.3. Honoré Daumier, from his series *Les Philanthropes du jour* (1844): "Pull hard, Gaspard . . . . He's going to drown—Leave me alone . . . you can see I know how to swim and I'm minding my own business—Keep pulling, Gaspard . . . . If we listened to them, we could never save anyone . . . we'll drag him like that to Bercy and the agent will give us 25 francs for what we've done . . . without counting the tip, which is on our big spender here!"

was tweaking the commonplaces of the tourist view. The point of Turner's artificial viewpoint is to emphasize the continuity between land, littoral, and water, melding nature and humanity, business and leisure, into a unified, heterogeneous urban zone.

Nothing of this sociability remains in the portrait of the Seine offered in Maxime Du Camp's *Paris, ses organes, ses fonctions et sa vie* (1875). In this magisterial work, casual panoramic writing has become serious history. For Du Camp, the Seine is an active zone of transport and commerce. The section devoted to the Seine describes the waterways crowded with "swift little boats . . . washhouses, baths, steamboats that heave the tow chain" and lined by "the great quays where the busy crowd swarms." Despite the bustle, Du Camp remarks of the average Parisian: "The Seine isn't anything special for him."[9] "We hardly notice it."[10]

The Seine appears similarly unremarkable in another work regularizing panoramic literature: the guide to Paris put together to commemorate the World's Fair of 1867, *Paris-Guide, par les principaux écrivains et artistes de la France*. In the volume on *Paris moderne*, the visitor finds fifteen entries on *Promenades dans Paris* by leading literary lights, devoted to spaces: parks, boulevards, squares, gardens. Frederick Lock's "Les Ponts, Les Ports, et les rues," despite its title, contains no mention of the city's ports, and the Seine, in Lock's view, does not play an important role in city life. "Given up to commercial navigation transporting wines, stones, gravel, asphalt and other materials, the Seine is only frequented when it is the season for cold baths by Parisians, who in all other weather, merely look at it from the height of the city's twenty-five bridges."[11] In the only other entry in the modern section of the *Paris-Guide* that treats the Seine, "Les places publiques, les quais, et les squares de Paris," Jules Clarétie describes a walking tour along the quays of the Seine, very much like a walk along a boulevard, where the river is represented as an outmoded presence. In Clarétie's words, the boulevards are "the very life of Paris."[12] Associating "the quays" with "its past and history," Clarétie proceeds to their role in social upheaval and their links to poverty, illness, and death, concluding with discussion of the gibbet at Montfaucon and the Morgue.[13] These moribund dangers contrast with the vital menace of river areas that fascinated writers a generation before, exemplified by the confusion between work and crime in the shady (lumpen) waterside activities detailed by Eugène Sue's *Les Mystères de Paris* (1842–1844).

What has happened to explain these two very different visions of the Seine found in literature on Paris in the 1830s through 1840s and the 1860s through 1870s? The development of rail travel certainly contributed to the demise of a sense of the waterway's vitality. Railways were in stiff competition with boats for commuter transport when they were first inaugurated in Paris in 1840. Across the 1840s and 1850s, railways became the most effective means of passenger transport. As a result, the port lost its importance in commuter travel, and the riverfront started to lose its place as a destination for urban sociability. When Flaubert had Frédéric Moreau choose the steamboat to return from his uncle's in Le Havre to his provincial home up the Seine in *L'Education sentimentale,* Flaubert blends attitudes of the late 1860s when he drafts the novel with attitudes of 1840, when the novel was set. The fact that Moreau chooses the steamboat because of its leisurely pace reflects an attitude of the 1860s. Moreau's experience of river sociability, which first brings to him a woman he will love, does justice to the vitality of the river in Parisian life at the beginning of the 1840s.

At the same time, the rise of the railways was only one piece of the story, for boats still figured in leisure activities. The decline of the obligation to use the river for travel might not necessarily erase its visibility; people could just as well be encouraged to use it for entertainment. Indeed, the first Parisian society of regattas dates to 1854. Similarly, the bateaux-mouches that still cruise the Seine to offer a tour of the urban panorama in our time date to the World's Fair of 1867, conceived as an initiative to promote tourism.

The demise of the urbanite's contact with the river can in part be credited to the modernization of the Parisian infrastructure, undertaken by Napoleon III with the help of his prefect, the Baron Haussmann, in the 1850s and 1860s. One major ambition of Haussmann's modernization was to sanitize the city's sewage disposal.[14] As is well known, this project produced a celebrated network of new sewer collectors. What is less remarked is that it simultaneously removed Parisians' access to the working waterways, as well as diminishing the visibility of the waterways in everyday urban life.

When the Canal Saint-Martin running through Eastern Paris was completed in 1825, it was a state of the art innovation valued for improving shipping into the city. By the Second Empire, the canal was known as an impediment to exponentially increasing street traffic. Napoleon III was also concerned with the way the Canal Saint-Martin cut central Paris off from the districts in the east that played an important role in the working class uprisings of the Revolution of 1848. How to cross "the Canal Saint-Martin without creating an obstacle either to navigation in the canal or to traffic on the street" was an engineering challenge. In David Pinkney's words, "[a] fixed bridge would have had to be very high and its roadway excessively steep. A moveable bridge would alternatively halt barges on the canal and block wagons on the street. The problem was ingeniously solved by lowering the water level of the canal twenty feet and vaulting over a section *more than a mile long* between the Place de la Bastille and the present Avenue de la République."[15]

"The area above the canal . . . became the Boulevard Richard Lenoir with two roadways on opposite sides of a center strip one hundred feet

Figure 3.4. Boulevard Richard Lenoir from Adolphe Joanne, *Paris illustré en 1870 et 1877,* 3rd ed. (Paris: Hachette, n.d.), 73. The illustration appears in David Pinkney, *Napoleon III and the Rebuilding of Central Paris* (Princeton, N.J.: Princeton University Press, 1958).

wide, embellished with lawns, trees, and fountains."[16] David Pinkney comments, "few projects directly served so many of Napoleon's purposes as did this solution, which . . . provided a new thoroughfare across a busy commercial district, gave the neighborhood a veritable park in its front yard in place of the dirty waters of the Canal Saint-Martin, and substituted a strategic way from which one could, Haussmann pointed out, 'take from behind all the Faubourg Saint-Antoine,' in place of the defensive position the canal had offered to insurrectionaries."[17] Note as well how the Boulevard Richard Lenoir blocked the city dweller's access to the riverfront along with his or her ability to see the work conducted on it.

The engineering feats of the Second Empire not only erased the visibility of the working waterways, but also created artificial spaces for viewing water that compensated for the loss. The Boulevard Richard Lenoir is a case in point. Even as boat traffic flowed beneath the urban strollers' feet, they could admire the play of purified water in the boulevard's new ornate fountains of stone and bronze. This separation of clean water to be enjoyed in leisure activities from the dirty water of work brings to the modern city transformations already at work in the emergence of seaside resorts a century before. In *The Lure of the Sea,* Alain Corbin notes that seaside tourism accompanied the transformation of fishing villages into picturesque resorts, when he traces the emergence of a connection between the waterfront and health in the eighteenth century.

The separation of the leisure-based enjoyment of water from the everyday city dweller's access to the working waterways is a result of Napoleon III's improvement of the Parisian parks. These parks had long been formal gardens that were notoriously dusty and hot during the summer months. In the 1840s, Louis Bonaparte spent time in London, where he was impressed by the English conception of landscape. On surveying the Bois du Boulogne, he is said to have remarked "we must have a river here, as in Hyde Park, to give [it] life."[18] Artificial waterways were planned and built for all the parks embellished during the Second Empire. In the grottos and cascades of Bois de Boulogne, Bois de Vincennes, Parc Monceau, Parc Montsouris, and Buttes-Chaumont, Parisians enjoyed not only a manmade version of flowing water, but also one directly taken from the Seine. Their "artificial stalactites and stalagmites" were supplied by river water diverted to flow over the "cut stone" of basins lined with cement and mortar.[19]

In obscuring the visibility of the working waterways in daily city life, Haussmann continued trends from urban planning begun in the Empire and Restoration. A good example of this continuity is his treatment of the notoriously polluted Bièvre River that ran through the tanner's area in the thirteenth arrondissement. By the early nineteenth century, the Bièvre was little more than an open sewer carrying the by-products of tanning and human waste into the Seine. To alleviate this pollution, Restoration urban planners conceived the plan to pave over the river entirely in 1828, though they did not execute it. In continuity with their aims, Haussmann included the Bièvre in his new system of sewer collectors. In Du Camp's words, "this filthy stream . . . finally received the only end it deserved: it became a sewer." Construction of this project was finally completed in 1910.[20]

The disappearance of a picturesque aesthetic of the waterways is evident in comparing depictions of the working waterfront in the July Monarchy and the end of the Second Empire. In part, this disappearance expresses cultural perceptions; in part, it does in fact respond to the changing aspect of the river. During this time, a number of picturesque *petits métiers* connected to the waterways and waterfront disappeared due to different aspects of nineteenth-century modernization. At the turn of the nineteenth century, floating mills dotted the river panorama. But the Empire's aim to improve the flow of traffic on the Seine led to the suppression of floating mills, outlawed with a decree in 1807. This decree also ordered a survey of river-based establishments on the Seine, as prelude to "suppressing all establishments that thwart navigation inside Paris."[21] During the Second Empire, the spirit of the 1807 edict was continued in the decree forbidding laundresses from washing directly in the Seine. The *porteur d'eau,* who brought water to the home from the river and wells is another figure who became increasingly rare with improvements in Parisian plumbing in the later nineteenth century. Panoramic writers lamented his disappearance for his picturesque aspect as well as his memorable call advertising his service.

Another *petit métier* to disappear from the banks of the Seine due to modernization in the 1850s was the driver who led the draft horses and mules towing barges along the Seine. During the 1850s, two kinds of engineering technologies replaced tow horses: tugboats, dependent on the advent of the steam engine, and a mechanically driven chain system.[22] From then on, horse-towing dwindled from the side of the river, though the practice initially continued to be used in the summer months when the low water level and the damming of the Seine made navigation particularly difficult. The disappearance of this *petit métier* affects not only the picturesque quality of the waterfront, but also the everyday Parisian's interaction with it. In central Paris, the draft animals used towpaths that abutted "the very quays of Paris."[23] These paths offered a hint of country life in the city and were a magnet for strollers. When the mules and their drivers disappeared, the towpaths were paved over, and Parisians lost one attractive riverside destination.[24] Once we grasp that the 1850s are the decade when drivers and draft animals are disappearing, Meryon's waterside views of the empty river from towpaths with horses, such as *The Apse of Notre-Dame,* become all the more regressive and nostalgic.[25]

The riverfront's demise as an urban destination also resulted from the disappearance of the small ferries that were one important mode of transport across the Seine at the beginning of the nineteenth century. Urban planners recognized the need to add to the Parisian bridge stock, and Haussmann made a decisive contribution when he modernized nine bridges and added four others, along with removing tolls for bridge use. Recalling Haussmann's improvements in the bridge system, we can grasp the thoroughly modern character to Lock's previously cited claim from the *Paris—Guide* of 1867 that the Parisians have an indifferent relation to their river, which they "merely look at . . . from the height of the city's twenty-five bridges."[26] With the extensive bridge construction, small crafts and the *bateliers* who piloted them disappeared, taking along with them one source of the Parisian's everyday contact with the waterfront.

Haussmann's admirable network of bridges certainly improved circulation through the city. It also evinces a cultural preference for a landlocked city of stone that is not driven by practicality alone. Consider the opportunities passed up to establish any connection to the Seine in buildings where practical matters do not play an overwhelming role. A case in point was the new Place du Châtelet linking the Right Bank with the Pont du Châtelet, completed between 1860 and 1862 by Gabriel Davioud, an architect known above all for his fountain design. Oriented around a square with a grand fountain, rather than open in any way to the river, Davioud's plan, like the Boulevard Richard Lenoir, erased the waterfront and offered as substitute water artificially enclosed and ornamentally displayed.[27] Another iconic Second Empire renovation evincing the cultural preference for a landlocked city was the project to modernize the central markets, Les Halles, accomplished by Victor Baltard in 1857. Baltard's plan was inspired by the design of Hector Horeau, sketched in 1845, where the Seine was to serve as a giant unloading zone for the Central Market, connected to specialized pavilions which were to line the length of the river.[28] One of Baltard's important modifications of Horeau's vision was to do away with any connection between the market and the Seine.

The minor role played by the river in the Second Empire spectacle of modern urban life is also evident in the design for the pavilions of the World's Fair of 1867, commemorating the commercial and cultural achievements of the Second Empire. Though these pavilions could potentially have extended from the Champs de Mars to the Seine, they were rather at a distance from the water and enclosed in a landlocked circle. Nor do they celebrate the river's ports or the engineering accomplishments of the river's movable locks. Rather, the Seine's presence is as a sideshow, a platform from which to admire the vista of the city. Even as a sideshow, it had a limited draw. Record exists of a summer "Fête des lanternes," where yachts from different nations lit up the night sky, flying their national colors. Newspapers recorded, however, that viewers turned out in disappointingly small numbers, in contrast to the successful river concerts, the canot-concerts, held thirty years earlier.

Social historians of nineteenth-century art such as Robert Herbert and T. J. Clark have suggested that the Impressionists' vision has profound affinities with the view of cultural modernity shaping Second Empire reconstruction. Impressionist treatment of Paris expresses a landlocked vision of urban modernity. Though the Impressionists were certainly interested in waterways and the waterfront, they did not depict Paris as a city of maritime commerce and quayside sociability. Rather, their waterways are generally removed from the urban landscape, situated in the suburbs or at the beach, and associated with leisure and contemplation, in opposition to business and transportation. Compare Turner's scene of riverfront Paris from the 1830's to the sunbathers congregated on the waterways at the edges of Paris in *Une Dimanche après-midi à l'île de La Grande Jatte* (1884–1886) by Georges Seurat or to Manet's *Argenteuil, les canotiers* (1874). In these images by Seurat and Manet, as in Monet's *Le Pont du chemin de fer à Argenteuil* (1873), we do see indications of the workaday world in forms that evoke modern industry, whether it is the train rushing by or the smokestacks in the background. But the painters have placed these industrial forms in visual contrast to rustic expanses of water plied by old-fashioned boats. Sometimes, the presentation of the bodies of water as backwaters is in stark contrast to historical reality.

In the *Baignade à Asnières,* Seurat depicts young men enjoying leisure bathing precisely where Haussmann's new sewer collectors dumped all the filth of central Paris back into the Seine.[29]

According to Clark, there is a tacit "rule" governing the representation of industry in Monet's paintings, specifically: "industry can be recognized and represented but not labor . . . Industry must not mean work; as long as that fictitious distinction was in evidence, a painting could include as much of the nineteenth century as it liked. The railway, for instance, was an ideal subject, because its artifacts could so easily be imagined as self-propelled or self-sufficient."[30] Clark notes "Once, and only once" was this rule "apparently disobeyed. Sometime in 1875, Monet painted a picture usually called *Les Déchargeurs de charbon* (1875). As Clark puts it, "Here . . . is a line of barges drawn up by the riverbank, the nearest filled with coal, and a few dim figures inside it filling their baskets with the stuff or balancing the new load on the back of their necks."[31] It is indicative of both the importance of the working waterways to Paris and the cultural work of erasing this connection that when Monet paints the reality of labor that is the exception that proves the rule, that, in Clark's words, "confirm[s] that fantasy and make[s] it safe," he should choose a dockside scene of a working port, recalling the men who convey the fuel that produces the attractive puffs of steam ornamenting the other water vistas.[32]

Clark's analysis of Impressionism underscores that there is an ideological as well as functional component to conceptions of city space. In the case of Impressionist treatments of the waterfront, the ideological element involves a reluctance to exhibit physical labor in the spaces associated with urban modernity. There are other aspects of port zones that violate conceptions of urban modernity dominating the later nineteenth century. Port spaces pose challenges to the disciplinary impulse so powerful in hegemonic nineteenth-century culture. They are porous and unruly zones, containing transient populations, mixing travelers, emigrants, immigrants, and sailors, from different cultures, classes, and races, from the city, the provinces, and across the globe.[33] For twentieth-century modernist French writers, the port zone would accordingly be celebrated as a zone of transgression. This celebration is evident in a novel like Jean Genet's *Querelle de Brest,* and Margueurite Duras liked port settings for this reason as well.

The later nineteenth-century distaste for the spectacle of the waterfront stands in marked contrast to its ideological power in the early modern era, when urban planners in both Europe and North America configured the city around its waterway access. Rather than perceived as dirty and chaotic, the disorder of the port staged the success of European urbanites as world citizens, celebrating the European conquest of the oceans and a first global wave of colonial extraction in the early modern era. Joseph Konvitz exemplifies this architecture using the design of Amsterdam in 1607, with its master "plan of three rings" unifying Amsterdam as a series of concentric canals.[34] "The plan was distinctive because it incorporated different aspects of city life into a single form shaped around the waterways, making them paramount not just in a city's infrastructure but sociability itself. Amsterdam's extended waterfront offered the city's residents multiple opportunities to witness maritime activities as part of their daily life . . . At a time when no one visited the seashore for pleasure, they made the city's waterways into a principal public arena for social life and for the aesthetic enhancement of the city's architecture. The waterfront developed as a civilized and domesticated space, while at the same time fulfilling the primary economic and political goals that had justified constructing the city as waterscape."[35]

Konvitz observes that in the later eighteenth century, this celebration of the city as port starts to change. The port remains a center of energy, but urban planners put the emphasis on its decorative beauty, an aspect potentially at odds with its commercial status. Konvitz writes, "[E]lites . . . embraced planning for its decorative value alone, and claimed front-row seats in the theater of the waterfront. They fixed upon the very features of the waterfront that made it a working space—light, room, access to water, and concentration of buildings and activities— and tried to orchestrate them into an aesthetic enhancement of the cityscape."[36] In France, the aim of beautification is vivid in plans for the Bordeaux waterfront around 1785. In the plan for the Place Ludovise drawn up by Victor Louis, the waterfront was already to open into networks across the globe. It was to be organized around "a great semicircular place with a statue of the king in its center and thirteen streets radiating inland from it . . . [which] represented the newly independent United States, with which Bordeaux's merchants traded so heavily."[37] Yet though this organization is the culmination of the waterfront's importance at the heart of urban sociability, it also is a harbinger of the landlocked type of urban modernity of a later era crystallizing in Paris with Second Empire urban planning.

Jonathan Hay introduces a distinction useful for characterizing the kind of orderly monumentality preferred by Haussmannization apropos of the architectural lexicon accompanying Shanghai's transformation into one of the major port cities during the second half of the nineteenth century. One side of this distinction is the imperial "architecture of permanence," what Hay defines "as a symbolic nodule, in which a pre-existing matrix of civic buildings symbolically defined the city's rootedness in the Chinese landscape—as an outpost of the state and the great religions."[38] Certainly, the sweeping boulevards and monumental buildings of the Haussmannian city emphasize its permanence and rootedness in the historical grandeur of the French state, inheritor of an imperial classical tradition. Napoleon III is said to have remarked, "I want to be a second Augustus, because Augustus made Rome a city of marble." This architecture of permanence was evident even in buildings designed for entertainment like Garnier's Opéra. Indeed, the allied qualities of monumentality, centrality, order, and location are so powerful that they extend to impermanent structures, such as the pavilions of the World's Fair of 1867.

Hay opposes this architecture of permanence to a transient "architecture of displacement." Such architecture is casually and unintentionally exemplified by the makeshift utilitarian constructions of the working waterfront, where passing ships from all parts of the world edge the unstable and eroding land of the riverbank and flimsy wood docks and warehouses, light enough to sit on the unstable banks without foundations, are constantly in the process of being destroyed by the harsh effect of the water and weather.[39] In later nineteenth-century Shanghai, Hay observes that this transience itself inspires a style, where it synthesizes with cultural hybridity, producing an "ad-hoc agglomeration of Western colonial houses and streets, new hybrid Sino-Western buildings, and buildings in purely Chinese style."[40] The case of Shanghai is in part a reminder that the landlocked metropolis of later nineteenth-century Paris is only one type of urban modernity, influential as it has been.

Another fruitful distinction for conceptualizing the landlocked type of urban modernity expressed in Haussmann's city of stone is offered by Manuel Castells. This is the distinction between what Castells calls *a space of places* and *a space of flows*.[41] A space of places is defined by location, fixity, and unity in space across time. A space of flows, in contrast, is a discontinuous network of "nodes" and "hubs," defined by connection and exchange; it is, in Castells's terms, a "process" rather than a place. Castells proposes the distinction between the space of places and space of flows when he seeks to characterize our own global, postindustrial era. For Castells, the space of flows is epitomized by the current flow of information and the kinds of global networks of information capitalism, which Castells contrasts with the located model of industrial production dominating an earlier moment.

If there is in fact a connection between eras that celebrate flow and an interest in the spectacle of the working waterways, it might be one ideological strand in the renewed interest in waterfront development at the turn of the twenty-first century. In recent years, revitalizing the postindustrial waterfront has been not only a commercial enterprise, but also an aesthetic project challenging innovative contemporary architects. It has resulted in works like Frank Gehry's Guggenheim Bilbao or the Yokohama International Port Terminal, completed in 2002 by Foreign Office Architects (FOA) for The City of Yokohama Port & Harbour Bureau. The directors of FOA, architects Farshid Moussavi and Alejandro Zaera Polo, are articulate about their goals as renewing urbanites' experience of mobility and flow against located monumentality, which they express using the terms of Deleuze and Guattari: "The artefact will operate as a mediating device between the two large social machines that make up the new institutions: the system of public spaces of Yokohama, and the management of cruise-passenger flow. The components are used as a device for reciprocal *deterritorialization:* a public space that wraps around the terminal, neglecting its symbolic presence as gate, decodifying the rituals of travel, and a functional structure which becomes the model of an a-typological public space, a landscape with no instruction for occupation." As a result, visitors can experience a continuously differentiated mutation of states, become altered within his or her singular identity, "from local citizens to foreign visitor, from *flâneur* to business traveler, from voyeur to exhibitionist, from performer to spectator."[42]

The renewal of the waterfront as a destination for urban sociability is making its way even to Paris, where a lack of interface with the Seine has persisted. As late as 1989, Paul Chemetov and Borja Huidobro's building for the Ministère de l'Economie et des Finances asserts the power of stone above water from its location on the edge of the Seine in the twelfth arrondissement. It dominates the river with supports plunged directly into it, offering a panoramic perspective on the city that bypasses the transition zone between city and river. But Parisians were momentarily encouraged to experience the waterfront in 2002, when Bertrand Delanoyer, mayor of Paris, inaugurated *Paris-plages*. This successful summer happening turned the usually underpopulated quays into an ephemeral leisure destination, as they were piled with sand, in a carnival for those urbanites unable to escape to the seashore because work ties them to the city.

The vision of Paris as a landlocked metropolis was evident at the time it crystallized to Charles Baudelaire, that prescient critic of what he called "modernity" and "modern life." It should thus come as no surprise that the disappearance of the urbanite's connection to the working waterfront framed Baudelaire's most famous description of the toll of Haussmannizations on the everyday city dweller, "Le Cygne" (1859), though little attention has been paid to this historical horizon for his poem. In the opening lines, "Le Cygne" describes the poet's itinerary across what was then bustling river traffic. The poet passes from the Left Bank, where he would have witnessed steam cranes unloading stone to complete Haussmann's buildings at the Port d'Orsay, to the Right Bank, fringed by the historic Port Saint-Nicolas right next to the royal palace. Under his feet flow commercial and commuter boat traffic, including a steamboat named "Le Cygne," itself inaugurated in 1859. The poet, however, has no interface with this traffic since he takes one of Haussmann's new bridges, Le Pont du Carrousel. His lack of commentary on the matter typifies the Parisian attitude toward the river characterized by Du Camp: "We hardly notice it."

But one of Baudelaire's favorite modes of representation is displacement. The absent Seine crops up transformed from "Le Cygne's" first image of Andromache frozen in a gesture of mourning by an artificial waterway: "Andromache, I think of you. That small river, poor and sad mirror where formerly / The vast majesty of your widow's sorrow shone . . . suddenly watered my fertile memory / As I crossed the new [place du] Carrousel."[43] The mirror evoked by Baudelaire is a simulacrum Andromache has had created of the Simoïs, the river running through Troy. Virgil has Aeneas observe that this simulacrum is distanced from the working port of the city; would the "false Simoïs" be the classical harbinger of the artificial waterways of the Parisian parks?[44] Certainly, the exiled Princess takes her place among a hybrid, transient population worthy of a port scene: the captive swan, Ovid's man cast out from Paradise, the black woman yearning for her African home, "sailors forgotten on an island," "captives," "vanquished," and "still many more."

In Baudelaire's cascade of images, the opposition between the city of stone and the city of water takes on psychological force. Baudelaire undoes the power of Haussmann's monumental stone with a procession of weeping exiles, who water the dry wasteland of the construction site of the Louvre with their tears. The figures have been exiled on or across bodies of water, yet those who have "lost what can never be found again" find a renewed connection to flowing liquid "with tears" as they nurse at "sorrow like a good mother wolf." The food of sorrow enables the past to be incorporated, transforming melancholy into mourning and undoing Haussmann's petrification of memory associated with the poet's melancholy for his lost city.

With Andromache, exiled Mediterranean princess, and with the dark-skinned woman exiled from her African home, Baudelaire turns his readers thoughts south to the Mediterranean and to the circuits of travel that bring Africans to France. In doing so, he indirectly evokes, along with the working waterways of Paris, the Suez Canal, whose construction began in 1859, the same year as Baudelaire's "Le Cygne." Indeed, this vast canal connecting the Mediterranean and the Indian Ocean was arguably the greatest engineering feat to emerge from the Second Empire, and certainly the engineering feat of greatest global significance. There are rich historical connections between the Second Empire history of entrepreneurship partnering with engineering integral to Haussmannization and the conception and realization of the Suez Canal. Once we understand the absence of the city-dwellers' connection to the working waterfront as a historically specific moment in the development of a type of urban modernity, we can reconnect the history of urban modernity, even at its most landlocked, with circuits of transport and sociability that span the globe.

NOTES

All translations are mine unless otherwise noted.

1. Isabelle Bakouche and Jean Millard are among the contributors to *La Seine et Paris,* ed. B. de Andia, A. Alexandres, and S. Boura, who provide convincing evidence for the continued importance of the Seine to the Parisian infrastructure across the nineteenth century.

2. The figures are from Alfred Fierro, *Histoire et dictionnaire de Paris* (Paris: Laffont, 1996), 1092. The figures are somewhat more modest according to Jean Millard, but the significance remains the same. They portray the explosion of heavy shipping and the massive growth of the ports of Paris across the nineteenth century. See Jean Millard's "Mutations du port (1850–1950)," in *La Seine et Paris,* ed. B. de Andia, A. Alexandres, and S. Boura, 111–15 (Paris: Action Artistique de la Ville de Paris, 2002).

3. See *La Modernité avant Haussmann, Formes de l'espace urbain à Paris, 1801–1853,* ed. Karen Bowie (Paris: Editions Recherches, 2001).

4. The "canot-concert" was a weekly summer event during the 1840s featuring a concert on board a boat named the *Smuggler.* Hundreds of pleasure boats were reported to follow in its wake.

5. Charles Nodier, *La Seine et ses bords* (Paris: publié par M.A. Mure de Pelanne, 1836), 8–9.

6. Eugène Briffault, "Une journée à l'école de natation," in *Le Tiroir du diable,* 123–24 (Paris: Hetzel, 1845).

7. An image of Turner's work can be viewed at The official Web site of the Tate Britain, http://www.tate.org.uk/servlet/ViewWork?cgroupid=77167&workid=52017&searchid=11580&tabview=image, accessed June 22, 2005.

8. Ian Warrell, *Turner on the Seine* (London: Tate Gallery Publishing, 1999), 236.

9. Maxime Du Camp, *Paris, ses organes, ses fonctions et sa vie,* vol. 1, (Paris: Hachette, 1879), 283.

10. Du Camp, *Paris,* vol. 1, 318.

11. Frederick Lock, "Les ponts, les ports, et les rues," in *Paris-Guide, par les principaux écrivains et artistes de la France,* vol. 2 (Paris: Librairie internationale, 1867), 1412.

12. Jules Clarétie, "Les places publiques, les quais, et les squares de Paris" in *Paris-Guide,* vol. 2, 1384.

13. Strolling along the deserted quai Voltaire, Clarétie observes the quiet bouquinistes who literalize how the Seine has turned to "the library

of Paris" (1385). The riverfront becomes increasingly more ominous when he passes the poultry market where the wicker baskets carrying chickens are "prisons . . . where the chickens cry out as if they understood that they were going to the knife" (1384). The quai Montebello recalls the terrible barricade fighting of 1848, the Hôtel-Dieu on the Ile de la Cité evokes illness, agony, and death; the quai de la Tournelle, lively with shops, poses a social problem because "the worker areas [quartier populaire] that need to be fed" are "brewing" there (1386).

14. I use the term as shorthand for a collective process. Not only can the process not be reduced to the work of Haussmann in conjunction with Napoleon III alone, but also many of its aspects intensify trends that date at least back to the Restoration, if not before. The Second Empire contribution is to implement them on a grand scale.

15. David Pinkney, *Napoleon III and the Rebuilding of Central Paris* (Princeton, N.J.: Princeton University Press, 1958), 65 (my italics).

16. Ibid., 65.

17. Ibid., 66. Barricade fighting had occurred around the Canal Saint-Martin in 1848. The involvement of the canal in insurrection contrasts with the iconography of 1848 as a landscape of street barricades made of furniture and paving stones (figure). Our mythic image of 1848 is in keeping with the blind spot to the waterfront and waterways of Paris in our vision of nineteenth-century urban modernity. Du Camp recognized a seditious aspect to the Seine when he wrote, "La Seine a connu toutes nos discords civiles et, si je puis dire, elle y a pris part . . . de nos jours, elle a porté jusqu'à la mer les livres, les manuscrits, les vêtement sacerdotaux, les vases de l'Archevêché, et pendant nos insurrections elle a roulé le corps de plus d'un combattant" (*Paris*, vol. 1, 286–87).

18. Ibid., 30.

19. Ibid., 9

20. Du Camp, *Paris*, vol. 5, 332.

21. Bakouche in *La Seine et Paris*.

22. The right to ply these services was accorded by the municipality. On the development of mechanical towing, see Du Camp, Paris, vol. 1, 320.

23. Ibid., 319.

24. In this context, one thinks of the appeal of the towpath and river banks to Charles Meryon, so fond of evoking a Gothic and sinister lost Paris, as in the desolate view of the Pont-Neuf from the vantage point depopulated towpath, drafted at the close of the 1850s, the decade when

towing practices were thoroughly transformed. In Benjamin's view, it was Meryon "whose subterranean connection with the great remodeling of Paris is least to be doubted." Walter Benjamin, "The Paris of the Second Empire in Baudelaire," in *Charles Baudelaire: A Lyric Poet in the Era of High Capitalism,* trans. Harry Zohn, 9–106 (London: New Left Books, 1973), 87. In the notes of *Central Park* collected together around 1938, Benjamin remarks on the aesthetic of the liquid and the fluid that fascinates Meryon, commenting on the "sea of houses, the ruins, the clouds, the majesty and fragility of Paris" (section 7:2).

25. An image of Meryon's *Apse of Notre-Dame* can be viewed at http://rmc.library.cornell.edu/adw/gravely/meryon.html, accessed June 22, 2005.

26. Frederick Lock, "Les ponts, les ports, et les rues," in *Paris-Guide,* vol. 2, 1412.

27. The absence of a vista on the Seine in the design of this square indicates one difference in the relation to the river of nineteenth-century Paris and London. In London, the Embankments project also cuts the urbanite off from the riverbank, in a manner related to Second Empire modernization. Nonetheless, built into the Embankments were opportunities for distant vistas of the Thames. This increased visibility of the waterway running through the heart of the city may be connected to the contemporary consciousness of England's status as a maritime empire.

28. On this subject, see Isabelle Bakouche's previously cited essay in *La Seine et Paris bords,* 98).

29. An image of Claude Monet's *Le Pont de Chemin de fer à Argenteuil* is found at http://www.insecula.com/oeuvre/O0013669.html. An image of Manet's *Argenteuil les Canotiers* is found at http://www.grandspeintres.com/manet/resultat.php#. An image of Seurat's *Baignade à Asnières* is found at the official Web site of the National Gallery http://www.national-gallery.org.uk/cgi-bin/WebObjects.dll/CollectionPublisher.woa/wa/work?workNumber=ng3908. An image of Seurat's *Une Dimanche Après-Midi à L'île de la Grande Jatte* is found at http://www.ibiblio.org/wm/paint/auth/seurat/grande-jatte/. All Web sites accessed June 22, 2005.

30. T. J. Clark, *The Painting of Modern Life* (Princeton, N.J.: Princeton University Press, 1984), 189–90.

31. Ibid., 190.

32. An image of Manet's *Les Déchargeurs de Charbon* is found at http://www.histoire-image.org/site/etude_comp/etude_comp_detail.php?analyse_id=17, accessed June 22, 2005.

33. It is in keeping with the mixed social groups associated with water-side spaces that Flaubert's hero first sees Madame Arnoux on the commuter steamboat going from Paris to his home with her black servant: "il la supposait d'origine andalouse, créole, peut-être; elle avait ramené des îles cette négresse avec elle?" Gustave Flaubert, *L'Education Sentimentale* (Paris: Bibliothèque de la Pléiade, 1951), 37. Flaubert's novel opens September 15, 1840; the Paris-Corbeil line connecting Paris to the east was inaugurated on September 17, 1840.

34. Joseph Konvitz, *Cities and the Sea* (Baltimore: Johns Hopkins University Press, 1978), 35.

35. Ibid., 37.

36. Ibid., 170.

37. Ibid., 175.

38. Jonathan Hay, "Painting and the Built Environment in Late Nineteenth-Century Shanghai," in *Chinese Art: Modern Expressions*, 60–101 (New York: Metropolitan Museum of Art, 2001), 67.

39. Hay finds this "architecture of displacement" "in the headquarters of commercial associations, warehouses, and certain shops, all of which had ties to specific areas of China." These building types "gave expression to the sojourner's experience of exile and memory of (also pride in) her native place" (70). Hay cites as an example "the red-lacquered 1857 Customs House," situated on the wharf (70). Its construction "using a mixture of Chinese and foreign elements . . . reflect[s] its symbolic role as the interface between China and the out-side world."

40. Hay, "Painting and the Built Environment," 67.

41. See Manuel Castells, *The Rise of the Network Society* (Oxford: Blackwell, 1996).

42. Foreign Office Architects, courtesy of Lewis Tsurumaki Lewis. See the documentation on this project, which was displayed in the Van Alen Institute's show Architecture + Water, in *Van Alen Report* 9, n.p.

43. Charles Baudelaire, "Le Cygne" (1859), in *Oeuvres complètes,* vol. 1, ed. Claude Pichois, 85–87 (Paris: Bibliothèque de la Pléiade, 1975).

44. An artificial waterway, indeed, distanced from the port in Aeneas's representation of the scene in Virgil. See Pichois's note to the citation in Baudelaire, *Oeuvres complètes,* vol. 1, 1005.

PART II

Competing Narratives of the City: Contested Inclusions and Exclusions

4

Assembling Douala
Imagining Forms of Urban Sociality
AbdouMaliq Simone

African cities appear wrecked, and the progressive disappearance of any
kind of work, formal or informal, makes it nearly impossible for Africans
to anticipate what tomorrow might bring. The capacity to maintain recognizable and usable forms of collective solidarity and collaboration
becomes difficult. A sense of being encompassed, drawn into, and acting
upon a circumscribed world of commonality is nearly impossible as the
previously relied upon practices of forging solidarity fall apart. Urban residents appear increasingly uncertain as to how to spatialize an assessment
of their life chances—that is, where will they secure livelihood, where
can they feel protected and looked after, and where will they acquire the
critical skills and capacities? At the same time, residents in many African
cities have displayed an inordinate capacity to generate, mobilize, and
deploy enormous financial, material, and human resources at great speed
in order to make substantial things happen.

Emerging Ephemerality

Over a period of many years, how have diverse cities across Africa lived?
One can see people on the go. Stations, *gare routiers,* and streets are always
crowded, and people are always in motion. Because people do not have the
resources to plan in advance, since frequent exposure to unanticipated
events and crises can radically disrupt any normal sense of routine, constant adjustments in how daily life is managed have to be made, and this
entails movement. Because it is not always clear where the best prices for
essential commodities can be obtained, it is not clear just what one has to
do each day to put bread on the table. Where cheap resources and good
opportunities are to be had is seldom something fixed in a single location.

But this provisional relationship with sources of input and opportunity is intersected with a large measure of the sedentary. With diminishing prospects of cultivating long-term relationships with institutions that can be used as platforms for exploring and negotiating new affiliations and domains of personal operation, individuals and households often are stuck in highly redundant relations with neighbors and family members. As cognitive proficiency—the ability to assess information and to adapt to new conditions—requires differentiation, where information is to catapult individuals into new abilities, a highly circumscribed, even narrowing social universe comes to be punctuated with many dramas and conflicts, if only to ward off atrophy.[1] So even though stability is retained in people dealing with a known set of others for much of their lives, this stability is incessantly put under risk—through disputes, jealousies, and provocations—to give the "social body" punctuation and texture. Family and neighborhood life often face incessant crisis, which require a series of compensations; these compensations become particular economies—particularly as illness, accidents, social fissions, and death have to be serviced. A locality or particular social field then borders on the incessant recycling of suffering and compensation—where there is a rhythm of movement and fluctuation, but one that does not seem to proceed anywhere in any development sense.

Now, the very ability to earn money from one's labor by staying in one place is increasingly doubted and held in suspicion.[2] The notion now is that limited savings must be directed toward ensuring a capacity to act flexibly in face of uncertain social, economic, and political conditions. This stems from a burgeoning anticipation that everything that will be possible to do in the future is necessarily provisional. This provisionality threatens to undermine all gains if actors are compelled to defend their positions in given territories rather than to acquire an increased ability to adapt to a wide range of them. With both increased affiliation and affinity with movement, a highly mobile collective subject is configured[3]—the identity of which, though unstable and not thoroughly consolidated, does resonate with long and multiple African traditions of how localities were to be understood.[4]

Additionally, this tendency is combined with a widening practice of using almost everything that exists in cities—infrastructure, documents, bodies, and tools—in many different ways, converting one use into another, so that any clear hierarchy of value is disrupted. Finds of all kind, even the most seemingly dilapidated or dysfunctional material, are incorporated into bundles of objects that take on widely disparate meanings for different actors. In a way similar to processes of financial derivation, the flexible use of urban resources and territories creates uncertainty over the meaning of the resources and territories, thus, at times, attenuating the prospects of fights over them.

The provisional is also marked in space with intensified conflict over urban territories which are commonly perceived as neither the purview of private household domains or available to widespread public occupation or use—but rather to the expression of individuated practices and sentiments. In situations where there exists a scarcity of services and limited infrastructure, the structures of shifting access to these interstitial spaces, neither public nor private, is weakened by their use as places of refuse, in part wasted by virtue of being receptacles of waste. In dense residential conditions, this shrinkage of space that belongs to no one, but instead sites varying occupations and uses, is registered as a form of intrusion and social hostility, interrupting delicate social fabrics of neighborliness and mutual support.[5]

Additionally, spaces full of garbage tend to be popularly perceived as outside municipal control, not subject to the authority or management of urban government. For the poor, the "trashing" of this space then also becomes the most available means of signaling the fact that they are not "held" by any form of legitimate municipal power and that, in turn, this situation of incessant provisionality is to be seen as untenable for any political regime. Local collaboration geared toward improving these environmental conditions thus faces strong blockages as such actions are often perceived as giving in to the highly arbitrary practices of governing that are interpreted as simply supporting the privileged.

There has been a widespread proliferation of associations and nongovernmental organizations (NGOs) that have come to the fore in efforts to mobilize citizen involvement in a range of activities from environmental cleansing, civic education, and the development of infrastructure to participative planning. At varying times and places, these efforts have both revalorized and sidelined waning communitarian structures. Sometimes new local initiatives take advantage of these structures' sometime willingness to rediscover social power through operating in new modalities of interinstitutional partnership. At other times, despotic reactions to new local initiatives have to be fended off. Frequently, ineffective and illegitimate municipal and state structures operate through these substantive elaborations of civic associational life in order to expand clientele networks while at the same time taking advantage of these more localized service delivery practices as an occasion to consolidate an even more privatized accumulation of urban resources.[6] Additionally, many local initiatives increasingly link development to a form of small-scale communal entrepreneurship that Elyachar calls "microinformality" that is centered, through its relationships to international organizations and NGOs, on incurring and distributing debt (microfinance). Here, mobilizing the supposedly economically generative dimensions of cultural practice is enshrined as a new form of social discipline.[7]

Structures of mediation diminish those institutions which hold individuals, families, and households in some continuous consideration of one another. In their place are tentative social conglomerations, including uncertain electorates, unstable social fields that try to act as communities. There is a tendency for those whose status, and thus access to opportunities, is dependent upon exercising power on and through the resultant conglomerations to try to enforce solidity through threats and violence. Whether they are extended familial arrangements, local polities, ethnic associations, or confessional communities, violence comes to assume an increasingly justifiable form of maintaining order as these corporate forms face crises of legitimacy and relevance.[8] On the other hand, violence ensues from situations where regulating institutions retain little efficacy, where there is little recourse to authority systems capable of problem-solving, little sense of what the likely outcomes are of acting in a particular manner, and where persons have little sense of being obligated to perform specific tasks or adhere to specific rules.[9] Here, violence becomes an instrument of making things happen or keeping things from happening, as well as a kind of pure supplement that "performs itself"—that is deployed simply as something to do, a gestured enactment that seeks nothing to happen but itself.[10]

In an increasing number of urban situations, everyday life borders on a situation of combat—that is, a direct exposure to radical contingency where there is no recourse to reason, planning, or spirituality as mechanisms of orientation or consolation. Here there is an inversion of ordinary life, where the basic elements of being able to account, predict, and take the measure of things is absent, and in this experience, the future as a moment of anticipation, deferral, or fulfillment ceases to exist.[11] Everything must be seized in the moment, regardless of its apparent value or usefulness. Sensation is reorganized with emphasis on aural acuity. Remy Banzenguiza-Ganga, the Congolese sociologist, has talked about how during the prolonged period of urban warfare in Brazzaville during the 1990s, households could develop a precise referencing system on just where missiles would land based on the specific sound of their trajectory.[12] At the same time, bodies live through a marked dematerialization, a sense of being impermeable and impervious to harm, as somehow invisible to all that surrounds and encounters them.

While this characterization of swathes of urban life as that of combat may be extreme, at least then more and more urban neighborhoods live through an accumulation of small yet relentless traumas. Life expectancy diminishes across urban Africa in the face of weakened immunities, deleterious environmental conditions, accidents, and social conflict. Yet the nearly catastrophic character of African cities generates what Rob Stone has called a kind of "redemptive etymology"—where recognized tropes of urban life bring forward a great deal of cultural material that stays for a long time in a largely uncodified, undigestible, and unintegrable state—material that has not yet been allocated to certain understandable and administrable historical processes.[13] Thus the weight of remaking urban everyday life lies in an attention to the gestural, contingent, and shorthand annotation instead of the memorial; exchanged glances and murmurs rather than documents; deportments, practices, and trades—all a kind of emergency democracy. This emergency democracy is discussed here as a modality of "assembling" the city of Douala. Here the emphasis is on more ephemeral forms of social collaboration that nevertheless register material effects and thus constitute a particular form of materiality at work in urban life.

Domains of Collaboration

Given these qualifications, how does collective action take place? Of course, there is a history. Older quarters of cities retained forms of local accumulation and regulation based on clearly understood and respected systems of local, commonly religious, authority—with their concomitant networks of enterprise and social welfare. Public salaries supported a heterogeneous range of extended family members, clients, and activities anchored in a logic that livelihood was best attained through securing diverse and relevant positions with and across multiple networks. Substantiality in the urban public sphere was largely created through the sheer intricacies and entanglements of various strands of everyday life which, without such entanglements, might only barely function in their own terms. In other words, the ability of households, social institutions, economic organizations, religious groups, judiciaries, and so forth to do what was expected of them (something not always definitively clear either in endogenous and exogenous terms of efficacy) necessitated complex interactions along highly porous boundaries.[14]

So while a broad range of "traditional" institutions persisted, the configuration of urban solidarity, realized at primarily local, neighborhood levels, took place through an interpretation of domains and sectors rather than through the consolidation of citizenship within well-defined and well-managed "modern" institutions.[15] Religion, business, politics, social welfare, training, mutual support, and identity claims intersected with each other, so that any modality of association was not really disconnected from any other.[16] While such arrangements provided multiple opportunities for problem-solving, especially the ability to compensate during times of crisis in what were largely fluid urban environments, they did often limit the generation of new forms of independent action and innovation that could be brought to the larger public sphere. The interdependencies among religion, governance, politics, family life, and business also meant that the stakes were high for any shift in the internal dynamics of any one sector. Again, the locus of independent action is constrained, at the same time as the resolution of any particular difficulty within one sector was potentially availed the influences and resources of another.

As the city grew and extended into more provisional, unserviced, and informalized settlements, the conventional rules and networks which governed most aspects of life in many of the older quarters found limited applicability—with points of entry and mechanisms for survival more diffused across often competing practices and associations.[17] Everyday life depended on more provisional assemblages of resources and alliances.[18] The explosiveness of urban growth has meant that the entry into the urban system over the past decade, while remaining largely family-based, was not as thoroughly controlled or inscribed in a wide net of social and family relations which formerly had situated the new urban immigrant within a more comprehensive or ordered field of activities and obligations.[19]

Intensifying economic difficulties have reaffirmed in some respects the salience of extended family networks as the primary locus of livelihood formation. Increases in the cost of health and schooling often produce a more blatant stratification of opportunities within these networks, as some children can be sent to school or provided other kinds of support, whereas others cannot. Under circumstances of economic hardship, labor mobilization once again becomes important, as youth, in particular, "donate" their labor in return for promises of future support. In some cities, while family size through increased birthrates has declined, average household size may increase due to tendencies to form households on the basis on both kin and nonkinship relations possessing complementary skills and advantages.[20] But overall, the ability of extended family systems to manage increased economic difficulties has grown more precarious.

A critical question then becomes the extent to which the extension and substantiation of associational life in new, more diverse forms is related to the diminution of extended family capacities, as well as embodying urban survival logic and strategic approaches to urban livelihood that reflect practices that are neither rural nor urban, or conversely, constitute elements of a progressive transformation of African urban life.[21] These are not mutually contradictory possibilities, so the thrust of new research endeavors might be to more comprehensively examine what new modalities of associational life are being used for— particularly in the elaboration of new livelihoods.[22]

In light of this urban history and in light of the constraints and prospects for collective action and associational life, consider urban circulation—not the infrastructure of physical transportation, although such considerations are significant, but how residents circulate through a wide range of meanings, styles, vantage points, experiences, ways of talking—tried on and discarded, and perhaps retried again. These elements thus come to belong to no one, even though strong claims can be made on them by particular groups at any given time. However pursued, there are a wide range of efforts undertaken on the part of urban residents to attempt to insinuate themselves into the lives of others, to become some part of their "stories," networks, and activities, without becoming too obligated, too dependent, or tied down.

This is a pursuit to keep things open, keep things from being shut down, and as such, there is a generalized displacement of mediating interventions—in other words efforts to avoid crystallizing stable frameworks and types of actors able to render definitive interpretations about what specific actions must mean or what are to be normative, good uses of all that which makes up an urban environment.[23] This tactic of circulation ends up being particularly precarious since in Cameroon, at least, the relationship of the state to the intimacy of everyday life is one where the state acts as if it is in charge of a kind of invisible circulation. In other words, that it possesses a capacity to bring the mundane, traceable activities, contexts, and relations relaunched on a daily basis by residents to seemingly impossible intersections with unseen forces, unknown lives, distant places, and a whole range of unspeakable occurrences. Residents who navigate the city never can be sure how their own existence may be implicated in the narratives of others. They can never be sure whether their immediate positions and actions inadvertently place them in some "line of fire"—on a trajectory of some conveyance capable of harming them.

This pursuit of keeping things open is also a difficult game to play because it can lead either to a debilitating ambiguity as to what could or should be done or to highly circumscribed maneuvers where individual urban actors attempt to take responsibility for nearly everything they can possibly manage. On the one hand, there can be the incessant dissimulation that the city offers—its sense of the spectacular, the manipulation of pretense, trickery, and the always available profusion of talk, new words, new images, and new styles around which one can posit the illusion of efficacy and success. This is not to say that talk is necessarily immaterial—certainly, to return to Douala, it has its concrete and often deadly effects.

But the profusion of new words requires the interminable task of refashioning, and its arbitrary quality can mean an always jittery trajectory—where success and failure are too close to each other for distinction. In other words, it is never clear who can really get away with what under what circumstances or whether one is really keeping up with the new words that purportedly provide the speaker with an aura of contemporariness or success. Because it is only those able to pass themselves off as the most seemingly socially connected or the most traveled or the most close to the ever-changing configurations of who is in and out—in politics, on the street, in religion, or in nightlife—that are able to "capture" fleeting resources and opportunities. Whatever money gained will need to be reinvested in new appearances and stories, as well as the ability to show up in new circumstances and settings.

On the other hand, tasks are subsumed into the ambit of the individual performer—the man or woman who sees to it, without depending on anyone else, that goods are acquired, transported, off-loaded, shipped, retrieved, and resold. These are individuals that attempt to retain an ever vigilant proximity to the concrete labor necessary to transform objects they buy or otherwise get their hands on into sources of value that constitute the platform on which they, themselves, are transformed. This is about work and more work, where dependency on others is kept to a minimum—whether it is on their words, promises, or managerial performance.

Between these two trajectories—increased dissimulation and a reinvocation of the individual at work—a wide range of collaborations has emerged based on maximizing the use of *both* the physical and cultural materials of the city.

DOUALA

Douala is sub-Saharan Africa's largest city without a history of being a political and administrative center. While national capitals have been relocated in Nigeria, Tanzania, and Cote D'Ivoire, the largest urban centers in these countries have largely been elaborated by virtue of their former administrative functions. Douala is thus unique in that its development trajectory is almost exclusively accounted for by commercial activities. This accords a character to the city that enjoins a sense of economic dynamism to what can often seem a markedly disarticulated social field.

As the commercial center of Cameroon, Douala certainly has a broad range of political institutions located within it. But as the city has not been primarily focused on administrative activities and the concomitant salaries upon which large numbers of extended family members throughout urban Africa have come to depend, surviving in Douala entails a larger measure of individual entrepreneurial initiative than is characteristic of many other African cities. Even with large numbers of unemployed, the overall sense of the city is one where residents are trying to make livelihoods happen.

At the same time, the relative absence of political institutions and a dependency on public employment means that important instruments of urban socialization are absent, that is, domains around which social collaboration and solidarity can be fostered. Historically, cadres of civil servants, public sector unions, and networks of local authority forged in relationship to negotiating positions in and resources from the state played a critical role in fostering a sense of social cohesion in many African cities. As the burden of survival in Douala is much more incumbent upon individuals and households, there is a greater valuation on the autonomy of operations rather than on fostering social interdependency.

This tendency also produces a greater divergence in the characteristics of individual quarters. Without strong gravitational fields generated by critical political and civil institutions, quarters are more inclined to "go their own way." Some are characterized by a strong sense of social cohesion forged through particular histories of settlement, ethnic composition, location, access to resources, and the nature of local leadership.[24] Other quarters have little to distinguish them as coherent places except for either an administrative designation or a particular reputation.

Without either strong institutional supports or impediments, some quarters have been able to proficiently mobilize local initiative and resources to provide essential urban services in a judicious and cost-effective manner. On the other hand, for some quarters, the absence of strong political incentives means that there is little basis for residents to come together for any significant form of cooperation. In these instances, quarters can easily become overwhelmed by the absence of regulation and planning, since there are few mechanisms for land use and waste disposal—particularly thorny problems given Douala's climate and physical setting.

While urban households may be adept at securing livelihood and opportunity, the largely ad hoc manner in which this is pursued means that there are massive problems with critical urban functions, such as circulation across the city, drainage, refuse collection, and security. At the same time, it is difficult to foresee how applicable the array of local solutions often effective as stopgap measures in many other African cities with more substantive histories of social cooperation would be in Douala. So the city combines heightened ingenuity, a high degree of urbanization of behavior and social outlook, a largely inadequate institutional framework for regulating urban processes, and a highly contentious relationship to the political regime in power—all dynamics which make innovative urban development planning both necessary and difficult.

When practices of livelihood formation are largely concentrated outside the scope of political and civil institutional life, no clear modalities of representing residents' interests come to the fore. In some quarters, local power interests clearly are invested in deferring substantial improvements in urban services and the quality of life. This is because either power and wealth accrues to them in terms of compensating for the misfortune derived from poor living conditions or because they control the space of mediation between the quarter and important political actors outside the quarter.[25] In quarters where substantial efforts have been made to secure a decent living environment, there is often a reluctance to expend much local political capital in engaging at larger metropolitan levels, even when there is recognition that continued growth and protection of local gains may require such engagement. In some "virtual quarters," zones on the outskirts of the city where current inhabitants are few but where hundreds of plots have already been sold, struggles for local predominance are already underway.

These dynamics raise the issue of who constitutes legitimate and effective interlocutors for the kind of social collaboration perceived as necessary by key municipal officials. With even the characteristics of contiguous quarters often highly divergent, it is difficult to institutionalize formats of local representation and planning processes in any formulaic way. For example, one of the difficulties faced by a new citywide organization known as Forum for Inhabitants is that the diversity of local power centers and interests makes the transfer of local problem-solving across quarters and the consolidation of a metropolitan advocacy force highly problematic.

As in many African cities, such impetus for urban change is likely to come from youth. But the trajectories of youth are also contentious as they explore different pathways to address what they perceive to be increasing exclusion and declining opportunities. On the one hand, youth are more likely to criticize the persistence of the old mores and values as impediments to change and effective social mobilization. On the other hand, youth are more likely to interpret contemporary urban crises as those of moral values.[26] Thus, they are more likely to either support the resuscitation of traditional values and institutions or to devote their time to a host of religious sects which aim to constitute a "holistic" universe for their devotees while discouraging participation in other activities. Intergenerational conflict is escalating, particularly since youth have borne the brunt of the security operations carried out under extraordinary power by the military—detention, nighttime raids, constant identity checks, and even assassinations. The militancy of youth is increasing. On the one hand, this derives from the escalating boredom experienced as youth; under these security operations, youth are constrained to what are perceived to be claustrophobic quarters and household situations. Conversely, it also derives from an increasing tendency for youth to live in household arrangements independent of the family. Along both trajectories, youth are demanding both institutions they can call their own and a greater part in the deliberation of local affairs.

Although nebulous and diffuse, many youth are trying to put together an urban identity that attempts to go beyond both the ad hoc entrepreneurial sensibilities and the lingering power of ethnic affiliation.

At the same time, this identity forges itself through reinvented memories of the practices that emerged during the formative periods of the city's original quarters. This is not so much a revisionist history as it is an attempt to identify elements of a dormant capacity for diverse residents to create a powerful urban life. The following sections look at some voices, incidents, and trends through which this reassemblage of urban life is taking place.

In the early 1990s, the political opposition, the Front Social Démocratique, attempted to temporarily shut down Douala as part of an effort to press for greater democratization. During this campaign, *les villes mortes*, efforts were made to close all businesses and shut down the transportation system. Organizers of the campaign, however, still needed to get around, and motorbikes were used to replace the taxis and buses that were being shut down. Following the end of the campaign, this form of motorbike transport became increasingly popular as the city's population grew and spread out across terrains that were impossible to navigate with other vehicles.

BENDSKINS

Presently, it is estimated that there are about 35,000 *bendskins*, as the motorbike drivers are called, which cover the bulk of Douala's transportation needs. These drivers are predominantly young men between eighteen to thirty-five years of age. The majority come from the ethnic Bamileke groups, whose origins are rooted in the region to the north of the city. While the Bamileke are considered to be the economic power of the city, the indigenes of Douala—the Sawa and the Duala—continue to largely view them as strangers. Mostly kept out of the civil service and many formal organized private sectors, young Bamileke men are forced to pursue various commercial activities, of which the consolidation of this transport sector has been a key one.

Unlike other modalities of transport, *bendskins* largely fall outside any institutionalized regulatory system. They are compelled to pay annual insurance fees, but otherwise they are unlicensed and thus vulnerable to the incessant harassment of police. Again, since the majority of *bendskins* are Bamileke, who perceive themselves as largely marginalized from the institutional life of the country despite or perhaps because of their reputation for economic dynamism, their domination of transport always borders on becoming a display of political possibilities. Bamileke have generally not supported the ruling party. The majority of *bendskins* not only share a common ethnic identity, but they also largely reside in the city's densest neighborhoods of Bapenda and Makepe, long singled out as targets of the state's active repression and indifference.

In the early morning hours of July 10, 2003, near the major market at Nkololoun, a *bendskin,* age nineteen, was reportedly killed from a blow to the head issued during an altercation with police. Several other deaths occurred in the immediate aftermath of this struggle. Within hours, after word of the incident spread like wildfire, the entire city was shut down, with hundreds of barricades set up using commandeered vehicles, equipment being used in the massive road repair project, and various corner stalls used for cell phone calls and lottery sales. While many youth who were not *bendskins* were quick to join in the escalating mayhem, *bendskins* were also seen in strenuous efforts to curtail looting and other actions not focused on simply shutting down the roads. Bridges, roundabouts, major axis routes, underpasses, and lateral arteries were all quickly cut, significantly delaying the possibilities for state security organs to provide reinforcements and allowing *bendskins* to burn down several police stations, as well as ferry significant numbers of their supporters to key strategic locations.

Without any centralized command operation, the speed with which the dispersion of blockades was accomplished indicated a remarkable proficiency in both disseminating information and ensuring a comprehensive coverage of the entire urban area. At key intersections, one could witness the convergence of scores of *bendskins* that then would immediately fan out in different directions, accumulating additional numbers along the way.

During the following days, many press articles speculated about what the events of July 10 meant and particularly focused on why it seemed that the city allowed itself to so readily be shut down. If the materials from the various focus groups can be seen as representative of a certain collective mood, it seems that many residents of Douala have concluded that their activities count for little. The potential resourcefulness of people moving back and forth, working together, socializing, and trying on new roles and activities has largely been subsumed as a productive way of life to the more opaque machinations of a state posing as the coordinator of an overarching sorcery. Instead of anticipating the development and transformation of lives within the city, the city is used as a platform to actualize some form of escape. With all of its possibilities, more and more people have concluded that there is no possibility to remain at home. Every participant in the ten focus groups reported having an immediate family member living outside of Cameroon, and almost all of the participants indicated that they were presently exploring concrete possibilities to leave as well.

Although the *bendskins'* actions to bring the city's transport to a halt lasted a mere eight hours before subsiding, it reiterated, almost by default, the extent to which circulation is at the heart of urban life. By concretely shutting down the possibility of circulation, *bendskins* restore to visibility its importance. Of course, many observers were interested in how the *bendskins* could so quickly mobilize their numbers to engage the substantial expanses of the city as a whole. While it would be important to know more precisely the logic of self-organization deployed, what is interesting is what the *bendskins* themselves say about their practices, particularly the quotidian procedures and orientations that accrue to provide them some capacity to act as "municipalwide" actors.

In fact, many *bendskins,* particularly those who occupied a small office in Akwa that acted as an interlocutor in dealings with the press and various government officials, indicated that this manifestation of July 10 was really only incidental to a larger objective of building commercial networks of greater scale from among the hundreds of small initiatives being undertaken by *bendskins* in addition to their transport function—for example, initiatives such as linking small workshops making school uniforms to those photocopying school curricular materials to those providing inexpensive lunches to school pupils.

When queried about acquiring a capacity to circulate across the city and to articulate bodies, events, actions, and resources—whether it be in anger over an attack in the market or aspirations of greater economic power—many *bendskins* pointed out that it was important to pay attention to how they eat. While meals are frequently taken at home and in each other's company, there is also a deliberate practice on the part of the individual *bendskin* to eat in a new place, with a new audience, and in a new neighborhood. Wherever one is and whatever one is doing, one must stop to eat, and in this context of eating in public, of sitting down with others in the thousands of makeshift restaurants across the city, conversations are not only overheard, but trajectories into different lives are also potentially opened up. As *bendskin* informants indicate, this is not only about witnessing the *terroir,* but of also continuing to "steer the roads"—that is, to direct conversation between others in particular directions, to suggest possible entry points among those sitting to take a meal into each other's dilemmas, stories, or activities.

Of course, those who stop to eat must be careful about what they say. Often they may share their food, but they will make sure to say nothing to give themselves away. Sitting down to eat is then engineered with a complex toolbox of declensions, fragmented words, smirks and grunts, tongue clicks, and glottals. But at the same time, *bendskin* informants say that the event of strangers eating with each other is also an opportunity to "get carried away." Unlike meals with households, there is no discussion about daily earnings and obligations, of responsibilities met or unfulfilled. They therefore try to use a battery of jokes, jousting, and stories to get those hurriedly working their way through the food to make a comment about what someone else has just said or to offer some advice or information.

One *bendskin* described a recent meal where there was a captain who has just slept with the fifteen-year-old daughter of his commanding officer in a bleak backstreet hotel, a university student who has packed a small bag and is meeting a truck that will deliver him across the first of many borders that lie ahead, a director of a women's marketing group faced with a choice of taking a small grant from a European country to send her daughter to a university in France, a thief who worried that his father would identify him as the one who held up his office a few hours before, and the director of the recently opened stock exchange who was delivering a crate of chickens to the aunt who cooked at this location for four decades—all sitting in an unpredictable animation, each at the cusp of each other's trajectories, somehow ready to move and be moved.

At the smallest of levels, *bendskins* were elaborating a particular political practice using the sheer event of eating as a site of potential circulation, of knowing the larger city better, of trying to provoke people from different walks of life to make some uncertain, unanticipated connections with each other, and of trying to operate outside the accustomed discursive sites of sociality and family and neighborhood conviviality. Although these latter continue to exist and remain important, *bendskins* are clearly indicating a need to exceed these familiar domains and routines.

NOCTURNAL MACHINES

In Douala, *mapan* is a term that refers to a particular architecture of lanes that wind their way as a kind of maze and often lead nowhere. The word also refers to the futility of trying to accord any urban resident a definitive location and identity. Moreover, it refers to any effort that attempts to make some kind of definitive link between resident and place, resident and scheme, resident and any specific story one might be tempted to elaborate on about them. As such, *mapan* links a description of space to a particular urban ontological condition. In a city that has a long history of pursuing highly varied forms of entrepreneurship largely unencumbered by the official economies and functions of the state, this critical component of the city's imagination also reflects a general concern about the operations of various apparatuses of control to which, no matter how much residents may deflect or circumvent them, attention must always be paid.

Bepanda Omnisport is a quarter in Douala shaped powerfully by the various connotations of *mapan*. The quarter borders on the city's primary sports complex whose construction made the area exceedingly dense. As a primarily poor yet highly urbanized Bamileke neighborhood—in terms of its relationship to Bamileke authority structures largely concentrated outside of Douala—and one of the most militant in terms of opposition to the ruling politics, municipal authorities simultaneously neglected it, in terms of service provision, and subjected it to heavy doses of police repression.

Many of the city's *bendskins* come from the quarter. Their particular vocation gave the place a great deal of knowledge about what goes on in the city as a whole. This quarter, along with Bakepe and Bonamoussadi, were critical in driving the grassroots push for political transformation that swept the city at the beginning of the 1990s and subsequently suffered the most in the state's efforts to keep Douala from becoming an effective center of such transformation.

Along the route that passes the stadium are a series of markets and stores that service both the quarter and the traffic along this busy thoroughfare. Next to the large Catholic church complex just to the south of the sports stadium are lines of used vehicles and vans that are for rent usually just for a few hours at a time, with minimal deposit and documentation. This proves very convenient for those who do not have the time to rely on porters with their wagons or whose load is too large for them or too small to hire other carters. The vans are usually in bad shape, relegated to this role as their last conceivable function, and those that run these lots are clearly trying to squeeze the last bit of profitability from these vehicles.

Across the road are lines of noisy bars and cafes, full even in the daytime and overcrowded at night. They embody the quarter's reputation for roughness and are places where all kinds of observations about the city—mostly garnered by the *bendskins*—are turned into speculative exercises by thieves, poseurs, and tricksters eager to supply their unemployment with quick money. The circulation of information was also aided by the scores of prostitutes, young and old, which worked these bars for small change and had to drop as many hints and speculations of their own. While the city takes on a rough visage in many different locales, the passing police vans and other security vehicles at night seemed to simply compel a surfeit of reckless posturing.

Late into the night the bars are usually still full. There are fights over beer and women; old family wounds are reassuaged countless times. On some nights—there seems to be no clear pattern—a group will emerge from those assembled and head toward one of the vans lining the opposite side of the street. The crew will never be the same. There will be those that go out frequently, and others for whom this will always be the first and/or the last time. At first, it was barely a blip in a loud and long night of subsidized drinking and keeping out of view, tucked into a corner of the bar with a bevy of research assistants and hangers-on. But after awhile it seemed odd how different men of different ages would suddenly stand up and head toward the vans, seemingly without signal or advance planning, without coordinating watches or waiting for a specific figure to take the lead.

There were usually at least three vans that would depart at the same time and then quickly split up, taking widely divergent routes. Given the police checkpoints and the fact that these vans and their drivers would in all probability never have the entirety of the insurance papers, ownership documents, inspection stickers, and commercial vehicle licenses demanded by the patrols, these vans took circuitous routes through various quarters and back roads. But they inevitably headed to specific sites, or as close to them as possible, where the occupants would proceed to walk, keeping shovels close to their chests.

Whether it was the New Bell Detention Center, Laquintinie Hospital, the naval base, the Bonanjo Detention Center, the villages of Edéa and Petit Dibambu, or the cemeteries in Bonapriso where extrajudicial detainments, torture, and executions were rumored to take place under the Operation Command, the occupants of the vehicles would fill empty rice bags with dirt, no more than two apiece, and hurry back to the vans with them, the operation completed in a matter of minutes. They would then retrace their route almost precisely back through Bepanda and then take off again to various destinations. In the space of two weeks, the bags of dirt were tracked to BonaMbappe, a precarious trip over the Wouri Bridge where police checkpoints are normally constant, yet on this night nowhere in sight, and then to the local head of the ruling party, the Rassemblement démocratique du Peuple Camerounais in BonaMbappe—where the guardian was hit over the head and the bags emptied by the entrance of the front gate. This scene would replayed in front of cheferies in Barcelone, entrepreneurs in Cité des Enseignants, and party officials in Bonamouti Deido.

Having never interviewed any of the participants as to their motives or never being able to determine how the recipients of these offerings, whose identity was usually determined in retrospect on subsequent days, were affected, if at all, it is not clear what is taking place. Even so, it can be surmised, without much qualification, given the sites visited, the residential location of the occupants of the vehicles, the object placed in bags, and the identities of the recipients, that something about the disappearances, the hauntings of the various security operations, and the continued arbitrary detentions of various individuals, sometimes with nothing to distinguish them at all in terms of any actual crime or prospective danger, was being worked out.

Over the last fifteen years, as various short-lived but vicious security operations have come and gone, have been forgotten, renamed, interrupted and made to appear as incidental, occasional, and exceptional, a continuous event has transpired—something with no respite even if discernible actions seem to come and go. As conventional forms of political opposition have usually fallen apart and inertia and fear predominate, not only is a certain memory kept alive in these nocturnal actions, but also put to work, as what has been attempted to be buried finds itself dispersed across various vectors of power and status.

CONCLUDING NOTE

New trajectories of urban mobility and mobilization are taking place in the interstices of complex urban politics. Distinct groups and capacities are provisionally assembled into surprising, yet often dynamic, intersections outside of any formal opportunity the city presents for the interaction of diverse identities and situations. But, across urban Africa, there is a persistent tension as to what is possible to do within the city and the appropriate forms of social connections through which such possibilities can be pursued.

Increasingly, more ephemeral forms of social collaboration are coming to the fore, and more effective formal governance partnerships often succeed to the degree to which they can draw on them. This emergence is a means of circumventing the intensifying contestation as to what kinds of social modalities and identities can legitimately mobilize resources and people's energies. Throughout these efforts lingers the question as to how urban residents reach a "larger world" of operations. What happens within the domain of the city itself that allows urban actors, often highly rooted in specific places and ascription, to operate outside these confines? How are apparent realities of social coherence and cohesion maintained while opportunities are pursued that would seemingly require behaviors and attitudes antithetical to the sustainability of such cohesion?

Many cities have increasingly become a nebulous world where security operatives, freedom fighters, terrorists, corporate raiders, gangsters, rebels, activists, militants, presidents, smugglers, communication technicians, hackers, accountants, consultants, and priests are like each other, but not the same thing—and where we have no language to adequately understand these "like" relations. Yet, the relations are the important thing and not the clear definition of the identities. For urban residents, this means operating in a world with an incessant and responsible crisscrossing of identifications, allegiances, and collaborations. It means constantly exploring creative lines of connections to orientations which are not theirs—to attempt to let them speak in their own terms, to be affected by them without necessarily having to understand them and fit them into what they already know.

NOTES

1. Suhail Malik, "Information and Knowledge," *Theory, Culture, and Society* 22 (2005): 29–49.

2. Savina Ammassari and Richard Black, *Harnessing the Potential of Migration and Return to Promote Development: Applying Concepts to West Africa* (Sussex, UK: Sussex Centre for Migration Research, University of Sussex, 2001).

3. Dennis Cordell, Joel Gregory, and Victor Peché, *Hoe and Wage: A Social History of a Circular Migration System in West Africa* (Boulder, Colo.: Westview Press, 1996).

4. John Hanson, "Islam, Migration, and the Political Economy of Meaning: *Fergo Nioro* from the Senegalese River Valley 1862–1890," *Journal of African History* 35 (1994): 37–60.

5. Jacky Bouju, *Les incivilities de la société civile, Espace public urbain, société civile et governance communale á Bobo-Dioulassso et Bamako (Communes 1 et 2)* (Paris: Programme de Recherche Urbaine pour le Développement, Institut des Sciences et des Techniques de L'Équipement et de L'Environment pour le Développement, 2004).

6. Frances Cleaver, "Institutions, Agency, and the Limits of Participatory Approaches to Development, in *Participation: The New Tyranny,* ed. B. Cook and U. Kothari, 36–55 (London: Zed Books, 2000).

7. Julia Elyachar, "Empowerment Money: The World Bank, Non-Governmental Organizations, and the Value of Culture in Egypt," *Public Culture* 14 (2002): 493–513.

8. Barbara Cooper, "Anatomy of a Riot: The Social Imaginary, Single Women, and Religious Violence in Niger," *Canadian Journal of African Studies* 37 (2003): 467–512; Pierre Janin and Alain Marie, "Violences ordinaries, violences enracinées, violences matricielles," *Politique Africaine* 91 (2003): 5–13; Bjørn Enge Bertelsen, "The Traditional Lion Is Dead: The Ambivalent Presence of Tradition and the Relation between Politics and Violence in Mozambique," *Lusotopie* 10 (2003): 263–81; Thandika Mkandawire, "The Terrible Toll of Post-colonial 'Rebel Movements' in Africa: Towards an Explanation of the Violence against the Peasantry," *Journal of Modern African Studies* 40 (2002): 181–215.

9. Dominique Malaquais, "Anatomie d'une arnaque: feymen et feymania au Cameroun," *L'Etudes du Ceri* 77, Centre d'etudes et de recherches internationals, Sciences Po; Charles Gore and David Pratten, "The Politics of Plunder: The Rhetorics of Order and Disorder in Southern

Nigeria," *African Affairs* 102 (2001): 211–40; Caroline Moser, "Urban Violence and Insecurity: An Introductory Roadmap," *Environment and Urbanization* 16 (2004): 3–16.

10. David Anderson, "Vigilantes, Violence, and the Politics of Public Order in Kenya," *African Affairs* 101 (2002): 531–55; Human Rights Watch, "The Bakassi Boys: The Legitimatization of Murder and Torture," *Human Rights Watch Reports on Nigeria* 14, no. 5 (2002).

11. Harvie Ferguson, "The Sublime and the Subliminal: Modern Identities and the Aesthetics of Combat," *Theory, Culture, and Society* 21 (2004): 1–33.

12. Remy Banzenguisa-Ganga, personal communication.

13. Rob Stone, personal communication.

14. Alice Conklin, *A Mission to Civilize: The Republican Idea of Empire in France and West Africa 1895–1930* (Stanford, Calif.: Stanford University Press, 1997); James Ferguson, *Expectations of Modernity, Myths, and Meanings of Urban Life on the Zambian Copperbelt* (Berkeley: University of California Press, 1999); Brian Raftopolous and Tsueneo Yoshikuni, eds., *Sites of Struggle: Essays in Zimbabwe's Urban History* (Harare, Zimbabwe: Weaver Press, 1999); Filip De Boeck, "Borderland Breccia: The Mutant Hero and the Historical Imagination of a Central-African Diamond Frontier," *Journal of Colonialism and Colonial History* 1 (2000): 1–44; Nicholas Thomas, *Colonialism's Culture* (Princeton, N.J.: Princeton University Press, 1994).

15. Andrew Apter, *Black Critics and Kings: The Hermeneutics of Power in Yoruba Society* (Chicago: University of Chicago Press, 1992); Catherine Coquery-Vidrovitch, "The Process of Urbanization in Africa: From the Origins to the Beginning of Independence" *African Studies Review* 34 (1991): 1–98; Mariane Ferme, *The Underneath of Things: Violence, History and the Everyday in Sierra Leone* (Berkeley and Los Angeles: University of California Press, 2001); Jane Guyer and S. Eno Belinga, "Wealth in People as Wealth in Knowledge: Accumulation and Composition in Equatorial Africa," *Journal of African History* 36 (1995): 91–120; Andrew Hopkins, *An Economic History of West Africa* (New York: Columbia University Press, 1973); Phyllis Martin, *Leisure and Society in Colonial Brazzaville* (Cambridge: Cambridge University Press, 1995); Claire Robertson, *Trouble Showed the Way: Women, Men, and Trade in the Nairobi Area 1890–1990* (Bloomington: Indiana University Press, 1997).

16. Nazneen Kanji, "Gender, Poverty, and Economic Adjustment in Harare, Zimbabwe," *Environment and Urbanization* 7 (1995): 37–55;

Annelet Harts-Broekhuis, "How to Sustain a Living: Urban Households and Poverty in a Sahelian Town of Mopti, Africa," *Africa* 67 (1997): 106–31; Lynn Schler, "Ambiguous Spaces: The Struggle over African Identities and Communities in Colonial Douala, 1914–45," *Journal of African History* 44 (2003): 51–72; Kenneth King, *Jua Kali Kenya: Change and Development in an Informal Economy 1970–95* (Nairobi, Kenya: East African Educational Publishers, 1996); Joe Lugalla, *Crisis, Urbanization and Urban Poverty in Tanzania: A Study of Urban Poverty and Survival Politics* (Lanham, Md.: University Presses of America, 1995); Kisangani Emizet, "Confronting the Apex of the State: The Growth of the Unofficial Economy in Congo," *African Studies Review* 41 (1998): 99–137.

17. Christian Lund, "Precarious Democratization and Local Dynamics in Niger: Micro-Politics in Zinder," *Development and Change* 32 (2001): 845–69.

18. Tom De Herdt, "Economic Action and Social Structure: 'Cambisme' in Kinshasa," *Development and Change* 33 (2002): 683–708; Marchal Roland, *A Survey of Mogadishu's Economy* (Nairobi, Kenya: European Commission/Somali Unit, 2002).

19. Richard Banégas and Ruth Marshall-Fratani, "Côte d'Ivoire, un conflit régional? La Côte d'Ivoire en guerre: dynamique du dedans et du dehors (Ivory Coast, a regional conflict?)" *Politique Africaine* 89 (2003): 5–11; Emile Le Bris, ed., "Espaces publics municipaux," Politique Africaine 74 (2000): 6–83; Sabea Hanan, "Reviving the Dead: Entangled Histories in the Privatisation of the Tanzanian Sisal Industry," *Africa* 71 (2001): 286–313.

20. Jane Guyer, LaRay Denzer, and Agbaje Adigun, *Money Struggles and City Life: Devaluation in Ibadan and Other Urban Areas in Southern Nigeria, 1986–96* (Portsmouth N.H.: Heinemann, 2002).

21. Hakim Ben Hammouda, "Guerriers et marchands: elements pourune economie politique des conflits en Afrique," *Africa Development* 24, no. 3 and 4 (1999): 1–18; Mark Duffield, "Post-Modern Conflict: Warlords, Post-adjustment States and Private Protection," *Civil Wars* 1 (1998): 66–102; Janet MacGaffey and Remy Bazenguissa-Ganga, *Congo-Paris: Transnational Traders on the Margins of the Law* (Bloomington: Indiana University Press, 2000); François Misser and Olivier Valleé, *Les gemmocraties: L'economie politique du diamant africain* (Paris: Desclee de Brouwer, 1997); Janet Roitman, Garrison-Entrepôt, "Cahiers d'Ètudes africaines, 37, nos. 2–4 (1998): 150–52; Brad Weiss, "Thug Realism: Inhabiting Fantasy in Urban Tanzania," *Cultural Anthropology* 17 (2001): 93–128.

22. Janet Roitman, "Unsanctioned Wealth; or, the Productivity of Debt in Northern Cameroon," *Public Culture* 15 (2003): 211–37.

23. Achille Mbembe, *On the Postcolony* (Berkeley and Los Angeles: University of California Press, 2002).

24. Dickson Eyoh, "Conflicting Narratives of Anglophone Protest and Politics of Identity in Cameroon," *Journal of Contemporary African Studies* 16 (1998): 249–76.

25. Cletus Acho-Chi, "Sustainable Self-Help Development Efforts in the Cameroon Grasslands," *Development in Practice* 8 (1998): 366–71.

26. Deborah Durham, ed., "Youth and the Social Imagination in Africa," special issue, *Anthropological Quarterly* 73 (2000).

5

CITIES WITHOUT MAPS
Favelas and the Aesthetics of Realism
Beatriz Jaguaribe

Perched on the mountains overlooking the beaches of Rio, sprawling horizontally at the edges of São Paulo, or facing the sewage-choked lagoons in Salvador, favelas are an overwhelming feature of city life in Brazil.[1] The contradictory relations between the favela and the city constitute a key issue of the Brazilian urban experience because they translate how the expectations of the modern metropolis have been both frustrated and partially fulfilled. They have been defeated because the material promise of modernity as access to goods and services has been undermined by the radical economic and social inequality between the rich and the poor. Yet, they have been also enacted because the modernizing urban scenario is a crucial site for the invention of new forms of social identity, democratic struggle, and individual social mobility.

Cast as both the locus of the "national imagined community" and as a "fearful stain" in the landscape of modernity, the favelas were often metaphorized as an emblem of Brazil's uneven modernization. Celebratory versions of the favela as a samba community composing carnival lyrics coexist with images of armed adolescents shooting police forces during drug raids. Since the 1980s, the increase of social violence produced by the globalized drug trade and the flow of media images, consumer goods, and new cultural identities produced a crisis of representation of the "national imagined community." Indeed, the overwhelming presence of the media centered foremost on television and the circulation of globalized consumer goods, lifestyles, and political agendas has transformed expectations and cultural identities. Such transformations are keenly felt in the invention of youth cultures where the former national samba has lost much of its influence to funk and hip-hop in the favelas of Rio de Janeiro and São Paulo.

Images and narratives of a globalized favela emerge as the former national portraits of Brazil become increasingly fragmented. The fraying of previous narratives and images of national identity has also brought to the limelight new cultural icons shaped by the media and popular culture. In the wake of these changes, contemporary literary and cinematographic productions are attempting to come to terms with new portraits of Brazil that focus on marginalized characters, favelas, drug cultures, and the imaginaries of consumption.

The main contention of this essay is that a crucial element of the fabrication of the new representations of the favelas is the usage of different forms of the "aesthetics of realism." Evidently, not all the cultural representations of the favela rely on a realist register, but those that have had a greater repercussion and press coverage have made use of the mimetic impact associated with the realist encoding of the "real." The pages that follow discuss a selective group of representations ranging from *Quarto de Despejo* (1960) to *Cidade de Deus*, the novel (1997) and the film (2002), in order to analyze how the differing usages of realism and the popularization of the realist cannon occupy a central role in the construction of an image of social exclusion in the city and how such images provide the "shock of the real." Carolina de Jesus's famous book anticipates the impact of testimonial literature but does so without the political agency that would later be developed in the writing and reception of such accounts in the 1970s. The well-known Cinema Novo films of the 1960s that depicted the favela are not considered here because their production is related to a political agenda of the social transformation of Brazil; their cinematic aesthetics had scant repercussion among popular cinema viewers. In contrast, both recent documentaries and fictional productions on the favela have not only catered to large audiences, but also more importantly they have established an interpretive code of realism that allowed them to become focal points of discussion concerning the reality of Brazilian cities.

Guided by Simmel's classic definition of the hyperstimulation of urban culture, these realist narratives and images produce the "shock of the real" by means of artistic defamiliarization.[2] The term "shock of the real" refers to specific representations in both written narratives and visual images that unleash an intense, dramatic discharge that destabilizes notions of reality itself. The "shock" element resides in the nature of the event that is portrayed and in the convincing usage of a "reality effect" that, nevertheless, disrupts normative patterns. Different from notions of the sublime or the catastrophic that suggest a breakdown of representation by events so large in scale or so unexpected in dimension that they momentarily surpass conceptual coinage, the "shock of the real" is related to quotidian, historical, and social occurrences—rapes, murders, muggings, fights, erotic exchanges, and any range of events that evoke strong emotional responses. In many ways, the "shock of the real" unleashes a cathartic discharge, but contrary to the response elicited by Greek tragedies or romantic poetry, the cathartic element here does not necessarily seek to provoke the classic sentiments of compassion and pity or spiritual transcendence. Rather, in many instances, the cathartic triggering is purposefully ambiguous. Such an ambiguity is not related to the subtle veiled ploys of the narrative or image. After all, realistic depiction of violence or strong emotional feelings is easily apprehended by readers or viewers. But what is not so easily understood is the meaning of such violence and emotion not only because reception varies, but also because there is no overarching interpretative ethos to provide solace and meaning to such cathartic representations.

In Simmel's account of the metropolitan experience, the rapid pace of the city, the anonymity of the metropolis, and hyperstimulation produced by new forms of transportation, commodities, and entertainment induced urban inhabitants to adopt a blasé attitude in their daily lives. The blasé attitude cushioned the city dweller from a bombardment of sensorial stimulus. In contemporary terms, urbanites may continue to shield themselves from urban chaos, but the blasé defensiveness is threaded by the perplexity of uncertainty. Cities have become increasingly difficult to map. Furthermore, the very territorial boundaries of the city no longer persist. The shock of the new and the culture of hyperstimulation that were formerly perceived as part of the metropolitan experience have surpassed the boundaries of the urban environment. The city itself no longer has readily defined limits. Yet, in a world of globalized branding and intense cultural hybridity, cities continue to provide what Baudelaire termed to be the "commotion of the modern." If the shock of the new and hyperstimulation can be bought and experienced in computer games, theme parks, tourist sites, and shopping malls, the "commotion of the modern" still implies experiencing the tumultuous rush of the urban maze. It evokes the street scene, the unexpected encounter, the meeting with the stranger, the presence of the crowd, and the sensorial impact of the sights and sounds of the urban realm.

Experiencing the city also implies creating a range of representations that express the different vocabularies of modernity. These maps of urban living and "stories of the street" are in continual dispute.[3] An overflow of media images and narratives coexist with personalized memories, historical events, architectural constructions, and lived experiences. Contemporary urban dwellers are not only subject to the "shock of the new" and the tumult of hyperstimulation analyzed by Simmel, but they are also increasingly caught in a maze of representations where local knowledge is combined with globalized representations. Furthermore, as cities gain complexity and become deterritorialized, the experience of being in the city entails varying degrees of direct exposure to metropolitan living itself. Gated condominiums, communitarian neighborhoods, and isolated slum areas emphasize, for better or for worse, territorial limits. Yet, what distinguishes these urban configurations from their similar nineteenth and early twentieth century versions is precisely the flow of global communications and commodities. This implies not only the emergence of urban lifestyles and forms of identity that surpass local and national boundaries, but it also allows narratives and images to circulate.

Transmitted by film, television, radio, the Internet, and advertising, such narratives and images also fabricate representations of the city itself, its enticement and allure, its danger and threat. The phantoms of fear that haunt cities have their specificities and historical avatars. They come in the shape of unexpected terrorist implosions in public places, they lurk as the menacing criminal in the dark corners of parking lots, they are featured as the riotous mob or dangerous individuals, and they are centered in particular urban zones of manifest violence and poverty.

For inhabitants of large metropolitan areas in Brazil, the fear of urban spaces is tied to the usual threats of rape, robbery, and kidnapping. But such forms of violence can occur in any section of the city and are viewed as part of the menacing experience of the streets. Yet, within the urban maze, the favelas—as is evidenced by the dramatic drop of real estate prices of houses and apartments located near them—are seen as specific danger zones of violence and poverty. To experience the city entails facing these contradictions, ambiguous spaces, and cultural contagions. Disparities between the rich and the poor are directly mirrored in the layout of urban scenarios where favelas face luxurious shopping malls, street children cluster around well-heeled pedestrians, and public spaces such as the beach in Rio de Janeiro are both a congenial meeting ground of different classes and arenas of tension.[4] Indeed, inhabitants of cities such as Rio de Janeiro and São Paulo are constantly assaulted by uncertainty, an uncertainty that feeds on the fear of violence, that mirrors the transformations of the urban design, and that grows with the fluctuations of a volatile economy that expresses the fast pace of cultural change.[5]

In such an uneasy terrain, the aesthetic options that are chosen to represent the favela and the city become narrative ballasts that insert the weight of the "real" in what appears to be a fraying tissue of a dissolving reality. The aesthetic of realism has a particular appeal because it establishes codes of representation based on the verisimilitude of quotidian existence. Imagined communities in cities and the construction of daily existence are created by a multiplicity of discourses where the language of realism in the press, television coverage, personal narratives, and social events has become a naturalized encoding of the "real." Yet, the disputes concerning the register of the "real" and "reality" reveal that the very fabric of social construction is being debated and that perspectives of the future are being called into question.

The close contact between "fiction" and nonfiction does not necessarily erase the boundaries between the "real" and the fictional, but they question the status of representation and our access to experience largely tied to the "culture of the spectacle" created by the media.[6] Yet, the frontiers between the "real" and the imaginary are also constantly being blurred in advertising, televised stories, and our own personal daydreams. Journalistic disputes over the narration of the reality insist on offering distinctions between sensationalist coverage and objective news. Despite the legitimacy of these distinctions, the overall spectacularization of daily life and the very nature of representation make it practically impossible to experience facts without the mediation of television, newspapers, cinema, or the Internet. The sense of the real becomes increasingly packaged, and yet the shock of the real is insistently sought.

OLD AND NEW REALISMS

More than any other aesthetic endeavor, realist aesthetics places large claims on the representation of both the real and reality. Similarly to the temporal instant that is lived and yet cannot be consciously understood until it has been processed by memory and language, the "real" is a disputed category that tests the limits of representation and exceeds the selective mechanisms of our conscious control. As a presence of the world beyond and outside ourselves, the real cannot be fully encompassed by our experience, and even experience itself becomes elusive while we are in the process of living it. By contrast, reality is a part of the real that has been processed by the cultural construction of society mediated by a variety of discourses, dialogical perspectives, and clashing worldviews. Enmeshed in a socially built reality, we seek to symbolize and produce meaning in the fabrication of representations, narratives, and images. Realism as an aesthetic representation is also a conventional and culturally engendered form of reality-making. In contrast to the repertoires of surreal defamiliarization or the inventions of the fantastic imagination, realist aesthetics can offer critical appraisals of "experiencing the world," not by rendering the representation of reality "strange" but by making it "real." In its various forms, realism is an aesthetic that may or may not make use of verisimilitude in order to conjure narratives and images of reality. Indeed, what makes the various realist aesthetics so persuasive is that ordinary and commonplace perceptions of reality are often understood as apprehensions of the real. Yet, as is the case with other aesthetic endeavors, the codes of realism often seek to go beyond socially produced mechanisms of reality in order to touch the elusive kernel of the "real" itself. Such realist narratives and images acquire a particular force when they are perceived not merely as a mirror of a socially constructed reality but as a reaching out to an underlying dimension that reveals the masks of the social.

In Eagleton's analysis, realism "can be a technical, formal, epistemological or ontological affair. It can also be a historical term, describing the most enduring artistic mode of the modern age."[7] In recent decades, the focus on realist narratives and images has been closely connected to the duplication of the real by visual culture and new technologies of the media. The debates concerning the "society of the spectacle," the disappearance of the real by the production of simulacra, or the deconstruction of realism as an aesthetic bound to an ideological reality maintenance principle are often at the center of discussions concerning the postmodern predicament.[8] For the purposes of this chapter, this debate is framed in relation to specific media and artistic productions and only selectively deals with the many dense conceptual implications of these terms.

When realism arose as a form of art, most notably in nineteenth-century France, it attempted to forge a connection between experience and representation not only by emphasizing the "reality effect" gauged by codes of verisimilitude, but also by endorsing a secular disenchanted view of the fabrications of the social world.[9] Realism, in its varied guises, was to produce the predominant naturalized vision of reality in modernity.

The popularity and exportation of the novel as a literary genre, the circulation of the newspaper, and the emergence of new image-making media such as the photo camera and later the movie camera were to further intensify the realist reduplication of the real. The separation between fact and fiction, the construction of knowledge on the basis of objective empirical data, the instrumental rationalization of social life, the promotion of a scientific outlook, and the industrial expansion of the bourgeois class and nation-state all conform to the canons of realist representation. Yet, as Raymond Williams contends, if the naturalization of realism constituted the backbone of the bourgeois Weltanschauung, critical realism, in its artistic guise, sought to cast a destabilizing glance on the norms, values, individual constructions, and social aspirations of these societies.[10]

In the more nuanced critical realist gaze, the pedagogical effort of revealing reality or producing indictments of a social malaise is not centrally given, and the social and aesthetic construction of the world emerges in a flux of discourses, subjectivities, and imaginations. In other cases, the construction of reality hinges very much on the impact of the "shock of the real" that, nevertheless, must produce meanings that are not readily decoded as being the usual spectacularized product of the televised media. Evidently, visual media has a far more compelling force than the written word. Yet, precisely because of the predominance of visual culture, cinematic and photographic representations circulate in saturated realms of image overflow. As the main source of mass media viewership, television produces daily doses of images that both shock and fatigue. The spectacularized quality of these images relates to their decontextualization, their abundance of information that does not entail comprehensive knowledge.

Filmmakers and photographers who are intent on producing the "shock of the real" must therefore finds ways of providing intensity without the wrappings that are usually associated to events of violence, conflict, or the incongruous. Such wrappings come in the form of readily packaged signals that forewarn the spectator that what he or she is about to see pertains to the realm of the awful, awesome, or violent. The reiterative nature of these media goods dulls, makes banal, and dispels critical appraisal because they become preordained discourses that seek to provoke stimulated responses. In order to break the naturalized causality effects of emotionally charged images and narratives, the "shock of the real" suggests a negative epiphany, and it presupposes an awakening to an intense experience that may produce cathartic release but does not necessarily offer redemptive contemplation.[11] Tragedy surfaces in the slaughtering of innocent people during shootouts between drug dealers and policemen; in the slaying of street children; and in the despair of the stricken, homeless, and helpless; but such tragic events, images, and narratives are not affirmative of any ethos. They cannot be monumentalized because although they represent a rupture of the normative, they are also silenced into banality. Aesthetic inventions of the "shock of the real" attempt to counter banality but offer no metaphysical solace and in fact often reduce complexity.

Since the 1990s, the Brazilian public has consumed an outpour of realist literary and cinematic representations of the favela. Such fictional productions were matched by a rising interest in documentary films, biographies, and journalistic accounts of firsthand experiences in places of extreme social hardship. The absorption of these new realist registers is far from being a Brazilian phenomenon. From the Dogma manifestos toward an authentic cinema to the debunkment of magic realism by a new generation of Latin American writers, new forms of the "return of the real" have emerged as globalized narratives. In Hispanic America, the differing usages of realism are also a response to the fatigue of magic realism and its reliance on a mythical enchantment of modernity that would reveal the hybrid roots of a Latin American sensibility; whereas in Brazil, the contemporary realist registers rely not only on a lengthy tradition of realist depictions of Brazilian "reality," but also on formulaic genres such as the detective novel, gangster film, and dirty realism of mean streets that have become available through the global circulations of the media.

Despite an immense variety of aesthetic codes and allegiances, such realist inventions are also a response to televised fabrications of reality and to the mainstream productions of the cultural industry. Yet, rather than insisting on the representation of "reality" uncontaminated by spectacularization and mediatic aesthetization, the demands of new realist fiction seeks to revitalize experience, producing a defamiliarized "shock of the real."

In the specific case of Brazil, the realist register has an embedded cultural trajectory that began with the naturalist and realist novels of the nineteenth century and continued to prevail throughout the twentieth century. In the 1970s, under the auspices of the military regime, television as embodied by the Globo Network expanded remarkably, and TV Globo became the hegemonic force of the media industry. Glimmering on the surface of Globo's screen, the narratives of "reality" gained greater visual impact and influence in journalistic programs. If the "Jornal Nacional" was the reality principle shaping the televised imagined community, the soap operas of Rede Globo were the realms of fantasy that connected millions of viewers to the same fictional narrative. The entrance of cable network and the weakening of Globo's hegemonic position altered the centralization of the "imagined televised community."[12] Furthermore, social and economic upheaval, the disruptive violence of urban centers, conflicting agendas for the future, and the demise of hegemonic discourses all contribute to a sense of crisis and perplexity. Evidently, the rise of realist aesthetics is not automatically conditioned by social forces, just as the very notion of what realism is varies immensely. Nevertheless, new realist codes that focus on marginal characters, urban violence, poverty, and extreme experiences are producing narratives and images that avoid avant-garde experimentation and cancel flights of fantasy that menace the pact of mimetic legitimacy with the spectator or reader. The predominance of such realist representations leads one to ultimately question how fictional imagination shapes our existence and how the option for a realist aesthetics was often at odds and a response to the enchantments of everyday life that we pursue in advertising, dreams, beliefs, and nonrationalized narratives. There is a discrepancy between "realist" depictions of the poor and the marginalized in the favelas and the realms of fantasy that are often at the center of so many Brazilian social fabrications, ranging from carnival practices to religious beliefs.

A key element of the prevalence of the realist register is also related to the perception of realism as being closely tied to the construction of modernity. Whereas religious beliefs, inner realms of fantasy, and collective carnivalesque practices may actually feature in realist productions, the controlling reality principle is given by the rationalist realist code. Realism brackets the realms of the imaginary, the transcendent, and the irrational by means of a predominant codification of an objective reality. Often, the dramatic center of realist fiction is precisely the conflict and discrepancy between internal subjective self-fashionings and the social perception of the self or between the desires of achievement of an individual or social group and the thwarting circumstances that deflate such expectations. Individual and collective imaginations are pitted against the reality principle informed by the realist register. As this code becomes a standard form of narration in media productions that provide news and information, it also serves as a generalized form of communication. This does not imply that contemporary realism cancels dialogical difference or that it censors subjective projections. Rather it suggests that different worldviews are translatable by means of a connecting communicative code.

REALIST FAVELAS

The importance of the realist code in artistic productions in Brazil was and still is largely tied to the necessity of providing a pedagogy of Brazilian reality and its contradictory modernity. The favela with its flimsy, unsanitary, and densely packed constructions was always the very opposite of modernist urban planning. But even more problematic, the poverty and unruliness of the favela was located at the very center of the modernizing project, inside the city itself. Modernist productions of the 1920s and 1930s altered previous early twentieth-century conceptions of the favela ruled by positivist paradigms and Eurocentric values. In the 1930s, the urban popular culture of Rio de Janeiro gained nationwide projection with the broadcasting of samba by the national radio. As the site of the popular culture, the favela was celebrated for withstanding the scarcity of services, goods, and means through a cultural hybridity that adapts, transforms, and upholds its ethos in the midst of adversity.

But if both experimental modernist and social realist depictions of the favela catered largely to middle and upper middle-class sectors, the cultural production of the favela itself was tied to samba and the mass media productions of radio and television. The importance of Carolina de Jesus's book, *Quarto de Despejo,* published in 1960, was precisely her authorship, the fact that she wrote a book about her life in the favela using her daily existence as a written documentary.[13] When Carolina de Jesus's diary was printed in book form with the title *Quarto de Despejo,* it achieved an astounding success. Nine editions were published, and the book was translated into thirteen languages. Carolina de Jesus had been "discovered" by the newspaper correspondent Audálio Dantas who wrote for *Cruzeiro,* then the most widely read magazine in Brazil. For Carolina de Jesus, the usage of the realist register was a form of testimonial evidence and access to memory in a metropolis where the poor were largely silenced. She is one of the first favela writers to emerge in the twentieth century. Her production, however, does not spawn an outpour of testimonial literature or induce a fabrication of literary favelas by favela dwellers. On the contrary, her book constitutes a singular event, just as her disengagement from any political party or grassroots movement made her personal narrative an exemplary and yet isolated phenomenon.

Diverse from the films of the Cinema Novo that depicted the favela and in contrast to the literary writings of modernist writers that expressed the lives of the poor, Carolina de Jesus's narration was not a product of the cultured intelligentsia. She was not even a writer who had overcome humble origins and entered into the domains of the artistic circles. Carolina de Jesus was a *favelada* who barely made a living by gathering paper and reselling her scraps to local shop owners. The title of her diary, *Quarto de Despejo* (Scrap Room), is not metaphoric but literally the rendition of her material circumstances. Making a living out of scraps, rubbish, and garbage, Carolina de Jesus and her children lived in utmost poverty in the shantytown of Canindé, situated at the margins of the river Tieté in São Paulo. She gained visibility where no poor black female slum dweller ordinarily would. She was not a samba star, a naïf painter, or a seeker of the limelight in carnivalesque television shows, nor was she a protagonist of a sensationalist horror story told by the press. Carolina de Jesus emerged as an author who used the written word as her means of expression. Furthermore, she made use of her daily existence as a form of narration.

The transcription of the "real" in the form of narrative realism is the key element that renders Carolina de Jesus's story so convincing, and the reality of her biographical existence is given photographic visibility in the pictures of herself in her slum dwellings. Her grim narrative of gathering paper, scraping meals, fetching water, and listening to the ruckus of neighbors is repetitive and exhausting, as pounding a living minute by minute can be. Yet, the bare bones of realism are often coated with lyrical musings, and a cultured literary usage of words appears amid numerous grammatical errors. The entrance into the domains of the letter is also a form of extricating herself from the sheer narrative of survival that was obtained from gathering waste paper. Despite negative references to politicians, a heightened perception of racial discrimination, and a pointed critique of male abusiveness in the favela community, Carolina de Jesus's voice is not affiliated to preestablished codes of political usage or social demands. The basis of her reception is conditioned by a humanitarian notion of the rights of citizens upheld, in her specific case, by her personal dignity in the midst of degrading circumstances and by her appreciation of "high culture," a "high culture" that is not, however, processed as mere emulation but is filtered through personal experience and seen as a source of redemption. Symptomatically, Carolina de Jesus read the saccharine nineteenth-century abolitionist novel, *The Slave Isaura* (1875), and wept with the plight of the chained slave.[14] In her published diary, she seldom mentions literary references, although she does specify her writing activities and the opinions surrounding her bookishness are incisively summed by the commentary of a neighbor: "I never saw a black woman like books as much as you do."[15] Yet, if she regards the act of reading as an "ideal," her written word becomes a form of denunciatory evidence, a confessional paper, a register of scarcity, a kind of epiphany. In all these instances, the crucial point is the vital connection between the written word and the lived experience, between her narration and her biographical truth.

But if the narrative represents an anchoring of memory and a projection of visibility into the future, the future of the favela itself is suspended in the void of barren necessities. The favela is not exoticized. It is not the "imagined community" of the nation; it is not the revolutionary terrain of the proletarian revolution. Rather, Carolina de Jesus's words reinforce the notion of the favela as a "fearful stain."[16] Despite her pronounced antipathy toward the politician Carlos Lacerda, Carolina de Jesus actually endorses what Lacerda himself would espouse in the 1960s, the eradication of the favelas by state authorities. It is therefore symptomatic that the day she left the favela of Canindé she was pelted with stones by her neighbors. She did not project herself politically as the voice of the oppressed, but rather she denounced her living conditions and expressed her adamant will to be free of the bondage of scarcity. The luxury of writing was the only means of breaking the cycle of mere subsistence. Media visibility through the domain of the written word became the way out of the favela. Yet, when Carolina de Jesus left Canindé, she also destroyed her access to the testimonial narration of life within the favela. The loss of that lived testimonial narration eventually closed all her paths, left her without readers, and placed her once again in appalling conditions of poverty. By then, she was too far gone and broken to articulate her word again. The novelty of her authorship had worn off, and Carolina Maria de Jesus died as she had lived most of her life: utterly destitute.

The same ingredients of the veracity of lived experience were also used to promote the narrative of a radically different book, Paulo Lins's bestseller *Cidade de Deus*. First published in 1997, the novel was hailed by prominent literary critic Roberto Schwarz as an "uncommon artistic adventure" as it articulated a new range of discursive strategies combining ethnographic research, literary naturalism, and cinematic flashes in order to reveal an explosive scenario of social exclusion and violence.[17] Although Schwarz's laudatory review veers away from personalizing the figure of the author, the overall reception of the novel was influenced by the fact that the author of the novel, Paulo Lins, was a former resident of the favela Cidade de Deus. Yet, the true novelty here was that his authorship was radically different from the writing of previous favela writers such as Carolina de Jesus. Lins was research assistant to Alba Zaluar, one of the leading Brazilian anthropologists on urban violence, favelas, and the drug trade. Zaluar had published a full-length study on Cidade de Deus entitled *The Machine and the Revolt* (1985), and also published the collection of essays, *The Condominium of the Devil* (1994).[18] As Zaluar's research assistant and as a resident of the favela, Lins acquired a dual role as anthropological researcher-informant and as community member. Both the legitimacy of his authorship and the subject matter of a new radically violent drug culture within the favela offered middle-class readers an insider's view of an unknown terrain. Moreover, if the subject matter had evident cinematic qualities manifest in the usual display of murders, escapades, and exchange of bullets, the social dimensions of such a warfare and the protagonists of the bloody feud were distanced from the aesthetics of violence as seen in American films or narrations. The multitude of characters is given scant psychological depth, their ethical conflicts surface minimally, and they are ruled by desires that are constantly thwarted by the very violence that constitutes and dissolves them. The literary "shock of the real" is fabricated by a series of brutal crimes, violent disputes, and tumultuous events where the possibilities of a banal quotidian, the maintenance of identities, are continuously destroyed. Children are not children in *Cidade de Deus,* and lives are worthless in the constant mowing of the drug disputes, police raids, and inner wars. Lins stresses that he is narrating a neo-favela since he initiates the novel in the 1960s and ends the narrative in the 1980s, where the scale of violence wrought by the drug trade and by patterns of social exclusion in a society mesmerized by consumption surpasses previous parameters. However, the social existence of Lins himself suggests a complex scenario where the relation of the favela to the city reveals contact zones based on radically unequal exchanges.

Viewed by millions of spectators, reviewed by all the major newspapers in Brazil, and granted critical acclaim in international film festivals, the film *Cidade de Deus* (2002), based on Lins's novel, galvanized public attention and was at the center of polemical opinions. With fewer characters and fewer episodes of straightforward violence, the film's narrative swiftness is achieved by a mutative camera eye that alters its visual register from documentary to video-clip montage in an accumulative narration that tells the saga of several outlaw bandits and drug dealers. The film has caused far greater impact than the novelistic original. Such an impact is not only achieved because of the sensorial quality of the visual medium, nor is it based exclusively on the cathartic mobilization of a public cinema viewing that caters to far larger numbers of people than the reading of a novel that is both solitary and demands literacy. *Cidade de Deus* became the focal point of a battle of representations concerning the nature of the "real," the fabrication of society, the viability of cities, and the nature of violence. It has been allegorically read as a synecdoche of the nation while being upheld as an example of realism. Conversely, it has been denounced as a spectacularized Americanized action film devoid of realism. Critics who have placed it in the category of an enter-tainment action film either extolled it as an example of a competent cin-ematic narration or disparaged the film as a "cosmetics of hunger" versus the previous neorealist tenets of the Brazilian Cinema Novo in the 1960s that extolled "an aesthetics of hunger."[19] In a brief newspaper review, anthropologist Alba Zaluar criticized the lack of white characters in the film and undermined the supposed analogy between the "similitude of the favela/American black ghetto, not withstanding the great racial and cultural differences between the American ghetto and the Brazilian favela."[20] Zaluar further questioned the racial inversion in the film where the most violent and ruthless gangster is black, when in real life he was an "almost white" northeasterner. Others emphasized that viewing the film was a "civic duty" or that aesthetic discussions concerning the qual-ities of the film were beside the point because the film brought forth the camouflaged fact that Brazilian cities are facing a war, a war wrought by social exclusion, poverty, injustice, and the rampant abuse of the drug trade, a war that has had a greater death toll than the city of Sarajevo when it was at the epicenter of an ethnic strife.[21] By contrast, MV Bill, famous rapper from Cidade de Deus, praised the aesthetic qualities of the film but announced that it would only benefit its makers, whereas the actual community of Cidade de Deus would be even further ostracized as a living hell, as the most violent favela in Brazil.[22]

Whether denouncing its lack of true realism or celebrating its realist impact, *Cidade de Deus* was largely judged in relation to its appraisal of a disruptive social situation. The demands of realism were sustained by the cast of unknown actors recruited from the favela communities of Rio de Janeiro. The acting talents of these unknown children and adolescents became a source of constant praise and a generalized consensus, but the dividing line between fact and fiction was further blurred by the social origins of these actors who escaped the fate of their fictional characters yet lived in direct contact with the contradictions of the favelas. The film itself insists on the ambiguity between the "real" and the fictional by pairing off at the end of the narration the pictures of the actors with the photographs of the real drug dealers that they had been embodying.

The question then arises why so much was read in a film whose focus is actually very narrow since it essentially depicts the violent disputes between outlaw characters in different periods of the favela. The diverse critical reception given to *Cidade de Deus* indirectly evoked the specters that expressed the quintessential Latin American dichotomy of the nineteenth century: civilization versus barbarism. In its nineteenth century configuration, the "barbarians" were cast as rustic rural remnants in the provinces or backlands, folks that would inevitably be obliterated by the exorable march of progress. In the cities, the "barbarians" identified as non-Europeans were to be subjected to educational reforms, sanitized, and modernized. Even in their nineteenth-century configurations such polarizations collapsed and often revealed the contradictory montage of social relations and legacies. The destabilizing element in the dichotomy was the very real presence and existence of mestizo cultures and of the ongoing processes of cultural hybridization that ensured a porousness of cultural influences. Such cultural influences are depicted in the film by the presence of a youth culture centered on drugs, music, sexual exchanges, and relationships of affection that surpass class boundaries and territorial divisions. It is also mirrored in the trajectory of the protagonist, the young man from *Cidade de Deus* who enters into the world of journalism as an amateur photographer, has an amorous encounter with a white woman journalist, and becomes a mediator between the city and the favela. Nevertheless, disruptive violence as featured in both the novel and the film *Cidade de Deus* produces a vision of otherness, of encapsulated worlds that revolve around an almost Darwinian survival of the fittest. In this process of social implosion, subjectivity and imaginative construction are undermined by the hammering of corrosive violence. Critical dismissal of the film's usage of video-clip camera movements and aesthetization obliterates director Fernando Miereles's attempt to essay a new form of realism, a realism that does not rely on the direct unfiltered documentary camera but introduces the aesthetization of daily life with the symbolic and cultural components that constitute the imaginary of the characters in the plot. The drug dealer's competition for the limelight, the search for some kind of mediatic notoriety, and the choice of consumer goods and musical genres, in this case, the presence of James Brown in the late 1970s and early 1980s, a choice that would later include funk and hip-hop, are elements used to evoke the role of the imagination in the fabrication of self-fashioning. What this "new realism" cannot do is produce totalizing images of the national narrative, even though the demands that are placed on it are centered on a vindication of a new portrait of Brazil.

The dispute for an apprehension of the "real" and the invention of a new realism centered on the favela and the urban poor has engendered different documentary and fictional films as well as literary productions. A documentary filmmaker such as Eduardo Coutinho provides an anti-aesthetics of the real, an antispectacularization of daily life by focusing on anonymous people in peripheral conditions who are struggling for a living and yet fabricate their lives in narrative tales told to the camera.[23] Once again, the favela is a favored documentary site, but in tune with anthropological arguments that stress the rights of self-representation, the participants in several of these films represent themselves as they are registered with minimal intervention and camera filters without special effects. Pauses in the conversation, redundancy, noises, and the presence of the interviewer or the vision of the filming camera emphasize that the spectator is viewing a film in the making. Thus, the effect of reality is rendered by the exhibition of the conditions of the filmic fabrication. What engages the spectator are not the aesthetic resources of the camera, nor the voyeuristic espionage of veiled intimacies, and even less the display of violent imagery since Coutinho's films avoid the "shock of the real." What arrests the spectator is the real-life narrative that pours from the lips of the filmed participants who engage the spectator's attention as they become personalities imbued with their own visions of the world. In films such as *Santo Forte* (1999), *Babilônia* (2001), and others, the camera movement is minimal, the aesthetic effects are practically nonexistent, and the register is direct without making its plainness a source of self-conscious nonaesthetization. Centered on the speech of the favela dwellers, the striking component in many of these films are the inner worlds, the realms of belief, the mobilizing force of personal and collective imaginations of people attempting to make sense of their lives, to rise above their circumstances, and to obtain their freedom through religion, politics, and consumption. Coutinho's films are dialogical in the ethnographic diversity of voices that emerge from the screen, but they adhere to realist representation as the imaginaries of the speakers are not projected as visual imagery. Coutinho's resistance to the lure of the image is also a form of sustaining documentary veracity against the spectacularization of the real undertaken by reality shows and sensationalist media coverage. It is a documentary grounding of authenticity imbued by a political agenda that seeks potential characters, humanizes anonymous people while holding at bay their efforts of fictional projection. This minimalist aesthetics controls carnivalization because the social inversion of roles or the fictional masks the interviewed people might wish to fabricate are solely available through their speech, as wish images, as instances of self-fashioning. As part of the portrayal of the lives of the poor, Coutinho has a selective panel of what represents "ordinary people." His narratives bypass the reworking of clichés of violence by avoiding the presence of drug dealers, bandits, and outlaws. Yet, by centering the focus on particular communities, they do not address the multiplicity of urban voices, mappings, and commotions that make cities arenas of change. At the end of the film *Babilônia*, a favela dweller invites people to come up to the hill of Babilônia and view the famous New Year's celebration on Copacabana beach from the favela overlooking the city. "People make wrong judgments about us," he claims.

The invitation to enter the domains of the favela and join the party evoked by the favela dweller of Babilônia would constitute a veritable impossibility in João Moreira Salles' documentary *News from a Particular War* (1999). Filmed in the favela Santa Marta, in police headquarters, and institutions for juvenile delinquents, the film offers a corrosive view of the ongoing dispute for the drug trade in the midst of urban poverty and rampant violence, yet it also focuses on the speech of the favela dwellers and the working class people of Santa Marta. Amid the violence of both the police and the drug dealers, a critique of social exclusion is undertaken even by specific sectors of the police. But the most grating image of the film is the depiction of the adolescent drug dealers who voice their passion for clothing, the acquisition of consumer goods, and their rejection of normative work ethics. What is telling in these interviews is not so much the social view that is being displayed in a favela world of brutal options but the dramatization of such a self-fashioning in front of the camera. Their heavy posturing and the drawling accent become an acting out of the gangster role playing that is overtly theatricalized and self-conscious.

This new mediatic visibility largely connected to television offers a range of representations of the favelas, the poor, and the outlaws. The new ingredient is given by the internalization of the media component by the drug dealers, the favela dwellers, and the poor. Those that manage to appear on the screen are able to voice their condition in front of television cameras, documentary films, video clips, and feature films.

REALIST DEFAMILIARIZATION

The realist register in recent representations of the favela in film and literary fiction has been variously used as a means of engendering both artistic "defamiliarization" and as a form of translating the new cultural experiences of the globalized favela. As the site of defamiliarization, art—according to the famous words of Victor Sklovskij—is what makes the "stone, stony" and its aim "is to convey the immediate experience of a thing as if it is seen instead of recognized; the device of art is the device of making things strange."[24] The strangeness of art as evoked by Sklovskij is related to a heightening of perception that peels away the wrappings of the customary and provides unfamiliar awareness. Avant-garde experimentation tended to provoke a dramatic rupture between the stone and its stoniness, whereas modernist experimentation often dismissed the aesthetics of verisimilitude in order to evoke another "realness." Realist representation in its many guises and epochs emphasizes the palpability of experience and lays particular claims to its capacity of making the "stone, stony." Yet, how to enforce the tangibility of the "real," essential to the realist experience in media cultures saturated with images, hyperstimulations, spectacularized events, and technological reinventions of nature?

In the case of the realist narratives and images examined in this chapter, the aesthetics of realism resurfaces as both a shock response and as a means of reworking the connections between representation and experience in an attempt to engender interpretive frameworks that produce a vocabulary of recognition in the midst of the tumultuous uncertainty of Brazilian cities. As the focal site of urban unease, the favelas are once again thematized, but now they are no longer buffered by modern narratives of future utopian redemption that prevailed in the agendas of the Cinema Novo and much of the previous modernist inventions. Contemporary depictions of the favela provide defamiliarization without radical aesthetic experimentation because this "strangeness" may demolish the petrification of daily habits, but it channels perception to specific interpretative vocabularies and aesthetic codes.

While the actual democratization of Brazil has failed to alter significantly economic and social disparities, it has, nevertheless, dramatically changed the production of cultural codes. Media culture and new forms of consumption have created new elites, celebrities, and role models. Yet, the same media culture and the allure of consumption also foment increasing frustration within the youth cultures of the urban poor hampered by harsh economic options that curtail consumer expectations and social possibilities. As never before these social frustrations, expectations, and desires are being voiced by a number of artists that come directly from the favela communities or from the ranks of the urban poor. Distinct from the lyrical productions of the former samba composers that relied on both Afro-Brazilian traditions and yet were also influenced by the poetical forms of a culture of letters, these new expressions of favela culture are shaped by local/global visual and musical cultures that are not necessarily connected to previous national narratives or elite models of expression. The prevalence of the realist code attests to a veritable anxiety of uncovering these pluralistic portraits of Brazil, while making both empathetic connections between the daily experiences of the urban centers and artistic representations. While televised soap opera productions still largely portray the romances and expectations of the urban middle classes, cinematic and literary realist productions have centered their attention on the poor, the excluded, and the marginalized as an attempt to instill a critical perspective and insure their access to a wide audience.

The impact of such productions forms part of an ongoing dialogue concerning the feasibility of the nation, the possibilities of urban living, and the agendas for the future. As a battle of representations unfolds around themes of urban violence, social exclusion, justice, and the depiction of the popular, the aesthetics of realism both forms part of the culture of the spectacle and yet it politicizes representation. Perhaps a crucial danger of the realist aesthetics is its masking of its own mechanism of fiction-making and its silencing of forms of imagination that subvert the codes of the realist real. Yet, in the most powerful realist productions, the reductive mechanism is countered by a convincing rendering of experience that brings to the surface the claims of authenticity that had been discarded by theoretical deconstruction and postmodern relativism. It is the debate surrounding social exclusion, urban violence, and security measures as exemplified by the conflicts of the drug trade in the favelas that are encouraging a plurality of voices to emerge and discuss the outcome of Brazilian society. The favelas—as seen under the lens of the "shock of the real"—are sites of contention in the cities of a nation that is now openly discussing the narratives and images that express its reality in the making.

NOTES

1. The word favela designates the slum areas without basic sanitation, infrastructure or legal ownership of the land that exist in almost all the cities of Brazil. The origins of the term favela began in the late nineteenth century when homeless soldiers returned from the backlands of Bahia after having exterminated the messianic rebel uprising of Canudos. While combating in Canudos, the soldiers had camped on a hill covered by vegetation known as favela. Upon returning to Rio de Janeiro, the soldiers never received the promised government housing and built makeshift shacks on a hill near the center of Rio. They named their location as Favela in a clear reference to Canudos.

2. In his excellent essay "Modernity, Hyper Stimulation, and the Beginnings of Popular Sensationalism" published in *Cinema and the Invention of Modern Life* (Berkeley: University of California Press, 1995), Ben Singer makes use of Simmel's classic essay "The Metropolis and Mental Life" and argues that the hyper stimulation of metropolitan living also fomented sensationalist press coverage and entertainment. My argument concerning the crisis of Brazilian cities and the aesthetics of "shock of the real" follows a similar reasoning by suggesting that realist aesthetics surface as a response to urban uncertainty as a form of competing with media fabrications of everyday life.

3. See Michel De Certeau, *L'invention du quotidian, 1a arts de faire* (Paris: Èditions Gallimard, 1990).

4. In the early 1990s, funk gangs provoked panic on the beach of Ipanema. The debate surrounding their representation in the press

and the role of funk culture in Rio de Janeiro has been studied by Micael Herschmann; see "As imagens da galera funk na imprensa," in *Linguagens da Violência*, ed. Carlos Alberto Messeder Pereira, Elizabeth Rondelli, Karl Erik Schollhammer, and Micael Herschmann, 163–97 (Rio de Janeiro, Brazil: Rocco, 2000). See also James Freeman, "Democracy and Danger on the Beach: Class Relations in the Public Space of Rio de Janeiro," *Space and Culture* 5, no. 1 (2002): 9–28.

5. The promise of the modern city was precisely the possibility of envisioning alternative futures distinct from the tradition-bound premises of the past and diverse from the hierarchical constraints of rural existence. As either the scenario of the revolutionary masses or the conquering ground of the enterprising individual, the modern city was to fulfill the dreams and aspirations of a better future. The persistence of such acute social polarizations reflects both the failures of modernizing projects as well as their triumphs. Favelas have increased throughout Brazil. Yet, the term favela encompasses such an urban variety that it no longer has a singular vocabulary that can account for its diversity. If there are many aspects to the lives of the poor and a diversity of cultures of poverty, there are also many forms of social critique that have increasingly surfaced within the urban tissues of the great cities. The global impact of the media, neighborhood associations, NGOs, and new role models set by the several agendas of identity politics provide a wide range of social options. The struggle for representation is particularly relevant in the depiction of the marginalized. It is strategic in the emergence of the new visions of the favela and instrumental in decoding the validity of the notion of the "divided city." In the case of Rio de Janeiro, dramatic social violence such as the massacre in 1993 of favela dwellers in Vigário Geral by police forces seeking revenge from local drug dealers and the murder of street children, also in 1993, in front of Rio de Janeiro's cathedral were among a host of events that spelled the carnage of unleashed violence. In the wake of these events, the term "divided city" coined by journalist Zuenir Ventura in his book of the same title gained currency as an apt description of Rio de Janeiro. Yet, such polarizations and even a close reading of Ventura's own book reveal that more than just being a "divided city," Rio de Janeiro is a tumultuous urban maze of inequality and social juxtaposition. Between the favelas and the neighborhoods of the rich and the middle class are numerous exchanges, and indeed it is the ambiguity of these contact zones that allows both violence and cultural socialization to simultaneously occur. For a discussion of the concept of the "divided city," see Zuenir Ventura, *A cidade partida* (São Paulo, Brazil: Companhia das Letras, 1994). For an analysis of press coverage of the favela, see Mariana Cavalcanti's master's thesis "Demolição, Batalha e Paz: favelas em manchetes," ECO/UFRJ, 2001.

6. Guy Debord, *La société du spectacle* (Paris: Editions Gallimard, 1967).

7. Terry Eagleton, "Pork Chops and Pineapples," *London Review of Books* 25, no. 20 (October 23, 2003).

8. Debord, *La société du spectacle*; Jean Baudrillard, "Simulacra and Simulations," in *Selected Writings,* ed. M. Poster, 166–84 (Stanford, Calif.: Stanford University Press, 1988); Fredric Jameson, *Postmodernism: Or, the Cultural Logic of Late Capitalism* (Durham, N.C.: Duke University Press, 1991).

9. For a discussion of the relations between realism as an aesthetic code and modernity, see Margaret Cohen's preface "Reconfiguring Realism," in *Spectacles of Realism: Gender, Body, Genre,* ed. Margaret Cohen and Christopher Prendergast, vii–xiii (Minneapolis: University of Minnesota Press, 1995).

10. Raymond Williams, *Long Revolution* (Peterborough, Canada: Broadview, 2001).

11. The term "negative epiphany" is used by Susan Sontag, *On Photography* (New York: Farrar, Straus, 1973).

12. For a discussion of the breakdown of TV Globo's hegemony, see Isabel Christina Esteves Guimarães's doctoral dissertation, "Populismo eletrôñico: Ratinho e a crise da tv brasileira" Rio de Janeiro, Booklink, 2002.

13. Carolina Maria de Jesus, *Quarto de despejo: diário de uma favelada* (São Paulo, Brazil: Livraria Francisco Alves, 1960). For a discussion of her diary, see Carlos Vogt, "Trabalho, pobreza e trabalho intellectual (*O Quarto de despejo* de Carolina Maria de Jesus)," in *Os pobres na literature brasileira,* ed. Roberto Schwarz, 205–13 (São Paulo, Brazil: Brasiliense, 1983).

14. Written by Bernardo Guimarães, the abolitionist novel, *A escrava Isaura* (1875), narrates in sentimental prose the plight of the lovely Isaura who was born a slave and was subjected to cruel torments by her lustful master. The crucial point about the slave Isaura is her complexion, as Guimaraes casts her as a white woman of African descent. Made into a soap opera by Globo Network in the 1970s, the *Slave Isaura* was a tremendous public success in Brazil and also in Cuba and China where it was exported.

15. Carolina de Jesus, *Quarto de despejo*, 27.

16. See Janice Perlman's critique of the "myth of marginality" cast upon the inhabitants of the favelas of Rio de Janeiro in her book, *O mito da marginalidade: favelas e política no Rio de Janeiro* (Rio de

Janeiro, Brazil: Paz e Terra, 1977). Carolina de Jesus's prose does not reinforce the "myth of marginality" because she does not endorse the clichéd view of the poor as "lazy," "slothful," and "backward." Yet, her portrait of the miserable conditions of the favela practically has no redeeming features as the people she depicts tend to lack solidarity or cultural inventiveness.

17. Roberto Schwarz, "Uma aventura artística incomum," *Folha de São Paulo, Caderno Mais,* September 7, 1997, 5–12.

18. The translations of the Portuguese titles are mine. See Alba Zaluar, *A máquina e a revolta: as organizações populares e o significado da pobreza* (São Paulo, Brazil: Brasiliense, 1985) and *Condomínio do diabo* (Rio de Janeiro, Brazil: Revan; Universidade Federal do Rio de Janeiro, 1994).

19. Film critic Ivana Bentes created the term "cosmetics of hunger," and her expression has circulated in the written and televised debates of the film *Cidade de Deus.* See her critique of *Cidade de Deus* in a review: "*Cidade de Deus* promove turismo no inferno," *Estado de São Paulo,* 2002.

20. See Alba Zaluar, "A tese do gueto norte-americano," in *Jornal do Brasil, Caderno B,* September 2, 2002. The English translation of Zaluar's quoted words is mine.

21. João Moreira Salles, the director of *News from a Particular War,* wrote a review on *Cidade de Deus* entitled: "Cidade de Deus: o que fazer?" in *no mínimo,* Internet newspaper, September 8, 2002. The title in English is "Cidade de Deus: What to Do?" In the review, he states, "In Brazil and especially in Rio de Janeiro we are and we aren't at war. It is true that there aren't formal declarations or clear aims—requisites of any war. Yet, more people died in Rio during the four-year siege of Sarajevo than in the city of Sarajevo itself that was directly ambushed and in open and direct conflict." The English translation of his words is mine.

22. See interview with M.V. Bill, "Rapper da Cidade de Deus diz que filme prejudica moradores," *Folha On Line,* August 28, 2002.

23. For a discussion of Eduardo Coutinho's documentaries, see Consuelo Lins, *O documentário de Eduardo Coutinho, televisão, cinema e vídeo* (Rio de Janeiro, Brazil: Zahar, 2004). See the excellent discussion of Consuelo Lins in her book.

24. D. W. Fokkema and Elrud Kunne-Ibsch, *Theories of Literature in the Twentieth Century* (London: C. Hurst & Company, 1977), 16.

6

FATEFUL TRIANGLES

Modernity and Its Antinomies in a Mediterranean Port City

Mark LeVine

In a groundbreaking 2002 essay in the journal *Public Culture,* Rebecca L. Stein analyzed the genealogy of Israeli tourism in the Arab world as an outgrowth of the Oslo process.[1] While the main focus of her article was Israeli tourism abroad, the city of Tel Aviv makes several crucial appearances in the narrative: as the center of Shimon Peres's vision of a globalized "New Middle East," as home to tens of thousands of foreign (often "illegal") workers, and as a space that would soon (it was feared) be invaded by tourists in the form of "black-clad women from Iran."

As Israel's "world city," Tel Aviv is not supposed to be hospitable to black-clad women, unless it is fashionably and suggestively black. The very idea of a religious symbol, let alone a religious person, parading through "secular," "normal," "cosmopolitan," "unabashedly sybaritic," and, most important, "modern" Tel Aviv would challenge the century-old imagination of the city as the complete opposite of nationalist and religious Jerusalem, with whom one is led to imagine there is a continuous struggle for the soul and destiny of Israel.[2]

The city-turned-Tel Aviv-neighborhood of Jaffa is also present in Stein's text, or more accurately, its absence discloses a powerful presence: as home to myriad illegal Jordanian and Egyptian (that is, "Arab") workers, to criminals and mobsters, and to enough "black-clad women" that a Muslim Jaffan friend of mine complained that Jaffa "looks like Teheran"; in its function as a touristic "Arab" space that "shore[s] up the boundaries of the Israeli nation-state"; and as a site for Oslo-era "geographies of leisure" that were shaped by a "renewed" curiosity in Palestinian culture— as long as it was (first) domesticated and (only then) "developed" by the forces of the globalized market.

It is now a commonplace that there is no such a thing as "the" city. The shadowy presences of both Tel Aviv and Jaffa in Stein's analysis remind us that cities are not just part of the modern, the national, and the global; they remain equally part of the colonial, the not-urban, the nonmodern, and the nonpublic, too. Moreover, cities are not just physical spaces or material places—they are the products of collective imagination of a diverse and sometimes competing set of social actors. Within this complex matrix and the plurality of forms and experiences of the city, we must search for sites where ideas and practices of the urban converge—where, for example, Tel Aviv as an ideological construct was and still is concretized in the myriad conflicting social interactions between Jews and Palestinians in the Jaffa–Tel Aviv region.

More specifically, Jaffa and Tel Aviv are interstitial spaces whose unique location at the boundaries (or frontiers, or margins) of Israeli and Palestinian identities offers important insights about the "modern" city and its cultures—chief among them that the city often reveals itself to be what it is not—not "urban," not "modern," and not "public" and thus in some respects perhaps not a "city." Yet if the city is not what it seems or claims to be, what is it? At the very least, the case of Jaffa and Tel Aviv reminds us that cities are as much "other" as what they claim to be: Tel Aviv, no less than Brasilia or New York, is a modern city in the fullest sense of the word, a colonial city, a capitalist city, and a nationalist city. But it is not modern in the way its protagonists imagined and idealized it, at least not most of the time.

One of the primary contributions of this volume to the sociology of the city is the focus on how important the imagination of the city is to its material construction and the conflicts surrounding this process over time. The ever-shifting collective imagination of the inhabitants of Jaffa and Tel Aviv have played a crucial role in the unfolding of this process there; both cities (and now the unified city of "Tel Aviv-Yafo" are clearly imagined spaces—but as Lefebvre instructs us, such imagination is embodied in two contradictory ways: the "spaces of representation" of the administrative/legal and ideological/nationalist boundaries that separated Jews and Palestinian Arabs in the Jaffa–Tel Aviv region and the "representational spaces" of the clandestine, or underside of life—that is, life as directly lived by the Jews and Palestinian Arabs who daily challenged the official cartography of the region.[3]

Such representational spaces, imagined and material, can serve as the foundation for the kind of plebian/subaltern public spheres that Habermas notes (although never investigates) as being the foundation of a potential counterpublic to the hegemonic—or, rather, in the case of Palestine, dominant—public spheres of the bourgeois (or with Zionism, socialist) nationalist leadership. Such a perspective is clearly important to understanding the space of Jaffa–Tel Aviv. While the war of 1948 saw the end of Jaffa's existence as an independent city, the half century leading up to the catastrophe/miracle of 1948 witnessed a much more ambivalent, if not conflictual interaction between three interrelated experiences of modernity: first, Jaffa's cosmopolitan Levantine/Mediterranean modernity, born out of the numerous and multiplying connections within and between Arab/Ottoman and European countries and empires; second, an exclusivist-colonial modernity that arrived with Zionism and attained hegemony under British rule; and finally, various "nonmodernities" within and surrounding the space of Euro-modernity in Tel Aviv— that is, in Jaffa and its surrounding villages—that were produced in response to the peculiar matrix of European modernity and its synergism with the discourses of colonialism, nationalism, and capitalism.

When deployed in varying formulations by the leaders of Tel Aviv and the larger Zionist movement, this modernity matrix constituted an extremely potent set of forces that enabled an "overthrowing" of the existing geography—social as well as physical—of the region, whose urban core (the Old City of Jaffa) was at the same time among the most ancient ports and cities in the world and in the midst of an almost century's long process of modernization and economic expansion.[4] Indeed, if we know from the work of Anderson, Taylor, and others that the modern nation is a reformulation of the collective imagination, the crucial determinant in this process is defining who is part of the collective that is doing the (re)imagining. Indeed, "imagined communities" usually involve collectives that are specifically narrow—to the point of causing conflict between competing groups who cannot envision the other within a shared imagined landscape. For Anderson, modern nationalism is enabled by the collective (re)imagining of identity brought on by new communication technologies, particularly print media and its use of a national vernacular language. Such media were certainly important among Jewish and Palestinian Arab communities in pre-1948 Palestine, but other, more specifically spatialized technologies— architecture and town planning—were equally important in shaping, literally, what he describes (following Winichakul) as the "geo-body" of the nation.[5]

Once we begin digging through the material and discursive archives produced by these media, the web of relations and forces that has always made Jaffa and Tel Aviv, and cities in general, "places of attraction," of possibility, meeting, and movement, comes to the surface.[6] We come to understand that the continuous if conflictual interaction between Jews and Palestinian Arabs in the Jaffa–Tel Aviv region, by conjuring imaginations of their two cities that challenged the official geographies, constantly challenged and blurred the nationalistically determined boundaries between the two cities, and thus the two nations.[7] We also understand why this challenge was intolerable to the leaders of Tel Aviv and the Zionist movement; indeed, it led them to consider every method at their disposal to create and enforce separation between Tel Aviv and Jaffa, between Jews and Palestinian Arabs, including "blowing up with bombs" (as the mayor of Tel Aviv exclaimed in 1940) sites such as markets—one of the defining institutions of the modern city—where such intermixing occurred.[8]

In this case study, one crucial part of that body, the Jaffa–Tel Aviv region, is central to the formation of the two national identities, which are understood as both socially, relationally, yet conflictually constructed in such a way that an ontology of otherness was a foundation for the collective imagination of each. So the most powerful weapon in Tel Aviv's arsenal was not a bomb, but rather modernist architectural and town-planning discourses. Evolving in good measure in colonial settings (where separation of the "races" was a primary concern), they generated and sustained a narrative of modernity and progress versus tradition and stagnation that constituted the grid for both Zionist Jews and the British to read and transform the constantly evolving landscape around them. Indeed, they helped realize a "discursive erasure" of the territory and history of Jaffa and its Palestinian Arab residents that would make possible the literal erasure of ninety percent of the population during the 1948 war.[9] It is the dissonance, indeed incommensurability between the various narratives and spaces produced by the two emerging nations that prompts us to consider whether the city is—or at least these two cities are—neither urban, nor modern, nor public.

CECI N'EST PAS UNE VILLE: WHEN THE CITY IS NOT THE URBAN

Modern "physicians" of urban space have long believed, as a French planner of the Hausmannian period described it, that "cleansing the large cities" was a necessary condition for the cleansing of the country as a whole.[10] While such tabulae rasa were difficult to create in Europe, they were much easier in the "backward" colonies, which were deemed ready for the radical (re)inscription of modern planning and development.[11] The resulting colonial urban modernity "vanquished" the indigenous urban populations, making them "premodern by contrast" to their newly constructed European neighbors, which in turn helped to solidify the European self-conception as modern and enlightened.[12]

If the leaders of Tel Aviv believed that it was from the "overthrow of geography" that Tel Aviv came into the world, then it was through the process of creative destruction that this action was realized, one whose power was especially strong in the space of the urban.[13] In terms of our understanding of the city at large, this raises the following questions: If Zionism as a modern nationalist movement is an inherently colonial discourse and Tel Aviv, the "modern capital" of Zionist Palestine and now globalized Israel, is a colonial city, then are all modern cities regardless of their location (i.e., metropolis or colony/"periphery") colonial cities? And can a colonial city ever truly be a "city"? To answer these questions, we must find the proper tools with which to explore the various permutations of modernity and its sister discourses, which link the nation to the urban colony through particular articulations of capitalism that enframed them both.[14]

CAN A CITY EXIST WITHOUT FRONTIERS?

There is a serious problem with any discussion of "Jaffa," "Tel Aviv," or other spaces in the midst of urban transformation: These names rarely corresponded to clearly and officially delineated places. We can speak of Jaffa or Tel Aviv, but do we really know where they were/are? More to the point, while one could speak of Jaffa's "Old City" as an urban core of the Jaffa–Tel Aviv region; beyond (what by the 1880s remained of) its walls, there existed a complex patchwork of interwoven and constantly evolving land use—agricultural, industrial, and increasingly residential—that defies attempts to characterize them as uniformly "urban," even after the boundaries of the two municipalities expanded to encompass them. Indeed, the Jaffa–Tel Aviv region contained numerous and "difficult" border/frontier regions that nevertheless were necessarily and continually traversed by inhabitants of both cities/nations, joining the urban and agrarian spaces of the region into one "wider system."[15]

In fact, the notion of a firm dividing line between urban/city and other types of land was not present in the late Ottoman Middle East (and likely everywhere), since existing Ottoman and Islamic legal codes did not recognize a clear territorial differentiation between town and country.[16] If we examine the opinions of the Hanafi school, which was historically dominant in Palestine, what we find instead is a "multidimensional definition." Conceptually, the city should be a comprehensive social and political entity; geographically the all embracing town was a large locality in which there are streets and markets, to which rural districts belong, and whose size and economic and military importance warrant the permanent stationing of a representative of the State in the form of a "governor."[17]

More specifically, the city was a "center of an agricultural hinterland." What distinguished rural from truly urban spaces was the very relationship of dependence of the latter on the former and, as important, the fact that cities played a crucial "public" function because they possessed a "Friday mosque" that was the center not just for public worship but for the interaction of the public and the State. In this sense, Jaffa was already a "city" decades before it was officially granted municipal status in 1871, even before the Ottoman governor built a new mosque complex to support the rebuilding of the town after Napoleon's brief but violent sojourn in 1799. Moreover, the "ordinary houses" in the city's outlying precincts were also crucial to defining its borders, precisely because of their ambivalent locations. In trying to define the border of a city and its surrounding countryside, it was hard to know where the former ended and the latter began, since there was no agreement as to whether "houses and dwellings around the town" but outside the "permanently inhabited built-up area" should be considered part of the city proper.[18]

The various definitions of the boundaries of cities placed them between three and ten miles outside the urban core, which would clearly include not just Tel Aviv but also the surrounding Arab villages as well. This means that the land upon which Tel Aviv would be built was clearly part of Jaffa's hinterland and could be considered *"fina' al-misr,"* or land that "served the common interests of town dwellers, not, however, the interests of individual, private persons."[19] This urban-rural system as a defining criterion for the city raises the question of whether a city in the sense it was understood in Palestine could retain its identity as such if its hinterland was removed from the control of the town (or literally erased by the urbanization of another, "enemy" town as in the case of Jaffa and Tel Aviv).

Similarly, the privatization of land heretofore in the "common interest"—a fundamental dynamic in the modern city—would clearly threaten the stability and identity of the urban core in an urban-rural system such as the Jaffa region. If we understand the *fina' al-misr* as "the spatial embodiment of the town dwellers as a collective unity," as a bridge between the built-up areas of the town, its agricultural surroundings, and the open countryside, the ramifications of the birth of Tel Aviv on the future of Jaffa as a city in its own right become clear.[20] However, if we delimit Jaffa's geography and borders, it is clear that the Jaffa region was becoming increasingly "urban" and "modern" during the late Ottoman period, as evidenced by the rush of activity and mélange of peoples and goods in her port and bazaars (which by a decade after the Crimean War were a *"pele-mele"* of foreigners and locals, of East and West, with immigrants arriving from as far away as Afghanistan).[21]

Given the ambiguity over Jaffa's borders, it seems appropriate, even necessary, to ask: Where in fact was Jaffa? Was Jaffa a city? A "district" (as it was in the late Ottoman period)? A "region" including the old town, newer neighborhoods, and surrounding villages? A cosmopolitan personality that was only vaguely related to an identifiable space with clearly defined borders? These are crucial yet difficult questions to answer. Indeed, by 1888, the year Jaffa's first Jewish suburb was established, the city's walls were completely dismembered—a major event in the cultural history of the city—and streets, homes, and shops were being constructed on the now filled-in mote, many using stones that months before separated the old town from the surrounding neighborhoods. This rapid development led the Government to commission a new map of Jaffa which was clearly intended to more precisely fix, or in modern legal/planning parlance, "settle" its borders.[22] Thus, within two years "every meter of suitable land for planting [could] be sold for a high price . . . the farms have achieved a prestigious place in the commerce of Jaffa and apart from their enormous income, they employ many hands."[23]

Not surprisingly in this situation, by the turn of the century, the "question of nationality" had become "the most difficult" in the city, with Jewish sources reporting that the Arabs feared that "the Jews came to impose a foreign Government upon us."[24] Thus, in 1907, the Qa'im-maqam of Jaffa, Muhammad Aṣaf, wrote to the MutaṢarrif of Jerusalem warning him that "a foreign foundation is now conquering the Jaffa region, important and most harmful, that threatens the future of . . . the country. These are the foreign Jews."[25] These Jews were "buying thousands of dunams of land and have turned the lands of Jaffa and its surroundings [the word for turn here is the Turkish equivalent of "overturn" or "overthrow"], all of which were state (miri) land, to private property (mulk) or "waqf" in a manner that contravened Ottoman land law.[26] Moreover, these lands were supposed to be "subject to Ottoman laws and urban planning," but when they fall into "foreign hands, the Government can't do anything."

That is, with the passing of the land of Jaffa and its environs into Zionist hands, the very nature of the space of the region was transformed. The patchwork of residential, market, industrial, and agricultural lands that constituted "Jaffa" was falling under the control of "Jews and other foreigners" who "live under various nationalities" yet only to pursue their own nationalist goals by "continu[ing] to build hundreds of buildings without permission, until they abut state land and the land of their neighbors."[27] At the very least, we can say that "Jaffa," what and wherever it was, was quickly becoming something other than what it had been and was on a trajectory to become before the arrival of Zionism.

In response to this situation, during the late Ottoman period, Jaffa became a center for "constructive . . . nation-building" among Palestinian Arabs, no less than for Zionist Jews.[28] Such a project was not an inevitable development but was spurred by two dynamics. The first was the fear, as an Ottoman official telegrammed the local Government, that "Ottoman culture has weakened . . . and foreign culture has become dominant" with the increased activities of European states in Palestine, especially the British and increasingly the Zionists who were simultaneously challenging Ottoman sovereignty at the same time as they were an attractive source of revenue through their land purchases.[29] The second, related to the first, was that the Palestinian population increasingly perceived the Ottoman Government as no longer able to or interested in looking out for their interests, which led to a natural shift in communal identity away from the "Ottoman" and toward the "Palestinian."[30]

The evidence presented here suggests that the particular constellation of forces in the space of the Jaffa–Tel Aviv region in the late Ottoman period blurred the boundaries between Jaffa as a "city" and its surrounding and increasingly contested hinterland. But it was not just Europeans and Zionists who were a "problem." The Ottoman Government was increasingly worried about "Arab nationalists" who were "inciting Bedouins and city-dwellers into insurrection against the Turkish community and Ottoman Government . . . and distributing newspapers to the villages" in and around both Jaffa and Haifa.[31] From an Islamic perspective going back at least to Ibn Khaldun, one of the most basic characteristics of the city and its attendant "urban" culture/civilization was precisely its distinction and separateness from that of the Bedouins. What are we to make of the increasing commingling of the two populations, and what does this tell us about the distinctive culture of the modernizing, increasingly nationalized Islamic/ Ottoman city?

The records of Jaffa's Shari'a, or religious court, also provide contradictory descriptions of what was and was not part of "Jaffa." In one land sale, the neighborhood in which the property was located, "Mahallah Sheikh Ibrahim al-Malahi," is labeled as "inside" Jaffa even though it is outside of the Old City, while the orchard (located between another orchard and a vineyard to the south of the Old City, along what was called *"al-tariq al-hilweh,"* most likely today's Yeffet Street) was considered "outside" Jaffa.[32] On the other hand, in a case involving the registration of the division of shares in a newly purchased vineyard, the scribe described the property as *"kharij Yafa al-mahdud"* (a technical term meaning outside a town/city's borders).[33]

What is clear from the Shari'a court records is that unlike Europeans, Palestinian Arab residents of Jaffa took a larger view of what constituted their town. This had several implications, first and foremost among them is that Arab residents of the Jaffa–Tel Aviv region would not have limited their evaluation of the city to conditions—that is, the noisiness, overcrowdedness, and poor sanitation—prevailing in the Old City,[34] especially after "modern" neighborhoods such as Ajami were established in the 1880s. Moreover, in the description of the preceding property, we learn that it included a vaulted house with a European tiled roof and kitchen/bathroom facilities. This blending of local Arab vernacular and European architectural styles, which we can assume was underway (at least) in the decade before this sale, demonstrates an economic and cultural interaction between Arabs and Europeans that belies the traditional historiography of this period.

We face a similar problem placing Tel Aviv in the larger region and delineating its boundaries, or better, frontiers. The difficulty is exacerbated because its origins lie in a narrative of sand and redemption that make it even harder to decipher its administrative, cognitive, and discursive boundaries. Indeed, one can say that Tel Aviv was always in the process of becoming a city, of overturning (or as LeCorbusier would describe it, "uprooting") more and more of the local geography as it gradually expanded to encompass the six surrounding Arab villages (one of which, Summel, was literally surrounded by the Jewish town yet remained independent until the early 1940s).

The land on which the first neighborhoods were built provides the most interesting evidence of this ambivalence, since it forces us to consider whether Tel Aviv was constructed on barren sand dunes waiting to be reclaimed or on a complex fabric of common land of mixed and changing usage and tenure that symbolized the evolving geography of "Jaffa." Known as "Karm al-Jabali" (that is, the vineyard owned by the al-Jabali family), it was located slightly more than a kilometer from the Old City and was originally sold by members of the family in 1905 to a Jewish broker from Jerusalem. It is unclear exactly how many owners the land had; moreover, the borders of the property are quite different in the original Arabic contract, the subsequent sale to Jewish building society Ahuzat Bayit, and in the official survey done in the Tabu, or deeds office, with the contract sold to the building society describing as "vacant" land that the other documents describe as vineyards or roads.[35]

In a very tangible sense, the various official documentations surrounding Tel Aviv's establishment are not talking about the same plot of land. Beyond this, the descriptions common to each demonstrated that the land of Karm al-Jabali was already "in play" for many years, had a mixed Arab-Jewish ownership, mixed usage, and mixed tenure. It was anything but "barren sand dunes." Yet the land was and remained contested by local semisedentarized Bedouins, who used it for grazing, occasionally farming, and to travel from the villages to the Old City, while the majority of the land in the region was either collectively owned or at least not parceled out, making purchases difficult. Even the Jaffa Municipality and the State each claimed the land, as "state" land, so that it could not be sold to Jews or be used freely by Bedouins.

What is most important about this situation is that while the founders of Tel Aviv ultimately won out and began building their town, for the Bedouins the region remained as it was before, and they continued to graze their flocks right through the town well into the Mandate period, much to the consternation of the Jews and British alike. Thus, even after Tel Aviv was recognized as a city by its Jewish inhabitants and the British administration, within the larger political and economic geography of the Jaffa–Tel Aviv region, it was not necessarily recognized as such by the surrounding "Arab" population.

As the Mandate period wore on and Tel Aviv's population rapidly increased, the borders expanded until they abutted Jaffa and the surrounding six Arab villages. This led to a continual "war over land" between the Tel Aviv Municipality and Zionist officials and the Jaffa Municipality and local villagers, most of the battles of which Tel Aviv won because it shared with the British—the ultimate arbiters in these conflicts—a common modernist discourse of development and urbanization that favored the "urbanization" of previously agricultural land over local Palestinian Arab (i.e., Islamic and Ottoman legal) categorization, usage, or narratives.

In this way by the 1940s, most of the land of the surrounding villages was incorporated into Tel Aviv's "town-planning area," if not its "municipal borders." Thus, at a 1937 meeting of the Boundaries Commission, Tel Aviv Mayor Rokach pressed for the annexation of the village of Summel and the adjoining part of Arab el-Jammasin el-Gharbi, then still part of the "Rural Area," into Tel Aviv's boundaries by explaining that "these lands are rural but have acquired an urban value."[36] Such lands were still considered "practically undeveloped," and it was considered vital to bring them under "complete municipal authority" because only the "legal and administrative machinery of a municipal corporation" would have the power to draw up a "creative or positive machinery of development" through which Tel Aviv could "redeem some of these defects which have deformed and stunted its past growth and to prepare for a better planned and more spacious urban future."[37]

Thus, we see that the modern city swallowed its "other" in the Jaffa–Tel Aviv region, as it has in so many other locations. In so doing what happened in Tel Aviv can be seen as a microcosm of the larger processes taking place in Mandatory Palestine. But the question this raises is: At what cost? Does not the violence at the heart of the processes of urbanization—especially in a colonial setting such as the Jaffa–Tel Aviv region—rend the very fabric from which the city, the civitas, and the nation are sewn together?

IS THE CITY MODERN?

The Jaffa–Tel Aviv region was a seminal space of colonial modernity, one where the urban and rural were woven together—and gradually rent apart—in an evolving patchwork of land uses and imaginaries. This unique tapestry suggests that the region differed from other sites of colonized modernity, since until the 1930s, Tel Aviv did not have the same degree of power to shape Jaffan spaces and social discourses as, for example, British colonialism had in India and also because a significant proportion of Arab inhabitants of the Jaffa–Tel Aviv region were not motivated by modernist ideologies or self-identities, as were Tel Aviv's inhabitants.[38] Some, like a wealthy and very conservative Palestinian Arab merchant who explicitly set out to build the most modern house in Jaffa or Tel Aviv, could and did utilize it as a strategy or idiom for self-definition and even social advancement, but many others did not so define themselves through modernity since they had already been "modernizing" their landscape for several generations without having to define it as such (as was the case with local farmers who had drained swamps around the 'Auja/Yarkon River north of Tel Aviv, a quintessentially modernizing activity for Zionism) or perhaps because that rubric was claimed by Jaffa's hostile and expansionist neighbor (and therefore represented a threat to Jaffa and Palestinians).[39]

Following Latour, the processes we are discussing suggest that even a "hybrid form of colonial modernity,"[40] let alone a pure distillation of the two discourses, was never a logical possibility, since modernity is (self-)defined by its refusal of hybridity.[41] Given the colonial basis of modernity, we could ask the following question: Can a space experiencing a colonial transformation such as the Jaffa–Tel Aviv region be modern? Can either the colonizer or the colonized within that space be modern? Latour's work suggests that only by taking full cognizance of what he has termed productive "nonmodernities," always produced alongside (and often by) modernity, can we begin to address such questions and challenge the existing spatializations concretized by modernity's creative-cum-destructive power.[42] Moreover, by acknowledging the presence of nonmodernities within and surrounding the space of Euro-modernity in Tel Aviv, the role of colonialism as the engine and prism (in the sense of actively distorting, yet in so doing clarifying) of modernity becomes clear.

Viewed thus, quintessentially modern places such as Tel Aviv rarely live up to the ideals of modernity; what is more, those colonized by modernity often see through the "ontology of sameness"—premised, as discussed at the beginning of this chapter, on an ontology of otherness—that produces modernity by simultaneously denying and creating the fundamental differences between modern and not-modern that are at the heart of the colonial project.[43] It is for this reason that Arab inhabitants of the Jaffa–Tel Aviv region often saw through the modern(ist) artifices of British and Zionist administrators, politicians, and technocrats, where the latter did not (at least not most of the time).[44]

This acuity of vision—and recognition of the ethical implication of planning—reminds us that the production of modernity "occurs *only* by performing the distinctions between the modern and non-modern, west and non-west," an activity which always carries the danger of "contamination and disruption by the latter on the former."[45] By refusing to make these distinctions, by seeing through the modernist discourses, many of the poorest and most marginalized residents of the Jaffa–Tel Aviv region can be seen as not modern, even if many of their economic and cultural practices (such as the capitalization of land) had been modern for several generations. But it needs to be stressed that here we are not referring to the nonmodernity of modernity's imagination (that is, the backwards "other" of its "spaces of representation"),[46] but rather the productive non-modernity of those who cannot stop "translating" modern ideologies into more hybrid realities.

Visualizing the Urban through the Modern: Architecture and Planning in Jaffa and Tel Aviv

Given that the need to reject existing indigenous Palestinian Arab or Jewish cultures was a defining feature of Zionist ideology, it is not surprising that the leadership of Ahuzat Bayit agreed that new land purchases had to be as far away from Arabs as possible[47] and should be based on the most modern planning and architectural notions from Europe. Thus, they adopted the Garden Suburb model of Ebenezer Howard, which was given a specifically colonial twist through the twin ideas of spatially and ethnically segregating Tel Aviv from "Arab" Jaffa.[48]

Architecturally, this process was reflected in debates over whether to build in "Arabic-Yafo" versus "European" styles; more important was that in adopting Howard's spatiality Tel Aviv's founders territorialized his "hatred of the city" as an "outright evil and an affront to nature," a perspective that did not recognize incarnations of the urban which "could not be abstracted to serve [Howard's] Utopia."[49] Of course, this sentiment could not, by definition, be directed toward *their* suburban-turned-urban utopia, and so it was directed with full force at Jaffa and the surrounding "Arab" geography. This necessitated—as in all territorializations of colonial modern urban discourses—the imagining of a "natural, non-historical conception of space, devoid [or better, made void—that is 'purified'] of all otherness."[50]

Tel Aviv as utopia could only be born by overthrowing—and just to be sure, erasing—the existing Arab landscape. Not surprisingly, by the 1930s, the heightened interest in town planning as a solution for the economic and "absorptive" capacities of the country,[51] coupled with the widespread adoption of modernist International Style/Bauhaus-inspired architecture as Tel Aviv's architectural motif, made possible the concretization of the dreamscapes of figures like Le Corbusier (several of whose Zionist Jewish students would work in the city), who believed that "where one builds one plants trees. We uproot them."[52]

The violence inherent in this process produced a paranoia that has lasted until today. Thus, if we look to the contemporary architectural styles on display in Tel Aviv, the eminent Dutch architect Peter Kook describes the present Tel Aviv "style" as "paranoia on the one hand, and the world wide trend of the worship of money on the other. The paranoia is reflected in the fact Israeli architects are closed to any outside styles, they only see what the Housing Ministry does, and not what's going on in the wider world. The power of money rules here in a dominant way on both aesthetics and on urban planning."[53]

This evident paranoia both reflects a failure of the process of "self-reflexivity" that is supposed to be a hallmark of the modern, especially in the space of the city, and betrays the most deleterious consequences of modernism as a colonial discourse. Yet if Tel Aviv's leaders were always paranoid, what is new in this equation is the increasingly prominent role of private interests in planning and development in Israel, and in Jaffa in particular, and how this development reflects the shifting of jurisdictions of exclusion within the State's land and planning system in order to maintain permanent Jewish control of as much territory as possible. Thus, when Jaffa's Palestinian inhabitants complain about a lack of affordable housing, Tel Aviv's planning authority responds, "What can we do, the market is the market."[54] In this manner, globalization's discontents intersect with the nation's as Israel's global city enacts new strategies to serve the interests of its State and nation.

Tel Aviv and its discontents and the contemporary experience of the urban reflected in this relationship reveal how little space for "public" discourse and debates exists in contemporary Jaffa or Tel Aviv. But can a city be modern without a public sphere in which modernity as a project is continuously debated, interpreted, contested, and reshaped? Can a "frontier" neighborhood such as contemporary Jaffa—which two hundred years ago was also considered a frontier, or *thagr*, in Ottoman parlance[55] —ever be fully urban, modern, or public? If not, what does that tell us about the "city" it surrounds?[56]

Here it is worth once again returning to Williams's seminal interrogation of the city and the country, in which he argues that the development of the modern European city (especially in his native England) could not have occurred were it not for the transformation of the traditional relationship between city and country wrought by colonialism/imperialism, a process that occurred on "an international scale. Distant lands became the rural areas of industrial Britain,"[57] while the country's own rural areas increasingly became a "site of play, of capital, not of land" at the same time that extreme poverty grew on the city's margins. The widened economic gap was in fact crucial "to the construction of the space of London as a city;"[58] today's "quaint, old" Jaffa, like yesterday's quaint English vicarage, has been transformed by the forces of globalization into a site of "amusement" for the nation's nouveau riche.

Such a dream is epitomized in luxury projects such as the Andromeda Hill condominium project,[59] whose faux Oriental design—similar to Kook's description of the role of the Housing Ministry in architectural design in Tel Aviv—was dictated by the Tel Aviv Municipality. Not surprisingly, perhaps, while from outside its imposing security gates the complex appears to be made of the once famous Arab-hewn stone, Andromeda Hill is in reality constructed using a man-made material called GRC, or "fake stone."[60] The fake style and materials are intimately tied to how the brochure imagines its position in Jaffa, as a "city within a city"—language that is almost identical to that used by Tel Aviv's founders to describe their position in Jaffa right before its establishment, as a "state within a state." Here we see how the city and the State—more specifically the "nation-state"—are inextricably tied together through "urban masterpieces"[61] such as Andromeda Hill. But in order to understand fully how the city, or at least Tel Aviv, functions as a synecdoche and spearhead of the State, we need to explore the nature of the public spheres and cultures that evolved in Jaffa and Tel Aviv during the last century.

Is the City Public?

Is Disneyland, or Disney World, a "public" space? The literature on mall culture, and on Disney as well, would seem to suggest that this most commodified of places can spawn momentary publics, although they possess neither the self-consciousness nor the "insurgent" potential to constitute a lasting public sphere.[62] But the question is much larger, territorially and morally: Can a "world" city that is simultaneously a vortex for processes of neoliberal globalization-as-privatization yet retains many characteristics of a colonial city sustain truly public spaces or cultures, let alone provide the spaces and materials out of which "insurgent citizenships" can be constructed, that is, identities that nourish and transform the larger city, public, and nation even if they never achieve hegemony?[63]

We can define the public spheres and cultures of the city as involving ongoing contests over terrain—not just physical territory but also public spaces such as newspapers, schools, and places of leisure. The struggles to shape complex historical and global processes within the public sphere generate "prismatic structures of modernity" that are simultaneously local and interactive with other cities and cultures and with modernity at large.[64]

In this context, the struggle between Tel Aviv and Jaffa over whose city, public, nation, and modernity would emerge victorious ended more than a half century ago, Tel Aviv having decisively won that battle in 1948. Yet from the discussions thus far, it should not be surprising that the pre-1948 city of Jaffa was home to a vibrant and powerful public sphere. Indeed, the mortal weakening of Jaffa's public sphere with the flight of the city's bourgeois elite in late 1947 and early 1948 made its conquest and takeover by Tel Aviv inevitable.

What was most important about the pre-1948 Palestinian public sphere was the fact that it was expressed through a complex articulation of the public and through the popular that was in many respects unique to Palestine. That is, the combination of popular culture and public sphere did not follow the model of other Middle Eastern states in the making, such as Egypt, where the public sphere was the State's partner (in some ways junior, in some ways senior) in disciplining and normalizing the emerging modern subjects. In Palestine, the Palestinian Arab public sphere was specifically *not* part of or in dialog with the colonial State structure and was often in conflict with it.[65] In this situation, public institutions such as the press, which were centered in large part in Jaffa, helped shape and sustain a specifically "resistance vernacular" (a particular species of Anderson's "print vernaculars") that created a common language for the emerging Palestinian nation.[66]

Being "Jaffan" thus involved a "simultaneity of multiple meanings and actions in public" that were a constitutive arena for the emerging "Palestinian" and "Zionist" national imaginaries.[67] Jaffa was the home of Palestine's most important schools, newspapers, and places of leisure by the first decade of the twentieth century. Indeed, Jaffa was one of the primary centers of Palestinian public life, a pride of place that owed in large part to its being the womb and center of the country's press.

But if Jaffa clearly had a vibrant and expanding public culture in the last decades of Ottoman rule, from the moment of Tel Aviv's establishment, the local Palestinian Arab population and Ottoman officials feared that Jaffa's potential for further development would be constricted because the space, culture, and economy of the Jewish enclave would be closed to them. As a telegram to the Pasha in Jerusalem decried, "The Jews in Jaffa are founding *a state within a state* in the new settlement of Tel Aviv"—which mirrored exactly the belief by Zionist leaders like Meir Dizengoff that the Jews had "created a state within a state in Jaffa" even before the establishment of Tel Aviv (and predicted the sentiments of the developers of Andromeda Hill as well).[68]

The question that this city–state dynamic raises is what kind of public sphere can exist in a city that is also a "state," specifically a colonial state whose leaders are intent on using legal, administrative, economic, ethnic, and religious technologies and ideologies to prevent those who do not belong from having access to a formerly well-traveled landscape? What impact do such restrictions have on the experience of Jaffa and Tel Aviv as cities by those thus excluded? There is no definitive answer, but it is clear that both communities increasingly saw the other city as simultaneously enemy territory and a space that needed to be redeemed for the good of the(ir) city and nation.[69]

Yet for Palestinian Arab residents of the Jaffa–Tel Aviv region, the issues were not so clearly defined, since whatever the hostility toward Tel Aviv by those attempting to mold Palestinian Arab public opinion, the reality was that Tel Aviv was a major site for cultural consumption by Palestinian Arabs from Jaffa and beyond during the Mandatory period for fashion, food, film, and other activities of cultural consumption.[70] Indeed, Tel Aviv's press used this fact as part of its campaign to "instruct" Jaffa's Palestinian population as to the beneficial and positive aims of Zionism for the country as a whole and for Palestinian workers in particular—especially in contrast to the corruption and lack of progress existing in Jaffa.

For its part, we must understand the role of the Palestinian Arab press as a crucial component of both the popular culture and the public sphere of the community. That is, the more people from the two communities mixed together, the more important it was for the public spheres and popular cultures they attempted to direct to (re)enforce the boundaries between them.[71] Perhaps most significant, the entrance of Arabs, or Arab symbols, to this Jewish space was viewed negatively, unless such penetration was an act of defiance against the city and what it symbolized.[72]

Here a crucial dynamic is revealed: At the same time the "elite" of the two cities-as-nations saw the other city as both irredeemably "other" and as a space whose redemption was crucial for the survival of the nation as a whole. Yet this dynamic made it impossible for there to arise a common public among the various communities inhabiting the Jaffa–Tel Aviv region, and the conflict between the ultimately divided publics surely made the core experiences of the urban, or the larger project of modernity, difficult to sustain.

This historical dynamic continues to define the Jaffa–Tel Aviv region today: As the *Economist* explained in comparing Tel Aviv and Jerusalem, that Tel Aviv "contains hardly any Arabs. It has swallowed the old Arab port of Jaffa, but in the main it was built by Jews, for Jews, on top of sand dunes, not on top of anybody else's home."[73] The matter-of-factness of the "swallowing" of Jaffa, not to mention the historically inaccurate claim of the city's birth and population (i.e., the majority of the area of Tel Aviv was not sand or barren and had various Arab communities living on or otherwise utilizing it), suggests that the city of "Tel Aviv-Yafo" is not a "public" place, since the existing Palestinian population is barely visible, let alone in the possession of equal civil, economic, and political rights to its Jewish neighbors.

If we understand public to mean an arena, or zone, where "different interests, commitments, and values collide and resolve themselves into a reciprocal, multi-voiced, perhaps even carnivalesque civic sense that is shared as a relation, not as sameness or consensus,"[74] can a colonial city ever have a truly "public" culture, or even a "public" at all? At the very least, the exclusion (or inclusion via strategies of ethnic/cultural difference and exclusion) of significant portions of the population from the public sphere of an urban space challenges the Habermasian depiction of the public sphere as an idealized and inclusive space[75] and raises the question of whether a public-less urban space can be said to constitute a city.

Appadurai has described a public culture as a "zone of cultural debate" that reflects a larger public modernity of the national space, one produced by an "uneasy collaboration between the cultural agencies of the nation-state and the private interests."[76] The mechanics and mechanisms of Tel Aviv's public culture are of colonial vintage, yet at the same time have adapted to the conditions of neoliberal globalization and engineered an "easy" alliance between the State and the market that has enabled the continued exclusion of Palestinian citizens from the public life of the city and the nation. Thus, the culture of Tel Aviv, and of Israel, is not public in the fullest sense of the word and indeed can more accurately be described as "ethnocratic" because the demos it sustains is profoundly determined by the politically dominant Jewish/Zionist ethnos.[77]

This situation raises a question that is central to understanding the relationship between the city and the nation: If one of the main characteristics of the modern city is that it continuously and matter-of-factly generates a public "culture" or "life" composed from "life in the streets and other public places,"[78] can contemporary Tel Aviv-Yafo be considered a "city" if it denies "public" participation to entire communities, no longer just "Arabs" but today also tens of thousands of "illegal" Nigerian, Thai, Romanian, and other workers who live in the city's poorer and marginalized neighborhoods? Do their embattled carving out of public spaces of autonomy and homeliness against the official policies of the Municipality and State provide the city with just enough bona fides to warrant its standing as a "city," perhaps even one of world standing? If at the heart of the metropolitan experience there is supposed to be a mechanism that connects various urban collectivities whose "coming together in fact constitutes the public culture of the city," the tenuous threads of (inter)community in Tel Aviv-Yafo, which are stretched even thinner by policies of segregation and discrimination, challenge us to (re)consider how the space of Jaffa–Tel Aviv is public or metropolitan.[79]

Conclusion: The Borders and Frontiers of the City as Nation

The founders of Tel Aviv were quite interested in the latest trends in planning and design in Europe and the United States. It is thus worthwhile to compare the planning discourses at play in the creation of Tel Aviv with those in New York, for example, where progressive urban thinkers saw the city as providing a "vital platform for men and women to think themselves into politics, to make themselves into citizens."[80] Indeed, the "modern city" was even "the hope of democracy."

In this context, if we peruse the list of books used by Tel Aviv's founders to educate themselves on the most modern trends in city planning in preparation for choosing a design for their new society, we would find no reference in them to writings such as Howe's *The City: The Hope of Democracy* published in 1905, the year the original land of Tel Aviv was purchased,[81] or Wilcox's *The American City: A Problem in Democracy* that was published a year later, when Ahuzat Bayit, the building society that would establish Tel Aviv, was founded.

Wilcox specifically argued that the "city is the center of the complex web of national life" and as such had the power even to "save the nation."[82] Woodrow Wilson (better known as the great advocate of the rights of nations) similarly saw the city as the locus primus for grasping the relations between societies and their politics and so believed that "participatory urban democracy" was the best means toward a democratic society. Yet he also warned that a city—and thus a nation—can be "whole and vital only when conscious of its wholeness and identity."[83]

It is within this perspective that Jane Jacobs argues that cities whose publics do not recognize the fundamental connections between the various diverse spaces, communities, and cultures out of which they are composed become "dull and inert," containing "the seeds of their own destruction and little else."[84] This may be true in the long run, but as argued throughout this discussion, the discourses of colonial urban modernity that power a city like Tel Aviv are designed precisely to misread, erase, and otherwise overpower such hybridity in favor of supposedly pure selves, with the "others" no longer in sight. So how can we determine whether a city is "successful" or not, particularly, if, according to Raymond Williams, the city is always somehow "false—every street a blow, every corner a stab"?[85]

On the other hand, all cities—Tel Aviv no less than London or New York—are potentially "fantastically dynamic places"; what makes them such is their simultaneous location as the nation's most "strategic" places and its function as the entrepôt of the "nonlocal, the strange, the mixed, and the public"—and therefore, if we recall Latour, of the nonmodern.[86] In this context, what Jacobs terms "unsuccessful cities" are thus those which lack the networks "intricate mutual support" that makes the nation's "others"—consciously or not from the State's perspective—central to its strategy of self-realization. The goal of holistic and transformative (in Jacob's words, "real") city planning and design must be to catalyze and nourish diversity and the "right to the city" by all its inhabitants.

This cannot happen, however, when a significant portion of the inhabitants of the city are, as Althusser, Butler, and Warner have variously described it, "interpolated" into a position of marginality and otherness vis-à-vis the dominant identity as collectively imagined by the majority population, so that their rights to the city are severely constrained (indeed, the interpolation, or hailing of gay or black men described by Althusser and others is quite similar to the interpolation of young Palestinian Arab men by Israeli police or security services, with the ability of the latter to "misrecognize"—refuse to respond to the interpolation limited by the significant disparity in power between them).[87]

As with the Jews, blacks, gays, or Chicanas described by Butler, however, even with the successful erasure of an independent Jaffan–Palestinian identity, at a certain point it becomes harder for the dominant ideology to "interpolate" Palestinian Arab residents of Jaffa outside the dominant subjecthood of Israeli identity. At this same time, residents of the quarter began interpolating themselves into the larger Israeli and Palestinian public spheres through the creation of their own collectively imagined "communication communities." Through them the residents of Jaffa simultaneously demanded entrance into the dominant public sphere and establish a counterpublic whose goal is explicitly to help them remain rooted on their land.[88]

Yet in this context, Islamic Law (and specifically the Hanafi school) would seem to agree with Jacobs in long defining the city as a "comprehensive social and political entity embracing various groups, rallying different factions into one community and uniting them under one leadership" in a manner that transcends ethnicity or tribal loyalties.[89] By this criterion neither Jaffa nor (especially) Tel Aviv would be considered cities. At the very least, from this discussion we can imagine that neither Jaffa nor Tel Aviv, nor their respective nations, were/are successful enterprises because only by fostering the broadest right to the city can nations sustain their own civilization. After almost a century of conflict, the right to the city and nation are still very much in dispute.

NOTES

1. Rebecca L. Stein, "'First Contact and Other Israeli Fictions: Tourism, Globalization, and the Middle East Peace Process," *Public Culture* 38 (2002): 515–43.

2. *New York Times*, April 30, 1998, A19; another report called Tel Aviv "unabashedly sybaritic" (Serge Schmemann, "What's Doing in Tel Aviv," *New York Times*, December 21, 1997).

3. Henri Lefebvre, *The Production of Space*, trans. Donald Nicholson-Smith (Cambridge, UK: Blackwell, 1991), 33, 39.

4. This creative destruction was helped by the emerging disciplines of geography, sociology, and political "science" which were in the

process of overturning existing ways of seeing, mapping, governing, and living in the world. Thus Said argues that "imperialism after all is an act of geographical violence through which . . . space . . . is explored, charted, and finally brought under control" (Edward Said, "Yeats and Decolonization," in *Remaking History*, ed. Barbara Kruger and Phil Mariani, 3–29 (Seattle, Wash.: Bay Press, 1989), 10.

5. See Bennedict Anderson, *Imagined Communities* (London: Verso, 1992).

6. Raymond Williams, *The Country and the City* (Oxford, UK: Oxford University Press, 1973), 1, 6. Thus, Tel Aviv was early on seen as having a "power of attraction" that played a central role in its rapid development from a neighborhood to a city. Also see *Hapo'el Hatza'ir*, October 17, 1914, 8.

7. For a discussion of these interactions, see Mark LeVine, *Overthrowing Geography: Jaffa, Tel Aviv, and the Struggle for Palestine, 1880–1948* (Berkeley: University of California Press), chs. 1–4.

8. Ibid., 205.

9. In his analysis of the role of modernist town-planning discourses in the creation of Brasilia, James Holston describes a fundamental feature of the discourses of urban modernism and modernization as being an "aesthetic of erasure and reinscription" that is closely linked to an ideology of development (cf. James Holston, *The Modernist City: An Anthropological Critique of Brasilia* [Chicago: University of Chicago Press, 1989], 5).

10. Quoted in Gwendolyn Wright, *The Politics of Design in French Colonial Urbanism* (Chicago: University of Chicago Press, 1991), 16; cf. 319, note 8.

11. Holston, *The Modernist City*, 83. The planners possessed a teleological view of history in which capitalist modernity signified an advance in human civilization that began in Europe and would spread to the "backward" regions.

12. Bruno Latour, *We Have Never Been Modern*, trans. Catherine Porter (Cambridge, Mass.: Harvard University Press, 1993), 39. Thus, the administrators of these spaces of victorious modernity understood the process of planning and founding a new city as "a civilizing event . . . giv[ing] form and identity to an uncivilized geography (Holston, *The Modernist City*, 68).

13. David Harvey, *The Condition of Postmodernity* (Cambridge, UK: Blackwell Publishers, 1989), 16; cf. Joseph Schumpeter, *Capitalism, Socialism, and Democracy* (London: Allen & Unwin, 1976); Timothy

Mitchell, *Colonising Egypt* (Berkeley: University of California Press, 1988), 165.

14. Cf. Mitchell, *Colonising Egypt*, for his use of "enframing" vis-à-vis the experience of modernization and colonialism in Egypt.

15. Williams, *The Country and the City*, 7, 264.

16. Indeed, our knowledge of how they differentiated between them and, in fact, the primary sources themselves is vague and has yet to be properly elucidated. Fortunately, there has been some work done on Hanafi writings on this topic, which are relevant to our case study because the Hanafi legal school was (and remains) the dominant Muslim legal school in Palestine/Israel. The most important writing on this subject has been done by Baber Johansen in two works: "The All-Embracing Town and Its Mosques: al-Misr al-Gami'," *Revue de l'Occident Musulman et de la Méditerranée*, 32 (1981–82): 139–62; and *Contingency in Sacred Law: Legal and Ethical Norms in the Muslim Fiqh* (Leiden, Netherlands: Brill, 1999).

17. Johansen, "The All-Embracing Town," 141–43, citing Abu Hanifa. That is, economically, the town was defined as the center of commodity production that supports every type of specialized craftsman to earn his living; militarily, its inhabitants should be able to defend themselves against outside attacks.

18. The need for such accuracy involved when the traveling Muslim was supposed to shorten his prayers (which according to tradition meant that he had to travel at least three days journey, but that raised the question of when the journey began, i.e., how far out of the main urban area before you start counting (Johansen, "The All-Embracing Town," 146). Further, and equally controversial, was how much "common" or "pasture" land on the outskirts of the town could be considered within its jurisdiction or lay outside the city (Ibid., 147).

19. Ibid., 147.

20. Cf. Ibid., 153.

21. M. V. Guerin, *Description Geographique, Historique et Archeologique de la Palestine* (Paris: Limprimerie Imperiale Guerin, 1868), 2–11.

22. BBA, Y.EE 132/29, Letter of Abdurrahman Zekai, Inspector of Land-Registry Office, to Shakir Pasha, date undecipherable. Another document reveals that the English were authorized to conduct a topographical survey of Palestine north of Gaza for a new map, although it is not clear whether this was ever undertaken (BBA, DH.KMS 6/25, 1332h). Unfortunately, the files do not contain the maps.

23. Smilansky, 1890, quoted in Eli Schiller, "Orchards and Farms of Jaffa," [Hebrew] *Kardom*, no. 15, 1981: 42–47.

24. TAMA, 1/20, article in *Kedima*, (1904): 435.

25. Jaffa Qa'immaqam Muhammad Aşaf to Mutaşarrif of Jerusalem, July 9, 1907, document contained in David Kushner, *Moshel Hayyiti Beyerushalayyim: Ha'ir vehamehuz be'einav shel 'Ali Akram Bey, 1906–1908* [A Governor in Jerusalem: The City and Province in the Eyes of Ali Ekrem Bey, 1906–1908] (Jerusalem: Yad Ben-Zvi, 1995), 62–68.

26. Ibid., 63.

27. Ibid., 64–65.

28. Rashid Khalidi, *Palestinian Identity: The Construction of Modern National Consciousness* (New York: Columbia University Press, 1997), 127.

29. BBA, DH.İD 34/18, 1329h.

30. See Khalidi, *Palestinian Identity*, for a description of these dynamics.

31. DH.ŞFR 39/19, vol. 1, no. 6561, R.21.1332, telegraph from Private Office to Syria and Beirut Provinces and Post and Jurisdiction of Jerusalem.

32. JICR, book 83 (1298H/1880), case # 1014, 3–4.

33. JICR, book 104 (1907/1325–1909/1327), 100.

34. A more thorough review of the *sijjil* during this period would no doubt find numerous instances of the placing of certain neighborhoods as being inside or outside of "Jaffa," the mapping (in both place and time) of which would yield much insight into the changing nature of the Jaffan conceptualization of the "borders" of their town as both urban and agricultural development increased.

35. MHTA, Achuzat Bayit Box/Neighborhoods, A/I Achuzat Bayit; undated contract of sale in Hebrew. For a detailed discussion of the various sources relating to Karm al-Jabali, see LeVine, *Overthrowing Geography*, chapters 2 and 3, from which the evidence in this discussion is drawn.

36. TAMA, 4/2667b, Minutes of Meeting dated July 13, 1937.

37. Interview with Y. Shiffman, in *Palestine and Near East*, 1/43, 12. Making the erasure of the surrounding nonurban region easier was what Raymond Williams has described as the "common image of country is as thing of the past and city an image of the future." That is, Jewish and British planners saw the existing landscapes and

networks of land use as belonging to the "past" and thus depicted its urbanization as an inevitable and bright future.

38. Thus, while for Abdallah Laroui Arabs only crossed the threshold of modern times in the pain of "defeat, occupation, and servitude," this was not the experience of modernity in Jaffa, at least until the 1930s, when the planning discourses of Tel Aviv grew powerful enough to facilitate the annexation or swaths of the surrounding Arab-owned territory (Abdallah Laroui, *L'idéologie arabe contemporaine: Essai critique* (Paris: Maspero, 1982 [1967]).

39. Cf. Mark LeVine, "Conquest through Town-Planning: The Case of Tel Aviv," *Journal of Palestine Studies* 17, nos. 1–2 (1998): 36–52, section II. I would thus argue that we cannot separate the ills of modernism and modernization from the positive goals and dreams of modernity as a project (as so many analyses of modernity attempt to do) because the very philosophies and epistemologies underlying both—humanism, progress, enlightenment, freedom, and equality—are inextricably tied to colonialism/imperialism. Indeed, the discourse of the Young Turk revolutionaries who assumed power in Istanbul in 1908 reacted specifically to this problem, displaying an ironic and often hostile view of "la vie moderne" symbolized by France and the other European powers (Palmira Brummett, *Image and Imperialism in the Ottoman Revolutionary Press, 1908–1911* [Albany, N.Y.: SUNY Press, 2000], 84).

40. As Timothy Mitchell argues in *Questions of Modernity* (Minneapolis: University of Minnesota Press, 1999), 24.

41. As García Canclini argues for Latin America, its being a land of "pastiche and bricolage" with many concurrent temporalities and aesthetics has made it a land of postmodernity for centuries (Nestór García Canclini, *Hybrid Cultures: Strategies for Entering and Leaving Modernity* [Minneapolis: University of Minnesota Press, 1995], 6).

42. Whose marginalization or elision of the non-West is even reproduced by a thinker as perceptive as Foucault (cf. Bhabha's critique of Foucault, as described by Mitchell, *Questions of Modernity*, 16, García Canclini, *Hybrid Cultures*, 7).

43. Cf. Ibid., 7; Vassos Argyrou, "Sameness and the Ethnological Will to Meaning," *Current Anthropology* 40 (1999): S29–41, particularly S35–37.

44. For a good example of this response, see *al Jam'iah al-Islamiyyah*, December 21, 1937, 3.

45. Mitchell, *Questions of Modernity*, 26, his italics. That is, there are two registers of difference, one providing the modern with its

characteristic indeterminacy and ambivalence and the other with its enormous power of replication.

46. Ibid., 27, clearly utitlizing Lefebvre's categorization.

47. TAMA, Protocols of Achuzat Bayit, 1908, 21.

48. Thus, it would have to be situated at a distance from the city in order to maximize its autonomy, and only Jews could live in the neighborhood (the by-laws prohibited the sale or renting of houses to Arabs; CZA, L18/105/4, L51/52, L2/578; TAMA, Protocols of Achuzat Bayit, June 6 and July 31, 1907). Apparently, as Katz points out (Yossi Katz, *The Business of Settlement: Private Entrepreneurship in the Jewish Settlement of Palestine, 1900–1914.* [Jerusalem: Magnus Press, 1994], 284), in purchasing the land at Kerem Jebali, the members of Achuzat Bayit felt that they were "beyond the city limits of Jaffa." The Jaffan authorities, not surprisingly, considered the area within their jurisdiction.

49. Cf. Jane Jacobs, *The Death and Life of Great American Cities* (New York: Modern Library, 1993 [1961]), 23–26.

50. Uri Eisenzweig, "An Imaginary Territory: The Problematic of Space in Zionist Discourse," *Dialectical Anthropology* 5, no. 4 (1981): 261–87, particularly 267, 271, 278, emphasis added.

51. This was reflected in the Colonial Development Act of 1929. For a critique of the idea of "absorptive capacity," see Mark LeVine, "The Discourse of Development in Mandate Palestine," *Arab Studies Quarterly*, vol. 17 (Winter 1995): 95–124.

52. Le Corbusier, *The City of Tomorrow and Its Planning*, trans. F. Etchells (London: The Architectural Press, 1947), 82.

53. "Yafo Is Disneyland, the North Is a Tragedy," [Hebrew] *Ha'ir*, June 12, 1997, 24.

54. Thus, for example, the pseudogovernmental Jewish National Fund announced in November 1998, that it was severing ties with the Israel Land Authority, the semigovernmental agency that administers both state and JNF-owned lands (and which heretofore has been composed of both government and JNF representatives), precisely because by going "private" it could buck the legal trend toward equality between Jews and Palestinians in the Government sector and ensure that its huge reserves of land remained "in the hands of the Jewish people" (*Ha'aretz*, November 6, 1998, A1).

55. Cf. JICR 7, 1797/1211, 12-13 and JICR 4, 6/J/1234h (1819), 118.

56. Moreover, if we view Jaffa as a frontier region—actually, as a frontier region of a frontier region, since Tel Aviv originally saw itself as a

frontier—it further becomes clear how the spatial policies of the Municipality are used as a powerful tool to exert territorial control over and physically shape this discursive yet material space (Oren Yiftachel, "The Internal Frontier: Territorial Control and Ethnic Relations in Israel," *Regional Studies* 30, no. 5 (1995): 493–508, particularly 494, 496, 498. For a more detailed analysis of this dynamic in the country at large, see Oren Yiftachel and Avinoam Meir, eds., *Ethnic Frontiers and Peripheries: Landscapes of Development and Inequality in Israel* (Boulder, Colo.: Westview Press, 1998).

57. Williams, *The Country and the City,* 280.

58. Ibid., 281, 292.

59. The project is billed as "the incomparable Jaffa . . . the New-Old Jaffa" and the heart of a "renewed Ajami district where the rich and famous come to live" (Andromeda Hill brochure, 1998).

60. As one of the architects described it to me, GRC is made out of silicon. It is less expensive, lighter, and easier to use. The video shown to prospective customers misleadingly implies that the whole project is being made out of stone.

61. "Andromeda Hill—The New Old Jaffa: Living an Original," 1998 brochure for project.

62. Cf. the contributions to James Holston, ed., *Cities and Citizenship* (Durham, N.C.: Duke University Press, 1999).

63. Ibid.

64. Arjun Appadurai and Carol A. Breckenridge, "Public Modernity in India," in *Consuming Modernity: Public Culture in a South Asian World*, ed. Carol A. Breckenridge, 1–22 (Minneapolis: University of Minnesota Press, 1995), particularly 15.

65. This is not surprising given the specific nature of British rule and the presence of a competing national movement, in Zionism, which had far greater political and financial resources to nurture its public and popular culture spheres.

66. For a discussion of "resistance vernaculars," see Russell A. Potter, *Spectacular Vernaculars: Hip-Hop and the Politics of Postmodernism* (Syracuse: State University of New York Press, 1995), 57; cf. Anderson, *Imagined Communities*, ch. 5.

67. Thomas Bender, "Metropolitan Life and the Making of Public Culture," in *Power, Culture, and Place: Essays on New York City*, ed. John Hull Mollenkopf, 261–72, (New York: Russell Sage Foundation, 1988), particularly 264.

68. As Tel Aviv's first and most famous mayor, Meir Dizengoff described it (Meir Dizengoff, *Leyedidei Noari* [To the Friends of My Youth] [Tel Aviv: n.p., 1931], 6–7). For the significance of Dizengoff's remark, see LeVine, *Overthrowing Geography*, ch. 7.

69. Thus *Falastin* called for the foundation of a society to purchase large plots of lands around the towns before Zionists could purchase them, and at least one notable who had conflicts with Jews over land surrounding Tel Aviv wrote for the paper against land sales to Jews (*Falastin*, August 12, 1913, 1; August 30, 1913, 1–2).

70. This is confirmed by numerous interviews, recollections, and memoirs of Palestinians who lived in Jaffa during the pre-1948 period, all of whom had memories of going to the beach, movies, shopping, and even prostitutes in Tel Aviv (see LeVine, *Overthrowing Geographies*, chs. 4–6, for detailed discussions of these issues).

71. See LeVine, *Overthrowing Geography*, chs. 3–7, for detailed examples of the role of the press in these conflicts.

72. *al-Jam'iah al-Islamiyyah*, September 6, 1932, 2.

73. "Survey of Israel at 50," *Economist*, April 25, 1998, 18.

74. Bender, "Metropolitan Life," 264.

75. That is, the bourgeois European public sphere excluded more than half the population—that is, women, the poor, and the working class—as participants, while Habermas himself has explained that its functioning has often been hindered by hegemonic political and economic power. Thus the public sphere—which is supposed to be a "free" space where the use of reason as the basis for communicative action is encouraged—has rarely been as "public" as we would imagine, since so many people are denied "free" entrance and because the network of economic, political, and cultural powers that control its institutions are usually more opaque than transparent in their workings (and thus not open to "public" scrutiny).

76. Arjun Appadurai and Carol A. Breckenridge, "Public Modernity in India," in *Consuming Modernity: Public Culture in a South Asian World*, ed. Carol A. Breckenridge, 1–22 (Minneapolis: University of Minnesota Press, 1995), particularly 4–7.

77. For a discussion of Israel as an "ethnocratic" state, see Oren Yiftachel, "Ethnocracy and Its Discontents: Minorities, Protests, and the Israeli Polity," *Critical Inquiry* 26, no. 4, (Summer 2000): 125–56.

78. Bender, "Metropolitan Life," 262.

79. Even if we go farther and recognize that the public culture of the city is "contested terrain . . . a local configuration of power and symbolism" where public meaning is made, inscribed, and deciphered (these three activities constituting the foundation for any synthetic "reading"— or better, performance—of the city [Ibid., 263]), how are we to decipher the public meaning of a mayor feeling the need to blow up his city's newest market, or closer to the present day, a Deputy Mayor's blithe assertion that the gentrification of Jaffa could well lead to the disappearance of the Palestinian population within a decade?

80. Thomas Bender, "Intellectuals, Cities, and Citizenship in the United States: The 1890s and 1990s," in Holston, *Cities and Citizenship*, 21–41, 21.

81. Cf. ibid., particularly 29.

82. Cited in ibid., 34.

83. Wilson, cited in ibid., 33.

84. Jacobs, *The Death and Life of the Great American Cities*, 448.

85. Williams, *The Country and the City*, 266.

86. Cf. James Holston and Arjun Appadurai, "Cities and Citizenship," in *Cities and Citizenship*, ed. James Holston, 1–20 (Durham, N.C.: Duke University Press, 1999), particularly 1–2.

87. See Louis Althusser, *Lenin and Philosophy and Other Essays* (New York: NLB, 1972); Michael Warner, *Publics and Counterpublics* (New York: Zone Books, 2002); J. Butler, *Bodies that Matter: On the Discursive Limits of 'Sex'* (London: Routledge, 1993).

88. Enrique Dussel, *Ética de la Liberación en la Edad de la Globalización y de la Exclusión* (Madrid: Editorial Trotta, 1998).

89. Johansen, "The All-Embracing Town," 141.

PART III

The City and the Vision of the Nation

7

THE IMAGINED COMMUNITY AS URBAN REALITY

The Making of Ankara

Alev Çınar

The relationship between modernity and the city is no doubt a complex one. Even though urban theory has been exploring this relationship thoroughly, this investigation has been limited by a Eurocentric conceptualization of modernity, thereby producing a skewed analysis that takes the Western urban experience as the norm. This limitation is augmented with the complexities and ambiguities arising from the diverse uses of the concept of modernity that can take many, sometimes contradictory meanings. For example, a textbook definition takes modernity as a "distinct and unique form of social life" characterized by a cluster of institutions such as the nation-state, capitalist economic order, industrialism, or secular, materialist, rationalist, or individualist cultural values.[1] Whereas for William Connolly, modernity is "an epoch in which a set of contending understandings of the self, responsibility, knowledge, rationality, nature, freedom, and legitimacy have established sufficient presence to shuffle other possible perspectives out of active consideration."[2] Yet another understanding is introduced by Marshall Berman, who draws attention to the difference between modernism as autonomous artistic and intellectual imperatives and modernization as "a complex of material structures and processes—political, economic, social—which, supposedly, once it has got under way, runs on its own momentum with little or no input from human minds and souls."[3]

As these accounts suggest, modernity can have such a wide range of definition so as to include a lifestyle, an epoch, a process, a structure, an intellectual movement, a culture, an economic activity, a value system, or a cluster of institutions. No matter how sophisticated these accounts may be, they cannot avoid the pitfalls of classical modernization theory that generalizes modernity as a uniform experience across time, space, or culture. Understanding modernity as an epoch induces a sense of temporal uniformity as if it has a consistent manifestation within a given time frame; as an exclusively Western experience imposes a sense of spatial homogeneity throughout the West; and as a lifestyle asserts a sense of an essential cultural experience. These totalizing definitions diminish the analytical use of the concept and make it difficult to examine its specific manifestations in different, particularly non-Western, contexts.

An alternative way of thinking about modernity, which avoids such Eurocentric and totalizing accounts, is to work with locally produced definitions and explore the ways it is evoked in a particular context. In Turkey, the concepts of modernity, modernness, modernization, and modernism have been at the center of political discourse since the early nineteenth century and have come to constitute the basis of the founding ideology when the new Turkish state was established in 1923. As the Turkish case illustrates, regardless of how it is defined, the idea of modernity can have an immense transformative and constitutive power in the ongoing formation of a social–political order, the constitution of the public sphere, and the shaping and transformation of urban life. In such a case, it is much more meaningful to study the specific meanings modernity takes locally and how such meanings take form in different modernization projects, rather than working with an overarching concept that locates modernity in particular institutions, cultural trends, or intellectual movements that are specific to select European experiences and thereby overlook locally specific manifestations. The significance of the historical creation of this local or vernacular modernity is no less and is in fact particularly rich in the case of a country like Turkey, where its founding ideology is so engaged with the ideal of European modernism.

This chapter examines how the making of urban space and the construction of a city lie at the center of the implementation of the modernization project in Turkey. Emerging as an idea that shaped the founding ideology of the new Turkish state, the specific conceptualization of modernity endorsed in the early years of the Republic dictated a new nation-building project which was implemented through the creation of a new capital city. In other words, the idea of modernity shaped the image of the new nation, which in turn was given material form in the construction of the capital, Ankara. This chapter also examines the making of the city of Ankara, which came into being and took on the material form that it did as a result of the central concern of constituting and institutionalizing a modernization project and establishing the state as the agent of modernity that inscribes the nation into space.

This study diverts from literature on urban theory in important respects. First and foremost, rather than taking the city as the locus of analysis, it focuses on the link between the building of a city and the building of a state. More specifically, it looks at how the city and its spaces were vitally instrumental in the building of a new nation-state. The making of Ankara cannot be adequately understood without a due account of the state-building efforts of the founding elite and the ideology that made the state possible. In other words, this study inevitably takes an interdisciplinary perspective that stands at the intersection between urban theory, political science, and sociology and seeks to show how the building of a state is realized through the building of a city. It looks at what it actually means to found a founding ideology by showing how the constitutive principles of this ideology take material form and are realized through the city.

Second, rather than employing an abstract and decontextualized definition of modernity, this study works with locally produced meanings ascribed to the concept and examines how these ideas play a constitutive function toward the formulation and implementation of nationalist projects. Finally, this study takes the city not just as a backdrop wherein modernism and nationalism are instituted, but as itself the means and the product of the material articulation of the modernization project, such that the building of the nation and modernity are realized through the construction of the city.

As such, this chapter is not so much about the making of the city of Ankara itself, but more so about the ways in which modernism as a founding official ideology came to constitute the social reality of its citizens through the making of a city.[4] Hence this study primarily addresses how an ideology becomes so embedded in daily life that it becomes the urban reality that dictates the ways in which a city (as well as a nation) is perceived and experienced.

A New Center for the New Nation

Ankara was built out of a small insignificant town after being declared the capital of Turkey in 1923 and became in a couple of decades the second largest city after Istanbul.[5] Referring to the building of Ankara, writer and journalist Falih Rıfkı Atay, who was a close acquaintance of Mustafa Kemal Atatürk and the honorary chairman of the Ankara Master Planning Commission, said "The Ottomans built monuments, the Turks are the builders of cities."[6] What is significant in Atay's words is the contrast drawn between the Ottomans and the Turks, as if they are two different societies, and the subtle derision of the 600-year-old empire to the benefit of the fresh new Turkish state. Such denigration of Ottoman times was an important part of official discourse at the time, serving as an effective ideological tool with which the founders established the foundations of their modernization project and a new sense of nationhood.

Ankara's geographical location away from the Ottoman state centered in Istanbul made the city a perfect candidate for representing the newness and modernness of the new state. The image of a new modern state was achieved exactly by the creation of a sense of a disjunctive break from the Ottoman times. The Ottoman was projected as traditional, Islamic, backward, incapable of effective governance, and unable to represent or defend the nation. Atatürk himself denounced the Ottoman dynasty for having "usurped the sovereignty of the Turkish nation by force, and carried on this corruption for six centuries."[7] This inferior image of the Ottoman allowed the new state to constitute itself as modern, secular, superior, and vested with the power and authority to capably represent and defend its nation living in Anatolia. Centering the new state in Ankara away from the Sultan's palace allowed for the spatial articulation of this distance toward the Ottoman system and all that it represented. The fact that Ankara was going to be built on more or less barren land that bears no significant marks of Islam and the Ottoman times made the city function like a blank screen upon which the image of a new modern nation could be projected. Consequently, what emerged in a matter of not more than a decade was a new city wherein every corner, street, and avenue and every building, statue, or monument embodied this official vision of the nation.

The creation of a new capital city is not only about the articulation of a new national identity, but also more importantly about the creation of the state itself. The state constructs itself by opening up new spaces, closing others, inscribing them with the marks and symbols of the nation and state power, and organizing urban space around foundational norms and principles. These are self-constitutive acts; the state constitutes itself as an agent of modernity vested with the power and authority to control space, dictate the meaning of urbanity, shape the evolution of the public sphere, and suppress contending ideologies. By constructing a city, the state becomes the agent of the nation, the author that inscribes the nation into space, hence creating the nation-state. Giving shape to urban space by monitoring the architectural styles, erection of statues and monuments, and placement of squares, parks, shopping centers, and public buildings allows the state to establish its power and authority in controlling and dictating the norms that guide daily public life. The arrangement and monitoring of public spaces serve the function of transforming ordinary city dwellers that, just by partaking in daily routine activity, are transformed into citizens. This is how, by creating the city of Ankara, the new Turkish state constructed itself as secular, national, and modern.

The making of Ankara also served to create a sense of national and territorial unity. It allowed for the homogenization of urban space and national land by functioning as a paradigm of the national city that will be replicated, as well as distributed through images after which various other towns and cities across the country will be modeled.

Ankara was built upon the pillars of the founding ideology, consisting of a West-oriented modernism, secularism, and Turkish nationalism that distinguished itself from Ottomanism, Islamism, and other contending national ideologies at the time. The latter ideologies had emerged as viable alternatives before and during the founding years, which had come together at the first National Assembly in 1920 that had consisted of elements from a wide political spectrum, including Islamists, Ottomanists, Kurdish nationalists, and Bolshevists. However, during the War of Independence that lasted until 1923, these rival ideologies were overpowered one after another to the benefit of the West-oriented secularist ideology of Mustafa Kemal, such that when the second National Assembly gathered in 1923, it was much more homogeneously congregated around the principles of secularism and a West-oriented nationalism under Mustafa Kemal's unchallenged authority. To this day, the plurality and heterogeneity of the first National Assembly is presented as a problem and an impediment to the realization of Mustafa Kemal's secularist and nationalist ideals by official national history.[8] It is in the midst of such contention that the principles upon which the new Turkish state was founded emerged. The cases examined here illustrate the ways in which the founding principles were instituted against their alternatives through the construction of the city, arrangement of its spaces, engineering of its appearance, and regulation of the flow of daily life.

However, the founding of the state does not mean that all contending ideologies are silenced and eliminated once and for all. On the contrary, the negotiation of Turkey's national identity around the issues of Islam, Kurdish nationalism, liberalism, or Westernism continued throughout the twentieth century and still constitutes the main point of contention and politics today. As with all nation-building projects, the building of the Turkish state and the consequent creation of Ankara took place amidst a field of contending ideologies and alternative national projects. The state's official version of secular-national modernity has never been the only project. Since the early years of the Republic, there have always been alternative projects and discourses of modernization that understand and exploit the term in different ways. Throughout the course of the twentieth century, several alternative discourses have been formulated and deployed not only by different political parties and movements, but also by forces of civil society such as the media, business associations, or religious groups that have interacted with and influenced one another in different degrees. The liberal/industrialist wave of the 1950s, the Marxist trends of the 1970s, and the Islamist discourses of the 1990s are some salient examples. Not all of these alternative views of modernity developed into full-fledged political programs, and while some have remained marginal, others have been so influential as to come to power, altering the official discourse on modernity in important respects. It is possible to trace the spatial and architectural articulations of competing discourses of modernity in Turkey in the evolution of cities in general and of Ankara in particular throughout the twentieth century. However, since the scope of such a study would be much too broad to be effectively dealt with here, this chapter examines only the early years of the Republic when the formation of the new state was achieved through the making of the city of Ankara.

THE TURKISH NATION: MODERN AND SECULAR

Modernity and secularism, constituting the core of the founding national ideology, were the main principles upon which the new nation-state and consequently the city of Ankara were built. These two concepts were so tightly connected and complemented each other that they came to be treated as one and the same thing. To this day, the word modern is widely used in Turkey to indicate a secular viewpoint. The following cases are all illustrative of the ways in which these principles concertedly dictated the emergence of a new city, a new sense of urbanity, and a new public sphere wherein a new nation and its citizens came into being.

The notion of modernity plays a central role in the constitution of the new Turkish nation-state. Modernity has been the single most important guiding force that has shaped the formation of societal and political institutions and the evolution of the public and private spheres since the early years of the Republic. As the basis of the founding ideology of the new state, modernity at the time was understood as the consumption of what was taken as a universal norm of civilization, but what was in fact French bourgeois culture. It was neither associated with Europe, nor specifically France that it actually modeled, but rather seen as a universal standard and style. On this note, Atatürk said,

> There are a variety of countries, but there is only one civiliza-
> tion. In order for a nation to advance, it is necessary that it joins
> this civilization. If our bodies are in the East, our mentality is
> oriented toward the West. We want to modernize our country.
> All our efforts are directed toward the building of a modern,
> therefore Western state in Turkey. What nation is there that
> desires to become a part of civilization, but does not tend
> toward the West? (*Atatürk'ün Söylev ve Demeçleri* [Atatürk's
> Speeches and Lectures], vol. III, 91)[9]

As suggested here, modernity and civilization were seen as one and the same thing, understood primarily as a way of life and a universal norm that all modernizing countries are expected to adopt. On a similar note, Atatürk referred to the new apparel and the top hat that was introduced with the Hat Law of 1925, as part of the "international dress" style that the Turkish nation is expected to adopt to show how civilized it is.[10] Understood as a lifestyle, an orientation, this universal culture of modernity and civilization would find its best expression in the outward appearance of citizens.

This conceptualization of modernity as an image of the nation was mobilized in the early years of the Republic and institutionalized as part of the nation-building process in the making of the city of Ankara. This new lifestyle was to be displayed in various realms of daily life from clothing, gender identities, family type, entertainment, sports, and leisure activity to architecture, urban planning, and the arts. New public spaces emerging under the supervision of the state became the stage from which this new "civilized" lifestyle was displayed. Acknowledging that cities and city spaces were the primary sites for the expression and institutionalization of modernity, Atatürk said, "Every place that is a home and shelter for the Turk will be a model of health, cleanliness, beauty, and modern culture."[11] With this particular goal in mind, Atatürk personally initiated various projects in Ankara including public parks and greens, the building of a new hotel and restaurant, and the establishment of a conservatory of music, an academy of performance arts, and the Halkevleri ("People's Houses"—centers for culture, sports, and arts). Several new buildings and public spaces such as the new Ankara Palas hotel, where dance receptions, Western classical music concerts, and other extravagant celebrations were held, became key public sites where this new lifestyle was performed and displayed.

Since the founding elite saw modernity as the culture and practice of what they understood to be Western civilization and since Islam was absolutely external to the imagination of the West, modernity, by default, had to be secular. For this reason, secularism has been the most essential part of the founding ideology and the most vital mark of modernity in Turkey. This insistence on secularism as a foundational principle was probably more pronounced than other experiences with secularism in Europe because of the role and place of Islam in Ottoman society. Islam was not only the single most important guiding principle around which social, political, and cultural life under the Ottomans were organized,[12] but also was so tightly associated with Turkey in the eyes of Europeans that dissociating it from the new Turkish identity required doubly concentrated efforts. Since Islam played such a constitutive role in Ottoman society, secularism as the foundational principle that was to replace it had to serve a similar function and act as a guiding principle that would organize the public as well as the private spheres. As a result, secularism emerged not only as a principle governing formal political affairs of the state, but also as a norm that would reshape the public and private lives of citizens and a matter of national identity that was to be displayed for the European gaze.[13]

For this reason, secularism in Turkey has acquired distinctively unique characteristics. Rather than following the common pattern where all religious affairs are separated from formal political affairs, the institutionalization of secularism involved the bringing of all religious activity under the direct control and monopoly of the *secular* state. In 1924, a Directorate of Religious Affairs was formed to act as the ultimate authority on the knowledge and practice of Islam. The Directorate would operate directly under the Office of the Prime Minister, and its chair and board would be appointed by the president. Simultaneously with the establishment of the Directorate, all other practices and authorities of Islam were outlawed, including the Caliphate, which had been the institutional ruler of Islam all over the world since the sixteenth century. Autonomous religious lodges (*tekke* and *zaviye*) and sufi orders (*tarikat*) were banned. A secular civil code was adopted (from Switzerland) to replace the previous codes based on Islamic law (Shariat) outlawing all forms of polygamy, annulling religious marriages, and granting equal rights to men and women in matters of inheritance, marriage, and divorce. The religious court system and institutions of religious education were abolished. The "use of religion for political purposes" was banned under the new secular Penal Code; the Ottoman dynasty was expatriated; the article that defined the Turkish state as "Islamic" was removed from the Constitution; and the alphabet was changed, replacing Arabic letters with Roman ones.

While autonomous Islamic authorities were dissolved one after the other, the Directorate of Religious Affairs was authorized to oversee the knowledge and practice of Islam, which included the supervision of all mosques and the public sermons given there, the appointment of imams, and the production and dissemination of Islamic knowledge.

State control over Islam also involved the strict regulation of its public visibility and presence. The Hat Law of 1925 outlawed the wearing of religious garb and the turban *except for* the staff of the Directorate of Religious Affairs and the imams of mosques. The unauthorized wearing of religious garb was severely penalized, not so much because secular authorities were against Islam per se, but because such "imposters" were confused with government-appointed religious officials and thereby "undercut the authority of the authorized personnel."[14] In other words, what the secular state was against was the visibility of Islam that was beyond its control.

One of the most controversial attempts to bring Islam under the control of the secular state was the changing of the call for prayers (*ezan*) from Arabic, the sacral language of Islam, to Turkish. In this case, "control" was attempted by the nationalization of a prevailing Islamic ritual. The first call for prayers in Turkish, translated into "pure Turkish" by the Turkish Language Association founded by Atatürk, was chanted in 1932 in the Ayasofya Mosque in Istanbul and then standardized throughout mosques around the country upon the orders of the Directorate of Religious Affairs.[15] Since the *ezan* is chanted five times per day from atop minarets scattered around cities, intended to be heard by everyone, it is a highly salient mark of the undeniable presence of Islam in the public sphere. By chanting the *ezan* in Turkish, the secular state not only brings under control Islam that has gained a unique presence in public through sound, but also submits it to nationalist discourse. This intervention, however, never became popular, could not be institutionalized, and was abolished by the populist Democrat Party regime in 1950.

As such, the institutionalization of secularism involved not exclusion, but a tightly controlled inclusion of Islam in the public sphere. While official Islam was given a limited and closely monitored place in the public sphere, autonomous Islamic practices were disallowed.

In sum, the new state was founded upon interventions that sought to institutionalize modernity-as-civilization and a unique understanding of secularism as a monopoly on Islam. This task involved the creation of a sense of a new, modern, and secular Turkish nation with a unique culture, history, and a lifestyle and instilling it in the collective imagination. This founding ideology was codified in the 1924 Constitution, but the declaration of the nation in writing was not sufficient. The founding principles that constituted the national subject as modern and secular had to be given material form so as to constitute the social reality of the citizens. No other means than the building of a city would serve this function better. In other words, the state started to build Ankara in order to give substance and reality to the nation that it conjured up.

ANKARA: CENTERING THE NATION

The image of the new nation found shape through various means, ranging from the writing of a new national history to the making of new social and political institutions, starting with the constitution. One of the important mediums of the creation of this new sense of nationhood has been the use and rearrangement of cities and city spaces. The interventions of the founding elite in space so as to build a new nation and to establish the state are illustrated in the designation of Ankara as the capital of the new Republic and the relocation of city centers away from central mosques to secular spaces marked by administrative buildings and national monuments in towns and cities across the country. In particular, the declaration of Ankara as the new capital and Ulus (Nation) Square as its center, marked by the new parliament building and the Victory Monument, served to inscribe the new modern secular nation upon space and establish the new state as the agent of this inscription.

Aware of the importance of the building of the new capital, the new state diverted an important portion of its scarce resources to the building of Ankara. The first task was to build the city center, a central square from which the rest of the city would expand. It was only natural that the most important building that would designate the placement of this square was the parliament building. Just as a sense of national community was being forged around its representative center gathered in the parliament, so was a sense of national territory being built around the territorial center at the central square of the capital city. Marking the center of the nation, this square was initially given the name Hakimiyet-i Milliye Meydanı (National Sovereignty Square), which later became Ulus Meydanı (The Nation Square).

Ulus Square stood at the intersection of İstasyon Avenue and Atatürk Boulevard, marked at its center by the Victory Monument and circumvented by structures and buildings representing the key axes of the new republic. The second parliament building (1924), which housed the National Assembly until 1962, marked the political significance of the square as the center of a new nation-state. The plaza on the side of the parliament was used as the central public space for the state to meet and address its citizens. This plaza was used not only for official ceremonies and commemorative gatherings, but also for the public execution (hanging) of the Independence Tribunal convicts.[16] These were usually people who had resisted or fought against Atatürk, his reforms, or the new state forming in Ankara, convicted either for collaborating with the occupying forces during the war or for leading insurgencies—often based on Islam— in Anatolia. These public executions served to display the authority and power of the state in incriminating alternative political ideologies and projects, particularly Islamism and Ottomanism, using the public sphere it created as its medium.

Perhaps the most significant building on the square after the parliament was Ankara Palas (1927), the hotel commissioned by Atatürk himself to serve as the official guesthouse, which, together with Karpiç Restaurant close by, served bureaucrats, politicians, diplomats, high-ranking bureaucrats, and other new constituents of Ulus Square. As discussed in detail later, Ankara Palas and Karpiç Restaurant became the main public space of the new republic where the West-oriented secular modern lifestyle of the Republican elite was performed and displayed. Another prominent building was Sümerbank (state-owned textiles and apparel company), facing the square with its showcase of textiles all produced in Turkey by Turkish workers, inscribing the symbol of national industry, progress, and state productivity onto the square.[17] Across from Sümerbank was the Türkiye İş Bankası (Turkish Business Bank), Turkey's first private bank founded with state support in 1924 to finance industrial development.[18] These two buildings represented the attempt to build a state-owned industrial base for a national economy and stood as testaments to the state-built foundations of Turkish capitalism.

The final landmark that faced the square from the bottom of Station Avenue was the central train station. At the end of World War I, Ankara station was the end of a minor route on the Baghdad-Basra line. Within ten years after the founding of the new state, which diverted significant resources to build "an iron web across the country,"[19] Ankara station had become the main hub at the convergence point of the national network of railways extending in all directions toward Turkey's new borders.[20] This placement of the train station accentuated the national significance of Ulus Square, which was now located not only at the center of the capital, but also at the convergence point of national territory.

At the center of Ulus Square stood the tall Victory Monument, with the figure of Atatürk in military outfit, riding a horse on top of a pedestal overlooking the procession of the new buildings on Station Avenue, starting with the parliament and ending with the station building. The height and the strategic positioning of this monument placed the new Ankara under the gaze of the iconic figure of Atatürk, as if he is closely watching the growth of the new city under his feet and with it the trajectory of Turkish modernity. This instillation was one of the first iconized images of Atatürk that would proliferate throughout the country during the following decades, turning him into a near-deity who is overseeing the

Figure 7.1. The Victory Monument, marking the center of the new capital and overlooking the construction of modern Turkey. From Ozan Sagdic, *Bir Zamanlar Ankara* (Ankara, Turkey: Büyükşehir Belediyesi Yayınları, 1993), 59.

development of Turkish modernity and nationalism in the direction he ordained.[21]

Modernism as the National Style

Another important intervention through which a sense of a homogeneous nation was created involves the emergence of a "national architecture" that reflects national identity and dictates the common style to be used in the new buildings, structures, and monuments across the country.[22] Regardless of the styles and forms endorsed by such national architecture, which change over time with every shift in national identity, the idea to adopt a common style is significant in and of itself in that it serves to create a sense of homogeneity in the construction and appearance of cities, thereby serving to nationalize space.

Until about 1927, Ottoman influences were still prevalent in national identity, reflected in architecture as Ottoman revivalism.[23] However, by late 1920s, the founding ideology that defined national identity in opposition to Ottomanism and Islam was sufficiently codified and institutionalized that it became impossible to sustain Ottoman influences in anything national, including architecture. The new urban elite in Ankara endorsing the founding principles started a campaign against Ottoman and Islamic influences in all domains of public life, condemning them as signs of backwardness and barbarism. As such, Ottoman revivalism was rapidly abandoned to be replaced by modernism as the new norm in defining national architecture. In order to lead this new modernist movement, architects and planners from Europe, mostly German, were brought to Ankara and the studios of the architects leading the Ottoman revivalist movement were closed.[24] German architects such as Ernst Egli, Clemens Holzmeister, who built the third parliament building that is still used today, and Hermann Jansen, who developed the master plan for the city of Ankara, were given initiative to lead the way toward the modernist phase of national architecture.[25] Since Europe was seen as the bearer of the ideal and model of modernity, the Turkish state chose to give European architects and urban planners the task to build a new and modern city as the sign of the modernism in the building of the city.

As such, starting with the 1930s, modernism came to dictate the style of all public buildings and significant monuments such as Atatürk's Mausoleum Anıtkabir, as well as residential buildings that were being built in Yenişehir (New Town), planned as the new residential district for the Republican elite. An influential newspaper at the time, *Hakimiyet-i Milliye* said, about this new style, that

> The Ministry [of Health] building has indeed become the most
> modern building of Ankara. It resembles the latest and most

modern buildings of Europe. That the building is erected in Yenişehir has additional significance because in planning our Ankara, we had adopted the principle of constructing grand and monumental buildings in Yenişehir (July 4, 1927).[26]

Modernity was dictating the contours of urban life in Ankara through such officially sanctioned buildings and activity, as well as private projects in house design and interior decoration. In his semidocumentary novel *Ankara*, Yakup Kadri Karaosmanoğlu denounces Ottoman influences in residential architecture salient during the initial years of the Republic and notes that this

> feeble and garish trend that prevailed due to the inexperience of the initial years was fortunately replaced by modern architecture. The towers attached to villas were torn down . . . and green glittering windowsills started to disappear. The facades of several buildings were changing, clearing up and becoming plainer just like the faces of these [modernizing] men who were shaving off their beards and moustaches.[27]

The modernist movement was not only shaping the public sphere, but also transforming domestic life. The Ottoman house with unspecialized spaces and furniture such as the divan and the tray tables rapidly left its place to specialized use of space in house design where rooms were differentiated according to their function and furnished with corresponding furniture.[28] Karaosmanoğlu depicts the enthusiasm of the new Republican elite in Ankara to redecorate their homes with the latest styles in modern furniture and decorations that they see in European magazines or learn from a "visiting engineer from Berlin."[29] Again, the presence of the European expert is evoked as a sign of modernism.

The modernist movement in national architecture was also introduced into school curriculums, thereby transforming architecture as a profession into a vehicle for the dissemination of the modernist ideology of the state. The emerging movement of national architecture was organized around the *Mimar*, a new professional journal of Turkish architects launched in 1931. According to Bozdoğan, this movement called *yeni mimari* (new architecture) "effectively legitimized the architect as a 'cultural leader' or an 'agent of civilization' with a passionate sense of mission to dissociate the republic from an Ottoman and Islamic past."[30]

In sum, by the 1930s, just as a new nation-state emerged out of the remnants of a capitulant empire, a new prospering capital city had materialized in place of an insignificant small town, emerging as the embodiment of national ideology. The signs of the nation inscribed all over the city, from its architecture and urban design to its squares and monuments, made Ankara the national model for all other cities of the country.

THE NATIONAL MODEL CITY

While building Ankara was an absolute priority for the new state, several towns across Turkey also needed to be transformed into national cities to complete the nationalization of the country. Using Ankara as the model, this transformation primarily involved the designation of a new location for the city center in each of these towns, displacing the former center that was marked by the main mosque. Before the Republic, an Ottoman town would be typically clustered around a central mosque, marking the main public area surrounded by the marketplace, inns, and lodges. The new center was moved away from the mosque to a new location that would be marked by a monument of Atatürk and would be invariably named the Republic Square.[31] Hence, while under Ottoman rule, Islam had marked the town center around which a sense of religion-based community was established, the new state moved and relocated city centers by inscribing the mark of the nation at the new center around which a new sense of secular-national community would be established. Marked by the iconic figure of Atatürk, this new center would be surrounded by municipal and administrative buildings, police headquarters, and other offices representing the secular power of the state.

Just as in Ankara, train stations in cities that connected to the national railway system were also built close to the central Republic Square surrounded by government offices. As such, through the network of railways, main cities of the new country were now connected to each other from Republic Square to Republic Square, further enhancing the sense of national unity and connectedness. The designation of Ankara as the model city served to create a sense of homogeneity and nationhood through the standardization of architecture and urban design. Atay, the honorary chair of the Ankara Master Planning Commission, said, "For the Turkish will, which sought, found, and made Ankara, building the rest of Anatolia was going to be like shaping dough in the same mold. . . . Ankara inaugurated the idea of modern urbanism in Turkey . . . [which is] manifesting itself at different scales in various towns scattered around the country."[32]

The city that underwent the most significant transformation was no doubt the former capital Istanbul. The pronounced presence of the marks of Islam and the Ottoman in Istanbul made it impossible for them to be hidden or slighted in any way. Sultanahmet Square, which served as the imperial center for 500 years, was surrounded by the royal Topkapı palace, grand mosques standing tall as reigning monuments of Islam, and other landmarks testifying to the imperial authority of the Ottoman state.

Instead of removing such marks of the Ottoman and Islam, authorities of the Republic chose to relocate the center of the city to a neutral location and inscribe the symbols of the secular ideology of the new state on a clean slate. This location was Taksim Square, a place that was sufficiently far from Sultanahmet that the grand mosques were not visible, yet still within the city limits. The only significant structure in Taksim that gave the square its name was the city's water distribution system, built in 1732. This building was the only structure in the area that was related to Ottoman rule and did not have any religious or imperial significance. Furthermore, Taksim was adjacent to Pera (Beyoğlu), the district where the majority of the non-Muslim population in Istanbul lived, the central churches and synagogues were located, and most of the European diplomatic missions and consulates were placed. As such, relocation of the city center in Taksim not only allowed for a sufficient distance from the Ottoman-Islamic center, but also a proximity to the culture of Europe.

Just as in most other cities of the Republic, Taksim became Taksim Republic Square and was designated the new center of Istanbul by the inscription of the mark of the nation, the Republic Monument, which was erected in 1928. The erection of the Republic Monument depicting Atatürk as the leader of the War of Independence and the founder of the Republic represented the displacement of the Ottoman center and stood as the spatial articulation of the political triumph of the new secular state over its predecessor, the Ottoman state.[33]

In the meantime, most of the monuments, palaces, and structures representing Ottoman power were turned into museums. Sultanahmet Square marking the imperial center was eventually museumified and presented for tourists as part of the old and distant past that no longer bears

Figure 7.2. The Republic Monument at Taksim Republic Square in Istanbul, with Atatürk Cultural Center in the background. Photograph by Zeynep İnanç.

any political presence or national significance. Both the deposition of Istanbul from capital city status and the relocation of the city center in Taksim Square served to display the power of the new Turkish state to enclose and confine the Ottoman era and its culture into spatial and temporal remoteness.

ANKARA PALAS HOTEL: MODERNITY
AS THE PERFORMANCE OF CIVILIZATION

Built upon Atatürk's orders, Ankara Palas opened near the parliament in 1927 to serve as an official guesthouse and to host local and foreign diplomats, high-ranking bureaucrats, and other important visitors. Its central heating and pressurized water systems, its *"alafranga"* (European style) toilets and bathtubs, and its powerful electric generator immediately made the hotel the most prominent symbol of modernity and civilization in Ankara, which was until then "accustomed to deem kerosene lamps."[34] The hotel was also famous for its restaurant, tearoom, and, particularly, the grand ballroom where dance receptions, banquets, and other official celebrations were held. Among these, the "Anniversary of the Republic Ball" celebrations were particularly popular where the new urban elite would have the chance to show off their knowledge and skills

Figure 7.3. Ankara Palas Hotel, where the West-oriented secular modern lifestyle of the Republican elite was performed and displayed. From Sagdic, *Bir Zamanlar Ankara,* 59.

in consuming French high culture, taken as the ultimate mark of civilization. The presence of diplomats and hence the European gaze made Ankara Palas the most pertinent place for the staging of the new civilized, modern lifestyle adopted by the Republican urban elite "who were eager to display their recently acquired taste in ballroom dancing, haute couture, and international cuisine."[35]

Alongside Ankara Palas, Karpiç Restaurant was opened up to host official dinners and receptions, also upon Atatürk's orders who personally asked for "Baba Karpiç," an Armenian Russian émigré, to be brought from Istanbul to run an exclusive, "modern" restaurant.[36] Due to their proximity to the parliament building and the CHP headquarters, Ankara Palas and Karpiç Restaurant became the main gathering place for parliamentarians, bureaucrats, and journalists where affairs of the state would be deliberated and important meetings would take place.[37] As such, these places also served as a modern public sphere (in the Habermasian sense of a site of public deliberation) during the early Republican years.

Another important aspect of this "modern" lifestyle forming around Ulus Square was music. There was a live band playing at all times in Karpiç Restaurant, and regular Western classical music concerts were held at Ankara Palas. The garden extending between Karpiç Restaurant and Ankara Palas, called the Millet Bahçesi (Nation Garden), was used as a recreational area where bands would play music and people would dance.[38] Once again, Atatürk personally initiated several projects to promote Western classical music, taken as another sign of the universal culture of modernity and civilization. One of these projects was the building of the Conservatory of Music in 1927–1928, where Western classical music, opera, and ballet were taught and institutionalized as the universal norms in music and art. Likewise, the Turkish Hearth was built in 1927–1930, as a national center for culture and art, where cultural programs and art performances were developed under the close supervision of Atatürk "who wished to foster elements of European culture while concurrently developing specifically Turkish forms."[39] For example, local performances of operas such as *Madame Butterfly* and *Tosca* were performed here sung in Turkish with all Turkish casts.

PROFANING ISLAM: THE ETHNOGRAPHY MUSEUM

The intervention of the secular state in the sacred realm of Islam is perhaps best illustrated at the Ethnography Museum, opened in 1930 upon Atatürk's orders to store Anatolian folk art and culture, consolidated as the basis of official nationalist policy.[40] The site for the museum was significant in that it was built on a prominent hill marking the threshold between the old and the new Ankara. The citadel behind its back and overlooking the new cityscape, the Ethnography Museum stood as if to show the new direction for the country. The Ottoman and Islamic past was to be left behind, and the future lay in the new, secular, and modern.

The Ethnography Museum building was placed on a stone terrace with a bronze statue of Atatürk at its center. The iconic figure of Atatürk on his horse in military clothing stood as the eternal guardian of the museum and the "cultural values of Anatolia" that were on display inside. The main exhibit consisted of various objects, clothing, and household items from different parts of Anatolia mostly used in agricultural production, ornaments, wedding ceremonies, or other activities, as well as artifacts from Roman and Hittite excavations from around Ankara. What were also on display were objects and artifacts confiscated from the Sufi orders and dervish lodges that were closed down only a couple of years ago in 1925. A majority of these items were ordinary things such as articles of clothing, furniture, rugs, and kilims that were still in use in daily life.[41]

By placing on exhibit Hittite and Roman artifacts, the state is dictating what particular histories are to be selected as constitutive of national history, hence displaying its authority and control over history and time. Likewise, the collection of rural artifacts from different parts of Anatolia serves to manifest state power over its own territory. What are perhaps unrelated cultural practices scattered around the region are brought together under the dome of a national museum at the capital and exhibited as constitutive of national culture, again serving to create a sense of a single nation with a unique and monolithic culture living on unified territory. These archeological and cultural artifacts serve to display the power and capability of the state to collect and bring together, under a national frame, things that are otherwise temporally and spatially disconnected, unrelated, and not readily accessible.

What is rather unexpected to be on exhibit in an ethnography museum alongside such cultural and archeological artifacts are the common items collected from Sufi orders and lodges after they were banned and all their property confiscated in 1925. Unlike the other artifacts, these items are in fact most easily accessible and have no special value other than the significance of the places from where they were brought. But the exhibit of these ordinary items in a museum alongside the historically and culturally significant artifacts serves to give just this impression, that they are indeed items that were previously inaccessible by virtue of being under the authority of Islam. Their museumification serves to display the power of the new state to break into the sacred realm of Islam and render it profane and a thing of the past that is neatly placed on exhibit in a museum. Hence, what was really museumified here was what Şerif Mardin calls "heterodox Islam" that had served to organize daily life under the Ottoman rule.[42]

In sum, the Ethnography Museum is another instance by which the foundational principles, nationalism, secularism, and modernity are institutionalized. The collection of items on exhibit at the Ethnography Museum is a testament to the power and authority of the state to control time, space, and religion, thereby constituting itself as the agent of the nation, its history, its space, and its relation to God.

ATATÜRK'S MONUMENT/MAUSOLEUM ANITKABIR

The Victory Monument at Ulus Square remained as the symbolic center of the nation well after the death of Atatürk in 1938, until his Mausoleum was opened in 1953.[43] Atatürk had already become the iconic figure representing the nation while he was alive, so his death in a way completed this metamorphosis that turned him into a total incarnation of the nation. His statues, busts, and pictures proliferated everywhere, placed in squares, parks, schoolyards, and public offices inscribed as the mark of the nation to express an allegiance to the founding principles laid by him. As such, the search for his burial site turned into a search for the most significant ground in Ankara. The parliamentary commission that was set up in 1939 to oversee the building of a mausoleum for Atatürk considered several locations before deciding on Çankaya, where the residential headquarters of the president is located. However, after a member of the commission suggested Rasattepe, which was on one of the few hills in the area that would allow for the monument to be visible from all around the city, and made a moving speech, the commission unanimously selected this location for the building of the mausoleum. The words that brought the commission around were,

> Rasattepe is like a star in the middle of a crescent reaching from Dikmen to Etlik [the southern and the northern corners of the city respectively]. The city of Ankara is the body of the crescent. If Anıtkabir is built here, it will be as if the city of Ankara has opened its arms wide to welcome Atatürk in its bosom. Hence, we will have Atatürk rest right in the middle of the star of the crescent on our flag.[44]

What used to be an empty piece of hill was now laden with such national significance, since it was designated to be Atatürk's burial site. The mausoleum was to become an inscription upon this hill, thereby marking the new center of the capital and the country, as well as the center of the national flag, which mapped the nation upon the city of Ankara, at the heart of which Atatürk's body would be resting.

Hence, Atatürk's Mausoleum complex, Anıtkabir, was to become the new symbolic center of the nation where all official ceremonies would be held and visitors would find a sense of citizenship. Paying respect to Atatürk's tomb would be the ultimate sign of allegiance to the nation. The project competition for the building of the mausoleum sought to further institute the image of Atatürk as the embodiment of the nation. The competition brief stated that the mausoleum should commemorate Atatürk "in whose person the entire nation is symbolized."[45]

Among twenty-seven competing projects, the Onat-Arda proposal won because theirs was the only project that "reflected the antique roots of Anatolia" and was not confined to Ottoman-Islamic traditions.[46] The architectural plans for the Mausoleum were changed many times after the initial project was accepted, eventually yielding an eclectic architectural style that is interpreted as being universalist beyond the confines of time and any given style, which is itself taken as a mark of modernity. Yet several features of Anıtkabir make references to specific historical-cultural contexts, such as the Hittite lions lined up along the processional alley leading to the main courtyard, the classical Greco-Roman temple style used in the mausoleum proper, the designs and carvings on the walls that are from Anatolian rug designs, or the use of a sarcophagus to symbolize Atatürk's tomb that is erected as the altar for visitors and the idea of a "mausoleum" itself that make references to pre-Islamic Greek-Anatolian traditions. These references express a deliberate disassociation from Ottoman-Islamic traditions and instead associate the Turkish nation with classical "world" civilization. In explaining their "design philosophy," the architects note that Turkish history "resides not in the Middle Ages but in the common sources of the classical world" and is a Mediterranean

Figure 7.4. Atatürk's Mausoleum Anıtkabir standing as the site of national pilgrimage and initiation into citizenship. From Nurettin Can Gülekli, *Anıtkabir Rehberi* [Anıtkabir Guide] (Ankara, Turkey: Kültür Bakanlığı Yayınları, 1993).

civilization that "starts with Sumerians and Hittites and merges with the life of many civilizations from Central Asia to the depths of Europe."[47]

The vast courtyard extending in front of the Mausoleum proper, called the Hall of Honor, was built as a ceremonial area to hold 15,000 people, facing the flight of stairs leading up to the mausoleum, which is lined up by reliefs on both sides depicting the War of Independence. The open courtyard is surrounded by ten towers, each symbolizing and named after a significant aspect of the foundation of the Republic, such as freedom, victory, peace, liberty, or national oath. The walls of these towers and the entrance to the Mausoleum are lined with several reliefs representing the suffering of the Turkish nation before the founding of the Republic, the War of Independence, the heroism of the anonymous soldier, the sacrifice of the peasant woman, and the might of the Turkish republic as opposed to the inadequacy of the Ottoman rule. These reliefs together with several statements by Atatürk inscribed on the walls throughout Anıtkabir concertedly provide a narrative of official national history. Anıtkabir was erected as the ultimate national monument that narrates the Turkish nation into being.

KOCATEPE MOSQUE: COMBINING ISLAM AND MODERNITY

While monumental structures of modernity and nationalism, such as the parliament, Ankara Palas, the Ethnography Museum, or the Turkish Hearth building were mushrooming in Ankara, the need for an official place of worship increasingly became evident. The project to build a mosque in Ankara started in 1944, very soon after Atatürk's death and the initiation of the Anıtkabir Mausoleum project. A committee was formed under the Directorate of Religious Affairs to oversee the project competition for the building of a mosque in Yenişehir, the district created as the model residential area to represent the modern lifestyle of the Republic. The idea was to build a mosque that would "adequately represent the Republic."[48] However, representing the modern secular aspirations of the Republic in a mosque soon proved to be quite a difficult undertaking. Building such a "state mosque," as it later came to be called, did not really contradict the official understanding of secularism and, in fact, was a direct outcome of its implementation. Indeed, by building such a mosque itself, the state would be keeping the central place of worship under its direct control. However, even though the necessity was recognized, the state was nevertheless reluctant in diverting already scarce funds to such a project, since it was not seen as a priority. Furthermore, the committee could not reach an agreement as to what constituted the acceptable architectural style for such a "modern" mosque. Hence none of the candidates in the first project competition were granted a prize.

As a result of controversy over its style, location, underlying ideological concerns, and related financial problems, the building of the mosque staggered for more than four decades and was finally opened in 1987. The current location of the Kocatepe Mosque was decided during the conservative Democrat Party government in 1956, which also initiated a new project competition and provided additional funds. Under the Democrat Party, the building of the mosque became a statement against the previous government's implementation of secularism.[49] Hence Kocatepe Mosque was built on a central hilltop right across from Atatürk's Mausoleum, where it is equally visible from all over the city, emerging as a salient rival symbol in representing the identity of Ankara and the nation, disrupting the centrality of the Mausoleum.

Figure 7.5. Kocatepe Mosque, informally noted as the "state mosque."

The controversy over the architectural style of the mosque took even longer to resolve. None of the thirty-six projects in the second competition in 1957 were found worthy either, except for the Dalokay-Tekelioğlu project, which was only found "feasible." However, after construction started in 1963, this project was also dropped for controversy over the endurance of the outer shell as well as the appropriateness of its modernist style. Finally, in the third competition held in 1967, the Tayla-Uluengin project won first prize with its classical Ottoman style. At the end of a long arduous process stretching over twenty-three years to find the right project, what ended up as the style to most adequately "represent the Republic" was the imitation of sixteenth-century Ottoman architecture that was preferred over the modernist style of the previous project. This is possibly one of the reasons why the project was never fully endorsed by the state and continually suffered a lack of finances. This controversy over the style of the mosque is an excellent illustration of the controversy over Turkish national identity: What is the status and place of Islam going to be in a country that aspires to be modern and Western? While architects such as Dalokay felt that it was possible to represent Islam through modernist styles in architecture, officials rejected this possibility and instead turned to traditionalist styles inspired from Ottoman architecture as the best possible way to represent Islam. The controversy over the appropriateness of Kocatepe Mosque in representing the Republic and the dispute over the role and status of Islam in Turkey which the Kocatepe Mosque symbolizes continues to this day.[50]

Kocatepe Mosque today is presented as a national place of worship that was built "combining sixteenth-century aesthetics with twentieth-century technology."[51] While Ottoman architectural styles and internal design was employed to represent Islam, modernity was represented through the use of technology, such as the elevators in the minarets, the mosque's conference room with high-tech lighting and speaker systems, or the central heating installed under the main prayer hall. The three-story megamarket and parking lot complex underneath the mosque arguably represent the ruling capitalist-consumerist ideology with a tint of Islam, marking the dominant understanding of modernity at the time.[52]

The Kocatepe Mosque is also prided for being the largest covered mosque in the Middle East and the largest domed temple in the world. With its capacity to hold 24,000 people for prayers at any one time, the mosque is certainly a grand place of worship intended for a massive community. Just as the effect of the Hall of Honor in Atatürk's Mausoleum, the vastness of the space conjures up a mass subject, similarly invoking a sense of national belonging, albeit through a different kind of affiliation based on Islam. This subject is invoked as national and not as Islamic because the audience that is addressed in the brochures, announcements, and sermons in the mosque is the "Turkish nation" and not the larger

Islamic community (the *umma*). This address is illustrated in the brochure distributed at the opening ceremony in 1987, where it is noted that "the streaming [of the faithful from surrounding provinces and regions] to Kocatepe, the greatest place of worship of the Republican period . . . explains the yearning of the Turkish nation for growing and uniting."[53] As suggested here, what makes Kocatepe a "state mosque" is not only that it was built using state funds and by a state agency, but also that it functions as a public space that serves to invoke a sense of national unity using Islam as a base for homogeneity.

In sum, the building of the Kocatepe Mosque by the state serves to institutionalize secularism by bringing the presence and practice of Islam (in this case, the regulation of the act of prayer as one of its essential rituals) under the direct and exclusive control of the secular state. This unprecedented understanding and implementation of secularism has been contested throughout the twentieth century by autonomous Islamist discourses, which have at times influenced policymakers and induced modifications in its implementation, such as during the Democrat Party period in the 1950s. The controversy over the location, architectural style, and the financing of Kocatepe Mosque is actually a direct result of this controversial status of Islam in the foundational ideology of the Republic.

CONCLUSION

This chapter examines the ways in which a city is conjured up so as to give materiality to the prevailing notion of modernity and the related sense of nationhood. The building of Ankara as the capital city of the new Turkish nation-state illustrates the ways in which the construction of a modern nation-state and the establishment of modernity and secularism as its founding principles is achieved through the building of the city and the engineering of its spaces, the erection of monuments, the endorsement of national architectural styles and construction techniques, or the monitoring of the use of public places.

The official discourse of modernity has altered with important regime changes after the coming to power of contending political ideologies pursuing different modernization projects, which in turn has resulted in corresponding transformations of the city of Ankara and its spaces. One of the most profound changes has been the decline of the famous Ulus Square as the celebrated center of the city as well as the nation and the shifting of the city center to Kızılay around the 1950s, which still remains the center of the capital city. Interestingly, there are no significant public buildings that mark Kızılay Square, and there is no Republic Monument or another statue of Atatürk marking the center of the square either. The name Kızılay (Red Crescent) was given to the square because the central building of the official Turkish Red Crescent stood in one of the corners of the square but was later taken down in the 1990s to be replaced by a shopping center. In other words, the only central square in Turkey that has substantially deviated from the national norm on urban design has been the one in the capital city where it lacks salient marks of official ideology. There is a monument in Kızılay, the Güven (Trust) Monument depicting Atatürk as a central figure, but it stands not in the center but in Güven Park, extending on one side of the square and is not even readily visible from the square.

Since Ulus Square was constructed as the material articulation of modernity as a founding principle, it is possible to interpret the decline of Ulus in favor of Kızılay, as a shift in the prevailing understanding of modernity as a norm constituting the Turkish polity. Indeed, this shift from Ulus to Kızılay is an excellent illustration of the ways in which the changes in the ideological composition of the dominant notion of modernity have found their material expression in transformations in the city and the arrangement of its spaces. During the early Republican years, the dominant understanding of modernity was one that identified it with a European-based (especially French) notion of civilization and high culture, which was reflected in the making of Ankara around Ulus Square; the first major ideological shift came in the 1950s with the advent of the multiparty system and the Democrat Party regime. The Democrat Party's political project, which has been referred to as a "technocratic ideology," was indeed an alternative discourse of modernity that took technological and economic development as the primary defining mark of modernization.[54] This new vision that saw the United States as the bearer of the true ideals of modernity, now defined around industrial development and capitalism, replaced the former official discourse. The shifting of Ankara's center from Ulus to Kızılay was a direct consequence of the new conceptualization of modernity introduced by the Democrat Party. This shift was initiated by the building of a new business complex (Ulus İş Hanı) in Ulus Square in 1955, thereby celebrating the idea of modernity as economic development and capitalism, which overshadowed all the other structures and monuments in the vicinity that represented modernity as a high culture and a way of life. The Victory Monument was also moved from the center of Ulus Square to the front plaza of this complex, thereby radically shifting the central emphasis of the square from the monument of the nation to this new business building. With the shift of the core ideals of modernity from high culture and civilization to capitalism and economic development, the significance of the Ulus area as the hub of social life where modernity as a lifestyle was displayed started to decline. Simultaneously, Kızılay was rapidly emerging as the main business district and becoming the center of city life. The moving of the parliament to a location closer to Kızılay in 1961 and the erection of the first high-rise in Turkey, again as a business complex erected here, made Kızılay the new city center. This high-rise not only represented advanced technology in building construction, but also paid homage to capitalism with its busy offices housing private businesses. The resulting relocation of the city center from Ulus to Kızılay symbolized the recentering of the nation and the displacement of the central norm of modernity from civilization to technological development and capitalism as symbolized by business centers and high-rises.

The dominant understanding of modernity changed again in the 1980s after late Turgut Özal's Motherland Party came to power in 1983, introducing local elements and traditional styles into the conceptualization of modernity accompanied by the celebration of consumerism.[55] Suddenly the most important and popular structures in the country as well as in Ankara became shopping centers and malls, emerging as the new temples of modernism. It was at this time that the project to build a "modern" shopping center in place of the old Kızılay building that gave the square its name was initiated. It was also at this time that one of the most prominent buildings in Ankara, the Atakule Shopping and Business Complex, was constructed, which was built as a towering structure standing atop Çankaya hill overlooking the city. Atakule is not only visible from all parts of the city, but also is now the second figure alongside the Kocatepe Mosque that constitutes the city's emblem that is engraved all around the city.

Arguably, the prevailing understanding of modernity is undergoing yet another transformation at the turn of the century with the coming to power of the AK Party that broke off from the former Islamist Refah Party under the leadership of Istanbul's former mayor Recep Tayyip Erdoğan, marked by a search for ways to wed Islam and modernity. Each of these ideological shifts has been articulated in the use of and rearrangement of public spaces, erection of new monuments, building of new structures, relocation or sometimes even the removal of statues and monuments, or renaming of streets, avenues, and boulevards. In other words, each ideological shift in power brought a different sense of nationhood and modernity, similarly using the city and its spaces as the medium for their material manifestation.

Another important change in the ideological climate as reflected on the city and its spaces is the Islamist interventions of the 1990s, when Islamist city administrations came to power in both Istanbul and Ankara after the 1994 local elections.[56] One of the most controversial interventions was a project developed by the Istanbul city administration under the mayoralty of Recep Tayyip Erdoğan to build a colossal mosque in Taksim Republic Square that would overshadow the secular monuments and buildings circumventing the square. This project was severely criticized by secularist circles and was finally rebuffed by the state. Another similar intervention has been the changing of Ankara's emblem by the Islamist city administration from the Hittite sun, representing the pre-Islamic Anatolian national roots, to the current emblem that depicts a mosque (arguably the Kocatepe Mosque) placed within a crescent, again making a reference to Islam. These interventions illustrate the ways in which the city and its spaces continue to be the main medium through which not only the dominant understandings of modernity and nationhood find their material expression, but also so do their contestations.

NOTES

All Turkish to English translations are by the author unless otherwise noted.

1. Stuart Hall, David Held, and Tony McGrew, eds., *Modernity and Its Futures* (Cambridge, UK: Polity Press, 1992), 2.

2. William Connolly, *Political Theory and Modernity* (Basil: Blackwell, 1988), 4.

3. Marshall Berman, *All That Is Solid Melts into Air: The Experience of Modernity* (New York: Penguin Books, 1988), 132.

4. I use modernism in this essay not as a specific architectural style or art form, but in the political sense, as in the ideology of modernity. The word "Modernlik" (modernism) is extensively used in Turkish, not as an art form, but as the ideology of modernity.

5. Ankara is estimated to have had a population of about 30,000 in 1920. Within two decades, this number had increased tenfold to a soaring 300,000. By the 1990s, it reached 3,000,000.

6. Falih Rıfkı Atay, *The Atatürk I Knew,* trans. Geoffrey Lewis, (Istanbul: Yapi ve Kredi Bankasi, Binbirdirek Matbaacilik, 1981), 233–34, cited in Turkish Daily News, October 13,1996, electronic edition: http://www.turkishdailynews.com/old_editions/10_13_96/feature.htm.

7. Cited in Tuğrul Akçura, *Ankara: Türkiye Cumhuriyeti'nin Başkenti Hakkinda Monografik bir Araştirma,* (Ankara: ODTU Mimarlık Fakültesi Yayınları, no. 16, 1971): 28.

8. Suna Kili, *Türk Devrim Tarihi*, 3rd ed. (Istanbul: Tekin Yayinevi, 1982), 66–69.

9. Cited in Mehmet Sarıoğlu, *"Ankara" Bir Modernleşme Öyküsü (1919–1945)* [Ankara: A Story of Modernization (1919–1945)] (Ankara: TC Kültür Bakanlığı Kültür Eserleri, 2001), 103.

10. For a detailed account of the Hat Law, see Alev Çınar, *Modernity, Islam, and Secularism in Turkey: Bodies, Places, and Time* (Minneapolis: University of Minnesota Press, 2005).

11. Cited in Mehmet Sarıoğlu, *"Ankara,"* 103.

12. Mardin establishes that because of the multiple functions of Islam in the Ottoman system as a legal frame for governance, a discourse of legitimization, a basis for social solidarity, and a system of social justice, the formation of a modern nation-state necessitated the formulation of an ideology that would replace Islam and fulfill these social and political functions. Mardin suggests that secularism as the founding ideology was developed to serve such multiple functions (Şerif Mardin, "Ideology and Religion in the Turkish Revolution," *International Journal of Middle East Studies* 2 (1971): 197–211).

13. For a more detailed account of the role and place of secularism during the founding years of the Turkish Republic, see Çınar, *Modernity, Islam, and Secularism in Turkey.*

14. Cited in Zeynep Kezer, "The Making of a National Capital: Ideology and Socio-Spatial Practices in Early Republican Ankara" (PhD diss., University of California, Berkeley, 1999), 212.

15. The Turkish ezan did not become a law until 1941, which was then annulled in 1950, and Arabic was resumed (*Diyanet Aylık Dergi,* no. 9, [September 1991]: 502–04).

16. Inci Yalım, "Ulus Devletin Kamusal Alanda Meşruiyet Aracı: Toplumsal Belleğin Ulus Meydanı üzerinden Kurgulanma Çabası," in *Başkent Üzerine Mekan-Politik Tezler: Ankara'nın Kamusal Yüzleri,* ed. Arif Güven Sargın, 157–214 (İstanbul: İletisim Yayıncılık, 2002), 194; see also Kezer, *The Making of a National Capital,* 213–15.

17. Sibel Bozdoğan, *Modernism and Nation Building: Turkish Architectural Culture in the Early Republic* (Seattle: University of Washington Press, 2001), 132–3.

18. Kezer, *The Making of a National Capital,* 134.

19. "We built an iron web across the motherland" is a line from the Tenth Anniversary March commemorating the tenth year of the foundation of the republic and referring to the network of railways built across the country.

20. Kezer, *The Making of a National Capital,* 121.

21. For a detailed account of the transformation of Ataturk into a cult hero figure and the proliferation of his statues, monuments, and busts, see Bozdoğan, *Modernism and Nation Building,* 282–6.

22. Yalım, "Ulus Devletin," 184.

23. Bozdoğan, *Modernism and Nation Building,* 16–55.

24. Ilhan Tekeli, "The Social Context of the Development of Architecture in Turkey," in *Modern Turkish Architecture,* ed. Renata Holod and Ahmet Evin, 9–33 (Philadelphia: University of Pennsylvania Press, 1984), 16.

25. Here, modernism is used as an ideology in the hands of the modernizing state, rather than a style or a phase in architectural or art history.

26. Cited in Afife Batur, "To Be Modern: Search for a Republican Architecture," in *Modern Turkish Architecture,* ed. Renata Holod and Ahmet Evin, 68–93 (Philadelphia: University of Pennsylvania Press, 1984), 76.

27. Yakup Kadri Karaosmanoğlu, *Ankara,* 6th ed. (İstanbul: İletişim Yayınları, 1997), 134.

28. Tekeli, "The Social Context," 17.

29. Karaosmanoğlu, *Ankara,* 134.

30. Sibel Bozdoğan, "The Predicament of Modernism in Turkish Architectural Culture," in *Rethinking Modernity and National Identity in Turkey,* ed. Sibel Bozdoğan and Resat Kasaba, 133–56 (Seattle: University of Washington Press, 1997), 138.

31. Kezer, *The Making of a National Capital,* 141–42.

32. Cited in Kezer, *The Making of a National Capital,* 138.

33. For a detailed account of the transformations in Istanbul and Taksim Square in particular, see Çınar, *Modernity, Islam, and Secularism in Turkey,* 110–21.

34. Yıldırım Yavuz and Suha Özkan, "Finding a National Idiom: The First National Style," in *Modern Turkish Architecture,* ed. Renata Holod and Ahmet Evin, 51–67 (Philadelphia: University of Pennsylvania Press, 1984), 56.

35. Yavuz and Özkan, "Finding a National Idiom," 56.

36. Yalım, "Ulus Devletin," 189.

37. Mehmet Kemal, *Türkiye'nin Kalbi: Ankara* (Istanbul: Çağdaş Yayınları, 1983), 62–66.

38. Yalım, "Ulus Devletin," 195.

39. Yavuz and Özkan, "Finding a National Idiom," 64.

40. Ibid., 63.

41. Zeynep Kezer, "Familiar Things in Strange Places: The Museumification of the Religious for the Creation of a Modern National Landscape in Early Republican Turkey" (unpublished paper presented at the MESA Annual Conference, Providence, R.I., 1996).

42. Mardin differentiates between orthodox Islam as the official religion of the Ottoman state practiced under the authority of the ruling ulema and heterodox Islam consisting of the wide range of sufi orders scattered around the Empire which is deeply ingrained in daily life, not only regulating ordinary daily activity, but also serving as a system of meaning and a buffer between the imperial state and the common folk (Mardin, "Ideology and Religion").

43. The decision to build the Monument in Anıttepe (then Rasattepe) was taken in 1939, a year after Atatürk passed away. The construction started in 1944 and ended in 1953. On November 10, 1953, Atatürk's body was brought to and buried in a special chamber within the Mausoleum.

44. Nurettin Can Gülekli, *Anıtkabir Rehberi* [Anıtkabir Guide] (Ankara: Kültür Bakanlığı Yayinlari, 1993), 14–15.

45. Cited in Bozdoğan, *Modernism and Nation Building,* 286.

46. Afife Batur, *"Anıtkabir" Cumhuriyet Dönemi Türkiye Ansiklopedisi,* vol. 5 (Istanbul: Iletisim Yayinlari, 1983), 1392.

47. Cited in Bozdoğan, *Modernism and Nation Building,* 289.

48. Sait Şan, "Camilerin Önemi, Toplum Hayatindaki Yeri Ve Kocatepe Camii'nin Ibadete Açılışı" *Diyanet Aylık Dergi* (August 2001), accessible online at http://www.diyanet.gov.tr/DIYANET/2001aylik/agustos/ayinkonusu.htm#.

49. The previous government was lead by the Republican People's Party (CHP), which was founded by Atatürk and ruled Turkey in a single-party regime until 1950.

50. For a detailed account of the controversy over the role of Islam in Turkey, see Çınar, *Modernity, Islam, and Secularism in Turkey.*

51. Ibid.

52. This is the neoconservative Motherland Party period under Turgut Özal's leadership (1983–1993).

53. Cited in Michael Meeker, "Once There Was, Once There Wasn't: National Monuments and Interpersonal Exchange," in *Rethinking Modernity and National Identity in Turkey,* ed. Sibel Bozdoğan and Reşat

Kasaba, trans. Michael Meeker, 157–91 (Seattle: University of Washington Press, 1997), 181.

54. Nilüfer Göle, "Engineers: 'Technocratic Democracy,'" in *Turkey and the West: Changing Political and Cultural Identities,* ed. Metin Heper et al., 199–218 (New York: I. B. Tauris & Co. Ltd., 1993); Göle examines how in the 1950s the notion of modernity changed from civilizational/cultural terms to acquire a new meaning with the advent of the Democrat Party regime, which took modernization as industrial development and technological advancement.

55. For a brief account of this shift and its effects on architecture and the urban scene see, Bozdoğan, "The Predicament of Modernism."

56. For a detailed account of these Islamist challenges and interventions, see Çınar, *Modernity, Islam, and Secularism in Turkey.*

8

URBAN SPACE, NATIONAL TIME, AND POSTCOLONIAL DIFFERENCE

The Steel Towns of India

Srirupa Roy

A tremendous amount of building is taking place in India and an attempt should be made to give it a right direction . . . so that new types may come out, new designs, new types, new ideas, and out of that amalgam something new and good will emerge.

—Jawaharlal Nehru (1949)[1]

Durgapur Steel Township today presents a notable example of lapse.

—Town and Country Planning Organization,
Government of India (1971)[2]

In 1957, the Indian state announced its second five-year plan. Explicitly borrowing from both the form and the content of Soviet-style economic planning, a program of nation-building through heavy industrialization was proclaimed that committed significant financial, political, and human resources to rapid state-sponsored industrial growth and the creation of large-scale projects such as hydroelectric stations; steel plants; locomotive, cement, and fertilizer factories; and shipyards. The mandate of the second plan (and the third plan with its continued emphasis on heavy industrialization) also included the building of several industrial townships in areas adjacent to the plan projects. The rationale for township development was expressed in terms that went far beyond practical or utilitarian considerations of providing housing for workers. They were described as entirely new kinds of places inhabited by new kinds of people who would directly participate in the grand project of building the nation: nation-builders in both the narrowest sense of physically enabling the manufacture of new industrial products and infrastructure and in the broadest sense of becoming the ideal "producer-patriots" of the new nation. In the words of a brochure issued by the Steel Authority of India (SAIL) to commemorate three decades of the Indian steel industry, "Nehru wanted the steel plants [and the associated steel townships] to be special places, inhabited by special people."[3]

If the postcolonial nation took the abstract form of a "dream we all agreed to dream,"[4] then industrial townships like Durgapur, Bokaro, Bhilai, and Rourkela, were its grounded and inhabited "dreamworlds,"[5] locations in which a dramatic and substantial reworking of existing spaces, times, and subjectivities could take place. As the state's Town and Country Planning Organization noted in a report on Durgapur steel township in West Bengal, an industrial township built to house the workers of the steel plant in the area, the expectation was that Durgapur would be a "grown-up city," its adulthood or coming-of-age marked by its "well planned nature" and by the fact that the state would, through the provision of superior civic amenities, enable the existence of a "better civic life."[6] Moreover, unlike the vexed task of planning and developing already existing and inhabited cities, the activity of planning and developing these industrial townships or "steel towns" offered the nation-state an opportunity to realize its vision *ex novo*. Located in backward and underdeveloped areas of the country, far from the large metropolitan centers of colonial India, steel towns would enable the postcolonial state to break new ground.

Fifteen years later, utopia was reworked as dystopia. Just as the promise of the steel towns had been expressed in reference to a larger scale, as a beacon held out to the nation, so was the problem of the steel town framed in national terms, as a problem of and for the nation. Thus, by the early 1970s, specific examples of crime, corruption, communal riots, residential segregation, labor unrest, and the inadequate supply and distribution of essential municipal services in steel towns were cited as material evidence for the multiple failures of the nation-building project, as proof of what happens when the pace of development is too rapid or when plans are carelessly implemented. The brave new citizen had become a "victim of haphazard and unplanned growth and uncongenial environment," the new city a place of "low and uneconomical densities, wastage of space and inability to optimally utilize existing infrastructure, ill-distributed facilities, loose planning, monotonous housing."[7]

The dreamworld of the steel town was renamed as a catastrophe, now cited as a "notable example of lapse" rather than a manifestation of the Nehruvian promise to realize "something new and something good."[8]

The journey of the steel town from promise to problem is the subject of this chapter. The interest here is not so much in the reasons for this downfall or in proclaiming what its definitive symptoms might be, but instead in the conditions of possibility and the stakes of such a narrative of the steel town as failed promise. How was the steel town produced as a dreamworld? What kinds of desires and expectations were invested in it, and what were the practices undertaken to realize the dream? What were the grounds on which its failure was proclaimed, and what were the solutions offered? Whose dreamworld or catastrophe was it anyway? Through addressing these questions, this chapter examines the spatial practices, locations, and dislocations that underwrite the formation of postcolonial nationalism.

I argue that the production of the urban as a specific kind of space inhabited by specific kinds of subjects is one of the central tasks to which the postcolonial project of building a sovereign, unified, and modern nation addresses itself. This goes against the grain of most discussions on the place of the urban in the postcolonial national imagination.[9] For instance, in the Indian context studies of Nehruvian nationalism have argued that the postcolonial moment is marked by a "frugal investment in the urban"[10] and that the legacy of the anticolonial movement and the shadow of the "Great Peasant" Gandhi[11] led to the village rather than the city being seen as the authentic heartland of India. Moreover, even when nationalism is seen to entail the valorization of "metropolitan modernity,"[12] this has been described in terms of a logic of abstract placelessness—the metropolis figuring as an idea or a symbol rather than a specific place targeted by specific sets of spatial practices. These arguments about the urban lack in the Nehruvian national imagination miss an important part of the picture, namely, the importance accorded to the spatial production of the *new urban*.

The Nehruvian state planned and developed several kinds of urban spaces from scratch: regional capital cities such as Chandigarh (Punjab) and Bhubaneswar (Orissa), refugee towns such as Faridabad, Nilokheri, Kalyani, and Ulhasnagar to rehabilitate the displaced people who had recently arrived from Pakistan, and industrial townships such as the steel towns of Bhilai, Bokaro, Rourkela, and Durgapur among others. These were all upheld as exemplary national spaces of the new India—spaces that would enable the birth of new citizens and bring forth the future of national time; spaces in which the state could foreground activities undertaken on behalf of the nation and thereby render visible its representative nature; and spaces in which the dream of "national integration" or the harmonious coexistence of diverse ethnic and religious groups would be realized. The new nation thus took shape in and through the production of the new urban.

By locating the discussion of the interrelationship between the urban and the national in the specific space of the steel town, the historical-metropolitan bias of urban studies is called into question—the conflation of the urban with the "big city" and the "old city." As this chapter suggests, the category of the urban is not exhausted by Bombay, Delhi, Calcutta, and Madras in the Indian context or, if we use a broader geopolitical canvas, by Istanbul, Paris, Karachi, New York, London, Mexico City, or Nairobi. In the formative years of the postcolonial nation, the urban spaces most celebrated by the discourses and practices of official nationalism had neither a significant geographic material nor a historical presence; they were instead unknown sites with unfamiliar and in many cases invented names, populated by relatively small numbers of people. While the spatial practices of colonialism were informed by strategies of centering—the building of capital cities that further replicated the centralizing imperative within their boundaries as the apex of colonial power rendered itself visible within newly demarcated city centers through the placement of imperial buildings, central promenades or avenues, parks, fountains, and monuments—postcolonial spatial practices were shaped by the imperative of decentering. Neither the capital city nor the borders of the nation-space were the primary objects of the nationalist gaze. Instead, it was to the "elsewheres" that lay between the center and the limits of the nation, to the new urban places filling in the abstract space of the national map, that postcolonial nationalism drew attention.

The main identity of the new urban was that of a new and state-made chronotope: a new space and a new time inaugurated by a new state. The formation of this statist chronotope entailed continual efforts to differentiate its physical location from the surrounding environment. The ground occupied by the new urban was cleared by inscribing a rigid boundary between what was inside and what was outside and by conceptualizing its site as a dehistoricized *terra nullius* or a blank slate upon which the state could freely realize its dreams on behalf of the nation. When dream turned to nightmare, this too was staged within the discrete, different, state-made time-space of the new urban. In both sets of understandings, dreamworld as well as catastrophe, the emphasis was on the radical estrangement of the new urban from its immediate environment and also from the "rest of the nation." The postcolonial nation thus took shape through spatial practices of differentiation and decentering rather than through the incorporation or subsumption of places within a seamless national whole.

To draw attention to these decentered elsewheres is not, however, to suggest that they are liberated from the "spatial incarceration"[13] of the nation—that the devolution of scale from the undifferentiated abstraction of the national to the specificity of the urban configures alternative structures and relations of power. This has been an implicit assumption of the recent body of scholarship that makes the persuasive case for locating citizenship in the city.[14] It is argued that a respatialization of citizenship offers new theoretical as well as political possibilities of thinking and acting beyond and against the "incarceration" of the nation and the deterritorializing practices and processes of national citizenship. Such discussions often draw upon and reproduce a dichotomous understanding of the relation between city and nation that is framed in terms of a difference between place and space. Thus to contrast the "irreducible antagonisms of the city" with the "abstractions of the nation-state" is to juxtapose the groundedness of urban place against the immateriality of national space. But what exactly is this ground occupied by the city—where and what is the city? How do we decide where the nation begins and the city ends, or where the city begins and the nation ends? To what extent and for whom is the urban a flexible, grounded, immediate community?

To address these questions is to examine the ways in which imaginations of the urban and the national are articulated within and against each other, producing the city as a particular kind of abstract and bounded national space with its own sets of exclusions and dislocations. The grounding of citizenship within the new urban was an integral component of the official nationalist imaginary in postcolonial India, practices of decentering and devolution were part and parcel of a centralized project of nation-building. Moreover, to produce the resident of the steel town first as ideal producer-patriot and then as failed citizen entailed an erasure of the lives, memories, and material practices of the inhabitants of the area, those for whom Bhilai, Bokaro, Rourkela, and Durgapur were lived place rather than exemplary space. Like the nation, the new urban thus excludes in order to include. This conclusion resonates well beyond the immediate case of Nehruvian nationalism and the Indian steel town, calling into question the "smaller is better" understanding of the urban, local, or subnational as spaces in which the constitutive exclusions of the nation form come undone.

New Amalgams

The origins of steel towns and industrial townships in India can be traced to the process of capital accumulation in the colonial period. Jamshedpur in eastern India was the first such planned settlement, built in the first decade of the twentieth century to house the workers of a steel plant located nearby. Subsequently, townships were also set up in the princely state[15] of Mysore and in Asansol, in conjunction with the development of steel industries in those areas. All of these townships, like the industrial projects with which they were associated, were developed primarily through the efforts of non-state or private capital—Jamshedpur was built by the firm of J. R. D. Tata, a prominent member of the indigenous colonial bourgeoisie, the Mysore complex reflected the capitalist aspirations of a princely state, and Asansol reflected the entrepreneurial activities of a private British firm, Burn and Company.[16]

In contrast, the steel towns built during the postcolonial period were all direct and exclusive creations of the national state.[17] They emerged within the framework of a state-led program of national development, not simply to house workers of steel plants, but workers of nationalized steel plants. Moreover, the manufacture of steel itself was invested with considerable national symbolic importance. Like other nodes in the Nehruvian "architecture of energy,"[18] steel was much more than mere industrial substance. Its production was an intrinsic part of the glorious task of "serving the nation," to quote the copy in a newspaper advertisement on the occasion of India's tenth Republic Day in 1953.[19] Postcolonial steel towns were thus sites in which the transition from the dependent colonial economy to the sovereign and planned national economy, from the unfree subject to the productive citizen proudly serving his or her nation, could be enacted in and through everyday practices—sites that, through owing their existence to the decisions and actions of the national state, proclaimed the birth of the sovereign nation.

The decision to build a series of steel townships was first announced in the context of the second five-year plan, and subsequent efforts at township planning and development were undertaken by the Hindustan Steel Company, a public sector corporation created by the national ministry of steel and mines to oversee the production of steel. The steel town was thus a state artifact in the most literal sense. It was built and supervised by the state, with every aspect of its existence, from its location to its street lighting, from local governance structures to the quality of fruits and vegetables being sold in its marketplaces determined by agencies of the national state. Moreover, being the creature of the state was also the chief identity of the steel town. Through an insistence on the steel town's *artificiality* or its centrally planned and "manufactured" existence, its *strangeness* or disconnection from the surrounding environment, and its *newness* or the fact that before it came into being there was nothing there, the steel town was built to bear witness to the agency of its creator. Like the other institutional and cultural-ideological innovations introduced in the early postindependence period, the building of steel towns was thus shaped by the imperative of "state visibility" or the effort to establish the difference of postcolonial India through making visible the representative activities undertaken by the newly sovereign state.

The first steel plant was built in Rourkela in the state of Orissa. Bhilai in Madhya Pradesh, Durgapur in West Bengal, and Bokaro in Bihar soon followed. The locations of these industrial complexes (plants along with residential townships) were largely understood to be empty. For instance, accounts of the sites in which the townships were developed describe how the advantages and disadvantages of its natural topography influenced the layout and design of the plan: the ways in which planners could take advantage of the natural incline of Bokaro to develop storm water drainage systems,[20] and how the existence of "beautiful and high hills" around the area of the proposed township of Rourkela would serve as an "excellent buffer to maintain the quiet character of the town from the noise of the steel plant, the state highway, and the main Calcutta-Bombay railway line."[21] In these accounts, the encounter between the planned township and its natural environment is staged in terms of the present—a present that is expected to bring forth a new and different future and that bears no traces of anything, anyone, or any place that came before.

But from these descriptions of the blank natural slate on which the steel township realized itself—the story of the encounter between the urban plan and nature, fleeting glimpses of other presences emerged. Thus, the land acquired for the development of Bokaro township was described to be "partly under intensive cultivation of paddy."[22] In another instance, the story of the development of the industrial township of Chittaranjan in West Bengal, built in 1951 in association with the locomotive manufacturing factory established there by the railway ministry, mentions in passing that people from the eight villages of Sundarpahari, Amaladahi, Fatehpur, Durgandi, Beramuri, Simjuri, Namkoshia, and Uparkeshia were displaced in the process of acquiring land for construction. Subsequently, three of the residential sectors of Chittaranjan township were named after these villages.[23] Is there a Sundarpahari, an Amaladahi, or a Fatehpur elsewhere? Did the villagers who left their names behind as they were relocated outside the urban area come up with new naming practices? These questions went unanswered in the official narratives, where the birth of the new urban was invariably described as an act of location rather than dislocation.

However, literal and metaphoric acts of dislocation and insulation were critical to the establishment of the steel town and to its symbolic significance as an exemplary national space. With all of the steel townships and steel plants built in areas where there was a high concentration of *adivasi* (indigenous-tribal) populations, the displacement of these groups and the rejection of their customary and collective claims to land was an integral part of the urban development process. Now placed outside the steel town and the steel plant, the indigenous population could only enter the areas in which it had previously lived as temporary "unskilled labor" in the plant and as domestic servants in the township. For instance, the Bauri community living in the areas outside the Bokaro township worked as maids, rickshaw pullers, and truck loaders. Within the steel plant, they were primarily employed in temporary positions or in "Grade IV" services as orderlies and sweepers.[24] There were thus significant numbers of people for whom the encounter with the nation-state was experienced as force, dispossession, "destitution,"[25] and insecurity. The fact that these experiences unfolded at a historical moment otherwise characterized by the widespread support and legitimacy of the Nehruvian project is a reminder that the character and effect of state power is more mixed and variable than uniform and that the authority of the nation-state is secured in multiple ways, harnessing registers of consent and affirmation as well as those of coercion and fear.

After being emptied in this manner, the spaces of the steel town were subsequently filled with the presence and the future promise of steel. The repletion took place in several ways. First, urban planning decisions about how much land to acquire and how many houses to build were shaped by a single calculation: How many workers does it take to produce one million tons of steel ingots, the initial production target assigned to each plant? Thus, the Town and Country Planning Organization estimated that 7,500 workers would be employed in the pursuit of the one million ton goal, and an "additional 2,500 persons will be required as secondary workers to cater to the various needs of 7,500 primary workers." Taking an average family size of five as the benchmark, planners set about the task of developing houses, shopping centers, schools, hospitals, police stations, parks, and entertainment centers for a community of 50,000 people.[26] Projections of the future growth of the towns were similarly shaped by calculations about increases in steel production.

Second, the question of proximity to or distance from steel informed determinations of the city limits and also the design of roads and transportation systems: How could these enable the ease and efficiency of journeys to and from the steel plant? For instance, the "circulation plan" for Rourkela—the layout of roads within the township—placed a "ring road" along its "main spine" that would connect the township to the steel plant, the railway station, and the highways beyond. All other roads within the town wound their way to this central avenue, the chief imperative being that each worker's house should be no more than a short walk away from any arterial road and consequently from the public transport vehicles of the steel plant.[27] At the same time, too much proximity was a bad thing. A critical distance from the "noise of the steel plant" also needed to be maintained, whether through the utilization of features of the natural landscape as buffers (such as the hills around Rourkela township) or through placing the township on another side of the railroad tracks or the highway. Both sets of considerations entailed understanding Rourkela in relation to steel.

Third, hierarchies of work were directly mapped onto the landscape of inhabitation. The development of different types of housing and their allotment among the residents were determined by the salary structures of the steel plant. As Benegal observes in the case of Bokaro township, "the size and location of a living quarter is directly proportional to the salary of the occupant. The cost of the house is recovered over a period of time by a 10% monthly deduction of salary."[28] In some townships, the spatial layout of the entire town reflected the relative earning power of its residents, since houses belonging to different socioeconomic categories were segregated into separate and "self-sufficient" residential sectors. In others, a conscious effort was made to ensure a form of (gradual) mixing—thus Grades A, B, and C would be clustered together in one residential block and the next three tiers of the socioeconomic scale in another.

Taken together, these three features of the steel town—its location, its roads, and its houses—defined its identity as a town of and for steel and consequently as a paradigmatically national space, given the central significance of steel in the postcolonial national imaginary. The nationalized production of steel symbolized one of the central pillars of Nehruvian nationalism: developmentalism or the progress and growth of the nation through the planned guidance of the state. The spaces of Rourkela, Bhilai, Bokaro, and Durgapur were also the sites for the realization of other (and related) aspects of postcolonial national desires, such as the Nehruvian insistence on newness as a defining characteristic of India and Indianness. In the Nehruvian imaginary, the newness of postcolonial India was to be its most distinctive feature and was juxtaposed against the colonial and precolonial past of "static conditions" and the resulting "weakness" of India. To quote Nehru: "[e]ven before the British came, we had become static. In fact, the British came because we are static. A society which ceases to change ceases to go ahead, necessarily becomes weak."[29] In contrast, India after 1947 would be marked by change and the relentless drive to move forward—impulses that would necessarily strengthen the nation.

The newness of India was also proclaimed in relation to an international canvas—the idea that the experiments underway in India would be different from those existing in the rest of the world. Thus, although the dominant imperative of the postcolonial moment was to "catch up" to "what has supposedly already happened elsewhere,"[30] the process of catching-up—the actual journey of development charted by the Indian nation—would take India beyond existing models and trajectories. In the logic of Nehruvian nation-building, there was no contradiction between practices of borrowing from modular templates and the proclamation of national uniqueness and distinctiveness. In fact, through such adaptive efforts, copies that were substantively distinct from and far better than the originals were expected to emerge. The formation of a "mixed economy" that combined principles of socialist and laissez-faire economics, the articulation of a "third way" foreign policy of nonalignment with the Cold War superpowers, the commitment to a "unitary federalism" that drew upon features of the centralized state structure of Britain as well as the federal design of the United States, and the enshrining of group rights as well as individual rights in the constitution were all examples of this effort to produce something new by combining features from disparate external exemplars.

The urban plans for the steel towns were also marked by this logic of newness as bricolage, or to use Nehru's words from the epigraph of this chapter: a belief that "out of this amalgam, something new and good will emerge." Planners selected concepts and designs from a wide range of often contradictory urban planning paradigms. For instance, while the idea of self-contained residential neighborhoods was derived from the "garden city" plan, other principles of the garden city such as the requirement of preserving an expanse of agricultural land outside the city[31] or the concentric-circle spatial layout were rejected. The urban planners' efforts to form the steel towns as spaces of modernity conceptualized the modern in a multifaceted way, with multiple imperatives and requirements. As modern, the new urban space was to be marked by independent living and self-sufficiency, hence the development of contained residential sectors, each with their own shops, schools, parks, and entertainment centers. At the same time, the new urban also had to respond to the modern imperative of legibility or transparency—to be unlike the inscrutable and inward spaces of the "old" city, which meant that the residential sectors could not be completely closed off into themselves. Thus, Durgapur as both garden city and "band town" had its self-contained residential clusters strung along a single arterial road instead of being laid out in concentric circles.[32] It was precisely through its synthetic combination of these different features, that Durgapur's newness was proclaimed; it was set apart from both Indian cities, as well as from past and present urban spaces in the rest of the world.

Along with the "planned hybridity"[33] of the steel town—the ways in which it consciously brought together (different kinds of) "western" and "Indian" spatial visions, the identity of the steel town as "made by the state" also enabled claims about its newness and distinction. Without the state and its concern to secure "balanced regional development," steel plants would not exist where they did and, consequently, neither would the steel towns. The state was quite literally the condition of possibility of the steel town's existence. Moreover, life within the steel town was also structured around the facilities and services provided by the state and its agencies. For instance, the plan for Bokaro was based on a "primary and secondary school district concept"—not recreational spaces such as parks or commercial spaces such as markets, but instead a primary school built by the state would be the center of activities for each residential sector, comprised of approximately 750 families in an area of forty or fifty acres.[34]

As the flurry of initiatives undertaken by the state in the initial years after independence suggests, the drive to educate India and Indians (in the most immediate sense of spreading literacy within an overwhelmingly illiterate population and in the broader sense of learning how to be the right kind of citizen-subject) was one of the central components of the Nehruvian nation-building project. From the documentary films produced by the Films Division of India that were compulsorily screened before the start of feature films at commercial theaters throughout the country[35] to projects such as the Labour and Social Service Camps or the National Discipline Scheme,[36] the relation between state and nation was articulated in and through a pedagogical framework: how the infantile nation could realize itself through the agency and direction of the (paternal and adult) state. In the steel town, we see a localized and concrete manifestation of this national discourse of infantility,[37] with the child's "need" of education and the state's response to that need placed at the center of urban life. However, only the educational needs of specific kinds of infantile subjects were taken into account; those who lived outside the township could not attend its schools. The existence of the school and the activity of schooling thus worked to differentiate the inside of the steel town from its outside, with the new possibilities and new subjectivities unfolding within the steel town visibly different from those existing elsewhere.

Along with the availability of education within the township, at least three other features marked the steel town as a state-made space of difference. First, the boundary demarcating the new urban spaces was a visible one—most townships were designed to have a specific entrance (and exit). For instance, the urban plan for Durgapur proposed the clustering of scientific and technical research and educational institutes in a single place that could serve as the "main entrance" to the town. By signifying "advancement through Educational Research,"[38] these buildings would make possible a conscious experience of arrival into a different space. In the case of the railway township of Chittaranjan, a "model industrial town with all available facilities of modern town life,"[39] the distinct experience of arrival was secured in a far more direct way: Chittaranjan was designed as a "protected area," with any nonemployee of the state-owned Chittaranjan Locomotive Works factory requiring a special permit to enter the town.

Second, community life and political participation within the steel town were very different from equivalent practices outside, with the presence and involvement of the state serving once again as the grounds for differentiation. All Indian towns and cities had structures of local government. Decentralized mechanisms of self-government were also being realized in villages at the time, with the directive principles of the Indian constitution committing the state to the active development of village panchayats or councils. The steel town, in contrast to other rural and urban spaces in postcolonial India, had no representative or participatory structures and mechanisms in place. All decisions were made and all policies were enacted by the officials of Hindustan Steel. The general manager of the steel plant (appointed by the Ministry of Steel and Mines) was the de facto mayor of the township, and his wife was the ex officio chair of the cultural clubs and organizations run by the "ladies" of the town.[40] The state thus took upon itself the tasks of expressing and meeting the present needs of steel town residents and also of anticipating their future desires. Liberated from the demands of political participation in this manner, residents of the steel town could occupy themselves with cultural, educational, and recreational activities such as the development of community gardens, the encouragement of "wrestling, freehand exercises, gymnastics and other [forms] of physical culture,"[41] and the organization of religious festivals. The resulting apolitical subjectivity of the citizen-resident—what we might even term "antipolitical" in that it actively denies the presence and possibility of political action—and the seamless or unmediated connection forged between state and citizen within the steel town set it off from the messy and sordid world of "profane politics" outside.[42]

Finally, the steel town was different because its spaces showcased both the diversity as well as the unity of the nation. While all Indian cities were marked by considerable cultural, linguistic, and religious diversity and heterogeneity is in fact taken to be the defining feature of the urban condition the world over, the steel towns of India were distinct in their ability to suture together these differences. With people from all parts of India living together in the joint pursuit of steel production, Durgapur, Bhilai, Bokaro, and Rourkela were concrete instances of the official nationalist mantras of "unity in diversity" and *hum sab ek hain* (we are all one).

It would take time before this dream of national integration was perfectly realized—before "living together" as empirical description translated into something meaningful and substantive. However, this was in keeping with the "logic of deferrence"[43] that dominated the Nehruvian national imagination and its conceptualization of the nation in terms of becoming rather than being. Thus, the existence of flaws in the present— worker-residents not producing as much steel as they should, citizen-residents neglecting to care for common spaces within the town, frequent glitches in the supply of water and electricity, and the fragmentation of associational life along religious, linguistic, or ethnic lines—did not interrupt the dreamworld of the steel town because they did not foreclose the possibility of the future. As Vikramaditya Prakash has observed in the context of a discussion of Chandigarh, the new capital city for the state of Punjab that Le Corbusier designed in the early 1950s at the behest of Nehru, the new urban spaces of postcolonial India were "not meant to be a prophesy of the future . . . but [were] intended as an expression of faith in the future—the belief that the modern way of thinking and doing things would allow the future to emerge."[44] So long as the spaces and practices of the steel town allowed the future promise of sovereign national time to unfold—people seen to be moving forward as they went about their daily lives as workers and as citizens and the nation growing and developing as a result of these individual actions, the power and the viability of the dream was assured. Thus, new space, new time, and residents who were both industrious workers as well as active citizens were the coordinates of the steel town promise.

To live up to these promises and in fact to even make them in the first place, the steel town had to conform to one vital characteristic. It had to be maintained as a time and place apart, as an elsewhere both in terms of its immediate surroundings and in terms of the nation at large. In a paradoxical move, the national significance of the steel town as promise was secured through emphasizing not its identity with but rather its difference from the nation. Simply put, its status as national paradigm derived from its existence as anomaly. Strategies of decentering and disconnection rather than of totalization and homogenization thus enabled the emergence of the postcolonial nation.

THE "LAPSE" OF THE STEEL TOWN

The steel town's identity as an exemplary national space was linked to its distinctiveness—the fact that the times, spaces, subjectivities, and practices associated with it would be manifestly different. As the utopian steel town was transformed into a lived reality, its distinctiveness did manifest itself, although in unintended and unforeseen ways—for instance, the imperative of state visibility, which was indeed realized within the steel town. However, given the multilayered understanding of the representative principle that structured the postcolonial political field, whereby centralized institutional interventions of planned development that represented the people by "acting for" them as well as democratic political structures that represented the people by "standing as" them were jointly authorized, to see the state was actually to behold multiple visions.[45] Thus, the state emerged as the "model employer" of the citizen-workers who inhabited the steel town; as the "developmentalist agent" that was laboring to realize the "fruits of advancement" for the nation as a whole; as the "pastoralist state" concerned with the minutiae of individual lives within the township, from the grocery shopping decisions made by housewives to the daily travel time of commuters; and as the "totalizing state" engaged in the task of integrating the national population;[46] these were but some of the multiple "faces of the state" that were encountered in the steel town.[47] The significant role played by international institutions, ideologies, and interests in the creation of the postcolonial steel projects also contributed to this effect. It was not simply the facilitating labors of an Indian state that were sighted in the spaces of the steel town, but sights and signs of German, Soviet, and British state authority as well. The lettering on the highway signpost that was placed outside the city limits of Rourkela illustrated this most vividly: "Wilhelmshaven: 10,000 km" it read, as a permanent reminder of the steel town's transnational constitution.[48]

Next, as the steel town became a reality, so, too, did its contradictions and aporias. Over time, the incompatibility between the different components of the nation-statist project became increasingly apparent. In the most general sense, the goals of "making workers" and "making citizens" led to conflicting outcomes, and the difference between the "industrial" and the "township" components of the industrial township or the efforts of capital and civic development, respectively, proved to be difficult to reconcile. For instance, the decision to allocate housing on the basis of workplace hierarchies entrenched class-based divisions within the township and acted as a barrier to the development of neighborhood solidarities and related forms of social capital and civic belonging.

One of the most persistent complaints about the steel town was its economic polarization and the manifest lack of cross-class interaction. Approximately one decade after the townships were built, a series of reports on the "present condition" of the steel town by urban planning agencies of the state as well as by non-state national and international organizations such as the Ford Foundation and UNESCO concluded that the tying of housing to salary—higher-paid workers at the steel plant got better houses than lower-paid workers—had led to a reinscription of workplace inequalities and hierarchies within the urban area. Moreover, since the residential sectors of the townships were largely homogenous with regard to housing type, this meant that for the most part poorer people lived together and in isolation from the more prosperous. The self-sufficient design of the residential sectors served as an additional deterrent to interactions between different economic groups since there was no reason for anyone to venture beyond the confines of his or her sector except to go to work, which was a similarly polarized space. In townships with mixed housing sectors, the situation was no better. In fact, the specter of relative deprivation and envy that hovered over all attempts to get the haves and the have-nots to share space possibly made matters even worse.

Economic polarization and segregation were considered to be especially problematic because of the ways in which the economic disparities between different categories of workers mapped onto colonial inequalities of caste, religion, and region. As the steel plant responded to the "full employment" mandate of the Indian state, it registered a steady rise in the numbers on its payroll without a corresponding increase in the amount of money available for distribution among its employees. Since managerial and other white-collar staff at the plant were considered to be nationally competitive, their salaries were held relatively constant. Consequently, the practice of overemployment had a disproportionately adverse effect on nontechnical, semiskilled, and unskilled labor: categories comprised of people who had been denied educational opportunities in the past. In short, instead of undoing old hierarchies, the new urban spaces of the steel town reproduced them.[49]

Pursuing the goal of rapid industrial growth also had other kinds of unintended consequences on life in the township. As the industrial capacities and outputs of the steel plant increased, so, too, did the size of the informal labor sector.[50] With this came the proliferation of camps, slums, and other forms of makeshift housing settlements on the outskirts of and also within the planned environment of the towns. There was an acute shortage of housing for formal employees of the steel plants as well. Thus in 1971, the Town and Country Planning Organization's data on employee housing at the Durgapur steel plant revealed that 47 percent of steel plant employees lived in shared housing, 27 percent in "labor camps," and 11 percent in *bustees* or slum dwellings. In other words, only 15 percent of the employees lived in their own houses within the township—a place that had been built to meet the housing needs of the steel plant![51] The fortunate few who had a house of their own within the steel town had their own share of problems to contend with: overcrowded schools, poorly equipped hospitals, and a "semi-developed market disguised as a Central Business District."[52] Residents often had to venture outside the township in order to satisfy their basic needs; vegetables were cheaper, schools were better, and even health care, though more expensive, was more reliable outside the steel town. As a result, the boundary between the inside and the outside of the steel town proved difficult to maintain, and the town's identity as a self-sufficient space was called into question.

Steel towns were also sites in which the constitutive contradictions of the nation-state's "mosaic nationalism" project—the idea of India as a unity of distinct subnational cultures—became apparent. Thus, on the one hand and in keeping with the multiculturalist logic of India's unity-in-diversity formula of nationhood, the existence of distinct ethnoreligious communities in steel towns was critical to its identity as a nationally representative space. On the other hand, these displays of subnational distinctiveness could very easily become expressions of insular parochialism, with intraethnic solidarities strengthened at the expense of interethnic connections. Steel town residents were commonly described as being trapped within the narrow prison houses of regional identity; instead of relating to each other as fellow "producer-patriots," they were seen to reproduce ethnic, linguistic, and caste barriers within the township.

According to Bagaram Tulpule, who served as the general manager of the Durgapur Steel Plant between 1971 and 1974, the frequent incidents of labor unrest during his tenure had a lot to do with the fact that Bengali employees of the steel plant were unable to get beyond their cultural milieu of *bhadralok* (genteel bourgeois) identity and to reconcile themselves to their status as "physical labor." In the account of this state official, the problem of "labor indiscipline" was linked to the persistence of parochial identity and the failure of the steel town to realize new, national attitudes and practices. Instead, Bengalis continued to be Bengalis; "discipline in the conventional sense of unquestioning obedience to or suppliance [sic] before their officers is naturally irksome to them."[53] Tulpule's account of labor unrest as ethnically derived behavior can be called into question. Of significance, however, is not his explanation of the steel town's problems, but the problematization itself: the fact that the very ethnoregional identity that the steel town was expected to protect, display, and foster was seen as a destabilizing threat to be kept at bay. The steel town was thus a site in which the inconsistent embrace of diversity in postcolonial India—the understanding that subnational diversity is something valuable as well as dangerous—found expression.

In a final example of the contradictions of the steel town project, while the meticulously planned nature of the steel town may have been a success as far as the goals of order and rationality were concerned, it had a negative effect on the quality and experience of life within the township. As one observer noted, "[w]ith dusk comes a lull over the town. Human activity almost comes to an apparent stop. There is very little communication between people. Everyone, as it were, recoils into his domestic cell. The life, activity, color, and gaiety of an urban area is strikingly absent."[54] The urban planning agency of the state concurred with this perspective, describing Durgapur in terms of the "monotony of the city environment" and of how the lack of a "skyline and visual urban effects" had "taken away the much desired element of human living."[55] In the state's own assessment, steel towns did not look or feel "urban," and their inhabitants did not behave like engaged and modern citizens.[56]

Perhaps the most unexpected outcome of the steel town project was the fact that it contributed to the proliferation and intensification rather than the erasure or transcendence of antagonisms and conflict. Reports about crime and law and order problems in the steel towns and the surrounding areas increased over the years. Contrary to the expectation that the steel town and the steel plants would transcend politics, there were significant interunion rivalries and frequent incidents of "industrial unrest."

The promise of shedding "atavisms" of identity was likewise belied. As Jonathan Parry's rich ethnography of workers in the Bhilai steel plant establishes, the policy of caste-based reservations of jobs for state workers meant that for many caste identity and the possession of a caste certificate was the means for entering the "caste-free" utopia of the world of steel.[57] Steel towns also proved unable to either transform or keep at bay one of the most pernicious atavisms of the old India: the problem of communalism or interreligious violence. Thus in March 1964, the town of Rourkela witnessed "indiscriminate killing, loot, and arson."[58] The police and the local administration proved to be either unable or unwilling to take any precautionary measures. Approximately thirty-four Muslims were killed over a twenty-day period, more than 5,000 left their homes, and researchers visiting Rourkela in the aftermath of the violence were struck by the high level of "communal mistrust among various sections of the people."[59]

Why did the riots happen? Explanations located the specificity of the violence in Rourkela within a larger narrative: The events in Rourkela were part of a contemporaneous wave of Hindu-Muslim violence that was affecting other areas of India and also of East Pakistan. Two weeks before the events in Rourkela, there were riots in the city of Calcutta, 225 kilometers away; a month before, there was extended violence in the East Pakistani town of Jessore. Moreover, these events appeared to be connected by something more than mere temporal coincidence. As trains carrying "Hindu refugees" from Jessore (via Calcutta) to the resettlement colony of Dandakaranya in the central Indian state of Madhya Pradesh stopped at Rourkela station and rumors about the events in Calcutta and Jessore reached the steel town, "the virus spread far and wide."[60] Efforts to insulate the steel town from nation and region and to preserve it as a distinctive and discrete space appeared to have failed. The Rourkela riots thus served to shatter the understanding of the difference of the steel town—it was just like the rest of India. Further, not only had the new space of the steel town failed to live up to its promise of bringing forth new practices of communal harmony and peaceful coexistence, but it may also have exacerbated communal violence. After all, most of the incidents of violence took place within the confines of the industrial township, and locations outside, such as the district town of Bonaigarh (40 miles away), were unaffected.[61] The involvement of *Adivasis* (indigenous peoples of the area) in the riots also suggested that the experience of living in and around Rourkela may have contributed to the emergence of communalism; before the establishment of the steel town, such incidents were unknown among the *Adivasi* population. Instead of enabling its citizens to move forward toward the future, Rourkela may have set the nation back quite a few steps.

While other townships did not experience either the directness or the intensity of the Rourkela riots, they were marked by a manifest absence of intercommunal communication and trust. As the findings of a 1980 study on the impact of urbanization in Durgapur note, "neighborliness in the city is quite lacking [sic] due to two factors: regional and caste prejudices . . . There is always an atmosphere of tension among neighbors and there is also the lack of commonness and specialized interests which could bind them together."[62] Like the visibility of economic inequality and the outbreaks of communal violence, the palpable "lack of commonness" in the steel town served to underscore the magnitude of its failure to realize the dream of an integrated and modern nation.

In sum, whatever else the steel town was, it was clearly not a space peopled by active, modern subjects whose "way of thinking and doing things would allow the future to emerge."[63] Unable to live up to the terms of its own promise of being a new and vibrant space filled with productive workers and engaged citizens, a nationally integrated and future-directed elsewhere that would bring growth and development to the surrounding areas of backwardness and yet maintain a clear distance from them, the dreamworld of the steel town was renamed as a catastrophe—holding up to the nation images not of its promised future but of its disavowed past.

Journeys Outside? The Spatial Incarceration of the Urban

Attention now turned to the question of whether salvage or recovery was possible, of how, if at all, the problem of the steel town could be fixed. The failure of the steel town was attributed to three specific causes: unrealistic plans, inadequate implementation, and hasty development. Accordingly, solutions considered how urban plans that met the needs of the people could be designed, how these user-friendly plans could be better implemented, and how the pace of growth and development could be slowed down. While the specific policy recommendations were diverse and wide-ranging, they all drew upon and reproduced a common set of assumptions. First, all efforts at problem-solving distinguished urban space from urban practice—the idea that built structure and inhabitants are two separable parts of a city and that it is possible to design structure to fit inhabitants and to change inhabitants by redesigning structure. According to the terms of this logic, the steel town was seen to have failed because the needs of its inhabitants had not been adequately known and anticipated. Therefore, carefully designed surveys and better demographic projections of population growth would make a difference. Alternatively, the problem was seen to stem from the passivity and inwardness of inhabitants. Therefore, the logic went, the development of more playgrounds and community halls were in order.[64] What was called into question (and what in turn presented itself for solution) was not the idea of nationally produced urban planning, but the specific flaws within the existing urban plan.

Next, solutions to the problem of the steel town continued to reproduce the assumption that the citizen-worker was the ideal subject of the new urban. How could residents of the steel town be productive and disciplined in the steel plant and neighborly and active in the township? How could a rich community life emerge from the shadows of a hierarchical workplace? In different ways, these questions attempted to grapple with the constitutive contradiction of the steel town—the fact that to the extent that the steel town fulfilled its goal of being a *steel* town, a place where docile workers lived, it failed to be a steel *town*, a space inhabited by engaged citizens. A radical revision of the conditions of work and the presumptions of citizenship may have been one possible way to mediate this contradiction, but this path remained uncharted.

Third, solutions offered to the problem of the steel town were, like the promise of the steel town, located and bounded within a specific urban area. Something had gone wrong inside the steel town, and reform efforts would accordingly focus on this inner space. In other words, the problem of Rourkela, Bhilai, Bokaro, and Durgapur was conceptualized as a problem within Rourkela, Bhilai, Bokaro, and Durgapur—a conceptualization premised on the assumption that urban and nonurban spaces could be differentiated and that problems and solutions were localized. Within this framework, the problem of economic polarization could be addressed by redesigning the system of housing allocation. Thus, if workers' houses were pegged to their family size rather than to their salary, economic disparities would be less visible within the town.[65] This solution did not engage with the question of structural inequalities—of how and why some people earn so much more than others. Such an interrogation would have called for a journey outside the urban and a rearticulation of the relationship between the urban and the national in terms of connection rather than of estrangement and differentiation. However, this path, too, remained uncharted.

Finally, though tribal communities lived (and continue to live) in Bhilai, Bokaro, Rourkela, and Durgapur, they were completely absent from the narratives of steel town reform, just as they were from the earlier narratives of promise and problem as well. The violence that generated the new urban spaces of postcolonial India found no mention in any of these state texts. There was no place for the stories of the forcible displacements that were undertaken in order to sacralize the new "temples of modern India:"[66] the dams, steel plants, locomotive factories, and other "fetishized figurations"[67] of postcolonial modernity. So the questions still remain: To whom does Bhilai (or Durgapur or Bokaro or Rourkela) belong? Who belongs to Bhilai? Whose dreamworld and whose catastrophe is it anyway? Their non-resolution is a reminder that efforts to realize the freedoms, dignities, and equalities that we take to be the positive substance of democratic citizenship need to do much more than call for the devolution of citizenship from the abstract scale of the nation to the more grounded scale of the city,[68] or alternatively, call for a reconnection of urban elsewheres with national everywheres. Unless the constitutive exclusions and amnesias of the urban are addressed, the deficits and exclusions of national citizenship and the spatial incarceration of the nation merely will be rescaled.

NOTES

I am grateful to Anand Vivek Taneja for research assistance and to Thomas Bender, Alev Çınar, and the participants at the Shehr Network workshop on "Gendering Urban Space" (Cairo, February 2004), especially Martina Rieker, Kamran Ali, Maha Yahya, Omnia El Shakry, Dina Siddiqi, and Thomas Blom Hansen for their helpful comments on an earlier version of this chapter.

1. Jawaharlal Nehru, letter to Le Corbusier, Fondation Le Corbusier, Paris, File P2-13, 292, cited in Vikramaditya Prakash, *Chandigarh's Le Corbusier* (Seattle: University of Washington Press, 2002), 10 (fn. 13).

2. *Durgapur Steel Township General Development Plan* (New Delhi: Town and Country Planning Organization, Government of India, 1971), 2.

3. Steel Authority of India, *Tryst with Steel: Nehru and the Public Sector Steel Industry* (New Delhi: Steel Authority of India Limited, 1988), 6.

4. Salman Rushdie, *Midnight's Children* (London: Picador, 1982), 112.

5. Susan Buck-Morss, *Dreamworld and Catastrophe* (Cambridge: The MIT Press, 2000).

6. *Durgapur Steel Township,* 2.

7. Ibid., 2–3.

8. See the opening quotations of this chapter.

9. A recent essay by Gyan Prakash on historicist understandings of the urban in Nehruvian India is a notable exception. See Gyan Prakash, "The Urban Turn," in *Cities of Everyday Life: The Sarai Reader, 27,* 2–7 (New Delhi, India: Sarai, CSDS and the Society for Old and New Media, 2002): 2, available online at http://www.sarai.net (accessed November 13, 2002).

10. Ravi Sundaram, "The Bazaar and the City: History and the Contemporary in Urban Electronic Culture," *Expand,* available online at http://www.expand.at/s/expand/expand.html (accessed November 13, 2002).

11. Sanjay Seth, "Nationalism, National Identity, and 'History': Nehru's Search for India," *Thesis Eleven* 32 (1992): 37–54; in a recent collection of essays, Ashis Nandy has argued that the postcolonial celebration of the rural amounts to an "ambiguous" valorization. See Ashis Nandy, *An Ambiguous Journey to the City: The Village and Other Odd Ruins of the Self in the Indian Imagination* (Delhi, India: Oxford University Press, 2001).

12. Sanjay Srivastava, "The Order of Men: Sentiments of the Metropolis, Settlements of Civil Society," in *Constructing Post-Colonial India: National Character and the Doon School,* 165–89 (London: Routledge Press, 1998).

13. Arjun Appadurai, "Putting Hierarchy in Its Place," *Cultural Anthropology* 3, no. 1 (1988): 37.

14. See, for instance, James Holston and Arjun Appadurai, "Cities and Citizenship," in *Cities and Citizenship,* ed. James Holston, 1–18 (Durham, N.C.: Duke University Press, 1999) and also the other essays in this volume.

15. Unlike the directly ruled British Indian provinces, princely states enjoyed nominal sovereignty during the colonial period.

16. For a discussion of these colonial steel towns, see Niranjan Krishna Benegal, "Township and Housing Design for Bokaro Steel Project, India" (master's thesis, North Dakota State University, 1966), 7.

17. A significant qualifier is necessary: All the public sector steel plants and townships of postcolonial India were built with financial and technical assistance from other nation-states. The Soviet Union collaborated on Bhilai and Bokaro, the British state on Durgapur, and the Federal Republic of Germany on Rourkela. Consequently, steel towns were international spaces as well. Significant numbers of foreign nationals lived and worked in the towns, especially during the initial years after their construction.

18. Ravi Sundaram, "The Bazaar and the City."

19. "Old Glory, New Achievement: Hindustan Steel," *Times of India* (Bombay ed.), January 26, 1953, 3.

20. Town and Country Planning Organization, *Town and Country Planning in India* (New Delhi, India: Town and Country Planning Organization, 1962), 91.

21. Ibid., 68–69.

22. Ibid., 87.

23. S. K. Bose, *Chittaranjan Township* (Delhi, India: UNESCO Research Center and the Indian Institute of Public Administration, 1960), 3.

24. The lack of educational qualifications was a significant barrier to the employment of Bauris in formal positions on the shop floor, where all positions above the grade of "operator" required education up to the eighth standard. See Nirmal Sengupta, *Destitutes and Development: A Study of the Bauri Community in the Bokaro Region* (New Delhi, India: Concept Publishing Company, 1979).

25. Sengupta's study of the effects of planned development on the lives of the Bauri community establishes that, contrary to the expectations that steel complexes would be "generative engines" of growth and development, the local communities experienced rapid increases in levels of poverty, unemployment, and general social-economic "destitution." See Sengupta, *Destitutes and Development*.

26. Town and Country Planning Organization, *Town and Country Planning in India* (New Delhi, India: Town and Country Planning Organization, 1962), 68.

27. Ibid., 69.

28. The highest paid employees of the steel plant (the managerial and administrative personnel) earned almost sixty times more than the lowest paid employee who was eligible for housing (non-contract or "casual" labor did not qualify for housing). Of the six grades of housing, Grade A, reserved for those at the highest end of the salary scale (earning approximately 3,500 rupees per month), consisted of a 2,100 square foot house with three bedrooms, "servants' quarters," and garden. On the other end, Grade F, reserved for those who earned less than sixty rupees per month, consisted of a room with a balcony, a shared bathroom, and a common passage. These rooms were clustered within two- or three-storied dormitory-style buildings (Benegal, *Township and Housing Design for Bokaro Steel Project, India*, 10), 20.

29. Jawaharlal Nehru, letter to Le Corbusier, Fondation Le Corbusier, Paris, File P2-13, 292, cited in Prakash, *Chandigarh's Le Corbusier*, 9 (n. 11).

30. Sankaran Krishna, *Postcolonial Insecurities: India, Sri Lanka, and the Question of Nationhood* (Minneapolis: University of Minnesota Press, 1999), xix.

31. In Ebenezer Howard's original vision of the garden city, the preservation of such an expanse of agricultural land was what would enable

the garden city to realize its role as a "town-country magnet." See Ebenezer Howard, *Garden Cities of To-Morrow* (London: Faber and Faber, 1946).

32. For a discussion of the different types of urban planning activity undertaken in the postcolonial period and the varied genealogies of these plans, see Otto Koenigsberger, "New Towns in India," in *Town Planning Review* 23, no. 2 (July 1952): 95–131.

33. Gayatri Chakravorty Spivak, "City, Country, Agency," in *Proceedings of Theatres of Decolonization,* ed. Vikaramaditya Prakash, 1–22 (Seattle, Washington: College of Architecture and Urban Planning, University of Washington, 1997), 3.

34. Town and Country Planning Organization, *Town and Country Planning in India* (New Delhi, India: Town and Country Planning Organization, 1962), 90.

35. For a discussion of the "pedagogical nationalism" of Films Division documentaries, see Srirupa Roy, "Moving Pictures: The Indian State and Audiovisual Depictions of Nationhood," *Contributions to Indian Sociology* 36, no. 1 & 2 (2002): 33–64.

36. Labour and Social Service Camps were introduced by the ministry of education in the 1950s, as part of an effort to increase interactions between city and countryside and to instill an appreciation of the "joys and dignities of manual labor" in urban youth. University students would live in villages for approximately ten days every year and undertake various kinds of "useful projects." The National Discipline Scheme developed a comprehensive list of activities for schools and universities that could make the youth of India more disciplined, industrious, and efficient. For a discussion of these projects, see G. D. Sondhi, *Youth Welfare* (Delhi, India: Government of India, n.d.).

37. A somewhat different notion of "infantile citizenship" has been developed by Lauren Berlant to draw attention to the way in which official and popular cultural discourses in the contemporary United States address the unborn fetus as the ideal civic subject. See Lauren Berlant, "The Theory of Infantile Citizenship," in *The Queen of America Goes to Washington City: Essays on Sex and Citizenship,* 25–54 (Durham, N.C.: Duke University Press, 1997). Here, I draw attention to a different discursive process—namely, the "infantilization" of the national collectivity (with the corresponding construction of the state as the paternal adult).

38. Town and Country Organization, *Town and Country Planning in India* (New Delhi, India: Town and Country Planning Organization, 1962), 83.

39. S. K. Bose, *Chittaranjan Township*, 2.

40. The memoirs of Bagaram Tulpule, general manager of Durgapur steel plant from 1971–1974, illuminate some of the complexities of this situation. See Bagaram Tulpule, *Amidst Heat and Noise: Durgapur Recalled* (New Delhi, India: All India Management Association, 1977), 85–94.

41. The "area committees" of Chittaranjan township were charged with these responsibilities. They were entrusted with undertaking certain kinds of prohibitory activities as well, such as preventing "acts of vandalism" and discouraging "wild rumor." For a detailed account of the role and responsibilities of the area committees, see S. K. Bose, *Chittaranjan Township*, 9.

42. Nehruvian nationalist discourse promoted the notion of a constitutive split, obtained between the domain of "profane politics" and that of "sublime politics." The state belonged to the latter, whereas all expressions of "ordinary" political behavior (whether by political parties, social movements, civic associations, or interest groups) belonged to the former. For a discussion of how Nehruvian nationalism secured for the state its sublime and transcendent location, see Thomas Blom Hansen, *The Saffron Wave* (Princeton: Princeton University Press, 1999), ch. 1.

43. Sankaran Krishna, *Postcolonial Insecurities*, 17; Krishna draws upon Derrida's concept of "différance" to argue for a reading of postcolonial nationalism in terms of its production of "the metaphor of nation as journey, as something that is ever in the making but never quite reached" (16).

44. Prakash, *Chandigarh's Le Corbusier*, 10, emphasis added.

45. For a discussion of the different categories of representation, see Hanna Pitkin, *The Concept of Representation* (Berkeley: University of California Press, 1967).

46. For a discussion of the "individualizing" and "totalizing" effects of state power, see Michel Foucault, "Omnes et Singulatim: Towards a Criticism of Political Reason," in *Power*, ed. J. Faubion, 298–325 (New York: The New Press, 2000).

47. The steel town also attested to the pluralized constitution of state sovereignty in Nehruvian India. For instance, the establishment of the steel town was an outcome of strategic bargaining among central and regional state elites, with the eventual accomplishment of building Rourkela, Bokaro, or Bhilai claimed by central and regional governments alike. The subsequent administration of the township and the

steel plant also brought together different levels of state authority and reflected the structuring imperatives of national as well as regional political fields. In sum, the "visibility of the state" in the steel town was about witnessing the *heterogenous* makeup of stateness and the *divided* character of state sovereignty.

48. Jan Sperling, *The Human Dimension of Technical Assistance* (Ithaca, NY: Cornell University Press, 1969), 120; within the steel township, there were numerous other ways in which "foreign presence" could be discerned: direct encounters with the significant numbers of German and Russian personnel who lived and worked in Rourkela and Bhilai, respectively; the development of residential areas and recreational centers set aside for the exclusive use of "foreigner residents" of the township; and the growth of a differentiated service economy (specifically, that of domestic service) catering to their "specialized" needs.

49. For an extended discussion of the macroeconomic reasons for the increases in economic inequality among steel plant workers and, by extension, among steel town residents, see Benegal, *Township and Housing Design*, 15–16.

50. For a discussion of the preponderance of "inside contracting" (the subcontracting of jobs that are then carried out within the premises of the plant itself, in contrast to a "putting out" system of subcontracting) and other forms of informal labor practices in the steel plant, see Nirmal Sengupta, *Contract Labour in the Rourkela Steel Plant* (Mimeo: 1980) and P. K. Mohanty, *Collective Bargaining in the Steel Industry in India* (New Delhi, India: Discovery Publishing House, n.d.).

51. *Durgapur Steel Township*, Appendix IV.

52. Ibid., 63.

53. Bagaram Tulpule, *Amidst Heat and Noise*, 14.

54. Benegal, *Township and Housing Design*, 1.

55. *Durgapur Steel Township*, 3, 67.

56. The conclusion about the inability of planned urbanism to realize an effective "urbanity" was also invoked during discussions about other planned cities. Ravi Kalia's commentary on Chandigarh is strikingly similar to the observations about the steel towns previously noted: "Chandigarh was meant to be something beyond a new state capital. But it lacks a culture. It lacks the excitement of Indian streets. It lacks bustling, colorful bazaars. It lacks the noise and din of Lahore. It lacks the intimacy of Delhi. It is a stay-at-home city. It is not Indian.

It is the anticity" (Ravi Kalia, *Chandigarh: In Search of an Identity* [Carbondale: Southern Illinois University Press, 1987], 29).

57. Jonathan Parry, "Two Cheers for Reservation: The Satnamis and the Steel Plant," in *Institutions and Inequalities: Essays in Honour of André Béteille*, 129–69 (New Delhi, India: Oxford University Press, 1999).

58. B. B. Chatterjee, P. N. Singh, and G. R. S. Rao, *Riots in Rourkela: A Psychological Study* (Delhi, India: Popular Book Services, 1967), 125.

59. Ibid., 132.

60. Ibid., 125.

61. Ibid., 15.

62. Jogendra Sahai, *Urban Complex of an Industrial City* (Allahabad, India: Chugh Publications, 1980), 180.

63. See fn. 49.

64. These are among the conclusions and recommendations offered by the Town and Country Planning Organization (1962).

65. This proposal is developed at length by Benegal, *Township and Housing Design*.

66. Jawaharlal Nehru famously referred to dams as the "temples of modern India," in the course of a speech at the inauguration of the Bhakra Nangal dam in 1952.

67. Benjamin Lee and Edward Li Puma, "Cultures of Circulation: The Imaginations of Modernity" *Public Culture* 14, no. 1 (2002): 193.

68. As noted in the introductory section, the city in contrast to the nation is often seen to offer a more grounded and less abstract space for the realization of citizenship.

9

"AMMAN IS NOT A CITY"
Middle Eastern Cities in Question
Seteney Shami

Amman is a much-maligned city. Its inhabitants complain endlessly of its dullness and lack of charm. The elites complain of the lack of cosmopolitanism and nightlife intellectuals complain of the lack of artistic or literary movements, merchants complain of a lack of market, university students complain of the lack of campus life, and ethnic groups complain of the lack of ethnic neighborhoods. Expatriates complain about the lack of authenticity. The poor, of course, have a great deal about which to complain. Each segment of urban society appears to be complaining about its own failure to realize itself. The inhabitants of Amman offer various political, economic, social, and cultural explanations for their malaise. However, they commonly agree on the underlying problem and explanation: that Amman is *not a city*.

Yet Amman has an attractive landscape of hills and valleys; it can claim an ancient history as evidenced by the Greco-Roman theater in the old downtown. It has 1.5 million inhabitants; it has a slummy East side and a fashionable West one. It has a crowded downtown with the requisite hustle and bustle; a small but lively financial district; a distinctive style of architecture; international luxury hotels, cafes, and restaurants; a McDonald's and a Hard Rock Café; swimming clubs and sports arenas; good health facilities; two or three theaters where local and foreign performances are given; art galleries; several universities; a cinema club; a writers' union; a tourist industry; professional unions; NGOs, foreign and local; and a continuous stream of international and regional conferences and colloquiums. It also has its share of political demonstrations and unrest. So what is it that Amman lacks in order to qualify, in the eyes of its inhabitants, as a city?

A cultural history of Amman highlights the specificity of the case as well as its relevance for broader questions of how urban culture and urban identity are constructed in relation to both personhood and nationhood. This chapter discusses the construction of urban imaginaries, discursive and spatial practices, and urban citizenship and belonging as they play themselves out in Amman through three moments in time: the late 1940s–early 1950s, when an emergent urban identity can be observed; the late 1970s–early 1980s, when oil wealth bisects the city into east and west; and Amman of the new millennium, which is witnessing fragmented though important attempts at constructing an urban narrative of its past and future. These moments are examined through the practices and discourses of two (reified) categories: "the bourgeoisie" and "the state."[1] These represent only some of the many actors and factors engaged in making Amman, but ones that play definitive roles in constructing Amman as a noncity, a negative case, a depository of discontent.

Tracking the urban imaginaries that play themselves out in Amman, helps in understanding processes that result in hegemonic urban spatial practices. Does the predicament of Amman lie in the panoply of fragmented narratives and inconclusive inscriptions in space? Is it that the overarching urban narrative in Amman is one that paradoxically emphasizes its fragmentation and deprives the city from claiming a unique urban identity? Why is the overall consciousness, the set of meanings, the hegemonic urban discourse concerning Amman one that *negates* its identity as a city? The answer partly lies in the ways that Amman's inhabitants construct their identities through references to a multiplicity of cities as well as to alternative identities that work against consolidating an Ammani identity.[2] The particular relationship of the state to and its policies toward its capital city and its inhabitants are also of central importance. Finally, it is crucial to realize that the "negative" discourse and its associated practices are quintessentially *urban* as well as distinctively *Ammani,* and historically situated.

If the negation of urbanness is itself an affirmation that Amman is a city, the challenge to interpretation is how to construe this absence as a presence in analytical terms. This cannot be achieved by recourse to prevalent explanations focusing on demography, physical layout, or event history, although all these play a part in the contingency that is Amman. Rather, the focus should be on processes through which a city's inhabitants construct their identities and the ways in which urban, national, and transnational identities overlap to create particular ways of belonging to and/or alienation from urban space. Equally of interest is how state actors—municipalities, planning agencies, public service providers— envision the cityscape and the consequences of the relationships between them and city elites for the ensuing urban fabric. Finally, how does the construction of citizenship and nation-building projects shape urban imaginaries and narratives? In the case of Amman, the inconclusiveness of nation-building projects explains to a large extent the prevalence of the maxim that "Amman is not a city." The ambiguity of official discourses on national identity, including the place of territory, of history, and of Islam within it, as well as the lack of institutionalized significations of nationhood, result in the partial and fitful nature of state-sponsored urban projects that attempt to inscribe national identity and its symbols in space.

Amman is not unique; worldwide there are many bland cities, cities of convenience, which do not engage its inhabitants in struggles over identity and belonging—or at least not in ways that turn into major urban projects or movements. However, the issue gains theoretical interest in the case of a *capital city,* rather than a provincial secondary urban settlement or an economically eclipsed town in a multiurban setting. How are we to understand a capital city which subsists on "thin" symbolism and is semiotically underdetermined? The view from Amman alerts us that the vast majority of contemporary cities in the region (and not only in this region) are not those of the Orientalist imaginary or of European modernity. They are emerging in a completely different historical juncture, socioeconomic context, and cultural current. This is not to deny the importance of historical and megacities, such as Cairo, Damascus, or Marrakech, but rather to confirm their continued significance in shaping perceptions of urbanity in the region. The "late" cities that have come into their own in the 1950s or 1970s (such as the cities of the Arab Gulf) continue to live in the shadow of the historically dominant ones, while reflecting fully their transnational settings and hybrid specificities. They present us with new, ambiguous, and challenging terrains for research.

Urban Imaginaries

In constructing their notions of a city, the inhabitants of Amman draw on a number of imaginaries that echo historical and scholarly constructs and often stem from the same sources. Both popular and scholarly discourses concerning urban life in the Middle East are modeled on three constructs and ideal types: the Orientalist city, the modern city, and the global city.

The Orientalist city or what is commonly referred to as "the Islamic city" exists, as many have shown, more in the imagination of the scholar than in lived experience. Orientalists wrote detailed descriptions of the urban features of Islam, which were understood to shape cities in the Middle East. However, generalizations were built on limited examples and handed down in two sets of *isnad,* or "chains of authenticity," one based mainly on the study of Fez and the other on Aleppo and Damascus.[3] These writings have left important, if often vaguely articulated, legacies of what cities in the region should look like: grand central mosques, covered markets, twisted alleys, and closed-in residential quarters. Amman has no such old city center, no "medina" or "casbah." Neither is there the equivalent in Amman to what, in Cairo, are called "the traditional urban quarters" or the "traditional popular areas," nor the equivalent of the Cairene social category *"ibn al balad"* (the son of the city).[4]

Likewise Amman does not have the grand boulevards or public squares and structures of the nineteenth-century modern city, which in the region was produced through European colonialism and in a dialogic relationship with the "traditional city." If modernity is marked by "free circulation of crowds and vehicles; impersonal and anonymous encounters of the pedestrian; unprogrammed public enjoyment and congregation in streets and squares; and the presence of people from different social backgrounds strolling and gazing at those passing by, looking at store windows, shopping, and sitting in cafes, joining political demonstrations or using spaces especially designed for the entertainment of the masses (promenades, parks, stadiums, exhibitions),"[5] then Amman has only a curtailed and partial modernity. Its quiet, empty streets and modest shopping and business centers do not display the required intensity of public life.

In many ways, Amman presents a postmodern cityscape: decentered, fragmented, privatized. However, it certainly does not display the nightmarish landscapes of fabulist consumerism or urban implosion described elsewhere.[6] Its scattered configuration and the bypassing of the city center are not due to deindustrialization or the reconfiguration of financial flows within the city.[7] Rather it is due to the migration of capital to the oil economies of the Gulf in the 1980s and more recently of regional political instability. Although many global currents swirl around Amman, they do not quite seem to settle in it except through some of the trappings of global consumerism such as fast-food chains and movie theaters. Amman does not function as a global financial center or a major destination for global tourism, in spite of much infrastructural investment in the latter.

World cities and their built environment are often seen as coherent spatial representations of tradition, modernity, or globality. In cities like Cairo, Marrakech, and Istanbul, different sections of the city are represented and exhibited to their inhabitants and visitors as historical stages of urban evolution through their different archetypical built environments, economic functions, the meanings and values they evoke, and through their inhabitants or stereotypes about them. The overlapping, interpenetrated, and mutually constitutive nature of these constructs appears to be separated analytically through and in space.

The point here is that in the lack of fit with presumptions of a progression from tradition to modernity and globality is born Amman's malaise.[8] Authors describing Amman's lack of "organic identity" use terms such as the "betrayal" of "the laws of the oriental Islamic city."[9] What do such analyses tell us about Amman? What do they tell us about our models? These constructs neither capture the identity, nor the empirical realities, of many contemporary cities. However, as popular models they are powerful. Amman, thus, belabors under the weight of the region's many historic cities. This is a region that hosts the oldest still-inhabited urban centers of the world, aged capitals of powerful past empires, major religious sites, and centers of learning as well as notable colonial creations. Damascus, Sana'a, Rabat, Baghdad, Cairo, Jerusalem, Isfahan, Aleppo, Mecca, Istanbul, Fez, Qom, and Basra: the names alone evoke the great regional significance and weight, the multilayered histories, and the contemporary vitality of these dominant cities. Amman has a very difficult act to follow. Thus, it is not only the lack of fit with abstract constructs, but also the lack of commensurability with historical parallels that makes it difficult to take Amman seriously. By whom, however?

While all of Amman's inhabitants partake in the laments about the city, these are articulated most often by the bourgeoisie as well as by writers, journalists, artists, architects, and other elites in ways that clearly implicate their own uneasy sense of distinction and class position. It is perhaps obvious that the bourgeoisie would be particularly concerned with issues of urbanity and urbaneness. The authenticity as well as the cosmopolitanism of the city is perceived by them as a direct reflection of and comment on their class distinction as well as their integration into global culture. How do Amman's bourgeoisie translate their identities onto the city through their discourses and practices?

On the other hand, how does the state deploy notions of the city in the making of Amman? Everything we know about state and nation-building would lead us to anticipate that the state would be vitally invested in inscribing itself into the cityscape and displaying nationhood as part of consolidating its power. How does one explain the lack of national monuments, a national museum, and other spatial markers of national time and space in Amman?

The identity of a city arises out of a combination of elements that identify it as urban first, as having particular characteristics that gives it an urban specificity second, and, finally, as reflecting and bestowing meanings larger than itself, such as nationhood, modernity, or globality. These identity-creating elements make the city (and its representation) recognizable as Istanbul rather than Ankara or Cairo rather than Fez, and their meanings are intertwined with but are not the same as people's identity as urban dwellers. All of the city's inhabitants participate in making and remaking the identity of the city through their labor and imagination. Urban dwellers are city people first, inhabitants of a particular city second, and, finally, the producers and consumers of larger narratives. The processes that give rise to the identity *of the city* are much less well understood in urban scholarship than the making of identities *in the city*. Discussions of imagined communities, collective imagination, and the public sphere rest more easily in local, national, or global spaces than in the city as the unit of analysis. We know how to interpret particularisms and universalisms, but not the articulation of the two, which is the unique attribute of the city.

DISORIENTATIONS: SPACE INTERRUPTED

It would appear at first that there are quite easy answers to Ammani laments, and these are readily offered up by many of its inhabitants. First, Amman is a recent city. It was refounded, after some centuries of depopulation, as a frontier settlement of the Ottoman state in the late nineteenth century. Secondly, its population has been formed by numerous waves of displacement and refugee movements. Thirdly, its economy is largely dependent on the fortunes of a rentier state rather than on industry or global financial flows. Finally, Amman has experienced continuous and rapid physical expansion, such that its urban fabric is "more of a construction site than a city."[10] History, economy, social composition, and spatial density are central elements in defining urban formations, and Amman's characteristics all seem to make for disruption, disjuncture, and disorientation. While these arguments may go some way in explaining Amman's malaise, taken separately or cumulatively, they do not provide the whole story of Amman and its discontent.

On the newness of Amman, according to conventional wisdom, the site was resettled in 1878 after a substantial break in permanent settlement. It became a town only after 1903 and a capital city only since 1921, and it is only since the 1970s or 1980s that most of its cultural facilities and activities were established.[11] However, more than 125 years of settlement, 100 years of urbanization, 80 years of being a capital, and a quarter of a century of transnational engagement constitute substantial periods of time. Cities elsewhere and in other times have been made in such durations and under similar constraints.[12] Given the creative imagination displayed cross-culturally in constructing historical identities and cultural imaginaries, there would appear to be fertile enough ground for the invention of a historically urban Amman out of the Rabath Ammon of the Ammonites (thirteenth century BC), the Philadelphia of the Greco-Roman "Decapolis" or confederacy of city-states (third century BC), and the Amman of the Ummayads (seventh century AD) and of succeeding Islamic empires.

A second explanation offered for the "fact" that Amman lacks an urban identity is that it is composed of displaced people who do not identify with it. A brief overview of the various displacements and migrations gives a sense of the multiplicity that forms the urban population as well as the circumstances that brought people to and through Amman.

In 1878, Circassian immigrants from the Caucasus established Amman when they were settled by the Ottoman state in its frontier areas. They were followed by merchants from Syria, Lebanon, Palestine, and the Arabian Peninsula, especially after the Hejaz railway, which was built along the pilgrimage route from Istanbul to Mecca, reached Amman in 1903. The population was then augmented by Arab nationalist political dissidents, especially from Damascus, seeking refuge from Ottoman and later French Mandate suppression, as well as Druze fleeing from the French and Najdi and Shammari refugees fleeing the Wahabi state of al-Saud. Other groups coming in include Kurds from Iraq and Syria, Bedouins settling in the environs of the town, and Bokharan Turks from Central Asia.

The establishment of the Transjordanian Hashemite state under a British Mandate is the major turning point in Amman's modern history.[13] The British brought in colonial administrators, land surveyors, and archaeologists, while the newly formed bureaucracy began to attract important influxes of migrants, especially Christians, from other Transjordanian settlements as well as from Palestinian cities. In the 1920s, Armenian refugees from the massacres in Turkey began to arrive. Palestinian merchants unable to compete with Jewish commercial and agricultural enterprises being established in Palestine, bureaucrats, lawyers, and bankers continued to settle in Amman.

The highly charged dates of 1948 and 1967 mark two massive influxes of Palestinian refugees following the creation of Israel and later the Israeli occupation of the West Bank. Refugee camps filled the city, expanding its size and population rapidly. In 1970, the bloody clashes between the Jordanian army and the PLO were followed by an exodus of the PLO militias and political sympathizers. It also led to a move by many of the bourgeoisie, and not just the Palestinians among them, to the supposed safety and commercial security of Beirut. The Lebanese civil war starting in 1976 brought back the bourgeoisie, as well as some Lebanese, most of whom moved on to Cyprus and Athens. More Lebanese came after the 1982 Israeli invasion of Lebanon.

The 1970s and 1980s also saw large in and out migrations due to economic reasons. These were the oil boom years when a significant portion of the labor market in Jordan, across all sectors and classes, went as migrants to the oil-producing countries of the Gulf. In the same period, a "replacement labor" pool of in-migrants ebbed and flowed, mainly Egyptians working in construction and semiskilled labor as well as domestic labor from Southeast Asia. The 1990–1991 Gulf crisis and war disrupted these patterns and brought back most of the labor migrants as well as around 300,000 Palestinian and Jordanian "returnees" who were second or third generation migrants in the Gulf and had never lived in Jordan, despite their citizenship. In addition, over two million "transit migrants" made their way to their home countries via Jordan. Small numbers of Bosnian refugees have also been added to the population. Since the 1990s, the most important in migration has been that of Iraqis: first as a result of the U.N. sanctions regime and then the 2003 war and ensuing instability. Official figures, largely seen as underestimations, range from 30,000 to 100,000, among whom intellectuals, professors, and artists figure largely, some seeking refugee status and resettlement in another country and some settling in Amman to wait out the current state of affairs.[14]

It would be difficult to see how urban coherence could be maintained through these upheavals, whether materially or discursively. All the more so, since the in-migration mostly represent forced rather than voluntary movements, reflecting as they do the region's turbulent history throughout the twentieth century and beyond. For most of these migrants, Jordan was a transit destination, although for many it ended up being their final one. Still their children or great-grandchildren continue to look in two directions at once: toward home/homeland and toward a preferred temporary destination or a "second home." Given this social composition, it is therefore perhaps not surprising that the inhabitants of Amman do not easily identify themselves as "Ammani."

Yet, paradoxically, while the extreme porosity of Amman may prevent identification with the city per se, it does provide people with a strong sense of proprietary interest in residential space and engenders a privatized "place attachment."[15] Accounts of settlement in Amman, whether the person speaking is Damascene, Palestinian, Circassian, Hijazi, settled Bedouin, or rural migrant, almost always elicits statements of pride and achievement: "There was no-one here before us, these were empty lands, wastelands, *we* made Amman." In performing individual as well as group identity, people often point out of their windows saying, "When I built my house here, this was all empty land, I was the one who first built a road, everyone followed me, there used to be wolves and wild animals in these hills when I moved here." The poor, refugees, and squatters echo the same sentiments. A Palestinian inhabitant of a squatter area called Wadi Al-Rimam (or the Valley of Dead Remains) is quoted as saying: "we (Palestinians) leave our fingerprints wherever we go. We changed this place from a valley of the dead to a valley full of life, as you see."[16] There is therefore a strong sense, both individual and collective, of having domesticated the space that is Amman, made it into a place, and laid the groundwork for future settlement and urbanization and indeed for civilized living and the existence of the state.[17] This would appear to be a powerful tool for forging a strong urban consciousness, especially of a capital city.

A final explanation offered by the inhabitants of Amman concerns the features of its built environment. The dramatic physical growth of the city from a small settlement encapsulated in a deep valley to an urban sprawl doubling in size every decade or so as a result of population influxes is manifest in the spatial disjunctures and the abrupt transitions that characterize Amman. The topology of Amman reinforces these disorientations; as new neighborhoods crept up the steep hills surrounding the original settlement, winding roads were constructed that followed the topography of the hills and the earlier paths made by animal and human traffic. Steep stairways rose up vertically to link the roads to each other for pedestrians. As new residential and commercial areas rapidly developed, Amman continued to creep up and down hills. The consequence is not only an exhausting experience for pedestrians, but also for drivers. The frequent steep turns and sudden drops offer unexpected glimpses and views of the city, juxtaposed in counterintuitive ways. This "third dimension" effect plus the explosive growth of the city and the small downtown which no longer provides a "center" makes it difficult to orient oneself while navigating the city; one never knows which way one is facing. Even the more recent construction of high-rise buildings that serve as some sort of landmarks do not help as they suddenly appear from unexpected angles, adding to the puzzle as to which direction one is traveling. Only in the outermost edges of the city, in the ring roads and highways recently constructed, is there some sense of longitude and latitude. While these parts of Amman are flatter and more easily navigable, finding one's way to the small clusters of houses and shops that intermittently spot the landscape is made no less easy by the open plan layout.

Economic forces shaping Amman as the capital of a rentier state[18] and a city built on remittances also make for morphologies of interruption. Starting with the 1970s, the commercial class became heavily involved in regional and international trade. Many moved with their families to the Gulf States while still maintaining bases in Amman, and professionals and small businessmen followed suit. Skilled and unskilled laborers also made their way to the cities of the Arab Gulf. This is when Jordan became "the world's only non-oil exporting oil economy," which led to the rapid growth of the public sector and to an "increasing appetite for land in and around urban areas."[19]

It also led to the kinds of incongruities captured by Jonathan Raban in his account of Amman from the late 1970s. After acknowledging, "I had been wary of coming to Jordan. I hadn't liked the look of its Gross National Product,"[20] Raban describes his first day in the city:

> I found Rainbow Street, bright with boutiques, jewellers, craftware curio shops and the sort of stationers where you can buy only deckle-edged "At Home" cards and amazingly expensive buff-colored scented notepaper which looks as if someone has knitted it out of painted horsehair. The street itself was full of amazingly expensive buff-colored people. There were more

Gucci bags on show than there are around Sloane Square; more Dior dresses than on Bond Street. The men had blow-dried hair and wore Italian crocodile-skin shoes. Everyone passed in their own fragrant bubble of personal cologne . . . They looked to me as if they were managing remarkably well on $460 a year.[21]

The 1970s saw the increasing stratification of the population and division of the city into east and west in ways that could not be captured through conventional "averaging" measures, such as the GNP. The smaller eastern part of the city was becoming evermore spatially dense as remittances from the Gulf were used to bolster zinc and cinderblock houses and to add extra rooms and second stories. East Amman is also where most of the squatter areas and refugee camps are located, which according to a conservative estimate, comprised more than 25 percent of the households of Amman in the mid-1980s.[22] In West Amman, on the other hand, remittances and oil-derived wealth were used to expand the city at a dizzying speed. Thus between 1972 and 1982, the surface area of the city grew from twenty-one to fifty-four square kilometers, and the period was marked by land speculation, increase in land prices, and widespread construction.[23]

West Amman emerged as a rapidly expanding area marked with an extremely low density of population, with spacious single-family villas built on large plots of land, separated from one another by tracts of agricultural land. The tenuous, though increasing, hold of urbanism is illustrated well by the common sight of luxury villas surrounded by agricultural lands still planted, harvested, and used as pasture by the inhabitants of the villages encapsulated within the boundaries of these new suburbs. This makes for an urban texture that simultaneously conjures up city and country.

This pockmarked urban fabric is encouraged by legislation which does not link the permission to subdivide agricultural land and its conversion to residential areas with the availability of infrastructure. Thus, "the common practice of landowners has been to obtain subdivision approval, and then pressure the municipality to provide the highly subsidized infrastructure services, which in turn significantly enhanced land values."[24] As Razzaz points out, the present planned residential areas in Greater Amman could accommodate a population of 3.3 million, or more than double the present population.

All these would constitute important explanations for why Amman is experienced and perceived as not being a city: its lack of fit with models of tradition, modernity, or globality and the incoherent cityscape it presents and its jumble of inhabitants thrown together by forces emanating largely from outside the country—the shards and debris of the politics and policies of regional and global powers. Yet it still remains to be explained why place attachment and "frontier" pride are not translated into identification, why an "Ammani" villa architecture is not celebrated, or why investments in construction and city planning do not create coherent public spaces and representations of Amman.

To go beyond macroprocesses that make of Amman a disjointed reality, we need to recognize the city as a product of people who make space and place, discursively and materially, negotiating macrolevel "forces" in culturally specific ways. The question then becomes who is invested in denying Amman's citiness and why?

Amman c. 1950: Bourgeois Formations

An important part of the construction and articulation of the identity of cities is struggles over space and meaning between different segments of the urban population. Geertz vividly describes the competition in Sefrou, Morocco, between established city elites and incoming upwardly mobile rural migrants over municipal elections and arguments over whether to paint the city beige or white.[25] Exclusion and inclusion between different segments of the urban population and between city dwellers and "outsiders" are thus at the heart of constituting urban culture. They are not only inscribed in space, through the presence or absence of certain buildings, institutions, and urban layout, but also marked by social and cultural practices. Consumption, quite literally, is an important part of these practices. In his memoirs of mid-twentieth century Nablus in Palestine, al-Masri describes how two kinds of the city's signature sweet delicacy, *kunafa*, would be prepared every day: one of lower quality for the peasants who come to the markets in the morning and one of higher quality for the city dwellers, the "Nabulsis," which would only be put out in the afternoons when the peasants had safely departed.[26]

Struggles for dominance over the city mark elite discourse and give it its political content. Negotiations, often bitter and perhaps violent, take place over the social and spatial boundaries between the "real" inhabitants of the city and the interlopers. Competing groups display and contest identity through the quarters they inhabit in the city, the types of housing in which they live, and their lifestyles in terms of dress, furnishings, food, and other consumption practices. In municipality politics, this competition takes the form of struggles over the design of public space, surface appearances of buildings, building of mosques or shrines or other public/religious buildings, and so on. It is important to point out that the struggles within segments of the bourgeoisie, or between the bourgeoisie and an incipient bourgeoisie, draws in the urban poor as well, linked as they are to these groups through patronage relations and economic dependence. In this way, dominant images of a city as well as notions of urbanity and urban belonging may be formed through sets of competing alliances between segments of the state, dominant groups, and subaltern groups.

Who are Amman's bourgeoisie? In which practices of inclusion and exclusion do they engage? The 1940s to 1950s is a good transitional period to explore, since in many ways it sets the stage and also shows what *might have been.* Amman of that day was a town of around 30,000 inhabitants and the capital of the British Mandate state of Transjordan ruled by the Hashemite Emir Abdullah.

Amawi describes the complex relationships between the merchant class and the state/palace as one of mutual constitution. Emir Abdullah encouraged the influx of merchants and attempted to draw them away from the city of Salt, whose elites had rejected Hashemite rule. On their part, individual merchants financed the Emir through nonreturnable loans when the British subsidy fell short of his needs for distributing largesse. They also donated ("cheerfully" according to a British observer) to the building of hospitals and schools and other public works. The chamber of commerce was created as early as 1923, and merchants had also formed a social club called the "Tuesday Club" and met in each other's homes to discuss affairs of the day.[27] When Sharif Hussein (Emir Abdullah's father) came to visit Amman, one of the merchants contributed to the welcome parade by building a metal, though somewhat skeletal, "triumphal arch" over one of the main streets of downtown.[28]

World War II was good to the merchants of Amman,[29] and their prosperity began to mark and structure the city in a new way. A study in the mid-1980s documented 140 villas of affluent merchants from that period that are still standing in Amman.[30] This is while many of Amman's 30,000 inhabitants were engaged in agriculture and living in simple one-story courtyard style houses. The distinctive personality of the merchant class was clearly being inscribed in space through a new architecture and the creation of elite neighborhoods, slowly drawing away from the core settlement in the valley and up the surrounding hills.

This class of merchant families saw itself as urban notables, invested in the newly established state and the facilities of its capital city. Identities of origin continued to be important, however, given that these families drew their wealth precisely from their continuing links with cities in Syria and Palestine and with branches of their kinfolk living in them. Merchant families sought their brides overwhelmingly from their cities of origin and continued to speak with their distinctive accents.[31]

Yet their identities were also being reconfigured. Amawi quotes one of her sources: "Budayr noted that in Transjordan, all Palestinians were called 'Nabulsi' and every Syrian was called 'Shami' (referring to Damascus) . . . This factionalism between the two groups was specifically evident during the annual celebrations of the birth of the Prophet Muhammad.

Each faction competed to organize a better parade than the other faction."[32] The tradition of organizing competing parades on holy occasions is known in other cities, especially in Damascus where they represented competition and rivalry between the notable families of different quarters of the city.[33] In Amman, in addition to a neighborhood competition, it also becomes a rivalry between two "ethnic" groups. Thus, the designations "Nabulsi" and "Shami" are Ammani categories since they would not carry the same exact meanings combining origin and occupation elsewhere, and yet these Ammani identities are simultaneously references to other cities, other places, and other times. This kind of incongruity continues to mark the bourgeoisie of Amman today.

Other practices and performances of identity were also being negotiated in Amman in the 1940s. Circassians remembering this period often mentioned that Damascene women veiled in public by wearing several layers of thin black crepe material over the face in a recognizably Damascene fashion. In contrast, Circassian women were traditionally unveiled, if unmarried, and only wore a head covering after marriage. The growing Damascene influence in Amman led some Circassian women to follow suit and to also cover their faces, while Circassian women in the surrounding villages did not. In a different recollection of the same issue in the same period, Munif states that "because Circassian women were Muslim, they set an example for others to be unveiled. This was further facilitated by the fact that Circassian tolerance had been matched by Bedouin tolerance . . . This facilitated the movement from veiling to unveiling, bypassing the obstacles of the fanatic urban mentality, which was full of complexes and taboos, and which governed several other Arab societies."[34] For Munif, Amman's dominant feature in the 1940s is a colorful pluralism that paves the way to modernity: "Mango Street in particular seemed like a carnival of different costumes and accents."[35]

Through oral histories and memoirs one can see the reconfiguring of identity in the space that is Amman. The merchant bourgeoisie contributed to the physical markers of this new Amman through their houses, their warehouses, the markets they built (such as the Mango Street mentioned by Munif, built by a prominent merchant family of the same name), and the public works that they sponsored as well as through organizing public events and making public spaces for the performance of Ammani politics, identity, and practices.

The state also marked and transformed the space of Amman. In describing how Amman was made into the capital of the Transjordanian state, Rogan emphasizes the fact that due to the pecuniary condition of the British Mandate government, the power of the new state was exhibited more through ceremonial parades than by the construction of public buildings.[36] One important ceremony was the Emir's ride from the palace to the mosque for the Friday prayer,[37] and then there were the parades of the newly formed army. Strict procedures were laid, and every step of the way, including the slogans to be repeated by the assembled populace, was planned. Thus, Rogan argues, it was through ceremonial rather than through construction of buildings that Amman was made into a capital city under the British.

Another type of mass presence and scripted public performance that marked Amman as a capital city and as an urban capital in this period is also well remembered: the political demonstrations and protests that took place in response to events in Syria, Iraq, and especially Palestine. In addition to the influence of ideologies such as Arab nationalism and Islamism, the identification of the people of Amman with regional events had a personal nature since they were often recently arrived from those very cities and countries in which significant events were taking place. As Munif points out, this was augmented by the influence of the first generation of young professionals, who had come back from studying in Cairo, Baghdad, Damascus, and Beirut and brought with them the political ideas and sentiments of those cities. It is also noted that high school students were very active in these demonstrations—these represented are the first generation being educated in the newly established high schools of Amman. Recollections of these protests reveal their simultaneously local and global character as well a mix of pragmatism and idealism. A Circassian man recounted this anecdote to me:

> A friend of mine used to go to a school near the Muhajirin quarter. This was in the early 50s, maybe 1951. Abbas Mirza was the Minister of Interior. The school was badly built, and the rain would come in and so on. So the students went out in a demonstration. They shouted two slogans: "Fix the school!" and "Down with imperialism!" They marched to the Ministry of the Interior, and Abbas Mirza came out on the balcony and asked what they wanted. They said they wanted the school to be fixed and down with imperialism. Abbas Mirza said: "As for the school, I talked to the Prime Minister, and we will do what you want. As for imperialism, leave that to me."

In these manifestations of identity and power, houses, veils, parades, and other means of marking domination in space, Amman was acquiring an urban identity marked by practices and politics of the merchant bourgeoisie and their alliances with the state, but also by the formation of an urban public of professionals, students, and "masses."

This emergent urban identity was augmented and yet fragmented by the 1948 influx of the Palestinian refugees. The Palestinians competed with and overwhelmed every incipient class, including the barely formed bourgeoisie, the new bureaucracy, and the small army. Dispossessed

Palestinian peasants provided the cheapest labor force, and refugee women entered into domestic work in large numbers.[38]

The new bourgeois segment of Amman, the Palestinian displaced middle and upper classes, was marked by deep ambivalence. On the one hand, they could easily participate in the discourse of having "made Amman" and civilized it. On the other hand, their identity was firmly rooted in the cities of Palestine and reinforced by exile as well as by the slight downward mobility resulting from displacement. One marker of this ambivalent bourgeoisie was the new Ammani housewife: middle class, unveiled, in Western dress, cooking intricate, refined, Palestinian *urban* foods and delicacies, but living in the basement apartments of the two-story villas that sprang up all over the then peripheries of Amman.

AMMAN CIRCA 1980: THE NOSTALGIC BOURGEOISIE

The 1948 and 1967 influx of Palestinians furthered processes of urban fragmentation in Amman. Many of the bourgeois neighborhoods that had been forming in the hills around the valley of the original settlement of Amman became the site of the "temporary" refugee camps, eventually leading the older inhabitants to abandon them to form new neighborhoods to the west. This became an Ammani pattern reinforced by the constant in and out migrations that followed; new neighborhoods would barely last ten years before new ones would spring up, more desirable and more indicative of wealth and status. As wealth was accrued abroad, it was invested in larger and larger dwellings always pushing the city westward into agricultural lands. As those owning the lands sold them at huge profits, they too became part of the creeping urbanization and villa colonization of the lands west of Amman.

Meanwhile, people's social networks and visiting patterns became less with neighbors but were rather scattered all over the city. The car became a necessity as public transport could not keep up with the growth of the city and as lifestyles became increasingly luxurious. Women took to driving with delight. The bourgeoisie were no longer invested in organizing events in public, open space to mark identity, status, and power but rather performed in private for one another,

> Every evening, in some villa on one hill or another, there was a party. At each one there was somebody who was giving a party the following night, and everyone was invited. So evening after evening, we went to the same party. The hills and the villas changed, but the occasion remained the same . . . the party seemed to have been going on for several years at least, and it had acquired the ritual quality of a church service. It was conducted in several different languages at once . . .

Sitting next to Gabriela Durra on one of these identical evenings, I began a sentence by saying, "Surely in a city of nearly a million people . . ." "No! No! No!" she said "you don't understand! Amman is not a city of a million people, it is a city of a hundred couples!"[39]

This circulation of elites in closed private space was reinforced by the move of their capital to the economies of the Gulf in the 1970s and 1980s. The massive labor migration to the Gulf led to a rapid upward mobility and changes in lifestyle, dwellings, and consumption. The expansion of the elites beyond the "hundred couples" meant a much more complex social composition and less homogeneity. For many, Amman became a *pied-à-terre,* a summer vacation stop on the way to Marbella on the Spanish Riviera or similar resorts, to escape the heat of the Gulf States, a place to invest in building a huge villa that remained empty most of the year. Built in a variety of styles from "Islamic" to "Arabesque" to postmodern, the villas of Amman's bourgeoisie conjure up Bedouin tents, Swiss chalets, turreted castles, Mamluke fortresses, and American ranch houses. Fethi and Mahadin attempt to classify the styles of villa architecture in Amman and conclude that many of them are marked by "acrobaticism":

> Structural acrobaticism refers to villas which employ an incredible array of structural and formal acrobatics, such as inclined walls, large cantilevers, suspended arches, curved elements and all sorts of architectural "tricks." Here the architect (and client) is showing off his best; that is, his imagination and masterly use of the full potential of reinforced concrete. Similar "fantastic" villas can be found in the Gulf region. This formalistic way of exhibitionism can either be related to a good sense of humor or simple cultural bankruptcy and egotism.[40]

While the architectural forms may be proliferating, these villas continue a process of marking wealth and building popular perceptions that first began in the late 1940s. Munif recalls popular sentiment about one of the first elite merchant houses: "When the Jeweller Muhammad Ali Al Ardakani built a palatial house near the First Circle Roundabout, many said 'Madness is an art.'"[41]

While building bigger and better houses, in an expression of individualism and consumerism that increasingly fragments the urban fabric, what the bourgeoisie maintain, in terms of urban discourses, are sentimental ruminations of other cities, of other spaces, and of other urban identities. This is not only in the case of Palestinians where the frustrations of continued Israeli occupation make identity construction a particularly nostalgic process,[42] nor is it a process that refers only to the long past.

But it marks all those who briefly lived the various golden ages of a succession of Arab cities: of Damascus, of Jerusalem, of Beirut, and now even of Kuwait and Baghdad, which have been added to the list of cities that they mourn.[43]

Performances of bourgeois identity do not only take place through building facades. In recognizably elite fashion, it also takes the form of marking luxurious interiors with antinomies of identity, such as displaying peasant embroidery and "folkloric" artifacts, as well as archaeological remains (often illegally collected) to decorate gardens. It takes the form of having a "Bedouin" sitting room as well as a "Western" sitting room. Men wear suits to social gatherings ("the Party"), but women may wear stylized designer-made dresses with "peasant" embroidery, usually the handiwork of women in refugee camps, increasingly producing for NGOs run by bourgeois women. Bourgeois identity also takes the form of what may be called the "consumption of foreign wives," such that a stratification of Ammani society could be quantified through the numbers and nationalities of foreign wives, creating new generations of Ammani elites who leaven their regionally hybrid identities with global admixtures.

Nostalgia is for the past but also for a future, one that is no longer marked by the search for locality but rather for unfettered modernity—a desire to escape and leave behind the messy processes of contested nationhood, of unrealized Palestinianess and Jordanianness, of unrequited nostalgia for a series of destroyed cities: Jerusalem, Beirut, and Baghdad:

> The Party really was a showpiece . . . A door had been open to the garden and at midnight a man called Victor had come in from the moonlight olive grove playing an accordion. He had started with moaning Arab tunes, each note stretched as if it was on an inquisitor's rack. He moved on to Czech folk dances, then to American pop, and finished up with "Viva la Spania" . . .
> The Party was roaring out—
> We're going to catch that Costa Brava plane!
> Vi-va La Spann-yaa![44]

Regardless whether bourgeois performances are seen as derivative cosmopolitanism or kitschy hybridity, it is not that the elites of Amman are not urban or not urban enough to sustain an Ammani identity. But rather that their urban identity is drawn from other cities from which they trace their origins or with which they profess a closer identity regardless of their citizenship (as in the cases of Beirut and Kuwait). They are a "nostalgic bourgeoisie," but the object of their nostalgia is not the Amman of the past but the past of other cities in the region. Also, as indicated by their Party song, the object of their nostalgia for the future is not Amman but the cities of the West, the modern and the global.

These practices and desires represent simultaneously a turning inward and an extreme boundlessness, the cultivation of personal space and of peripatetic exercises. It would seem from some discourses and per-formances, that the locality, the nation, and the city were transcended. However, this would discount powerful continuing discourses of the past (of other cities) as well as the rise of new practices in marking public space. One example was the growing phenomenon in the 1980s of wealthy individuals building mosques in various parts of the city. As Rogan describes, this private philanthropy was often one way in which migrant remittances were invested in the city and intersected in interest-ing ways with a state plan to "Islamize" Amman. Other segments of the bourgeoisie built cultural foundations and centers and established art galleries and poetry clubs. Yet others were active in businessmen's asso-ciations and the Rotary Club. Women, previously active in charitable organizations, transformed these into NGOs. New buildings representing these activities began to dot the cityscape and present new kinds of "public" interaction from the most open (mosques and some NGOs) to the most closed by class and status (film clubs and crafts boutiques.) In spite of the public nature of these new spaces, none of them are open spaces, leaving the city's public terrain as the sole territory of the state.

Amman 2000: Citizenship and the State

If the bourgeoisie are unable or unwilling to sustain a sense of place, of here and now, what about the state and its projects, both national and urban? As mentioned, the early years of statehood were marked by a state-bourgeoisie alliance in marking space but which was fluid and did not stabilize the meaning of urban places. In the 1950s, more systematic planning began to take place, and master plans for Amman were drawn up though not implemented. As of 1963, the phrase "Greater Amman" was used, but the first master plans for the greater metropolitan area were only drawn in 1985. Greater Amman now encompasses about 520 square kilometers and is divided into twenty administrative districts, forming a "city region." The importance of the master plans lies not only in the reshaping of the cityscape, but also in determining the nature of the authority that has jurisdiction over the city and its inhabitants. Along with the idea of "Greater Amman," the structure of governance was changed to appoint a "Lord Mayor" who presides over a forty-member municipal council, from which eleven committees are formed to oversee various aspects of city administration. None of these are elected offices.

The role of Amman's inhabitants in the making of the city is thus not through formal representation and committees, nor through negotiations over public space and facades, but rather by strategizing to lay claims on privatized spaces. In the case of West Amman, this leads to inefficient municipal infrastructure trying to keep apace with bourgeois ambitions. In East Amman, the poorer parts of the city, state power plays itself out in a different way. Here the state is part of people's daily lives as they struggle to gain access to services as well as cope with the benefits and problems wrought by a variety of urban projects, from squatter upgrading to sites and services, to housing projects and income-generating schemes. Most of the urban projects in Amman are funded through foreign aid, channeled and implemented through governmental agencies and, increasingly, through NGOs. While these are important projects shaping Amman, they do not generate an Ammani narrative. Rather, in keeping with general urban practices aimed at the poor, they partake of global discourses about planning, rationality, and hygiene.

Among the poor we find another paradox of Amman. The city's poor, working classes, and rural migrants are rarely, if ever, referred to in general and official discourse as the "urban poor," which would perhaps marginalize them but still include them as part of the urban population. Rather the two salient categories are "refugees" and "squatters." The former refers to Palestinian refugees inhabiting camps run by the United Nations Relief and Works Agency (UNRWA). The latter refers to Palestinian refugees not inhabiting the camps and an assortment of rural migrants and immigrant labor who find shelter in illegal settlements scattered throughout the city. While their designations render them temporary, these segments of Amman's urban population are equally invested as the elites in their housing and engage in important struggles claiming rights in their streets and neighborhoods.[45] These enduring struggles lead to a mix of identities that simultaneously articulate inclusion and exclusion. For the Palestinian poor in Amman, neighborhood belonging is strong, but refugee identity is stronger. Most importantly, the third and fourth generation inhabitants of these areas are invested in cultivating their "village" identity in reference to their village of origin in Palestine and, more generally, their "peasant" identity as an important component and claim to Palestinian nationhood.[46] Within Palestinian identity, the peasant/urbanite distinction (fallahi/madani) is a crucial social categorization and dichotomy.[47] With poor Jordanian rural migrants one similarly sees the cultivation of tribal as well as village identities. One finds formal and informal village associations and tribal associations all over Amman, which do sometimes articulate with neighborhood belonging. An interesting example is provided by an attempt in a neighborhood of East Amman, largely composed of one tribal group, who lobbied the municipality unsuccessfully to assign names of tribal ancestors to the streets of the neighborhood, to inscribe genealogy in space as it were.[48] Street names in Amman are generally from Arab and Islamic history and are quite long and difficult to remember. Thus no one uses street names as addresses in Amman, rather using landmarks, such as well-known restaurants or malls, to assign unofficial popular names to streets. Once again, we see how state policies and the multiplicity of identities do not serve to thicken an Ammani identity but rather to dilute it.

Symbols of state power began to become more visible all over Amman in the 1980s. Key ministries such as the Ministry of Planning have large and impressive buildings, although many other government offices are housed in modified residential buildings. The King Abdullah Mosque, named after the great-grandfather of the current king and the founder of the country, sits next to the recently built parliament and has replaced the old Husseini mosque in downtown Amman as the official mosque used for prayers by royalty and statesmen on religious holidays and state occasions. It competes with the downtown Roman theater as the image of Amman which graces official posters of the city and is often used as a backdrop for CNN reports from Amman.

Although the state marks space in its capital city, few of the plans and schemes that it embarks on are accompanied by attempts at constructing a hegemonic narrative or story of Amman as a city or as a capital. State planning for Amman is generally marked by technocratic considerations and by global rather than local or national narratives. State-driven attempts to reshape Amman and affect its outward appearance and use of space are attempts toward integrating it into meta-narratives that evoke different worlds than Western modernity.

In the 1980s, in the aftermath of the Iranian Islamic revolution, this desire took the form of "Islamizing Amman" through legislating certain architectural features, such as arches, shopping arcades, and white facades for public spaces, as well as trying to arrive at a fixed understanding of "Islamic architecture."[49] While this process was truncated and did not lead to a sustained remaking of the city, the debates and examples it generated together with the proliferation of philanthropic mosque construction have had consequences for the city. In addition to the highly aesthetic and pleasing architecture of these mosques that have become a regular feature of neighborhoods, the mosques impart a particular rhythm to daily life in the city. Growing numbers of people, mostly men but also women, now observe daily prayers in the mosque instead of at home as in the past. Islamic practice stipulates that, whenever possible, the Friday noon prayer should be observed communally, and at those times, streets are often congested with parked cars for several blocks around the mosques. The sermons, as well as the call to prayer, are transmitted over the mosque amplifiers, making everyone in the vicinity a participant.

Stressing the Islamic identity of Amman, however, though of consequence for both its built environment and for the nature of public life, does not provide a sustainable or distinct narrative for Amman, but rather integrates it into the meta-narrative of Arab Islam. The past few decades have seen state attempts to construct more specific identifiers of the city, such as designing a logo and landscaping it onto hillsides near the new underpasses and overpasses. In a juxtaposition of symbols, the logo of the city shows the word "Amman" topped by three arabesque arches, with the middle arch embracing the royal Hashemite crown. However, such attempts represent interrupted practices, the visions of one mayor or another whose works stop when he departs or of a government commission that gradually stops meeting and becomes defunct. Malkawi describes how the various urban plans for Amman ended up with little or no implementation at all. He argues that "planning discourse, as it exists in Amman, is produced by several contesting political and ideological elements. The combination of these elements is too powerful to allow one element to prevail and completely dominate the discourse. Hegemony is embedded in the discourse by its association with the various elements, rather than with one single element."[50] The "association of tribalism with national identity on the one hand and the king as the guardian of both on the other" represent the discursive limits of urban planning.[51]

Hourani makes a similar point, but rather than "tribalism," he argues that it is the financial interests of powerful elite families that tend to sustain or subvert urban planning projects.[52] These important insights suggest interpreting Amman's malaise in terms of the disjuncture between the country and the city—a country established by a deterritorialized royalty, which sets the tone for the peculiar construction of deterritorialized national identity. The nation thus identified is constructed not in terms of autochthony and territory but loyalty to the regime and the royal family. The capital city, though marked by spatial practices as a realm of power, is erased of symbols of belongingness, such as old neighborhoods, markets, coffeehouses, or old public buildings, and not allowed to create new signifiers such as legible street names. Thrown into high relief through this erasure is the Roman amphitheater in the midst of contemporary structures, a juxtaposition that highlights disjuncture and marks an "alien" (also "Western") presence in the ostensible heart of the city. The fragmented urban fabric reflects in turn an inchoate national identity. Amman, the porous city that assimilates all the groups that come to it, reflects their imprint but does not transform them into an entity that is Amman. Amman does not celebrate its ability to integrate or absorb different groups but continues to construct their practices as essentially alien and not "Jordanian," while not elaborating in positive terms what "Jordanian" or "Ammani" might comprise. Here is an Ammani, incidentally a Circassian, attempting to explain things to the travel writer:

> What you see in Jordan is often not 'Jordanian' at all. The Palestinians are the big-city people. They know about night-clubs and restaurants; the Jordanians know very little of these things.

Then there are the Lebanese. They all came to Amman in 1970 when things became too bad in Beirut. You know Rainbow Street? That is all Lebanese. Before it was just little shops, very dark. The Jordanians do not know about shop-windows and boutiques, they do not have a feeling for that kind of style. So the Lebanese bring this *chic* to the city . . . [53]

Recent activities starting in the mid-1990s and accelerating in 2002 are witness to a different state approach to Amman. The downtown area has been the scene for much state building activity. The restored Roman amphitheater, which dates back to the second century AD, was flanked by the "Hashemite plaza" and public gardens and a town hall with a parade ground and exhibition and conference halls was built in the western part of the downtown, partly on the site of demolished neighborhoods, including one of the older Circassian quarters. According to the Web page of the Amman municipality, the rationale is to revive the downtown area, to integrate the different parts of the city, and to "connect ancient Amman with the modern one," as well as to provide tourist facilities. An artificial lake and aqueduct are planned as well as a mosque, cultural center, national museum, and park.[54] Some of this reimaging of the downtown area is being funded by the Japanese International Cooperation Agency as part of an overall plan to develop international tourism in Jordan.

As Hourani shows, these plans are mostly aimed at making Amman a destination for large-scale tourism, which implies the need for a "traditional" set of commodified cultural products. For this purpose, the downtown area is being visualized as a series of "tourist trails" that will leave the visitor with certain "images." Hourani describes how these plans are being contested and many elements are being abandoned due to the role of prominent architects in constructing visions of "traditional" Amman that are different than that of the municipality and the state. He also documents the anger but helplessness of local residents and shopkeepers who are unable to maintain their small enterprises in the face of land speculation and investment by large companies.[55]

In spite of this heightened investment by the state in constructing authenticity, these activities and passions are focused on "imaging" Amman rather than narrating it. They are consistent with the aims of earlier plans for making Amman commensurate with other Arab cities,[56] rather than looking for the specificity that is Amman. While global tourism demands authenticity, this can be generically produced through images and representations rather than being grounded in a narrative of belonging. In another state enterprise, however, we begin to see the makings of such narratives. The activities around the declaration of Amman as the "Arab Cultural Capital 2002" for the first time includes attempts sponsored by the municipality to write the history of the city, to publish archival documents on the city and its different neighborhoods, and to sponsor art exhibitions and cultural performances that represent the "memory of the city." Abdul Rahman Munif's memoirs of Amman were republished in a special glossy edition, and other works commemorating Amman were commissioned.

In the increasingly familiar, quintessentially Ammani paradox, Amman begins to find its specificity and to write its history, not to emphasize its uniqueness but rather to claim a legitimate place among the array of Arab cities that continue to provide the norm and to set the standard of city life and culture. As its history, demography, and social composition suggest, Amman is a city that participates fully in its transnational setting—from receiving the refugees created by regional conflicts to its attempts at integrating a number of competing ideologies and identities. However, it does so by emphasizing regime over state and territory, the monarchy over the state, evoking meta-identities such as Islamism and Arabism, and by adopting an abstract modernism that permits no landmarks of identification and spaces of particularism.

CONCLUSION

While the discourses about Amman have been and continue to be frag-mentary, contradictory, and resistant to institutionalization, this does not mean that contestations over space are nonexistent or unimportant. Regardless of how they figure in discursive practices, the *making* of cities always takes place through struggles over space, struggles that manifest themselves in different locales and are undertaken by different segments of the population. As many have argued, one can read the landscape of power such that struggles over space are political ones and political struggles (whether class, ethnic, or national) will manifest themselves as struggles over space. As Soja states, "spatial fragmentation as well as the appearance of spatial coherence and homogeneity are social products and often are [an] integral part of the instrumentality of political power."[57] In Amman, struggles *among* segments of the population over space have constantly been appropriated by or delegated to the state, which becomes the site of the *dominant* struggle in the urban process. One could argue that in the Jordanian case the state/regime has under-taken to create itself at the expense of the nation and the city at the expense of urbanism. The historical contingency that is Amman, there-fore, has to be understood in a particular context of economy, state-building, and cultural production.

Cities like Amman are not among the prototypes which have for long provided and continue to provide the models for theories of urbanism. The particularities of Amman defy standard generalizations about the historical formation of cities, urban morphologies, population structures, political economy, or the social and cultural dynamics of class, community, and family. In all these topics, there is an uneasy fit between the data from Amman and governing paradigms. It is commonplace among both scholars and residents of Amman to attribute this "lack of fit" to a "missing" ingredient of Amman itself, to a crisis arising from some inherent lack of urbanity. The approach taken here shows the city as constantly changing, absorbing, and responding to spatial and social practices, state policies, and transnational linkages. How the city is constituted in official and popular discourses and practices may not reproduce the scholarly obsessions of a different urban heyday, but undoubtedly illustrate the profound modernity of the city that is Amman.

Notes

This chapter is based on long-term ethnographic fieldwork in Amman and directing a multidisciplinary project on the city sponsored by CERMOC (Centre d'Etudes et de Recherches sur le Moyen Orient Contemporain) in 1992–1996. Earlier versions of this chapter have benefited from discussions at a number of forums. Special thanks goes to Farha Ghannam and Bruce Grant for their comments and to Rami Daher for keeping me abreast of recent developments.

1. While I could use the (equally reified) categories of "the rich" or "the elites," I prefer for the purposes of this discussion to use the term "bourgeoisie" for several reasons. I would like to highlight the city (burgher) identity and merchant character of the elites in question as well as to acknowledge the local Arabic terms *"burjwaziyyah"* (the bourgeoisie) and *"barjaza"* (to act bourgeois) that are often used to refer to such elites and their lifestyles.

2. The suffix "-i" in Arabic indicates belonging, thus "Ammani" means "of Amman" as well as "from Amman."

3. Janet Abu-Lughod, "The Islamic City—Historic Myth, Islamic Essence, and Contemporary Relevance," *International Journal of Middle East Studies* 19 (1987): 155–76; Dale F. Eickelman, "Is There an Islamic City? The Making of a Quarter in a Moroccan Town," *International Journal of Middle East Studies* 5 (1974): 274–94. For the other two constructs, the paradigmatic modern city is Paris, and the global city is Los Angeles. See David Harvey, *Paris: Capital of Modernity* (New York: Routledge, 2003); and Mike Davis, *City of Quartz: Excavating the Future in Los Angeles* (London: Verso, 1990).

4. Sawsan El-Messiri, *Ibn al-Balad: A Concept of Egyptian Identity* (Leiden, Holland: Brill, 1978).

5. Teresa Caldeira, "Fortified Enclaves: The New Urban Segregation," *Public Culture* 8, no. 2 (1996): 303–28.

6. Mike Davis, *City of Quartz*; Arjun Appadurai, *Modernity at Large: Cultural Dimensions of Globalization* (Minneapolis: University of Minnesota Press, 1996), 192–94.

7. Edward W. Soja, *Postmodern Geographies: The Reassertion of Space in Critical Social Theory* (London: Verso, 1993).

8. For an expanded discussion, see Seteney Shami, "Introduction: Researching the City," in *Amman: The City and Its Society*, ed. Jean Hannoyer and Seteney Shami, 37–53 (Beirut, Lebanon: CERMOC, 1996).

9. Guy Loew, quoted in Eugene Rogan, "Physical Islamization in Amman," *The Muslim World* 86 (1987): 24–41 (quote from 30).

10. Lecture by Dr. Taleb Rifai, Architect, CERMOC, Amman (1992).

11. The arrival of the Hejaz railway to Amman in 1903 is a convenient marker of the transition from village to town. The arrival of Emir Abdullah in 1921 and the choice of Amman as his headquarters and then his capital is the second important event. Amman was officially declared a capital in 1928—thus for seven years, Transjordan was a state without a capital.

12. In the region, one can think of Tel Aviv for an intriguing parallel, as well as Ankara.

13. For a good discussion of the choice of Amman over Salt, which was a more likely urban center as a capital, see Eugene Rogan, "The Making of a Capital: Amman 1918–1928," in *Amman: The City and Its Society*, ed. Jean Hannoyer and Seteney Shami, 89–107 (Beirut, Lebanon: CERMOC, 1996).

14. In all the flows described previously, Amman was not the only receiving city or town in Jordan. However, as a capital city it tended to always draw the largest numbers, even in the case of Palestinian refugees where attempts were made to establish camps away from the urban centers.

15. Irwin Altman and Setha Low, eds., *Place Attachment* (New York: Plenum Publishing, 1992).

16. Aseel Sawalha, "Identity, Self, and the Other among Palestinian Refugees in East Amman," in *Amman: The City and Its Society*, ed. Jean Hannoyer and Seteney Shami, 349 (Beirut, Lebanon: CERMOC, 1996).

17. See my description of the Circassian version of what I term the "foundation myths of Amman" in Seteney Shami, "The Circassians of Amman: Historical Narratives, Urban Dwelling, and the Construction of Identity," in *Amman: The City and Its Society*, ed. Jean Hannoyer and Seteney Shami, 303–22 (Beirut, Lebanon: CERMOC, 1996).

18. Reiner Biegel, "Urban Development and the Service and Banking Sector in a 'Rentier-State,'" in *Amman: The City and Its Society*, ed. Jean Hannoyer and Seteney Shami, 379–403 (Beirut, Lebanon: CERMOC, 1996).

19. Omar Munif Razzaz, "Law, Urban Land Tenure, and Property Disputes in Contested Settlements: The Case of Jordan" (PhD diss., Harvard University), 104–5.

20. Jonathan Raban, *Arabia through the Looking Glass* (London: Flamingo, 1983, first published 1979), 304.

21. Ibid., 307–8.

22. Hisham Zagha, "Housing Problems, Policies, and Solutions in Jordan," in *Housing and the Urban Poor in the Middle East—Turkey, Egypt, Morocco, and Jordan*, ed. R. Keles and H. Kano, 178–96 (Tokyo: Institute of Developing Economies, 1987).

23. Razzaz, "Law, Urban Land Tenure, and Property Disputes in Contested Settlements," 127.

24. Ibid., 126.

25. Clifford Geertz, "Toutes Directions: Reading the Signs in an Urban Sprawl," *International Journal of Middle East Studies* 21 (1989): 291–306.

26. Malik al Masri, *Nabulusiyyat: min bawakir al-dhikrayat wa-al-wujuh wa-al-ṣuwar al-sha'biyah* (Amman: Al-Dar al-Urduniya lil-Thaqafa wa-al-I'lam, 1990).

27. Abla M. Amawi, "State and Class in Transjordan: A Study of State Autonomy" (PhD diss., Georgetown University, 1993).

28. Arslan Ramadan Bakig, *Amman: Yesterday and Today* (London and Ipswich: W. S. Cowell, 1983).

29. Amawi, "State and Class in Transjordan," 421–544.

30. Taleb Rifai and Ruba Kanaan, *Buyut Amman al-Ula* [The First Houses of Amman] (Amman: The University of Jordan, 1987).

31. Amawi, "State and Class in Transjordan," 482. Amawi, personal communication.

32. Ibid., 396, n. 82.

33. Philip Khoury, "Syrian Urban Politics in Transition: The Quarters of Damascus during the French Mandate," *International Journal of Middle East Studies* 16 (1984): 507–40.

34. Abd Al-Rahman Munif, *Story of a City: A Childhood in Amman*, trans. Samira Kawar (London: Quartet Books, 1996 [Arabic original published in 1994]), 103.

35. Ibid., 106.

36. Rogan, "The Making of a Capital," 103–6. Even where colonial and national states invest in the built environment, ceremonial displays are always important means of marking power in space.

37. This is in clear imitation of other, more powerful sovereigns, for example, the Ottoman Sultan whose ride to the Friday prayer in Istanbul was the scene of performances of power and populace.

38. This demographic factor leads many observers of Amman today to call it a "Palestinian city." To my mind, this is an unfortunate adoption of discourses that ignores the kind of cultural history that is reviewed in this chapter and participates in describing the city through ideological agendas.

39. Raban, *Arabia*, 323.

40. Ihsan Fethi and Kamel Mahadin, "Villa Architecture in Amman: The Current Spectrum of Styles," in *Amman: The City and Its Society*, ed. Jean Hannoyer and Seteney Shami, 171–82 (Beirut, Lebanon: CERMOC, 1996).

41. Munif, *Story of a City*, 224.

42. The role of the Israeli occupation in the physical transformation of Jerusalem and other West Bank cities as well as escalations in violence, which most recently in 2002 led to the destruction of the historic city center of Nablus, continues to fuel this nostalgia with concrete "objects of memory" (Susan Slyomovics, *The Object of Memory: Arab and Jew Narrate the Palestinian Village* [Philadelphia: University of Pennsylvania Press, 1998]).

43. There is an interesting shift in sentiment concerning Kuwait after the 1991 Gulf War and the forced displacement of Palestinians and Jordanians from the Gulf States. Before the war, there were many complaints of discrimination and second-class citizenship. After the war, Kuwait is remembered in terms of a lifestyle that was not only affluent, but also "modern."

44. Raban, *Arabia,* 337–38.

45. Razzaz, "Law, Urban Land Tenure, and Property Disputes in Contested Settlements," 160–263; Seteney Shami, "Domesticity Reconfigured: Women in Squatter Areas of Amman," in *Organizing Women in the Middle East,* ed. Dawn Chatty and Annika Rabo, 81–99 (London: Berg Publishers, 1997).

46. Aseel Sawalha, "Identity, Self, and the Other among Palestinian Refugees in East Amman," in *Amman: The City and Its Society,* ed. Jean Hannoyer and Seteney Shami, 345–57 (Beirut, Lebanon: CERMOC, 1996). Randa Rafiq Farah, "Popular Memory and Reconstructions of Palestinian Identity: Al-Baq'a Refugee Camp, Jordan" (PhD diss., University of Toronto, 1999).

47. Seteney Shami, "Studying Your Own: The Complexities of a Shared Culture," in *Arab Women in the Field: Studying Your Own Society,* ed. Soraya Altorki and Camillia Fawzi El-Solh, 115–38 (New York: Syracuse University Press, 1988).

48. Interview with an engineer in the Amman municipality, 1996.

49. Rogan, "Physical Islamization in Amman," 30–31, n. 27.

50. Fuad Malkawi, "Hidden Structures: An Ethnographic Account of the Planning of Greater Amman" (PhD diss., University of Pennsylvania, 1996), 8.

51. Ibid., 137.

52. Najib B. Hourani, "Amman Needs a Picture: A Political Economy of Place-Making in Jordan" (unpublished paper).

53. Raban, *Arabia,* 319.

54. Municipality of Greater Amman Web site, http://www.access2arabia.com/moga (accessed January 31, 2000). For recent developments and textual representations of the city see the new Web site of the municipality at www.ammancity.gov.jo.

55. Hourani, "Amman Needs a Picture."

56. Malkawi, "Hidden Structures," 93.

57. Soja, *Postmodern Geographies,* 126.

10

LET THE DEAD BE DEAD

Communal Imaginaries and National Narratives in the Post–Civil War Reconstruction of Beirut

Maha Yahya

In a conference in Beirut in 1999 titled Memory for the Future, a prominent local politician declared: "We should let the dead be dead. It is the only way forward." Coming at the end of three days of discussion in which the postwar experiences of Lebanon, Rwanda, South Africa, and France and the role of memory in postwar reconciliation were discussed, compared, and contrasted, this statement seemed quite remarkable for the purported pragmatism it presented.

The Lebanese civil war ended in 1990, nine years prior to the preceding statement. A massive reconstruction effort had been launched by the Lebanese state. This chapter intends to examine the place of the dead and of memory in the post–civil war reconstruction of Beirut's urban and architectural landscape and with it Lebanon's national identity. It will raise a series of questions regarding the place of the city in the contradictory project of defining national identity, in delineating the boundaries of modernity and often of urban citizenship. Arguably, some of these issues have shaped modernist discourse about the city in the past two centuries. The interpolation between identity politics, cultural histories, modernism, and planning in and through the city makes it an ideal locale from which to examine various issues. For a wide variety of scholars, cities have been the place from which to try and understand the impact of modernity on the social, political, and cultural fabric of society. While various works have pointed to the ways in which modernism was used to mask the unevenness of national development in different contexts, the uneven spread of modernity itself has seldom been discussed. Cities certainly bring this issue to the fore. In various cities around the world, the iconography of modernity seems to be located in select sites and areas while displacing from discourse and view the material realities of the other city—the "unintended city" that is never part of the official history/story.[1] This unevenness does not imply incompletion as Habermas argues.[2] Rather it lies at the heart of the experience of modernism.

In the case of Beirut, a city that historically has stood for the country, the confluence between globalism and post–civil war identity-making in its urban architecture brings up a series of questions such as how was the disaster [of a long civil war in this case] addressed through the work of the city's planners and what image of city and nation was implicit in its postwar reconstruction? In what ways does the double-sided character of nationalism—that is, its need to project outward, as well as inward—redefine the boundaries of city and nation? What is its impact on the politics of memory and rights to the city? Given the legacy of civil war—that is the penultimate point at which the official markers of national identity were violently challenged by a multitude of alternate voices—these questions acquire a certain critical urgency. This became manifestly clear in 1992 in a series of conflicts, which erupted over different spaces in Beirut. In what follows, a particular reading of one of those incidents is used to inform and structure this analysis of the postwar context for Lebanese nation-building and the centrality of Beirut, the capital city for that project.

Off with Their Heads

In May 1992, during the demolition of the last two medieval suqs in the historic city center of Beirut, the remnants of a mausoleum suddenly made headline news.

Located within the military zone that divided Beirut during the war, the mausoleum, made visible by war bombing that partially destroyed the building in which it was hidden, was immediately claimed to be a shrine housing the remnants of a Muslim Shi'a mosque caretaker. Hizbu'llah[3] quickly cordoned off the structure and the building was declared a religious monument, thus indestructible under the mandate of Solidere, the real estate company that owns the area. For the following weeks, nearby inhabitants transformed the structure into a small shrine for "pilgrims" from around the city, especially its southern suburbs where the majority of the city's Muslim Shi'a population lives.[4] As stories of strange events and miracles were being reported in city cafes and parlors, rumors of voices, sightings of ghosts, and the inability of those in charge of demolition, despite repeated attempts, to destroy the building proliferated in the local press.[5] Reports of the broken hinges of the first bulldozer, the shattered motor of the second, failed dynamite attempts, and the smell of orange

Figure 10.1. Ibn Arraq Mausoleum (right) at the end of Suq el Tawile in Beirut's historic center at the end of the civil war and prior to the commencement of reconstruction efforts. Photograph taken by the author in 1990.

Figure 10.2. Ibn Arraq Mausoleum after the demolition of the rest of the surrounding urban fabric. Photograph taken by the author in 1992.

blossom filtering through cracks in the wall recurred in these articles. A few days later it emerged that even though the structure, a seventeenth-century Mamluk building, was indeed a tekkiya dedicated to Ibn Arraq, he had been a Muslim Sunni rather than a Muslim Shi'a. Ironically, his effective hatred for Shi'as had led him to condone their death by any means!

Several questions are brought to the fore by this incident. The most obvious and immediate question is why would Hizbu'llah rush to proclaim a shrine in an area where the Shi'a community, a traditionally rural population that began to migrate into the city at the turn of the century, was not historically present and thus did not own property? How does one interpret this incident in the framework of post–civil war reconciliation and more specifically in the scope of proposed urban/architectural schemes for this country? Why this turn to the supernatural at this precise juncture in time, and who were those ghostly specters haunting the (re)consolidation and (re)construction of the nation and of national identity?

Rebuilding Beirut: Political and Economic Imperatives

Fifteen years of protracted violence (1975–1990) left approximately 200,000 dead, around 300,000 injured, and 800,000 permanently displaced in a population of around 3.5 million. The state was marginalized and lost its

Figure 10.3. The Green Line cut through Beirut's historic center and carved the city in two. Throughout the war, this zone was a no man's land between warring factions. Photograph taken by the author in 1990.

physical, institutional, and territorial control over the country. The capital Beirut was severely fragmented and partially demolished, its historic center and the areas extending out from it transformed into a no man's land between the warring factions.[6]

Successive episodes of conflict between different militias further fragmented the city into a series of smaller enclaves. Population displacement transformed squatting into the most basic strategy of survival and the principle form of urbanization during the war years and transformed Beirut into a complex web of property disputes ranging from the illegal to the quasi-legal.[7] A large portion of those displaced settled in the city's informal settlements along its southern suburbs, especially the coastal strip of Ouzai, a mix of publicly and privately owned land and which witnessed unprecedented growth during the war years.

Lebanon's infrastructure was also significantly damaged. The World Bank and other international agencies estimated total financial losses at $25 billion, real per capita income half of what it was prior to the war, while an estimated 200,000 professionals and skilled workers had emigrated out of the country.[8] Another 17,000 citizens remain missing.

With the signing of the Taif agreement in 1991, the "end" of the Lebanese civil war was announced.[9] As much the result of changed regional as well as internal conditions, this "end" coincided with the conclusion of the Gulf War and thus a reshuffling of the political checks and balances in the region. In Lebanon most of the militias were dismantled

Figure 10.4. The informal settlement of Ouzai in Beirut's southern suburbs. These were once luxury chalets that were occupied by populations violently displaced from their homes at the beginning of the Lebanese civil war. Photograph taken by the author in 1990.

with many members absorbed into the Lebanese army, parliamentary elections took place, and militia heads were integrated into the state.[10]

Using urban practices distilled from earlier periods, the postwar Lebanese state unevenly confronted a conundrum similar to that faced by French and Lebanese administrators and architects during the establishment of Lebanon as an independent nation-state, that is, how to give shape to a national identity when confronted with conflicting communal and ethnic identities.[11] The state embarked on a wide scale reconstruction plan to both rehabilitate its institutions and physically rebuild the country. The most important and grandiose urban rebuilding projects focused on revitalizing Lebanon as the "Switzerland of the Orient" and on (re)building the capital Beirut. Two large urban development projects were launched: the Lebanese Company for the Development and Reconstruction of the Beirut Central District (Solidere) for the rebuilding of the historic city center and the project for the reorganization of the city's southern peripheries, particularly Ouzai (Elyssar). The latter area is the site of the city's largest informal settlements that housed around 10,000 families or 50,000 individuals in 1992, a large majority of whom are lower-class Shi'a war-displaced or economic migrants. It is also an area that is partially controlled by Hizbu'llah. The Solidere project was to reconstitute the heart of the city into the financial and business center of the region, and Elyssar was to transform the southern coast of the city into its leisure zone. While the former was emptied out of its inhabitants by the war, the inhabitants of the latter were to be redisplaced into more "appropriate" areas in the project. In what follows, this chapter will focus on the city center project and refer to the project for the southern suburbs where needed.

However, before moving to these projects a few issues should be clarified. The exigencies of immediate postwar reconstruction—as in post WWII Japan and Germany—demanded a deliberate forgetting rather than remembering of the war, of atrocities committed during the war, and of the traumas inherent to having survived and adapted to fifteen years of violence which reached into every niche of daily activity. Through official discourse, popular journals, daily papers, and so forth, the fifteen-year-old civil war in Lebanon was presented as an aberration, the "war of others on our land" by intellectuals, politicians, and the populace alike. Official history accounts, including the newly rewritten school history books, have purged all references to communal and individual responsibility for the war. As the director of the project would claim, the approved history of the country "must eliminate everything that creates conflict between the Lebanese" so as to facilitate reconciliation.[12] Like the mythical phoenix to which Beirut is likened, the country in postwar discourse was to resurrect itself from its own ashes in its ever familiar form. In this discourse, the construction of a new beginning meant that history would simply pick up where the country left off in 1975. Lebanon, according to leading policy-makers was to reclaim its economic role as the "Switzerland of the Orient," irrespective of regional changes. As we shall see shortly, driven by the need to project a stable image to the outside that would inter-nally appeal to its disparate populations, state discourse represented official Lebanese "national" identity as a process of retrieving the rem-nants of a prewar golden past, while narratives of war, death, and sur-vival were written out of public discourse, relegated to the realm of the private, the biographical, thus in official accounts the ahistorical and apolitical.[13]

URBAN ACTORS

Postwar reconstruction of the city center included a variety of local urban actors representing the public and the private sectors as well as local inhabitants.[14] In addition, local militias in control of areas occupied by displaced populations also played an active role in initial negotiations around the center. However, not all of these actors played an equally effective role. In short, the Council for Development and Reconstruction (CDR), the official body in charge of the reconstruction effort, hired Dar Al-Handasah Consultants[15] (DAR) to submit designs for the area and organize the reconstruction process. At the same time, members of Oger Liban, an international firm based in the Gulf and owned by Prime Minister Rafic el Hariri, were either appointed to senior positions or acted in a consultative capacity to CDR, thus placing private capital in control of the foremost planning agency in the country.[16] Designs were carried out in Cairo, in DAR's main office for the Middle East. At the end of sev-eral months, members of the CDR were invited to Cairo for the unveiling of the project. Upon approval, the project was then brought to Lebanon as the endorsed master plan for the city center. It was presented at a series of meetings both in DAR and at various organized events in government offices, hotels, and universities.[17]

THE PLAN: COLONIAL IMPERATIVES AND NATIONAL POLITICS

As presented, this project proposed a radical reconstitution of the city center at the procedural as well as the programmatic and design level. A private real estate company, Solidere, was created to reconstruct the area within boundaries that had been delineated in past plans. This company had a dual basis: an imported model and local planning laws. The format of the company was based on a model created in Saudi Arabia for the renovation and reconstruction of areas surrounding the holy shrine in Mecca.[18] However, the general provisional laws for a real estate company existed in Lebanese planning laws. Initially envisioned as a public-private partnership for the purposes of large-scale urban renovation and regeneration, these laws were amended in 1991 to allow the total privatization of the reconstruction of the city center. Under the new formula, property boundaries were eradicated, and ownership was transferred to the company.[19] Fifty percent of the shares of the company were distributed among current property owners in a ratio equivalent to the value of their property.[20] The remaining 50 percent of the shares would be bought by investors, none of whom could control more than 10 percent of the shares at any one point.

At the programmatic and design levels, the proposed plan included a quasi complete overhaul in the urban and architectural character of the area as well as its economic functions. In brief, the city center, 119.1 hectares of an existing urban fabric, named by the planners as the "traditional" Beirut Central District (BCD) was supplemented with an additional 45.8 hectares of land reclaimed from the sea. Relying on a synthesis of picturesque planning and Haussmanian civic monumentalism, the plan was characterized according to its planner by "the themes of grandeur which mark the center of a capital city; the 'Grand Axes'; high buildings; new roads and boulevards; the new city park; the public and religious buildings."[21] These three parallel "grand" axes cut through nodes deemed of "national significance," the two Sérails or the military barracks constructed by the Ottomans in the nineteenth century and today housing the prime ministry and the CDR; the Place de L'Etoile, with the parliament and national library, all constructed between 1926–1930

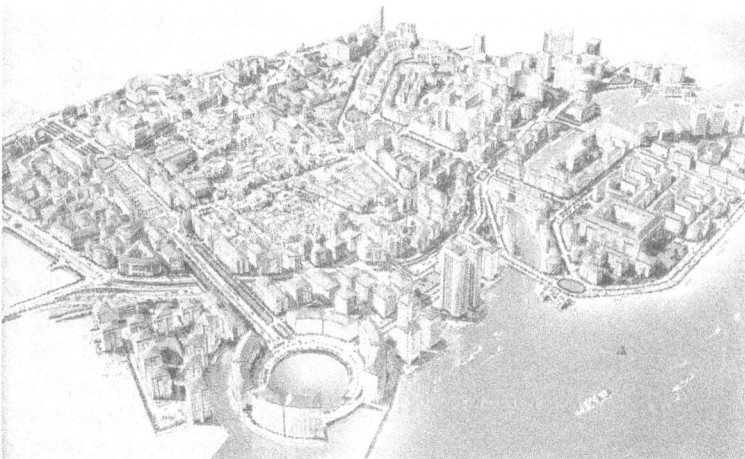

Figure 10.5. First postwar master plan for Beirut's historic city center (1991), showing the three "Grand Axes." Courtesy of Dar Al-Handasah.

by French authorities during their mandate over Lebanon; and the Place des Martyrs, named after the Arab nationalists that were hung by the Ottomans in 1916.

In addition to all religious edifices and a select number of residential buildings, these venues formed the crux of the preservation, conservation, and renovation aspects of the project. The company also instated a selective program of recuperation of historic buildings along with a series of archeological digs undertaken with the assistance of UNESCO and the Directorate General of Antiquities.[22]

The 4,000 displaced citizens who had resided in the peripheral regions of the city center during the war were given monetary compensation and made to leave,[23] while the rest of the urban fabric was destroyed and replanned, with new street layouts, zoning, and building criteria. This new layout was comprised primarily of financial districts, built to the Manhattan model, and residential areas, such as Saifi, created as contemporary "urban villages." Most of the previous functions that the center housed, especially those that catered to the lower and lower middle-class sectors of the Lebanese population, were eradicated.[24]

Figure 10.6. Second postwar master plan for Beirut's historic city center (1994). Preserved historic or cultural buildings are colored in grey. Most of the remaining fabric was demolished. Courtesy of Dar Al-Handasah.

LOCAL AND INTERNATIONAL:
THE TWIN FACES OF NATIONAL IDENTITY

This enactment of the project is not very surprising. Post–civil war nation-building required the projection of a stable, cohesive, and easily recognizable image, both externally to the outside world and internally over a fragmented territory, one that would counter the bloody associations brought about by long years of conflict. Put differently, this dual vocation created a tug of war for the city planners between the denationalization of urban space inherent to global capital and the need to nationalize and unite the postwar city and the capital of the country. This imperative of Lebanon's postwar reconstruction drive and specifically the rebuilding of the city center of Beirut was identified at the onset by Prime Minister Rafic el Hariri as a way to recapture Lebanon's "national vocation" as the financial capital of the East and to reinsert Beirut into a global narrative. In other words, Beirut was to "recuperate" its prewar position as an international capital for global capital. He also described these efforts as the "transformation of [Beirut's central district] into a modern financial and commercial center [and] as symbolizing the rebirth of the country and the determination of the Lebanese to rebuild their capital." These themes echoed earlier descriptions of the project as the "national heart" of the country, thus linking the rejuvenation of both economy and nation to the rebuilding of the center of the city. Inadvertently, it also identified this economic role once more as the most salient aspect of Lebanese national identity.

To project a cohesive image externally and thus (re)claim Beirut's position on the global scene, the center and with it the city's identity had to be deterritorialized, "liberated" from all existing codes and reference points to both past and present. It was transformed—to paraphrase Marx's famous discussion of money—into a purely ideal mental form necessary for understanding the ultimate abstraction of capital. Lebanon's national identity had to be projected through the city center as a comprehensible whole, as its capital Beirut becomes a node in a network of global cities, identified by Saskia Sassen as cities which no longer depend on their immediate hinterlands for their economies. Defined by flexible production and transnational economies, these cities make nonsense of national boundaries, national trade movements, and often even of national politics.[25] Inside those cities a new politics of centrality and marginality is created with massive investments in downtowns and little resources in the peripheries. Outside the central business district, the rest of the city is characterized by an urban space that is increasingly differentiated in social terms, even as it is functionally interconnected in some ways beyond the physical contiguity of neighborhoods. This recaptured economic vocation was to neatly extend Beirut's historic role as an important node in a larger network of Ottoman port cities and its more recent postindependence role as the financial capital of both the East and West in the region onto a global stage.

Internally these reconstruction plans were informed by a series of primary political concerns. To reestablish its power, the state needed to enact its territorial imperative in a physical space not implicated in the territories of any of the warring factions. The city center was to be "recovered" from the vagaries of war as the locus upon which the state could express its existence and spread its hegemony in opposition to the fragmentation of national space induced by the war. At the same time, Ouzai, Beirut's largest informal settlement located in its southern periphery, was directly identified with the chaos of war and the direct absence of the state during the war years. While the reconstruction of the city center was to signal the "recovery" of prewar Beirut's position of eminence in the region, the second proposal for the southern peripheries was to index the "liberation" of the city from the effects of this conflict.

Spatial Densities and Right to the City

At the urban level and to achieve the goals mentioned previously, the state employed a radical and purely utilitarian approach to defining privately owned property. Planners suggested that the total privatization of the center was necessary since the parcelization of private property due to inheritance, the war, and complex rental laws would hinder the reconstruction process and prevent the quick rehabilitation of the city center— a goal identified as paramount right at the end of the war.[26] However, this approach by the planners reduced property to a physical entity rather than a set of social relations and a system of rights between individuals and with the state. In other words, property rights in the city center were not just about the property itself nor just about the rights of property owners to their own properties but were also about the rights of citizens to their city. As Bentham maintains, property is not composed of physical objects only, but of expectations of deriving certain advantages from the thing we are said to possess.[27] In some instances, the definition of these expectations, *property rights,* the "official" interpretations of rights to land, conflicts with individual notions of rights and access, or *property claims,* hence citizen definition of these expectations. More often than not these conflicts, regardless of context, result in the same recurring phenomenon: lands of an ambiguous *property status* where the control of one group over space is challenged by others.[28] By collapsing these distinctions, the state negated all alternative claims to the city.

This narrowly defined approach to property neglected other more intangible aspects of property. As a social institution, property delineates

rights, obligations, power, and privileges, reflecting, reinforcing, and sometimes challenging certain power structures in society.[29] By transforming the
entire area into one privately owned lot of land and giving owners and
tenants a "share" in the company, Solidere transformed territory into an
abstraction. In the process, property rights, which previously encompassed
rights to use, to construct, to build, to reside, and so forth, were reduced
to a right to revenue, thus transmuting the social institution of property
into a binary relationship between investors and property owners and
between larger or smaller shareholders.

This effacement of property boundaries and various commercial
functions in the city center had significant consequences on the social
fabric and memory of the city. Reducing Lebanon's identity to its economic
vocation and thus transforming the center into the internal shopping
"mall" of Beirut provoked a compelling amnesia toward the social context
and myriad communities of the city. Severed from its social production,
space was fetishized, presented as an independent object, politically neutral, and not, as Lefebvre argues, one produced by the very conflicts over
its uses and the meanings attributed to it by its users.[30] By eliminating all
distinctions between property rights and claims, the project succeeded in
physically erasing and radically altering a critical component of social
memory. Transforming property into an abstract space eradicated the
subjective aspects of property, such as its confirmation for many of personal identity, family lineage, or inheritance, and severed its constitutive
role as a "site" for collective memory. Both the past and the present were
unanchored, deterritorialized. While this dissociation between property
and "right" to the city could potentially have spawned a radically new
discourse about the city, the forms it took foreclosed any alternative discussions. Property was redefined purely as a system of exclusions, effectively transforming it into an abstract entity removed from both physical
reality and its social context. At the same time, the hierarchy of social,
economic, and political relationships inherent to various tenure arrangements was flattened into a two-dimensional structure in which both
property owners and renters became partners in the company. Individual
rights to the city were reduced to the company's marketing logo at the
time of: "Buy a share in the reconstruction of your city."

These actual and symbolic practices enacted by the project concretized at different levels and in unanticipated ways both the imperatives of colonial planning as well as the urban transformations that
occurred during the war years. The appropriation of publicly and privately owned land for the benefit of a private company brought the
socioeconomic and political transformations of Beirut begun by French
Mandate authorities to their ultimate realization.[31] At the same time, this
project also symbolized the cumulative end to the "emptying out" of the
center enforced by the militias during the war period. Separated from its

prewar social context by fifteen years of violence, the eradication of property rights, and the obliteration of previous functions that the center used to house through the destruction of their buildings insured a quasi-total divorce between the center and its socio-urban context and redefined, once more, rights of access to the city. It also limited the range of citizens whom the center would service. Without getting into the moral and ethical question of appropriating private property on behalf of a private company, the implications of these actions on citizen rights to their city were manifold.

This attitude toward identity and rights to the city is further betrayed in the politics of representation utilized. With the eradication of the existing urban fabric and the voiding of the social content of property, architecture's relationship to the sociopolitical context within which it is active is not addressed. At the urban level, representations of the center envisage it with no apparent links to the rest of the city or country. Premised on the selective destruction and (re)construction of war and postwar efforts, the proposed plan presents a vision of future Beirut and Lebanese national identity in drawings where Beirut is erased and the center presented as an exclusive entity floating in a nonexistent city.

A perspectival tradition dominates the planning process, with the organization of facades to be looked at and vantage points to see from. The streets are wide and clearly visible, terminated with high towers from which one can have a totalizing view of the city. The panoramic vision provided by such images has been described by Michel de Certeau as one that "transforms the bewitching world by which one was possessed into a text that lies before one's eyes."[32] In other words, by using this panoramic bird's eye view to present the city, daily spatial practices, the accidental and nonmonumental, are effectively maintained external to the viewer's frame of reference and expunged from the future of Beirut. Such overarching gestures are rendered into an expression of power and authority. According to Mr. Chalak, the president of CDR at the time, "if you have a strong central power, the streets of the city are wide. They are straight. When political power collapses, they change into winding streets with dead ends."[33] One then wonders if what is desired is the eventual extension of this apparent order to the rest of the city. This direct association of disorder and "winding streets" with the era of the war implicit in such statements appeared even more equivocally in the underlying logic of the Ouzai project in the southern suburbs.[34]

More critically perhaps, assigned the status of an object, a symbol and a signifier, the architecture of the project regresses into a picturesque pastiche that reaches out beyond the immediate boundaries of city and nation. Descriptions of the three main axis of the project recall the "modern" capitals of Europe and America. Paris is evoked through the Champs Elysee, which cuts through Borj Square, Washington through the Serail complex now Capitol Hill, and New York through a mini-Manhattan to be constructed on land reclaimed from the sea. This language, used to describe the project, seemed to be subscribing to the collective memory of expatriate Lebanese to entice them back to a now worldly capital.[35] Yet the iconographic images used plundered the city's fabric for motifs ostensibly representative of this elusive national identity. At the same time, Beirut's last remaining medieval suqs were destroyed in the name of creating a new center for the city and then reconstructed under the guise of "preserving" its Mediterranean identity.

The drive informing "recuperative" initiatives was not the preservation of a particular urban fabric or a specific lifestyle or the restoration/conservation of one period in the city's history. It was about the preservation of elements deemed emblematic of one aspect of identity, a selective plundering that saw in the center's historic structures components open to interpretation and the nostalgic recall of a bygone past. For example, the architecture of the Saifi "Urban Village" used elements such as arches and columns from existing Ottoman and French Mandate residential buildings that had been destroyed as surface ornaments.

The cumulative impact of these actions is a patchwork center with renovated pedestrian and office areas from the French Mandate period and a series of isolated monuments, historic and religious, standing amid large stretches of empty undeveloped land and parking lots. Helen Sader, a leading Lebanese archaeologist argued that the reconstruction operation launched such a destruction frenzy in Beirut's center that it lead one to wonder whether the outcome would simply be "une destruction de l'histoire." More critically, isolating religious edifices, such as mosques, churches, and synagogues, from the urban fabric and daily living rhythms they once occupied transforms these structures literally and metaphorically into icons of the postwar era.

While the project decontextualizes architecture by eradicating the city's historic fabric, the new proposed sites manipulate scenery, ornament, and facade to create a site loaded with historical allusions. The project of memory in this instance is quite selective in the details of what it includes and what it omits.[36] In an attempt to create the modern space of Lebanese identity, difference is suppressed, and details are forgotten in the actual renderings of the project. The architect omits the more immediate past to reach out to an idyllic and revered time, the eternal past just waiting to be rediscovered, the designated prewar "golden age" of Beirut. Beirut, according to its planners, is to "regain" its status as a Mediterranean port city, the gateway between the East and West, the "Paris" or "Switzerland" of the region. This past, discussed as if it simply existed, overlooks the fact that it is actually a paralyzed past that is being plundered. Memory thus is not about addressing the trauma associated with neither the civil wars, nor the strife over national identity and belonging to the city. Memory is now about closure of that past, about forgetting, that is, the replacement or displacement of that past with another. The conflicts over the meaning of Lebanese nationality which have plagued the country since its creation are not questioned, while persisting attempts by all the religious communities in Lebanon to fabricate a politically distinct and almost sovereign "imagined community" of their own are abjured. By rejecting multiple notions of identity as a precondition for reconstruction, the project preempted the multiple experiences that different communities have undergone. The fragmentation enforced by the war and the coercion implicit in peace-generated homogeneity are in this sense commensurate.

These representations present a self-enclosed narrative, be it programmatic or historical, which uses perspective to close and seal the rest of the city whenever it can. Urbanity and national identity are transformed into a complete picture with a constructed past and future; the present is simply foreclosed, bracketed out of the image. The past here is transformed into a question of representation and not of responsibility, and here the representation voids private memories and painful histories.

This "tabula rasa" approach to reconstruction was not limited to the city center but was also forcibly embedded within the legislative framework of the country. At the end of the war, the Lebanese parliament issued a law declaring amnesty for crimes against humanity committed during the war, including full-blown massacres of civilians and entire communities, acts of mass torture, and so forth. Excluded from this amnesty were assassination attempts against political or religious leaders and foreign diplomats or crimes sent to the judicial council by the Council of Ministers as threats to national security. In other words, the postwar Lebanese judicial system sought to prioritize individual over collective responsibility. The arguments used were that it was time to forget and turn the page or else the country could not move forward.[37] It was an attitude, which, as Nizar Sagiyeh argues, succeeded in basing the process of national reconciliation upon a politics of suppression and denial. Not surprisingly, it was also reflected in the representational mechanisms the state utilized in its bid to reassert its authority over its renegade fragments.

GHOSTLY SPECTERS AND ALTERNATE MEMORIES

If the city center project seemed to isolate memory, it also invoked the extremes of forgetfulness. It acted as a form of denial, not of memory and forgetting, but of the ability to tell the difference between remembering and what it means to forget. However, as Maurice Halbswachs has argued, memory is not free-floating but in fact needs a social framework within which to function. Through this framework, memory is to guide experience by linking one to traditions, customs, and religious beliefs. As he points out, "a man who remembers alone what others do not remember resembles somebody who sees what others do not see. It is as if he suffers from hallucinations."[38] In other words, memory had to be linked to lived experience, retained and transmitted through generations through a complex web of social relations. The 4,000 displaced residents who lived in the center were forced to relocate, as were many of those who lived in its immediate peripheries or who owned properties there. For many of those inhabitants of the city center and its previous owners, the end of the war and the start of reconstruction did not signify an erasure of the war and a new beginning, but rather the beginning of their own loss, that is, the beginning of a different kind of war. In a series of interviews conducted by researcher Yasmin Arif into the impact of the Solidere reconstruction project on the current residents of the downtown, recurring tropes of loss and desertion at the end of the war rebound. In the words of Abu Fouad, "for us the older generation who grew up together, no matter what will happen to the Burj now, we don't care. What we care for is the years that were gone from our lives—and now after the war—we look back and realize that all the places that we remember are no longer there—they are a desert land now." His wife continues, "there was war but it was safe [here] . . . it was very stable . . . When you look around now, you see only destruction and despair . . . there is no one anymore. The people that you talked to will also have gone by the end of the month. I am here today, but I don't know if I will be here tomorrow."[39]

In these instances, individual memories and acts of remembrance intertwine in complicated and unpredictable ways with the declared need to "forget" the war, to erase it from collective existence. Lebanon's history is isolated in the project to the monumental/topographic sites of institutional significance, transformed into the nation's sites of memory, sites which, according to Pierre Nora, emerge when there is a perceived break with the past, while the accidental politics of everyday city life are eradicated. History and memory are represented as purely temporal and chronological rather than spatial and relational. History is used to privilege particular readings of political identity and national subjectivity as "real." Arrival into this "national" history, as represented in the project, erases not only the past of the viewer, but also that of alternative communal histories. *"I am here today but I don't know if I will be tomorrow."*

However, knowing the past is no longer, if it ever was, confined to the compulsory time frames of national historiography. The reality is that the nation is not, if it ever was, the site or frame for memory, and national history is no longer the measure of what people know of their past. Official attempts to channel memories constantly face the intangible and unexpected surfacing of the past not only in individual narratives, but also in the form of haunting, in the return of the ghost which as Gordon points out only comes into play when memory cannot recall the violent event to which it has been subjected. In her *Ghostly Matters,* Gordon uses the figure of the ghost as a sign that a haunting is taking place, "a seething presence, acting upon and often meddling with taken for granted realities."[40] Her primary concern with such haunting is to offer a critique of representation by taking into account the politics of governmentality, past exclusions, and silencings. It is a way of linking social critique with the imaginary and of negotiating the unsettled relationship between what we see and what we know. From this perspective, what could the emergence of the ghost around the Mamluk mausoleum, in the inner recesses of the city center and in the midst of ongoing demolitions no less, represent but the ghost's insistence on justice by bringing into view the thousands of dead and "disappeared" and displaced for whom no place could be found in the project? Can one not read this act perhaps as a symbolic protest against a program that was extending the politics of exclusion enacted by warring factions during the war into the reconstruction and reconciliation process?[41] The ghost in this instance cannot be tracked down to a single loss or trauma but rather to an entire sociality of being. Jacques Derrida's understanding of specterlity is also useful here for reading the appearance of the ghost, an eternal, timeless, and ephemeral presence, within the politics of reconstruction and of history. For, as Derrida suggests, to speak of ghosts is to also address the questions of inheritance and of different generations.[42] History in other words is the site of contradictions and haunting, and ghosts are not just the return of the past or the dead but a reckoning. Leaving aside for the moment Hizbu'llah's political interest at the time in establishing a territorial foothold in the city center, the wide scale currency of the ghost in the city epitomizes the furtive and ungraspable visibility of the invisible, a demand for justice and ethics from both the future and the past by the ghost, which *"begins by coming back."* Read from this perspective, this event can be interpreted as a symbolic rejection of a post–civil war reconstruction approach that relied on the suppression of varying rights and claims to the city.

This incident drives us to rethink the location of the city in memory and its role in the process of defining modernity and national identity. By virtue of its historical and topographic position, Beirut's city's center inaugurated a crisis of representation for successive postwar governments—for many to possess its image was tantamount to possessing the future (and history) itself. In this sense this project became emblematic of an ambiguous kind of political imagery. In the absence of a clearly defined national identity, the project strove to construct an ideal space for a postwar society redefined selectively and along singular class lines. Its imagery attempted to reconfirm the political center's territorial repossession of the historic center and thus secure a "secular" vantage point liberated from the binds of religious affiliation that underwrite political participation in Lebanon. Through the selective displacement of citizens or their removal from view, the state reclaimed the process of constituting national and political identities from within the heart of the capital city. The physical destruction of the city and its long (re)construction become forms of collective therapy in which the "death" of the city—its "cleansing" so to speak—is meant to rid the nation of memories of the multitude of deaths that continue to haunt its making.

RECOVERING THE CITY: POSTWAR URBAN IMAGINARIES

Unlike the urban plans proposed for the city, this double articulation of territorial restitution and ambivalent loss is clearly reflected in postwar literature and film production, many of which combine fable and fact to devise a language reflective of Beirut's new, multiple realities and the perceived loss of history. In these works, Beirut, recovered as the crucible for lived experience denied in the postwar reconstruction process, is the place in which and through which efforts to come to terms with the civil war and the place/role of the city in that war resonate. It is the site through which alternate historical, sociological, and political readings of the experience and implications of living through war are expressed. The centrality of the capital Beirut to narrative imaginaries is nothing new to Lebanese fiction. From themes of rural/urban confrontation which dominated prewar literature,[43] many novels today use individual biographies, personal narratives, and the micro patterns of daily life to reflect on the inanity of the war, its incomprehensibility, and the contradictions of postwar reconstruction and nation-building so as to recover Beirut's and Lebanon's historical and social memory. Two such novels are Rashid al Daif's 1995 autobiographical *Dear Mr. Kawabata* and Huda Barakat's *The Tiller of Waters*.

Al Daif's novel is written as a series of autobiographical letters to a Japanese friend. Like the dismembered and fragmented city, the writer's inner landscape is dissected by fabulous accounts and reflections on the past and the present of Lebanon and the larger Arab region, intersecting with some of the horrors of daily Beirut. The dissolution of Beirut into civil war is a mantra for the disintegration of various ideals and ideologies such as Arab nationalism and, more particularly, his engagement with Marxist comrades when they thought themselves to be the makers of history. The dreadfulness is such that only through hallucination is recovery possible. As the main character states up front: "it seems to me with the beginning of the war . . . that my mouth became filled with ants, and my lips were sewn tightly together, as one would sew a deep wound only with a solid strap . . . and I became convinced, with the war still in the beginning, that only hallucinations can accurately describe this intractable situation."[44] This hallucinatory condition is extended through the narrators'/author's reflection on Beirut, a postwar city that he no longer recognizes and can no longer navigate and an inner landscape with which he is no longer familiar. With this loss of the personal and communal comes the declaration that he hates history.

The density of the city's social memory and the sense of loss in postwar Beirut is also forcefully evoked in Huda Barakat's *The Tiller of Waters*.[45] Following the death of his parents at the beginning of the war and the occupation of his house by displaced refugees, the protagonist Nicholas moves to the textile shop of his father in the old suqs of Beirut's historic center. The no man's land of the now empty center becomes his sanctuary as he wanders through its deserted alleyways. Using the history of various textiles, Nicholas exquisitely weaves Beirut's history, its different landmarks and physical spaces, with that of the different peoples that once made up this city—the Greeks, Turks, Armenians, Kurds, Arabs, and a myriad of other foreigners. It is a history of the world and of civilizations through one small store in the heart of the city. Through these narratives Nicholas relives his affair with Shamsa, his Kurdish servant, while the cosmopolitan social life of prewar Beirut is skillfully brought to life against the now physically devastated center and the smell of corpses and wild dogs. Against this background of lost lives, "out there," that is, life outside the war zone, becomes the aberration with which he is unable to cope.

The novel ends with the "invasion" of artificially manufactured cloth that signals the end of the war and the rampant commercialism that overtakes the physical reconstruction of the city. This end not only reveals the "loss" of history through the texture of the city, but also unearths the mythical reconstruction underway. Like Abu Fuad for whom the heart of Beirut is now a "desert land" that he no longer reads, the city is dissected by war atrocities and postwar reconstruction efforts, Nicholas wakes up after the end of the war and his own death to discover a city he no longer recognizes. Describing Martyr's Square he states:

> I looked around me not believing what I saw. A level ground, empty, like an open palm, a horizontal extension, paved over and unmarred by any extensions or protrusions. A smooth desert without sand . . . nothing, no stone, no vegetation, no animal occupies the land. I turned around myself another time. Nothing. I walked a few steps and then stopped because I lost direction. I said the sea. I must find the sea. If I do not find it then I must be either dreaming or hallucinating.[46]

This sense of loss and the recovery of the city in the postwar context are also prevalent among young filmmakers who use personal narratives, constructed biographies, and individual memories. For example, in *Around the Pink House,* Joreish and Haji Touma use the story of an old nineteenth-century house inhabited by a family of squatters (or displaced individuals) to reflect on the ways in which physical reconstruction is fast outpacing social reconciliation in the city. Walid Raad, on the other hand, uses multimedia presentations that create individual, fictional documentations of the civil war in the form of personal notebooks, diaries, home videos, personal testimonies, photographs, and archives, presented in a live performance, to question the means through which historical narratives are constructed, namely: "How does one witness the passing of an extremely violent present?"[47] Familiar sites and neighborhoods in the city are integral to this process. Urging us to consider his own constructions as "hysterical symptoms," Raad slips in between historical and fictional narrations, creatively using different means to continuously dislocate the drone of official accounts of the war such as statistics, chronologies, reports, and so forth that try to explain the at once immediate yet removed "events" of the war. Consequently, while disrupting the notion of a complete historical explanation of the war, Raad relocates the act of memory within individual narratives and accounts of the physical objects that testify to/witnessed the war (such as the make, year, and color of cars used as car bombs during the war). As Raad puts it, "these projects do not document what happened, but what can be imagined, what can be said, what can be taken for granted, what can appear as rational, sayable, thinkable about wars."

WHOSE CITY IS THIS ANYWAY?

That the war was catastrophic for the Lebanese is undisputed, but the legacy of incomprehensibility, which lies at the heart of this catastrophe, has yet to be recognized. In the absence of any open and public discourse on the constitutive role of the civil war and on questions of national history and individual memory, the state's actions are preempted by the ghostly specters of sectarian bloodshed, which seem more real today than twelve years ago when the war ostensibly ended. By focusing their efforts on the reconstruction of the capital city and simply "letting the dead be dead," successive postwar Lebanese governments effectively reasserted the hegemonic role of the city as the geographic local and of the economy as the symbolic terrain for identifying national identity. In this context, rights to the city are reinterpreted from within the logic of postwar reconstruction that evokes an international role for the city rather than a process of reconciliation that turns the city inward—onto its own territory.

However, as Cathy Caruth suggests, "history like trauma, is never simply one's own, . . . history is precisely the way we are implicated in each other's traumas."[48] Liberating the city from the binds that tie it to its reality does not necessarily release it from responsibility toward its citizens. The coupling of the state and of private capital in Beirut produced a powerful historicist discourse that acts upon urban space and population. However, the historicism of this discourse fails to grapple with the challenge of spatiality that the city poses. As Gyan Prakash argues, not only is the urban built environment defined by its position as a pivotal node in the geographical landscape of capital, but it is also defined by "the very organization of the city as society entails spatial divisions and relations and not distinctions between different stages in the march of history."[49] Middle-class neighborhoods and slums are differentiated by space, both physical space as well as the space of power, and not by the timely unfolding of history and transition into modernity. One manifestation of the problem that the historicist discourse encounters in dealing with the sociospatial organization of Beirut is that despite the promise of a new beginning that this slate of emptiness created by the project offered, the development of the downtown is still unable to reconcile the numerous needs of a pluralistic and unintegrated society. Despite the multiple changes that the master plan had undergone since its inception in 1991, partly in response to social and economic conditions, the heart of the city is unable to open the way for a more substantive project of social reconciliation in the remaking of Lebanese nationalist identity. Transitory interactions between citizens are taking place namely in dense commercial spaces focused on consumption. As a recent study on approximately 2,000 car users indicates around 70 percent of those visiting the city center were from within its municipal boundaries (around 50 percent) and adjacent Mount Lebanon (another 20 percent) and not from Beirut's marginalized peripheries.[50] Furthermore, a large majority of residences in the city center are currently occupied by expatriate populations that visit the city periodically.[51] This heightened consumption has been coupled with strikingly visible religious buildings.

Another manifestation of the problems encountered by this historicist discourse is posed by what Ashis Nandy calls the "unintended city," that is, the city that was never part of the formal master plan but always implicit in it. This "unintended city" is comprised of the large and growing number of poor living in the informal settlements and inadequately organized areas in Beirut's various suburbs, such as Ouzai, inhabitants who provide the cheap labor and services without which the "official" city could not survive.[52] Disenfranchised, the existence of this other is not acknowledged by the official city as part of itself. Viewed from the lens of postwar reconstruction, often taken to mean modernization, the return of the ghost in the center can be read as an indication that this displaced and evicted mass of Lebanon's growing urban poor refuses to "bow out of history"[53] and exhibits a consistent willingness to return and "illegitimately" occupy large public spaces. As Prakash suggests, the refusal to "bow out of history" highlights one of the problems inherent to the nation-state's historicist discourse of modernization—the inability of its linear narrative to acknowledge the spatiality of historical processes, the possibility of multiple temporalities, the uneasy coexistence of the modern and the "traditional," the incursion of the rural into the urban, and the integrated growth of official and unintended cities. From this perspective, the successive modifications and negotiations that have occurred in the plan for the city center since its inception and the as of yet unimplemented large development project, Elyssar, proposed for the informal settlements in the southern suburbs of Beirut, are part and parcel for a redefinition of urban citizenship, one which includes diverse forms of identification with Lebanon as a nation and Beirut as a city. These also raise a series of questions about the notions of center and periphery or the rural and urban. The permeability of spaces and their constant appropriation and mutations also questions the viability of discussing city boundaries, especially in places such as Lebanon where the city is the country.

POSTSCRIPT

Space is never politically and socially neutral, as events in Lebanon over the last two years have shown. Since the assassination of Prime Minister Rafic el Hariri along with Minister and Member of Parliament Basil Fuleihan and twenty others on February 14, 2005, the city center of Beirut has become the most politically and socially charged space in the city, open and amenable to diverse forms of reclamation by citizens from across Lebanon. For more than two months following the assassination, Martyr's Square in particular was the site of daily demonstrations and weekly mass rallies to protest the killing of Prime Minister Hariri and to demand the withdrawal of Syrian troops from Lebanon. These protests culminated in a massive rally on March 14, 2005, when citizens flocked to the center beneath the most emblematic symbol of the nation: its national flag. Simultaneously, a small public space in front of the Martyr's Square statue was transformed into "Freedom Camp," set up by youth activists from different political parties and civil society organizations, all of whom remained in their tents until Syrian troops withdrew from Lebanon in April.

At the same time, on March 8, 2005, Riad el Solh Square, adjacent to Martyr's Square, was the site of a massive rally by the opposition camp at the time to thank Syria for "helping" Lebanon. More recent protests against the current government by the same group have developed into a makeshift "tent city" along its edges, also brandishing the Lebanese flag. Set up in Riad el Solh Square and along one edge of Martyr's Square, in parking lots, on private land, and underneath overpasses, this new "unintended city" is occupied primarily by Shi'a mainly protesters as well as some Maronite from the southern suburbs of Beirut and from peripheral zones in the country, many of whom had never before set foot in the center. Moving from the margins of Beirut and Lebanon to the peripheries of the city center, these protesters have made visible the spatiality and multiple temporalities of modernity for which the linear nationalist discourse is unable to account. Exhibiting an obstinate refusal to "bow out of history," the ghost has returned this time in the shape of a large number of urban and nonurban poor that are asserting themselves as central to the making of Lebanon's contemporary history and identity. The significance of the site of the city center for such action cannot be overlooked. It is evident in ongoing debates by both the government and the opposition around the "forced imposition" and the "occupation" by marginalized populations of areas they were once excluded from, bringing with them cultural habits "foreign" to this particular part of the city. Putting aside the declared and undeclared political goals of the demonstrators and as part of the dispute that ensued indicates, these protests are one element in an ongoing redefinition and negotiation of Lebanon's national identity in a new regional and global context and of the contours of urban citizenship. They are a demonstration of the ways in which the city is directly implicated in the consolidation of the nation-state and in articulating and perhaps reconciling contending notions of nationhood. They are also about who has the right to the city.

NOTES

During the course of writing this chapter I have benefited from the insights of various individuals. I would like to thank Walid Raad, Abidin Kusno, Bashar Haidar, and the blind peer reviewers for reading and commenting on various drafts of this chapter. I also gained from discussions with Tom Bender, Seteney Shami, AbdouMaliq Simone, Michel Agier, and Ramzi el Hafez. The debates that followed the Locating the City conference in Antalya were particularly useful. A version of this chapter was subsequently presented at the Center for Contemporary Culture in Barcelona, and I would like to thank Josep Ramoneda and Judit Carrera for the opportunity and their intellectual generosity.

1. Ashis Nandy uses this term to refer to the informal settlements located in many cities, areas considered outside of history and do not appear on any map of the city. The work of urban sociologists has been at the

forefront of this discourse for the last three decades and is too numer-
ous to cite here. Among others see Henri Lefebvre, *The Production of
Space*, trans. Donald Nicholson-Smith (Oxford, UK: Basil Blackwell
Ltd., 1991); Manuel Castells, *The City and the Grassroots: A Cross-
Cultural Theory of Urban Social Movements* (Berkeley: University of
California Press, 1983); and David Harvey, *Social Justice and the City*
(Baltimore: Johns Hopkins University Press, 1975).

2. Jürgen Habermas, *The Incomplete Project of Modernity* (Cambridge,
Mass.: MIT Press, 1989).

3. Hizbu'llah or the "Party of God" was founded by a group of dissi-
dents in 1982 during the Israeli invasion of Lebanon. One of the
largest political parties in the country, Hizbu'llah also runs a system
of NGOs that provides various social services. Among others see
A. R. Norton, *Hizballah of Lebanon: Extremist Ideals vs. Mundane
Politics* (New York: Council on Foreign Relations, Feb. 2000);
Waddah Shararah, *Dawlat Hizb Allah: Lubnan mujtama'an Islamiyan*
[The State of Hizbu'llah: Lebanon as an Islamic Society] (Beirut,
Lebanon: Dar AnNahar, 1996); Lara Deeb, *An Enchanted Modern:
Gender and Public Piety in Shi'a Lebanon* (Princeton, N.J.: Princeton
University Press, 2006); Maha Yahya, "Forbidden Spaces, Invisible
Barriers: Housing in Beirut" (unpublished PhD diss., Architectural
Association, School of Architecture, London, 1994); and Mona
Fawaz, "Islam, Resistance, and Community Development: The Case
of the Southern Suburb of Beirut City" (unpublished master's thesis,
Massachusetts Institute of Technology, 1998).

4. Shi'as and Sunnis are the two major sects in Islam that emerged from
the conflict over succession following the death of the prophet
Mohamed. Since then, the Shi'as, a minority in the region, have faced
persecution at the hands of different political dynasties. In some
regions, remnants of this conflict persist to this day with adherents of
a conservative strand of Sunni Islam accusing the Shi'as of being
heretics (such as the Wahabis in Saudi Arabia). In Lebanon, these
divisions are not prevalent and tend to flare up only at times of
extreme sectarian tensions among small sectors of society.

5. The person in charge of demolition relayed to me at the time that they
had avoided using live ammunition and dynamite in the vicinity of
the mausoleum and had resorted to bulldozers because they were
afraid of damaging it (private interview, May 1992).

6. Maha Yahya, "Reconstituting Space, the Aberration of the Urban in
Beirut," in *Recovering Beirut, Urban Design, and Post War Reconstruction,*
ed. Philip Khoury and Samir Khalaf, 128–66 (New York: E. J. Brill,

1993). See also Nabil Beyhum, "Du Centre aux Territoires, La Centralité Urbaine a Beyrouth," *Maghreb Machreq,* no. 123/126 (July-September 1989): 177–89, for the historic importance of the city center.

7. During the long years of the war, successive population displacements took place under violent conditions. See Yahya, "Forbidden Spaces," 139–44; Maha Yahya, "Right or Claim; Housing in Post-War Beirut," in *Urban Triumph or Urban Disaster? Dilemmas of Contemporary Post War Reconstruction* (York, UK: World Monuments Fund, York University Press and the Aga Khan Foundation, 1997). Among others see also Boutros Labaki, "Confessional Communities, Social Stratification, and Wars in Lebanon," *Social Compass,* XXXV (April 1988): 533–62.

8. It is not clear whether this includes actual material damage to infrastructure only or whether it takes losses incurred from the loss of potential capital investment in the country over the period of the war into account.

9. See Ahmed Beydoun, *The Torn Republic: The Fate of the Lebanese Formula after al Taef* (Beirut, Lebanon: Dar Annahar, 1999) [in Arabic].

10. All the warlords were given ministerial posts in the Lebanese cabinet.

11. See Maha Yahya, "Unnamed Modernism: National Ideologies and Historical Imaginaries in Beirut's Urban Architecture" (unpublished PhD diss., Massachusetts Institute of Technology, 2005).

12. The aim of updating school history books was to direct citizens to a new common past while purging all references to the religious sectarian discourse of the war.

13. I intend to explore the ramification of this reconfiguration of the public and private in a forthcoming piece on the politics of recuperation.

14. Public sector representatives also included the Beirut municipality, the Directorate of Urban Planning (DGU), and the General Directorate of Antiquities (DGA); the private sector also comprised property owners, tenants, and different trade associations; and civil society included various NGOs concerned with architectural heritage.

15. Dar Al-Handasah Consultants is the largest engineering company in the Middle East.

16. Al Fadel Challak, founder and head of Oger Liban (1982), owned by Prime Minister Hariri, and head of the Hariri Foundation (1984), became president of CDR in 1991.

17. These meetings, held at different venues around the city, generated considerable debate and dissent. See Nabil Beyhum et al., *Imar Beirut*

wal-Fursah al-Dhaiah [Rebuilding Beirut and the Lost Opportunity] (Beirut, Lebanon: Rami al-Khal, 1992).

18. Upper Council for the Development of the City of Riyadh, *Bournamaj Tatweer Mantaqat Qasr el Hokom; Al Mar'hala Al Thaletha* [Program for the Development of Kasr el Hokom Area; Phase Three] (Riyadh, Saudi Arabia: Upper Council, 1995); Yahya, "Forbidden Spaces," 241–45.

19. Select property owners were allowed to retain ownership of their properties according to very strict criteria.

20. Legal commissions were formed to estimate the financial value of those properties. With minimal venue for appeal, owners had little choice but to accept whatever estimates were made. One main point of contention was that estimates were based on the value of the land at the time—that is, substantially destroyed properties in a derelict part of town—and not on the potential value of centrally located property.

21. Council for Development and Reconstruction, *Beirut Central District, Planning and Urban Design* (Beirut, Lebanon: Dar Al-Handasah, 1994), 60.

22. Solidere was accused of destroying significant archeological sites for developmental purposes. See Helen Sader, "Lebanon's Heritage: Will the Past Be Part of the Future?", in *Crisis and Memory in Islamic Societies,* ed. Angelika Neuwirth and Andreas Pflitsch, 217–30 (Beirut, Lebanon: OIB, 2001).

23. These displaced families, namely of Shi'a origin, were squatting in abandoned buildings in Wadi Abu Jamil. Most took the compensation money and moved to the Hizbu'llah and Amal-controlled southern suburbs, to either the informal settlements or more recent low income housing developments.

24. Smaller businesses deemed inappropriate such as barbers, grocery vendors, and so forth were prevented from returning to the center through complex and prohibitive rules for the recuperation of previously owned or rented properties. As one of the company's lawyers stated in an interview, "we made sure that undesirable functions did not return to the area" (private interview, 1997).

25. These cities usually require leisure areas, vast business zones, investments in infrastructure, and so forth; Saskia Sassen, *The Global City: New York, London, Tokyo* (Princeton, N.J.: Princeton University Press, 1991).

26. Inheritance laws in Lebanon follow the religious affiliation of individuals. This has resulted in hundreds of descendants of the same family

becoming part owners in the same lot of land leading to paralysis in real estate transactions over these plots.

27. Jeremy Bentham, "Principles of the Civil Code" reprinted partly in C. B. Macphearson, *Property Mainstream and Critical Positions* (Oxford, UK: Basil Blackwell, 1978), 52.

28. Omar Razzaz, "Group Non Compliance: A Strategy for Transforming Property Relations: The Case of Jordan" (unpublished PhD diss., Massachusetts Institute of Technology, 1992), 4.

29. Peter G. Hollowell, *Property and Social Relations* (London: Heinemann, 1982); Macphearson, *Property Mainstream,* 1–13.

30. Lefebvre, *The Production of Space,* 26–59.

31. Yahya, "Unnamed Modernism," 340–76.

32. Michel de Certeau, *The Practice of Everyday Life* (Los Angeles: University of California Press, 1984), 92.

33. Quoted in Ousama Kabbani, *The Reconstruction of Beirut* (Oxford, UK: Center for Lebanese Studies, 1992), 38.

34. Yahya, "Forbidden Spaces," 248–88.

35. Lebanon has a long history of immigration that dates back to the nineteenth century. Current estimates are that around eight million Lebanese of different generations reside around the world. Of particular interest to the government were the financially affluent expatriates, many of whom live in the major capitals of Western Europe and the United States. See Jad Tabet, *Al I 'mar wa al Fursa al Dai 'a* (Beirut, Lebanon: Dar el Jadid, 1994); and Nabil Beyhum, "The Crisis of Urban Culture: Three Reconstruction Plans for Beirut," *Beirut Review* 4 (1992): 43–62, for a critique of the architecture of this project.

36. For further discussions on memory and postwar reconstruction in Beirut, see Saree Makdisi, "Laying Claim to Beirut: Urban Narrative and Spatial Identity in the Age of Solidere," *Critical Inquiry* 23 (1997): 661–705; and Jens Hanssen and Daniel Genberg, "Beirut in Memorium," in *Crisis and Memory in Islamic Societies,* ed. Angelika Neuwirth and Andreas Pflitsch, 231–62 (Beirut, Lebanon: OIB, 2001).

37. Nizar Sagiyeh, "The Memory of War in the Lebanese Legal System," in *Memory for the Future* (Beirut, Lebanon: Dar Annahar, 2002), 205–21.

38. Maurice Halbwachs, *On Collective Memory* (Chicago: University of Chicago Press, 1968).

39. Yasmin Arif, *Presentation on Research Findings* (Beirut, Lebanon: Center for Behavioral Studies, American University of Beirut, 1997).

40. Avery Gordon, *Ghostly Matters: Haunting and the Sociological Imagination* (Minneapolis: University of Minnesota Press, 1997), 8.

41. Given the politics of this event as well as the partiality of all religious communities in Lebanon to stories of the supernatural, one can read this incident "outside" its location within the specificities of the Shi'a community. In other words, the relevance of ghosts to Muslim Shi'as are less important in this particular case than the political and inadvertently symbolic value that this haunting took on among a forcibly displaced and in some ways politically exiled community.

42. Derrida's *Specters of Marx* is a social critique of the post-1989 new world order and the supposed triumph of economic and political neoliberalism. It revolves around a central conception—the notion of the past and the future as temporalities not fully subsumed in the present time. Spectrality from this perspective entails temporal disjuncture; it expresses that which does not exist solely in the "chain of presents." Such a politics is characterized by Derrida as one of responsibility to the past, to the dead—victims of war, violence, and oppression—and to the future, to those not yet born (Jacques Derrida, *Specters of Marx: The State of Debt, The Work of Mourning and the New International*, trans. Peggy Kamuf [New York: Routledge, 1994], 21). Christopher Wise takes Derrida to task for ignoring the textual and ontological distinctions inherent to Christian and Muslim belief systems and subsuming them to the historical and political specificity of Judaism through his particular interpretation of messianicity. He argues that Derrida's contention regarding the irreducibility of the religious model allows him to ignore present geopolitical conditions that require us to rethink the question of religion (Christopher Wise, "Deconstruction and Zionism Jacques Derrida's Specters of Marx," *Diacritics* 31, no. 1 [Spring 2001]: 56–72). Notwithstanding this "religious" criticism of Derrida's specters, his discussion of haunting as a way for taking into account past exclusions and injustices remains relevant for the purposes of this chapter.

43. Even though published during the war, the novels of Hanan el Sheikh, *Hikayat Zahra* [The Story of Zahra] (Beirut, Lebanon: Dar el Adab, 2004, 4th edition) first published at her own expense in 1980 and Hasan Daoud, *Benayat Mathilde* [Mathilde's Building] (Beirut, Lebanon: Dar el Tanwir, 1983) are exemplary in this respect.

44. In this novel, the author and the narrator exchange places regularly, as his meandering through the postwar city are used to reflect on history, politics, memory, and the relationship between past and future and between places and the events that take place in them (Rashid Al Daif,

Azizi Mr. Kawabata [Dear Mr. Kawabata] (Beirut, Lebanon: Riad el Rayyes, 2001).

45. Hoda Barakat, *Hareth al Miyah* [The Tiller of the Waters] (Beirut, Lebanon: Dar el Nahar Press, 1998).

46. Barakat, *Hareth al Miyah,* 172.

47. Raad usually presents his work in a multimedia/performance entitled *The Loudest Muttering Is Over: Case Studies from the Atlas Group Archive.* It includes several fake short documentaries. This body of work, according to Raad, is to be read as "hysterical symptoms" of sorts that "investigates the possibilities and limits of writing a history of the Lebanese wars (1975–1991)."

48. Cathy Caruth, *Unclaimed Experience: Trauma Narrative and History* (Baltimore: Johns Hopkins University Press, 1996), 24.

49. Gyan Prakash, "The Urban Turn," in *Sarai Reader 2002: The Cities of Everyday Life,* 5, http://www.sarai.net/ (accessed May, 3, 2004).

50. This study undertaken in July 2003 by transportation experts on a sample of approximately 2,000 cars should not be treated as a scientific study. Rather it should be considered as a relevant indicator of visitors to the area.

51. According to Solidere, around 60 percent of residences in the Saifi "Urban Village" are owned by local Lebanese, and 40 percent are owned by expatriates and Gulf Arabs. On the other hand, new residences constructed along the coastal zone are owned mainly by Gulf Arabs and Lebanese expatriates (private interview, May 2004).

52. Unacknowledged and at best tolerated, these informal areas have been making up for the inefficiencies of public land management and have provided a large segment of the urban population with buildable urban land, especially those displaced during the war, others displaced by large-scale infrastructure and development projects such as highways and Solidere, low income populations with limited access to the housing market, and migrant workers. In the absence of a comprehensive survey, existing data on the size and demographic characteristics of these areas is sporadic at best. See Wafa Charafeddine, "Formation des Secteur 'Illegaux' dans la Banlieu-Sud de Beyrouth" (unpublished PhD diss., Université de Paris VIII, 1985); Yahya, "Forbidden Spaces," 136–230; Mona Harb-El Kak, *Politiques Urbaines dans la Banlieue-Sud de Beyrouth* (Beirut, Lebanon: Centre d'Etudes et de Recherches sur le Moyen Orient Contemporain, 1996); Valérie Clerc, "Les Principes d'action de l'urbanisme: Le projet Elyssar face aux quartiers irréguliers de

Beyrouth" (unpublished PhD diss., Université de Paris VIII, 2002); and Dar Al-Handasah Consultants (Shair and Partners), *Action Area 2: Preliminary Planning Report, Existing Conditions and Development Strategies* (Beirut, Lebanon: Dar Al-Handasah, 1996).

53. Prakash, "The Urban Turn," 5.

CONCLUSION

Reflections on the Culture
of Urban Modernity

Thomas Bender

The study of urban culture over the past quarter century has been largely a search for the modern city or urban modernity. These chapters, in their self-conscious address of the particularity of cities, make an important and timely point about that quest. They argue against the notion of a universal urban modernity, and they raise questions even about the idea of alternative modernities. The latter formulation implies a hierarchy of modernities (or at least a pattern of precedence), while the former collapses under the weight of the manifold differences among cities and cultures. These chapters emphasize the value, indeed the indispensability, of focusing on *specific urban modernities*.

History in a broad sense produces this necessity, for history is formative of many moderns or comodernities. If the rhetoric of the modern emphasizes its break with the past, all specific instances of the modern are defined in dialogue with the past. The modern, like anything else in the social world, is a product of history and of a place, and that means it is shaped by the particularities of distinctive historical experiences. That, more than anything else, is what these chapters demonstrate. History, modernity, and particularity are inseparable and mutually constituted. The relation among these terms varies by time and place. But in all cases the particularity that is the legacy of history demands constant attention, lest we miss crucial differences and elements of city culture in the modern era. Taking such legacies seriously, we must be careful not to overlook those aspects of history that are marked colonial, the not-urban, the not-modern. The production of modernity depends not only upon distinctions, but also on complex relations between the modern and the not-modern, between the West and the non-West, metropole and colonial. To fail to bring these highly political binary elements into relation with each other in our analysis makes us more likely to misconceive and misunderstand urban modernity.

Efforts made to grasp, to define, to even describe *the* city founder on the plurality within cities and the multiplicity of cities. Once there was the walled city. It was a container, and the city was defined by the wall that distinguished it from the larger landscape. Even after the wall disappeared—finally in the nineteenth century—the city's inside and outside were still legible. The rhetorical categories of city, suburb, and rural seemed to hold into the middle of the twentieth century, even if they were no longer precisely descriptive of the social history of the era. But today such descriptive terminology, to say nothing of analytical categories, is no longer available. There is not even a settled name for the agglomerations of populations on all continents that are larger than any in history. Not only are they more extensive than could have been imagined as recently as a half century ago, but they are also increasingly multinodal metropolitan regions, with a variety of translocal connections: capital and labor movements, networks and diasporas, and fragments weakly integrated with unclear boundaries. Such apparent incoherence raises the question of whether there is in fact either a city or city culture. Precisely this question has been pointedly asked by Nestor Garcia Canclini, and his report from Mexico City raises serious doubts about the effective existence of urban culture.[1] He finds no sense of the whole or of a shared culture or experiences in the city. His surveys revealed a limited range in respect to individual experiences; the daily life of residents in the Federal District, even among fairly elite respondents, did not embrace the whole city, not even its distinctive cultural institutions.

Much can be said to challenge the protocols of this survey, but the argument rings true. Surely Amman, Jordan, to give a striking example, reveals the problem Garcia Canclini finds, as in their different ways would other cities examined in this volume: Rio de Janeiro, Los Angeles, Douala, and Jaffa–Tel Aviv. The list could be much extended. The social phenomenon of limited use, of limited connections, of little sense of the whole seems widespread. Close consideration of class and geography and the way they condition the experience of the city would further highlight the phenomenon. Yet the question of the meaning and significance of the finding remains open. Here the chapters in this book help. Collectively, they reveal the complex and shifting mix of the imagined, the perceived, and the experienced. These capture different spatial and temporal dimensions of the city. They do not—and need not—overlap or completely converge, and there is no reason to insist that the articulation or elaboration of each one of these domains be equally filled out. The challenge presented to urban studies is the exploration of the relations among them and their different roles in shaping the way individuals locate themselves in social life, including multiple scales of time and geography.

In the case of global cities like Los Angeles, images or representations tend to precede experience, and they contribute to the constitution of experience or, better, the interpretation or meaning given to experience. No doubt the intensity and detailed grasp of everyday experience is richer than representations of the city—and may challenge those representations. But there are reasons for holding onto the representations. The byplay between perception and experience can produce some dissonance, uncertainty, and thus uneasiness about identities, boundaries, and the meaning of affiliation in the city. But such heightened awareness enables negotiation and renegotiation of their interrelations, and it creates spaces of liminality that can enable moments of freedom and innovation.

There are limits to what representation can resolve. There are instances of urban dissolution that go well beyond what Garcia Canclini found in Mexico City. Referring to Kinshasa, one scholar has called this urban devolution the "villagizing tendency," and it includes the collapse of infrastructure, markets, public life, and political access.[2] The phenomenon is evident as well in Douala, where it is described as a "fractal" city, nothing quite so severe as in Kinshasa, which is a fragmentation that comes from a fortress mentality and withdrawal. Here it is a collapse of connections and the means of making connections. In Douala, for example, one finds a city spaced out in "all directions without clear aleatory channels or implications." The burden of urban leadership in Douala and cities in its circumstance is to find appropriate forms of social connections that will bring aspiration, perception, and action into better alignment.

Perception and experience come together to form a cognitive map that gives meaning to and orientation in the city. What Kevin Lynch called the "image of the city" is an almost cartoonish clutch of visual cues and objects that either invite or permit a sense of association. They carry a very limited but real meaning of the city. Not everyone carries the same images in their heads, but there are some shared ones—often a park, or a monument, or a building, or a cultural institution that gives focus and meaning, even if one rarely—if ever—actually goes to that place.[3] In some cases one of those places might be a place of danger, but it still sustains orientation and identification. Residents could not navigate the city without such legibility, but it is about more than movement. It points to questions of affiliation, inclusion, and exclusion. Affiliation with the city is in part, a significant part, an act of imagination. If that affiliation cannot be imagined, the city becomes in a quite fundamental way inaccessible, and urban citizenship is diminished. If one cannot imagine oneself into the city, make oneself at home in the city, one may be in it but not of it—marginalized. For Lynch the legibility of the city contributes to the empowerment of city dwellers. He believed city planning ought to have this in mind; the city has as much responsibility to make itself legible to its citizens as the citizen has to imaginatively project herself or himself into the city. Making the city legible can, however, point in less democratic directions. In some hands—whether in those of a Haussmann or the managers of modern media—the quest for legibility and perceptual control invites the possibility of social control.[4]

The imagined city is as important as the experienced city. No one made this clearer than Walt Whitman. Lewis Mumford once observed that anyone who touches Manhattan comes into contact with Walt Whitman, whether they realize it or not. Perhaps it is equally the case that anyone who reads *Leaves of Grass* imaginatively enters Manhattan. Whitman's best poems fuse the long lists of Manhattan's chaos of peoples, things, movements, and ideas into an imagined but never finished whole that seems to include them all.[5] Likewise, that is what Frederick Law Olmsted's Central Park was intended to provide, and on occasion it does. When Olmsted described the park as democratic, he did not refer to governance nor did he claim that it could overcome the social and economic structures that divided the city. But he thought that in such a great public space there could be *moments* of transcendence when the whole could imagine its collective selves there. He thought individuals could imagine themselves into the whole that was represented by the public space of the park—and they could do so whether they were actually in the park or not.

Just as the imagined community we call a nation forms a collective identity that is not actually experienced as such, the urban imagination can do the same. It is the cultural work of art to enable such an imaginary. But it is also the work of everywoman and everyman; their imaginative participation in the city is what makes city culture. In just that fashion the public culture of the city is sustained. If city culture can and occasionally does work that way, then Garcia Canclini's work stops short at experience. His findings indicate not an absence of city culture or a collective identity, but rather they should be understood as the starting point of city-making, the conditions for the work of city culture and the formation of urban affiliations. These chapters provide numerous insights into both the condition he describes and the process I am invoking here.

There is another condition and process crucial to urban affiliation, and it is urban citizenship. These chapters, with two exceptions, do not address politics and political institutions directly. While the writers are interested in public space and the public, they do not directly examine the politics of making these spaces, places, and institutions. The special appeal that the exploration of public life, of people out of doors, and the representation of this experience has among contemporary urban scholars, following in a tradition of analysis brilliantly developed in a line from Georg Simmel, Walter Benjamin, and Hannah Arendt, displaced another form and meaning of representation.[6] This is the actual institutionalization of political representation. Yet this institutional space of democracy, places of deliberation and decision, the places of citizenship are as important as the free-flowing performative spaces, where issues of identity and difference and tolerance are resolved—or so we hope.[7] The relation of the two demand far more exploration.[8] Most importantly, are there paths of access from the politics of the street, the world of identity, to that of places where decisions are made, the domain of citizenship?

With recognition of these two related but analytically distinct spaces of democracy, the debate between Jürgen Habermas and his critics among social historians finds some resolution. Perhaps because Habermas attended only so glancingly to the space of public culture or the public sphere, he and his critics are talking about different spaces of democracy without grasping the significance of that confusion. Habermas has in mind something more like the Greek theatre, a formal space for the enactment of public policy or a focused discussion in a café or salon, while his critics have in mind the agora and the street. The two are not mutually exclusive forms of public culture or places of representation; they are in fact complementary. The form of communication or expression is different in the two places. The rational discourse that Habermas assumes and that his critics see as elitist and narrow belongs in one place but not the other. On the street bodily presence represents politics, while in the cafe or legislative hall reasoned argument is appropriate and political choice is the issue. The roles of the two forms of representation are different as well. For the street it is recognition of difference and the encouragement of a culture of acceptance or inclusion, while the deliberative space of Habermas is oriented toward decisions. That is not the work of Whitman's bodily presence or his "barbaric yawp" in the street. Neither mode of representation is sufficient; one needs and can have both.[9]

The special appeal of the street as the locale of urban sociability and the public life of the city is a fairly recent historical development. Streets are as old as cities, but they were often not axial or focal. Before the street, it was the port—the surroundings of the wharves—that until the mid-nineteenth century provided the major site for public life as well as economic life, thus making these points of intra- and extra-urban connection perhaps a richer public space than the street today celebrated in urban studies. Current scholarship, in line with the *Paris Guide* of 1867, identifies the boulevards with "la vie meme de Paris," while "les quais c'est passé, c'est son histoire." But it is precisely such relocations and definitions of urban vitality—in the instance of Paris literally banished by Haussmannization—that mark the historical layering inherent in the modern city. We should not overlook the twentieth-century campaign by Le Corbusier and his ilk of architectural modernists to abolish the street, the *rue corridor,* as they called it.[10] By recovering such lost pasts and challenges to them, we gain some critical perspectives on our own fascinations.

These chapters also reveal the limitations of the language of flow that theories of globalization, especially those of Manuel Castells, have emphasized.[11] Some people, things, and knowledge move easily around the world and across borders, but others, even most, do not. The absence of connectivity is clearest in Douala, where there is an almost total disconnect between aspiration ("spectral" possibilities) and actually possible acts. But one sees a version of this break in the portrayal of Los Angeles in *El Norte* and in the actual experience of particular classes of people. Furthermore, we must not overlook the massive movement of refugees, those who have lost their homes, escaping only with their lives. They represent global movement, but probably it is not what is envisioned by the gentle metaphor of flow. When we take apart this metaphor, other complexities about the movement of people, money, and things become clearer. Among the more important matters that emerge are those concerning the relations between legal and illegal movement. Recently, the near hysteria in the United States about security and increasing worry in the European Union about immigration makes this issue larger by the day. It marks the difference between cities and nations. Cities cannot close their borders, or they lose their principal function as a place of meeting and exchange of commerce and culture. But the modern nation-state has from its emergence in the nineteenth century been highly protective of its formal territory and its borders.

The logic of the nation on this matter is often undercut in the daily life of cities, and we see an example in the Laleli quarter of Istanbul. Here we see the movement of people and goods mediated and eased by ties that are at once commercial and personal, even intimate. The language of romance and multiethnic social bonds secured through sexuality in Istanbul's Laleli quarter is utterly obscured and grossly distorted by talk of global flows, as well as by the rhetoric of border security. Only close ethnographic study of actors in specific urban areas and specific translocal and transnational markets and networks will reveal the dimensions of everyday life.

Latin America scholars have recently emphasized the tradition of the "lettered city," by which they mean an elite city, the city of the literate, even literary, but especially the city of planning and order. The popular classes have a very different experience of the city and often resist such a vision.[12] Moreover, the literary tradition of "magic realism" sustains the authority of literature even as it undermines the lettered city. Brazil, though a land and culture of enchantment, has a strong tradition of secular modernity that pursues and foments a social dialogue and diagnosis of the real. The real and the magic do not compete, but the proliferation of realisms produce conflict and contestation that is played out in the media, locally, nationally, and globally with various claims to be the really real. The capacity and the claim to narrate the real gains urgency with the intensification of crisis in the favelas of Rio de Janeiro. The narrative of the real, however, is less the product of direct experience than of mediated images, as often inflected by global as by local tropes. Understanding and managing the circulation of narratives of the urban real is an important challenge in exploding cities of the "global South," something today sustained for the young people of the favelas of Brazil's largest cities by hip-hop lyrics.[13]

Fear in and of cities not only eats away at the civic sense and public life of the city, but it also threatens the city's relation to its indispensable global constituency, whether bankers or tourists. As cities rely more and more upon outsiders, the category of temporary urbanite who must be maintained in comfort—free from fear or a certain class of fears that may be particular to them—becomes more and more important to cities. Governments feel compelled to weigh the needs of the permanent citizens against those of the temporary ones. Indeed, the search for a plausible narrative of urban progress is often motivated more by a concern for the temporary "citizens" than for the actual citizens of the city, thus severely compromising the meaning of urban citizenship and civic life.[14]

Looking about the world, particularly toward the cities of the "global South," one sees all too many examples of the failure of urban and national dreams. Were they only dreams? Some were nothing more, but others found material expression. In their moment some seemed to proffer the promise of transformed experience, but too often the promise dissolved. The new industrial cities in India called the "steel towns" began as dreamworlds in the 1950s. By the 1970s, however, they had been renamed as a "catastrophe." For such places, among others in the global South, the phrase "modernist ruins" rings all too true.[15]

Those ruins haunt the future. Agreeing to dream is insufficient for realization of the dream. Both internal resources—cultural, moral, and political as well as economic—and external ones must be not only sufficient, but also properly aligned and coordinated. Cities are increasingly aware of existing in a global gaze, seeing their fate in the perception of that gaze. Whether or not the world (meaning mostly the North Atlantic investment communities) is in fact looking, their presumed gaze is part of the urban imaginary in our global era. So *City of God* becomes a meaningful and consequential event not only in Brazil, but also internationally and especially in the North Atlantic. But the presumption of a global gaze is a problem in another way; it diverts attention from what can be done locally with the resources at hand. It obscures local responsibilities; some of the worst injustices are locally sponsored and sustained and thus have local solutions.

The narrative of the city—or that of some cities—is understood to stand for the narrative of the nation. If nations displaced cities as the political community of primary affiliation in the early modern West, there remains a representative and practical role for cities in nation-building, whether in the case of capital cities (Ankara and Brasilia) which were consciously planned for that purpose, to several historical cities recast as part of national building (Istanbul and Rio de Janeiro), or special purpose cities, such as the "steel towns" that were to represent and actually move nations into economic and perhaps social modernity. The cultural work assigned to Ankara and Brasilia was to rewrite the national past and project a future. The rewriting of the past is striking in the exhibits the Ethnography Museum established in Ankara as part of the creation of the new Republic of Turkey. The visitor sees the ancient Hittites elevated to precursors, while the immediate forerunner of modern Turkey, the Ottoman Empire, fades to near invisibility. Similarly, Brasilia was to be as much as possible the opposite of Rio de Janeiro, the historical capital. While most cities grew by accretion, these cities (Brasilia, Ankara, and the steel towns of India) were developed more or less in an instant as the result of massive commitments by the national governments seeking to establish a national narrative of modernity through strategic city building.[16]

If the Republic of Turkey made Ankara, it remade Istanbul. The historic center of Istanbul, dating from the time of Constantine but also the locale of the Sultan's Topkapi Palace, was displaced and turned into a museum. The new center of the city, emphasizing its modernity and difference from Sultanahmet, was built across the Golden Horn at Taksim Square, almost as an extension of the European sector of Istanbul.

What happened in Beirut is a warning to all cities; they are vulnerable. If the example of the Soviet Union shows that nations can dissolve into chaos, the Paris of the Levant shows that it can happen with cities. Beirut may be an unusual case, simply because it seemed—far more than most capital cities—to represent the nation, perhaps even experientially to contain it. A national crisis destroyed a city as militarized political factions turned urban fragmentation and pluralism into battle positions. Yet here, too, history may come to the rescue. The imagination of the city, largely a product of the past, has propelled a rebuilding that seeks to recover a cosmopolitan public life that is grounded in a very particular history of imagined and real experiences.

Whether unique or not, Beirut does and should haunt our urban future. Though its lesson has been discussed in this volume and elsewhere as an architectural matter, with much debate about the architectural vision guiding the redevelopment plans, there is a deeper worry that Beirut should prompt. Urbanists need to probe ever more deeply into the social and political circumstances (and urban dynamics) that brought the city down.[17] One wishes Beirut were in fact unique. Kinshasa is no longer a city, Bogota barely sustains its urbanism, the cosmopolitanism that was once Sarajevo has been destroyed, and witness Baghdad, on the site where urban civilization may have first emerged. One lesson to be gained from all of these cases—and others that could be named—is that there is a vital, complex, and fragile relationship between cities and nations that keeps the different values of urbanism and nationalism in some viable relation to each other.

Urban leaders will measure themselves not only against cities that seem to work, but also those that seem not to work. That is good, no doubt. There are important lessons to be learned across the urban landscape; comparative study is crucially important for scholarship and for policy. But to return to the point made at the beginning, each city must understand its own particularity. One of the oddities of our present historical moment is that urban planners, developers, and architects are creating urban forms and places of consumption around the globe that seem to be selected from a catalogue, almost in a mix and match fashion, the same catalogue, perhaps, as that used by the builders of hotels in Las Vegas. Equally odd and important, urban consumers, at least a certain class of them, embrace these developments that bear no relation to local history and culture. This phenomenon is as much a product of local deficits in self-confidence as it is of the ambitions of transnational capital and communication. Amman, so unsure of its urban status, looks anxiously at other cities. Houston-style homes with columns familiar to the American slave South populate the city's most exclusive neighborhood. Such emulation will not resolve the question of urban identity; it will only confuse and weaken it.

To the extent we focus upon these bizarre dreams that hardly connect with—indeed, actually abuse—the history of particular cities we risk being misled. We are vulnerable to the false truism that globalization means homogeneity. There is no more reason—and a good deal less reason—to think that globalization implies homogenization than the creation of nations in the nineteenth century meant homogeneous cultures and landscapes. Both nationalism and globalism are carriers of an ideology, a representation, of uniformity over space, but these ideologies conceal—and are probably intended to conceal—uneven development. They also obscure historical particularities that scholars and citizens overlook only at the cost of misunderstanding for the former and mistaken policies for the latter. What these chapters offer is an antidote to such failures of insight. Here the focus is on specific urban modernities, their relation to specific pasts, and the highly particular culture of cities.

Notes

1. Nestór Garcia Canclini, "Mexico. Cultural Globalization in a Disintegrating City," *American Ethnology* 22(1995): 743–55.

2. René Devisch, "Frenzy, Violence, and Ethical Renewal in Kinshasa," *Public Culture* 7 (1995): 593–629.

3. Kevin Lynch, *The Image of the City* (Cambridge, Mass.: MIT Press, 1960). For a remarkable example of knowing the city as representation without experiencing what is thus known, see the New York fiction written for children by Horatio Alger Jr., *Ragged Dick, or Life among the New York Newsboys* (Boston: Loring, 1868).

4. See also Michel de Certeau, *The Practice of Everyday Life,* trans. Steven Rendall (Berkeley: University of California Press, 1984), ch. 7.

5. In this point, see Thomas Bender, *The Unfinished City: New York and the Metropolitan Idea* (New York: The New Press, 2002), ix–xii.

6. See Hannah Arendt, *The Human Condition* (Chicago: University of Chicago Press, 1958); Walter Benjamin, *The Arcades Project,* ed. Rolf Tiedemann, trans. Howard Eiland and Kevin McLaughlin (Cambridge, Mass.: Harvard University Press, 1999); and Georg Simmel, "The Metropolis and Mental Life," in *The Sociology of Georg Simmel,* ed. Kurt H. Wolff, 409–24 (New York: Free Press, 1950). For all of these writers, the public is as much an aesthetic as a political phenomenon.

7. Richard Sennett, "The Spaces of Democracy," *The Harvard Design Magazine* 8 (Summer 1999): 68–72.

8. See Bender, *The Unfinished City,* ch. 13.

9. For the state of the debate, see Craig Calhoun, ed., *Habermas and the Public Sphere* (Cambridge, Mass: MIT Press, 1992).

10. Sigfried Giedion, *Space, Time, and Architecture: The Growth of a New Tradition* (Cambridge, Mass.: Harvard University Press, 1954, orig. 1941), 725.

11. See especially Manuel Castells, *The Rise of the Network Society* (Oxford, UK: Blackwell, 1996), *The Power of Identity* (Oxford, UK: Blackwell, 1997), and *The End of the Millennium* (Oxford, UK: Blackwell, 1998).

12. See Angel Rama, *The Lettered City,* trans. John Charles Chasteen (Durham, N.C.: Duke University Press, 1996).

13. Teresa Caldeira, "Re-Imagining Inequality: Hip Hop, the Urban Periphery, and Spatial Segregation in São Paulo" (paper presented to the Davis Center for Historical Studies, Princeton University, February 2005).

14. See Guido Martinotti, "A City for Whom? Transients and Public Life in the Second-Generation Metropolis," in *The Urban Moment,* ed. Robert Beauregard and Sophie Body-Gendrot (Thousand Oaks, CA: Sage, 1999), 169.

15. Beatrice Jaguaribe, "Modernist Ruins: National Narratives and Architectural Forms," *Public Culture* 11 (1999): 294–312.

16. For Brasilia, see James Holston, *The Modernist City* (Chicago: University of Chicago Press, 1989).

17. For a start, see Michael Gilsenan, *Lords of the Lebanese Marches: Violence and Narrative in an Arab Society* (Berkeley: University of California Press, 1996).

CONTRIBUTORS

THOMAS BENDER is University Professor of the Humanities and professor of history at New York University. His books include *Toward an Urban Vision, Community and Social Change in America, New York Intellect: From 1750 to the Beginnings of Our Own Time, The University and the City: From Medieval Origins to the Present, Intellect and Public Life, The Unfinished City: New York and the Metropolitan Idea, Rethinking American History in a Global Age*, and, most recently, *A Nation among Nations: America's Place in World History*.

ALEV ÇINAR teaches political science at Bilkent University. She is author of *Modernity, Islam, and Secularism in Turkey: Bodies, Places, and Time* (University of Minnesota Press, 2005).

MARGARET COHEN teaches French and comparative literature at Stanford University. She is author of *Profane Illumination* and *The Sentimental Education of the Novel*.

CAMILLA FOJAS is associate professor and director of Latin American and Latino studies at DePaul University. She is the author of *Cosmopolitanism in the Americas* and recently completed a manuscript on Hollywood border films.

BEATRIZ JAGUARIBE teaches in the transdisciplinary graduate program at the Federal University of Rio de Janeiro. She is the author of *Fins de século-lo* and *Mapa do Maravilhose no Rio de Janeiro*.

ANTHONY D. KING is emeritus professor of art history and professor of sociology at the State University of New York, Binghamton, and now lives in the United Kingdom. His most recent books include *Spaces of Global Cultures: Architecture Urbanism Identity* and, as editor, *Re-Presenting the City: Ethnicity, Capital, and Culture in the Twenty-first Century Metropolis* and *Culture, Globalization, and the World-System*.

Mark LeVine is associate professor of modern Middle Eastern history at the University of California, Irvine. He is the author of *Why They Don't Hate Us: Lifting the Veil on the Axis of Evil, Overthrowing Geography: Jaffa, Tel Aviv, and the Struggle for Palestine, 1880–1948, An Impossible Peace: Oslo* and the *Burdens of History* (forthcoming), and *Heavy Metal Islam* (forthcoming). He is coeditor (with Armando Salvatore) of *Religion, Social Practices, and Contested Hegemonies: Reconstructing the Public Sphere in Muslim Majority Societies* and (with Sandy Sufian) *Reapproaching the Border: New Perspectives on the Study of Israel and Palestine.*

Srirupa Roy is associate professor of political science at the University of Massachusetts, Amherst. She is the author of *Beyond Belief: India and the Politics of Postcolonial Nationalism* and coeditor (with Amrita Basu) of *Violence, Modernity, and Democracy* in India.

Seteney Shami is program director at the Social Science Research Council in New York.

AbdouMaliq Simone is professor of sociology at Goldsmiths College, University of London, as well as a visiting professor at the Institute of Social and Economic Research, University of Witwatersand, and is the author of *In Whose Image? Political Islam and Urban Practices in Sudan* and *For the City Yet to Come: Changing Urban Life in Four African Cities.*

Maha Yahya is the founder and editor of the *MIT Electronic Journal of Middle East Studies (MIT-EJMES)*, author of *Towards Integrated Social Development Policies in ESCWA Countries: A Conceptual Analysis*, and coeditor (with Alev Çınar and Srirupa Roy) of *Secular Publicities: Visual Practices and the Transformation of National Publics in the Middle East and South Asia*. She consults for international agencies and has taught at the American University of Beirut. Yahya is currently project director for the National Human Development Report at the United Nations Development Program in Lebanon and is working on a book-length manuscript entitled *Staging Modernisms: Historical Imaginaries and Identity Politics in Beirut's Urban/Architectural Narratives (1888–2005).*

Deniz Yükseker is assistant professor of sociology at Koç University, Istanbul.

INDEX

adivasi population, 188, 198–99
aesthetic of realism, 101, 103–4
affiliation with a city, 269–70
Africa. *See also* Douala: associational
life, extension and substantiation
of, 84; aural acuity, emphasis
on, 82; catastrophic character of
cities, 82; collaboration, domains
of, 83–86; commodities, search
for, 79; Douala, 86–89; economic
difficulties, 84; environmental
conditions, local collaboration
for, 81; ephemerality, emerging,
79–83; garbage, perception of, 82;
gare routiers, 79; interdependencies
among sectors, 83–84; life
borders, everyday, 82; life
expectancy, 82; local initiatives, 81;
mediation, structures of, 82, 85;
microinformality, 81;
nongovernmental organizations
(NGOs), proliferation of;
provisional relationship with
sources of input and
opportunity, 80; "redemptive
etymology," 82; reinvocation of
the individual at work, 85–86;
social coherence, 95; social
collaboration, 95; urban
circulation, 84–85; urban
growth, 84; urban mobility, 95;
urban solidarity, configuration
of, 83; urban territories,
conflict over, 81

agricultural hinterland, 125–26
Ahuzat Bayit, 138
Ajami, 128
alafranga, 166
Aleppo, 212
al-tariq al-hilweh, 128
Amman: bourgeois
formations, 218–22; bourgeois
identity, 222–25; bourgeoisie,
views of the, 212; capital,
migration of, 211; Circassian
immigrants, 214; citizenship and
the state, 225–30; citizens
views, 208; city center, lack
of, 210–11; cultural history, 208–9;
dominance of the city, struggles
for, 218–19; elites, circulation
of, 222–23; factionalism, 219–20;
Greater Amman, 225; Gulf
crisis, 214; identity clashes,
218–22, 226; imaginaries, urban,
210–13; international trade, 216;
Islamic identity, 227–28;
landscape of, 208; merchant class
and state/palace, relationship
of, 219–20; migrations,
mass, 214–15; newness of, 213;
nostalgic bourgeoisie, 222–25;
organic identity, lack of, 211;
Palestinian refugees, influx
of, 214, 222, 226; partial
modernity, 211; peasant/urbanite
distinction, 226; Philadelphia of
the Greco-Roma "Decapolis," 213;

place attachment, 215; population struggles among segments, 230; porosity of Amman, 215; postmodern cityscape, 211; private philanthropy, 225; proprietary interest, sense of, 215; Rabath Ammon of the Ammonites, 213; spatial disjunctures, 215–16; state approach, 229–30; state power, symbols of, 227; stratification of the population, 217; structural acrobaticism, 223; transit migrants, 214–15; Transjordanian Hashemite, establishment of the, 214; tribalism and national identity, 228–29; urban identity, lack of, 213; West Amman, growth of, 217

Amman of the Ummayads, 213

Amsterdam, design of, 68

Andromache, 71

Ankara: *alafranga*, 166; Ankara Palas, 160–61, 166–67; Atakule Shopping and Business Complex, 176; Atatürk's monument/mausoleum Anıtkabir, 169–71; Atay, Falih Rıfkı , 153; Caliphate, Outlaw of, 158; call for prayers, changing of the, 158–59; city center, development of the, 159–62; civil code, adoption of a secular, 158; Conservatory of Music, 167; cultural work, 274; Dalokay-Tekelioglu project, 173; declaration as the new capital, 159; denigration of Ottoman times, 153; development of, 153; Directorate of Religious Affairs, formation of, 158; Ethnography Museum, 167–69; *ezan*, 158–59; founding of, 155; geographical location, 154; Hat Law, 157, 158; heterodox Islam, 168; image of a new modern state, 15, Islam, role of, 157, 158; Islamist discourse, 155; Istanbul, transformation of, 164–66; Karpiç Restaurant, 160, 167; Kemal, Mustafa, 155; Kızılay, shift towards, 174–76;

Kocatepe Mosque, 171–74; liberal/industrialist wave, 155; Marxist trends, 155; *Mimar,* 163; modernism as the national style, 162–63; modernity and secularism, relationship of, 156–59; Motherland Party, 176; music, role of, 167; national and territorial unity, creation of, 154–55, 155, 160; national architecture, 162–63; 1920 National Assembly, 155; national identity, 54; nationalism, role of, 155; national model city, 164–66; Ottoman influences and revivalism, 162, 163; Ottomans and the Turks, contrast of, 153; religious court system and religious education, abolishment of the, 158; religious garb and turban, outlawing of, 158; secularism, 155, 157–59; secular-national identity, 155; self-constitutive acts, 154; state-building efforts, 153; Sümerbank, 160; Taksim Square, 165–66; train station, 161, 164; Turkish Business Bank, 160; Ulus (Nation) Square, 159, 160, 167, 175; Victory Monument, 159, 161, 169, 175; War of Independence, 155; West-oriented modernism, 155; *yeni mimari,* 163

Ankara Palas, 160–61, 166–67

antagonism and conflict, proliferation of, 197–99

anti-immigrant phobia, 37

Arabic-Yafo *versus* European styles, 132

Arab nationalists, presence of, 128, 244

Arabs and Europeans, cultural interaction between, 128

Arcades Project, 55

architectural and town-planning discourses, impact of, 124

architecture of displacement, 69

Around the Pink House, 255

artistic defamiliarization, 101–2

Atakule Shopping and Business Complex, 176

global imaginary, 5
Global Indian, 9
globalization, 272, 275; acceptance
of, 5; emergence of the world
or global city, 5; exchanges
and flows that link cities, 5;
historical process, as a
long term, 8
Greater Amman, 225

Hat Law, 157, 158
Haussmannization, 56, 57, 68,
71, 271
heterodox Islam, 168
hierarchies of work, 190
homogenization, 275
hybridity, planned, 191–92

Ibn Arraq Mausoleum, 238
identity-creating elements, 212
Illegal Immigration Reform and
Immigration Responsibility
Act (IIRIRA), 39
imagination of the city, 122
imagined city, 270
immigration patterns, 38–39
imperialism, 10
incarceration of the urban, 199–201
India: adivasi population,
188, 198–99;
antagonism and conflict,
proliferation of, 197–99; Bauri
community, 188–89;
Bhubaneswar (Orissa), 184;
Chandigarh (Punjab), 184;
chronotope, formation of
statist, 185; colonialism, spatial
practices of, 185; community
life, 191–93, 197; cross-class
interaction, 195, 196, 198;
displacement and dislocation,
188–89; economic polarization,
195, 196; education, role of,
191–92; failure of urban planning
and urban space, 199–201;
Faridabad, 184; incarceration of
the urban, 199–201; inhabitation
and hierarchies of work, 190;
Kalyani, 184; labor unrest,
197, 198; mosaic nationalism

project, 196–97; national
integration, dream of, 184,
193–94; national space, 190;
nation-building program, 182–83;
nation-statist project,
incompatibility of, 195; Nehruvian
nationalism, 184–85, 193–94;
Nilokheri, 184; origins and
establishment of steel towns,
186–94; planned hybridity,
191–92; political participation in
the steel towns, 192–93;
postcolonial modernity, 200–201;
postcolonial period, 187, 190–91;
quality of life, effect of steel towns
on, 197; rapid industrial growth,
effects of, 196; reform efforts, 200;
respatialization of citizenship, 186;
Rourkela, 189, 198–99; Steel
Authority of India (SAIL), 183;
steel townships, vision of the,
183–84; subnational
distinctiveness, 196–97; tribal
communities, presence of,
200–201; Ulhasnagar, 184;
unity in diversity, 193; urban
planning, 184–91
individual, reinvocation of
the, 85–86
industrial urbanization, 10
inhabitation, 190
insurgent citizenship, 134
interpersonal relations, role of, 17
Isfahan, 212
Islam: discourse, 155; identity, 227–28;
role of, 157, 158
Islamic city, 210
Israel: agricultural hinterland, 125–26;
Ahuzat Bayit, 138; Ajami,
establishment of, 128; al-tariq
al-hilweh, 128; The American City:
A Problem in Democracy, 138;
Andromeda Hill condominium
project, 134, 135; as an
ideological construct, 122;
Arabic-Yafo versus European
styles, 132; Arab nationalists,
presence of, 128; Arabs and
Europeans, cultural interaction
between, 128; architectural and

informality in, 22–24; informal market exchange, 17; interpersonal relations, role of, 17; Kurdish presence, 24; Laleli Businessmen's Association (LASIAD), 22; migrant merchants and petty traders from former Soviet Union (FSU), 17; migrants, predominance of, 24; "Natashas," 29; "no trade diasporas," 21; prostitution, 29; public culture of, 24–29; sexual relationships in business relations, role of consensual, 18, 29–31; shopkeepers and workers, non-local, 19; shuttle trade, 18–21; state regulation in economic transactions, absence of, 17, 19, 22; suitcase trade, 18, 19; Sultanahmet, 19; terrain of discontinuity, 21, 22; transnationalism, 19, 20; trust, role of, 26, 27, 28–29; urban borderland, as an, 21–22; urban space, as an, 18; women's presence in the informal economy, 25

language: mother tongue, as a, 9
Lebanese civil war, 214, 236
Lebanon, revitalizing, 241
"Le Cygne," 70, 71
legibility of the city, 270
les villes mortes, 89
lettered city, 272–73
liberal/industrialist wave, 155
life borders, 82
lived experience of the urban, 2
Los Angeles: anti-immigrant phobia, 37; *Bread and Roses*, 44–52; capitalism, geography of, 41; colonial urbanization, 12; colonization of, 12; communication, rise of technologies of, 37; cultural citizenship, 38; *El Norte*, 37, 38, 40–44; "Hispanic Hollywood," 38; Illegal Immigration Reform and Immigration Responsibility Act (IIRIRA), 39; immigration patterns, political forces of, 38–39; immigration reform, 39; Immigration Reform and Control Act of 1986, 37, 39; Latino films, impact of, 37–38; marginalization of the indigenous population, 12; migration, 37, 40–44; neighborhood boundaries, 37; North American Free Trade Agreement (NAFTA), 37; origins and development of, 12; Personal Responsibility and Work Opportunity Reconciliation Act, 39; populations, marginalization and ghettoization of, 41; SOS "Save Our state" ballot measure, 39

Machine and the Revolt, The, 111
mapan, 92–95
marginalization of the indigenous population, 12
Martyr's Square, 257
Marxist trends, 155
Mecca, 212
mediation, structures of, 82, 85
memories, social framework of, 250–53
merchant class and state/palace, relationship of, 219–20
Meydani, 160
microinformality, 81
migrations, mass, 214–15
Mimar, 163
modernism as the national style, 162–63
modernity: Berman's definition, 151; city, relationship of the, 151; classical modernization theory, 151–52; Connolly's definition, 151; diverse uses of, 151; epoch, as an, 152; locally produced definitions, 152, 153; matrix, 123; partial, 211; production of, 267–68; promise of, 100, 102–3; secularism, relationship of, 156–59; textbook definition, 151
Monet, 57
mosaic nationalism project, 196–97
Mustafa Kemal, xxiii, 153, 155. *See also* Atatürk

political representation,
    institutionalization of, 271
populations, marginalization, 41
porteur d'eau, 64
postcolonial cities, 5
postcolonial modernity, 200–201
postimperial cities, 5
postmetropolis, 11
postmodern cityscape, 211
postmodern urban condition, 11
print capitalism, 10
proletariat, 11
proprietary interest, 215
public culture, 18, 22, 24, 25, 29,
    30, 32, 135, 137, 271
public discourse, 133
public employment, 86
public spheres, plebian/subaltern, 122
Punjab: *See* Chandigarh

Qom, 212

Rabat, 212
Rabath Ammon of the Ammonites, 213
race, 9
realism; as a form of art, 105; realism
    as an aesthtic representation,
    104–8, 106
redemptive etymology, 82
religion, identification by, 10
representational spaces of the
    clandestine, 122
resistance vernacular, 135
respatialization, 186
Riad el Solh Square, 257–58
Rourkela, 189, 198–99

Sana'a, 212
Santo Forte, 114
Sarejevo, 274
secularism, 155, 157–59
secular modernity, 272
secular-national identity, 155
self-constitutive acts, 154
self-contained unit, city as a, 1
"self-reflexivity," 133
Shanghai: 69
social coherence, 95
social collaboration, 95
Soviet Union: *blat,* 27; favors of

access, 28; market economy,
    transition to the, 27
spatial: densities, 246–50;
    disjunctures, 215–16
street, representation and recognition
    of the, 271–72
structural acrobaticism, 223
subnational distinctiveness, 196–97
suitcase trade, 18, 19
Sultanahmet, 19
Sümerbank, 160
Suq el Tawile, 238

Taif agreement, 240–41
Taksim Square, 165–66
Territory unity, creation of, 154–55,
    155, 160
*The American City: A Problem in
    Democracy,* 138
The City: The Hope of Democracy, 138
The Tiller of Waters, 253–54
Third World cities, 5
time and geography, impact of, 268–69
topoi, 55
Transjordanian Hashemite,
    establishment of the, 214
transnational flows, 17
transnationalism, 19, 20
transnational migration, 8
transportation, role of modern, 2
tribal communities, 200–201
tribalism and national identity,
    228–29
trust, role of, 26, 27, 28–29
Turkish Business Bank, 160
Turkish state, establishment of the, 152

Ulhasnagar, 184
Ulus (Nation) Square, 159, 160,
    167, 175
United Nations: establishment of, 10
unity in diversity, 193
urban and national dreams, 273
urban circulation, 84–85
urban culture; hyper stimulation,
    101–3
urban experience, 100
urban growth, 84
urban identity, 2, 208, 209, 213, 224
urbanism, 6

urban mobility, 95
urban planning, 184–91
urban planning and urban space,
    failure of, 199–201
urban-rural system, 126
urban socialization, 86–87
urban solidarity, 83
urban territories, 81

Victory Monument, 159, 161,
    169, 175
visual culture, 105–6
voluntary migrations, 8
vulnerability, 274

West-oriented modernism, 155
world city, conceptualization of the, 5
world economy, cotter pins of, 5

yeni mimari, 163
youth, militancy of, 88
youth cultures, intervention
    of, 100–101

Zionist movement, 123, 124–25,
    127, 135
zone of cultural debate, 137

www.ingramcontent.com/pod-product-compliance
Lightning Source LLC
Chambersburg PA
CBHW020825270326
41928CB00006B/446